Writing Indian Nations

Writing Indian Nations

Native Intellectuals and the Politics
of Historiography, 1827–1863

MAUREEN KONKLE

The University of North Carolina Press
Chapel Hill and London

Designed by Jacquline Johnson
Set in Minion
by Keystone Typesetting, Inc.

Manufactured in the United States of America
The paper in this book meets the guidelines for
permanence and durability of the Committee on
Production Guidelines for Book Longevity of the
Council on Library Resources.

Library of Congress Cataloging-in-Publication Data
Konkle, Maureen.
Writing Indian nations : native intellectuals
and the politics of historiography, 1827–1863 /
by Maureen Konkle.
p. cm.
Includes bibliographical references and index.
ISBN 0-8078-2822-x (cloth: alk. paper)
ISBN 0-8078-5492-1 (pbk.: alk. paper)
1. Indians of North America—Historiography.
2. Indians of North America—Treaties. 3. Indians of
North America—Government relations. 4. United
States—Intellectual life. 5. United States—Race
relations. 6. United States—Politics and
government—19th century. I. Title.
E77.K65   2004
973.04'97—dc22
2003017455

cloth   08 07 06 05 04   5 4 3 2 1
paper   08 07 06 05 04   5 4 3 2 1

THIS BOOK WAS DIGITALLY PRINTED.

*For my mother and
in memory of my father,
Robert C. Konkle Sr.
(1935–1985)*

CONTENTS

ILLUSTRATIONS

Writing Indian Nations

Doubtless there are many who think it granting us poor natives a great privilege to treat us with equal humanity. The author has often been told seriously, by sober persons, that his fellows were a link between the whites and brute creation, an inferior race of men to whom the Almighty had less regard than to their neighbors and . . . whom he had driven from their possessions to make room for a race more favored. Some have gone so far as to bid him remove and give place to that pure and excellent people who have ever despised his brethren and evil entreated them, both by precept and example.

Assumption of this kind never convinced William Apess of its own justice. He is still the same unbelieving Indian that he ever was.

—*William Apess,* Indian Nullification of the Unconstitutional Laws of Massachusetts, or, The Pretended Riot Explained *(1835)*

INTRODUCTION

Everything about human history is rooted in the earth, which has meant that we must think about habitation, but it has also meant that people have planned to have more territory and therefore must do something about its indigenous residents. At some very basic level, imperialism means thinking about, settling on, controlling land that you do not possess, that is distant, that is lived on and owned by others. . . . Just as none of us is outside or beyond geography, none of us is completely free from the struggle over geography. That struggle is complex and interesting because it is not only about soldiers and cannons, but also about ideas, about forms, about images and imaginings.
—*Edward W. Said,* Culture and Imperialism *(1993)*

AMERICANS

After the xenophobia unleashed by the attacks of 11 September 2001, the Advertising Council produced a public service announcement that featured one person after another saying to the camera, "I am an American." The people in the ad were of various identifiable races and ethnicities, with regional and foreign accents, in cowboy hats and wheelchairs. The PSA included a young man on a college campus who would be described as "Middle Eastern" in appearance and who seemed hesitant or even fearful when saying his line, as if he wasn't sure he'd be believed, and ended with a little girl, dark-complexioned, maybe Hispanic, wearing a T-shirt with a *101 Dalmatians* cartoon puppy on it, waving a U.S. flag. I looked for the Native person in this ad every time I saw it, which was fairly often. Given the multicultural tenor of the PSA, its producers would have had to include a Native person, although they wouldn't have been obvious about it—that is, they wouldn't have shown the person in beads and feathers, as in the famous antilittering PSA first aired on Earth Day in 1971 that ends with a close-up of a tear trailing down the cheek of an Indian man who has just had a bag of trash thrown at his feet from a passing car.[1] I think the Native person in the 2001 ad was a stocky man of about thirty or thirty-five years old with long wavy hair, wearing a baseball cap that had some kind of design on it. "*I* am an American," he said, with special emphasis.[2]

When I asked students in my classes who the Indian was, they always pointed to this man, although they couldn't say exactly why. I think it was how the man spoke. Despite the PSA's apparently straightforward message about the need for tolerance of cultural diversity in the United States, the man's emphatic "*I*" echoes the point made by countless Native peoples—and countless representations of Native peoples—from the beginning of colonization that they were "here first." Almost invariably, people who are not Native receive that sentiment as a declaration of chronological precedence rather than a claim to geography: of course, although it cannot be denied that Indians were here first, they've been outnumbered and superseded by us and ought to get used to the idea. But the emphasis points to a distinction between America as geographic space and the United States as a political entity that is common in Native discourse: Native peoples' connection to land precedes and persists through European colonization and the formation of the United States to the present day. In 1744, British colonials recorded the comments of Canassatego, an Onondaga who spoke on behalf of the Iroquois at a treaty negotiation held at Lancaster, Pennsylvania, in regard to a dispute over land. "When you mentioned the Affairs of the Land Yesterday, you went back to old Times, and told us, you had been in Possession of the Province of Maryland above One Hundred Years," Canassatego told the assembled officials of Maryland, Virginia, and Pennsylvania. He continued:

> But what is One Hundred Years in Comparison with the Length of Time since our Claim began? since we came out of this Ground? For we must tell you, that long before One Hundred Years our Ancestors came out of this very Ground, and their Children have remained here ever since. You came out of the Ground in Country that lies beyond the Seas, there you may have a just Claim, but here you must allow us to be your elder Brethren, and the Lands to belong to us long before you knew anything of them.[3]

Statements such as this are often played for sentiment, as this account, early as it was, may have been: the poor Indians refuse to see their own impending doom. But however Native traditions account for the relation of the people to the land, their connection to America is to a geography that is historically theirs in a way that it is not for those of us who are not Native. From this perspective, the United States is not an origin or an inevitability but rather an event in time—catastrophic, but still an event in time, on their land.

Native peoples' connection to land is not just cultural, as it is usually, and often sentimentally, understood; it is also political—about governments, boundaries, authority over people and territory. The problem for European settlers has always been what to do about these "indigenous residents," as Edward Said puts it, how to gain authority over this land and then incorporate the fact of the existence of Native peoples—who, inconveniently, didn't just disappear—politically and imaginatively within the boundaries of that authority. One of the major impediments to the successful incorporation of Native peoples over time has been the existence of treaties Europeans made with them from the beginnings of settlement. The colonizers of North America and their successor, the United States, made treaties to form alliances with Indian nations for mutual protection, to regulate trade, to recognize boundaries and jurisdictions, and particularly with the rise of the United States, to legitimate EuroAmericans' acquisition of territory. No other instance of European colonization produced as many or as significant treaties. The historian Frederick Hoxie writes that treaties made between Europeans and Native peoples in North America and the United States are singular in the history of such documents in their numbers and "in the sense of sovereignty they embody."[4] The British in Canada negotiated far fewer treaties with Native peoples; in New Zealand, one treaty was negotiated in 1840, and in Australia, none. No treaties were negotiated in Latin America.[5] These treaties became part of the legal system in North America and the United States, where they remain today; despite the pervasive discourse of "broken treaties," treaties had and continue to have legal authority.

This presents a significant problem to Europeans and a significant opening to Native peoples, especially because treaties invoke two concepts fundamental to the formation of the United States itself: the contract as a model for social relations and the principle of consent to enter into a contract. A treaty is a contract between nations, and a contract cannot be made with an incompetent or an inferior; it requires the free consent of all parties. Reasoning from the inescapable fact of treaties having been made, it was a logical conclusion in the eighteenth- and early-nineteenth-century United States that Native peoples formed governments with boundaries and laws that had to be recognized. Native peoples' free consent required that they also be free to *refuse* to consent—which carried with it the implication that they must be capable of free will and rational thought as irrational savages could not make legitimate contracts. In political relations, then, at least the appearance of Native peoples' consent was crucial in order to establish the legitimacy of treaties and therefore the legitimacy of EuroAmerican control of land. Throughout the first half of the nineteenth century, on the western and southern borders of EuroAmerican settlement east of the Mississippi, one Native tribe after another made treaties with the United States giving up territory while preserving a smaller part for themselves. Then, like the Cherokees, many reached the point where they felt they could not give up any more land if they wanted to preserve their governments and autonomy and refused to consent to the proffered agreements. Hence the "removal" period ensued, as the United States and state governments resorted to coerced treaties, outright violence, and forced displacement to establish U.S. authority over land.

Historians have long contemplated the complex position of the United States as both a product of and a participant in European imperialism.[6] With respect to Native peoples, European imperialism takes a paradoxical form in North America and the United States. The agreements EuroAmericans made with Native peoples in order to establish their own authority over land in essence contradicted their claims to inherent superiority. EuroAmericans' asserted natural superiority could be refused by people who were understood to be mere savages incapable of adhering to the rule of law or forming governments. That legal mechanism for relations with Native peoples, the treaties, became locked into the U.S. political system in two cases the Cherokee Nation brought to the U.S. Supreme Court, *Cherokee Nation v. Georgia* (1831) and *Worcester v. Georgia* (1832) (known as the Cherokee Nation cases), which remain the key cases of Indian law. At present, the meaning of treaties going as far back as the eighteenth century has enormous significance in current efforts by Native peoples to secure land, governmental authority, and economic stability across the United States. The Native man in the multicultural PSA— ironically made to reinforce the ideal of national coherence at an especially divisive moment in U.S. history—embodies perhaps a trace of this movement.

This book takes the conflict over the meaning of treaties in the early nineteenth century as its ground, a conflict that was both a political struggle and a struggle over knowledge, what counted as true and real. From the EuroAmerican perspective, the only way out of the implications of treaty relations was to insist, ever more vociferously, that Native peoples were intellectually and morally incapable of forming true governments. Native peoples were held to be so different, an anachronistic relic of an early moment in the history of man locked in a state of nature without history and without a future, that they would rapidly disappear when confronted with the pinnacle of human civilization, the new United States. No matter how decimated Native populations might have been, the hypothetical disappearance of Indians carries with it a certain amount of wishful thinking. If Indians disappeared, EuroAmericans could retain the legitimacy they needed from the treaty documents and be relieved of the lurking possibility that Indians could equally legitimately refuse to concede to white superiority. Knowledge about the racial difference of

Indians is therefore an especially volatile political matter in the United States because that difference must cancel out a very tangible claim to autonomy and equality. Faced with treaties that, to say the least, complicated their history on the land, EuroAmericans wrote accounts of Native peoples that valorized EuroAmerican moral superiority in making treaties in the first place and positioned Native peoples as the rapidly receding predecessors of the new state. Native peoples had to be incorporated, explained, and superseded.

While the autonomy conceded in treaties did not necessarily make life easier for Native peoples, it provided a mechanism for resistance to EuroAmerican authority and an opening for critique on the part of Native intellectuals and political leaders in the nineteenth century that has only increased in importance in Native political struggles over time. The struggle over treaty rights motivated the emergence of the first significant body of Native writing in English in the first half of the nineteenth century. A small but relatively vocal group of Native writers—Cherokee, Pequot, Ojibwe, Tuscarora, and Seneca—used the evidence of treaties to argue exactly what the treaty signified in European discourse: the autonomy of Native political formations and the equality of those political entities to other political entities and of Native peoples to other peoples. All of the writers discussed here were at least nominal Christians, and several were ordained ministers. The majority of the writers were tribal leaders who were either called upon or felt compelled to explain the tribe's position to mainly white audiences in oratory, historiography, journalism, and official documents. Only two writers of the period, the Pequot William Apess and the Ojibwe George Copway, were able to publish more than one book in their lifetimes. Although they differed in the details of their criticism of what they understood as EuroAmericans' egregious misrepresentations of Native peoples, they essentially endorsed two points: the prior and ongoing autonomy of Indian nations from subordination to EuroAmerican authority and Native peoples' authority over their traditional knowledge, history, and contemporary experience. They all maintained that EuroAmericans' knowledge about Indians' racial difference was politically motivated and therefore Indians' representations of themselves were crucial to their political struggles.

In his history of Indian law in the nineteenth century, Sidney Harring observes that whatever EuroAmericans thought, Native peoples behaved as if they were sovereign nations.[7] The archetypal moment when the civilized cavalry faces the beautiful but doomed savages arrayed on the crest of a hill, about to descend, has an entirely different significance when viewed from the other side. This book begins with how Native writers described themselves and their political organization in the early nineteenth century and takes as its primary assumption that Native peoples did not wish to be subordinated to Europeans, that they insisted on their political autonomy, however they defined it. It is sometimes objected that an "Indian nation"—a phrase that became common in Anglo-American legal discourse by the mid-eighteenth century—is not really "Indian" because it is a product of colonization and settlement, an argument that reifies culture as the only real freedom for Native peoples.[8] The effects of Eurocentrism are a condition of modernity—in most societies around the world, they cannot be escaped. As the historian Arif Dirlik points out, to posit that colonized or indigenous peoples are at their most authentic when they are least effected by Eurocentrism is to deny their experience in time.[9] It is also often maintained in literary criticism, historiography, and popular discourse that Indian nations do not have that much real power or autonomy relative to the United States and never really did, which implies that to speak of Indian nations' political authority is deluded if not absurd. But relative size and power does not stop Andorra and Liechtenstein, for example, from being considered sovereign nations.[10] While this book is in part an attempt to describe what kind of authority Indian nations have in U.S. discourse, the emphasis here is on what Native writers who were engaged in political struggle wished Indian nations to be and what role writing, and specifically writing history, played in that struggle. Whatever the relative authority of Indian nations in the nineteenth century or the present, this book figures them as the location of struggle and aspiration rather than as static entities.

Like the "Indian nation," history—the progressive narrative of past, present, and future—is also an effect of Eurocentrism, and it is one that Native peoples engaging with EuroAmericans on the meaning of treaties must use. The principal means of undermining the political significance of treaties for Native peoples is EuroAmericans' denial of Native peoples' existence in time, their exclusion of Native peoples from history. For Native intellectuals, then, time is a political necessity: they write historical accounts of their traditions and experiences of European colonization and settlement in order to write themselves into a political future. According to all of the writers included here, Native peoples already had governments. Even the writers most inclined to dispense with traditional knowledge and practices concluded that in this respect, Native peoples already were civilized. When they presented themselves to white audiences, these writers set out to undo the effects of EuroAmerican knowledge about racial difference by writing history. This necessary engagement with EuroAmerican thought was not a simple or straightforward process. This book describes that process of engagement, which in the works of the writers included here involves analyzing the psychological and political effects of the knowledge about racial difference, struggling with its naturalization in the period, and attempting to reconcile tradition and modernity. These topics are complex and remain significant, arguably even fundamental, in Native discourse today.

The political autonomy of Native peoples remains generally absent from the scholarship on the representation of Native peoples and on Native writing. In literary criticism at least, treaties are understood to have been all "broken" and therefore of no real consequence other than as signifiers of white perfidy; images of Indians have been understood as the products of either white racist prejudice or partially redemptive sympathy; and although scholarship on early Native writing has recognized Native criticism of white violence and oppression, it has for the most part largely attended to the problem of explaining how an Indian who is a Christian and writes in English could still be an Indian.[11] Native American literature has been incorporated into a narrative of the multicultural coherence of the United States, where Native peoples constitute one of many ethnic groups to be recognized and appreciated through their literary works. Native political struggles and their ongoing effects also remain for the most part absent in much of the scholarly commentary on racism, colonialism, postcolonialism, and imperialism, where they are often glanced over, considered if not exactly insignificant, at least a settled point. According to this commentary, Native peoples were victims of conquest, and the few who survived are now rightfully incorporated into the United States, given their individual civil rights, and allowed their cultural heritage, including their "nations."[12] The inordinate focus on Native difference and cultural identity, while accepting at face value the moral correctness of Native incorporation into the United States, and the relative absence of Native peoples in the United States from the discussion of global colonialism and imperialism are themselves effects of the relations peculiar to U.S. colonialism that this book describes.

By way of introduction, this book begins with a description of the intellectual and political setting of U.S. colonial discourse that Native writers confronted in the early nineteenth century and how elements of that discourse persist in the thinking about Native peoples today, especially in literary scholarship on Native writing and the representation of Indians. The collision of Enlightenment theory of Indian difference and the practical necessity of political relations with Indian nations produced a convoluted discourse on Native peoples that, for all the apparent rigidity of the knowledge about Indians' difference, inferiority, and disappearance, was also peculiarly volatile because of the presence of treaties.

THE THEORY OF INDIAN DIFFERENCE AND
THE PRACTICE OF TREATY-MAKING

Vine Deloria Jr. and David Wilkins argue that federal Indian law is neither logical nor consistent, related neither to international law nor to domestic law, despite claims made to the contrary. Federal Indian law, they observe, "is a loosely related collection of past and present acts of Congress, treaties and agreements, executive orders, administrative rulings, and judicial opinions connected only by the fact that law in some haphazard form has been applied to American Indians over the course of several centuries."[13] The U.S. Constitution recognizes Indian nations as separate political entities and establishes the federal government's jurisdiction over relations with them in the Commerce Clause, which gives Congress "the power to . . . regulate Commerce with foreign Nations, and among the several States, and with the Indian Tribes."[14] In 1790, Congress passed the first Indian Trade and Intercourse Act, which further reinforced the principle that the federal government was the only authority for dealing with Indian nations, in this case mandating that Indian traders be licensed by the federal government. Several trade and intercourse acts were passed between 1790 and 1834, regulating relations with Indian nations and maintaining the federal government's authority over those relations. In 1871, Congress declared that the era of making treaties was over. In 1887, the infamous Land in Severalty or Dawes Allotment Act mandated the distribution of reservation land to individuals, which had the effect of further weakening tribal governments and divesting Native peoples of millions of acres of land.[15] In 1924, Congress declared Native peoples citizens of the United States, which effectively gave them triple citizenship: federal, state, and Indian nation.[16]

The most important arena for determining relations with Native peoples has been the Supreme Court, particularly in treaty-rights cases.[17] In treaty-rights cases, the legal scholar Charles F. Wilkinson writes, the Supreme Court "cut directly against the normal inclinations of Anglo-American judicial decision making by enforcing laws of another age in the face of compelling, pragmatic arguments that tribalism is anachronistic, antiegalitarian, and unworkable in the context of contemporary American society."[18] In other words, despite the historically prevailing view in U.S. society that Native governments are not really governments because Native peoples are essentially different from Europeans and their societies represent an earlier, primitive moment in the history of mankind, the existence of treaties continues to counter that prevailing view in ways that might seem mysterious, at least at first glance.[19] Why this is the case, Frederick Hoxie writes, is not immediately evident or reducible to one or two causes. Hoxie observes that the treaty's authority is not an invention of the U.S. government but followed from practices extant from the beginning of European colonization in North America, during which competition among European groups for control of land made treaties a principal means of establishing the legitimacy of Europeans' own political authority. "Questions of ownership, sovereignty, and legitimacy stalked the nations who came here and colored their relations both with each other and with the continent's native people," Hoxie writes; "treaties—or formal agreements between the leaders of the parties involved—were the principal means of resolving these questions of sovereignty and legitimacy."[20] In the early years of the republic, the U.S. government was forced to negotiate with Native peoples who could ally themselves with the Spanish or the British because it could not afford protracted Indian wars politically, militarily, or economically. The federal government also established its own authority against that of the individual states by claiming jurisdiction over relations with Indian nations. As Hoxie notes, "Ironically, Indian treaties were originally a badge of sovereignty for the national government." Finally, Hoxie observes, "there was the ideological reason: treaties seemed the fairest, most just way for a new nation to proceed, especially a nation which claimed to represent justice and liberty." Treaties continued to have authority even after the United States was able to militarily and politically control Native tribes, Hoxie argues, because they produced a system for dealing with Native tribes and "an orderly way to acquire native lands." At the same time, the federal government's claim of supremacy over state governments in negotiations with Native tribes continued to be a means of maintaining federal authority.[21]

From the perspective of the theory of Indians' difference in the era, the fact that Native peoples could be accorded any political authority is quite remarkable. According to Enlightenment theory of Indians' difference, Native peoples inherently did not have the moral or intellectual capacity to form governments. In the United States, the early policy for relations with Indian nations attempted to reconcile that theory of difference with practical conditions, producing a contradictory discourse on Indians that remains difficult to describe historically even today. Two accounts of Indians and Europeans' relations with them that were influential in the late eighteenth and early nineteenth centuries illustrate this collision between theory and practice. The Scottish historian William Robertson's *History of the Discovery and Settlement of North America* was first published in London in 1777 and quickly became, to judge from its publication history, the standard reference on Indians in North America in both Europe and the United States through the mid-nineteenth century, and Secretary of War Henry Knox's report to George Washington and Congress in 1789 on the state of Indian affairs set out a rationale for U.S. Indian policy that persisted through the confrontation over removal in the 1830s. References to Robertson's views on Indians are quite common in the works of others who wrote about Native peoples in the United States throughout the period examined here. Indeed, once the book was published in the United States after the Revolution, it was often reprinted in New York, Philadelphia, Cincinnati, and Albany, at least once along with the Declaration of Independence and several times as a school textbook with questions for students.[22] Written from the metropolitan center of London, Robertson's book presents the theory of Indian difference, which holds that Indians cannot rise out of their state of nature because of their inherent moral failings, which are demonstrated in their inherent traits that exclude them from the universal human. Knox's Indian policy attempts to accommodate the theory of Indian difference but is complicated both by the history of treaty-making, which could not be ignored, and by the ideological foundations of the United States. To solve these problems, Knox hypothesizes that if Indians could be persuaded to change their practices to EuroAmerican ones, fundamentally with regard to the issue of property, they would willingly submit—consent—to EuroAmerican authority. A modernizing Indian nation—an autonomous Indian nation in time—is inconceivable within the theory of Indian difference; the only civilized society possible is that of EuroAmericans. Knox's hypothesis would be disproven in the coming years as some Native peoples became literate, Christian, and farmers but still refused U.S. authority.

Robertson begins with the familiar argument that because Native peoples do not have the same relation to property as do Europeans, they are inherently inferior. His account of Indians also describes the entire logical structure built on that primary assertion, a logic that is important for understanding the intricacies of thinking about Native peoples in the United States. While individual stereotypes of Indians are well known, Robertson's history shows how those stereotypes make sense in relation to one another and in relation to historical and political conditions. All of that knowledge, in Robertson's telling, is balanced on the first principle: that because Indians do not appreciate the importance of property, they are morally and intellectually incapable of perceiving the tenets of natural law and therefore incapable of forming governments administered by the rule of law and of being civilized, political subjects.

Although the favorable environmental conditions in the New World "facilitate the progress of [the European] inhabitants in commerce and improve-

ment," Robertson observes, "the native inhabitants of America are strikingly unimproved."[23] With the exception of the ancient Incas and Aztecs, Indians in the Western Hemisphere existed in a "state of wild unassisted nature" on a "continent . . . possessed by small independent tribes, destitute of arts and industry, and neither capable to correct the defects nor desirous to meliorate the condition of that part of the earth allotted to them for their habitation. Countries occupied by such people were almost in the same state as if they had been without inhabitants" (126). The usual historical or critical interpretation of such statements is that they simply convey the fact that Europeans felt justified in taking land from Indians because Indians did not "improve" the land. Their lack of European-style agriculture is considered a moral failing, however, and a product of their incapacity to perceive the tenets of natural law. The fact that Europeans own property that they desire to improve is a matter of moral superiority; it propels them into the future and determines their government, domestic relations, art, and industry. According to this view, without the desire to improve themselves, Indians have no interest in anything other than satisfying their immediate needs, refuse to labor, do not understand time, have no abstract ideas, have tenuous domestic relationships, and, most important in view of the economic and political interests of EuroAmericans, do not form real governments.

Beginning with Indians' bodies and advancing through their governments, Robertson provides the scientific knowledge to demonstrate Indians' moral inferiority. Indians are "incapable" of "toil"; their "beardless countenance and smooth skin . . . indicate a defect of vigour"; they do not even possess much of an appetite for food (140–41). Indians' lack of desire for improvement, he writes, extends to their "insensibility . . . to the charms of beauty, and the power of love"; they "treat their women with coldness and indifference. They are neither the objects of that tender attachment which takes place in civilized society, nor of that ardent desire conspicuous among rude nations" (142). The "political and moral causes" of their bodily "feebleness" are tied to their lack of desire, ultimately, for property. "Wherever the state of society is such as to create many wants and desires, which cannot be satisfied without regular exertions of industry, the body accustomed to labour becomes robust and patient of fatigue," Robertson observes. But in their "simple state," Indians' "demands . . . are so few and so moderate that they may be gratified, almost without any effort, by the spontaneous productions of nature," and therefore "the powers of the body are not called forth" and Indians cannot "attain their proper strength" (142).

Bodily feebleness leads to intellectual feebleness. Since Indians' lack of desire for improvement confines their thinking to the concerns of their bodies, they have no capacity for abstract thought, "like a mere animal," Robertson observes (149). "Wants and appetites keep the mind in perpetual agitation, and, in order to gratify them, invention must be always on the stretch, and industry must be incessantly employed," he writes (151). Indians, however, are too comfortable in their reduced existence. "Where a favourable climate yields almost spontaneously what suffices to gratify them," he observes, "they scarcely stir the soul, or excite any violent emotion" (151). Limited to the immediate concerns of their bodies, Indians have no capacity for sustained domestic or political association with one another. Marriages among Indians are tenuous, again because of Indians' unwillingness to concern themselves with little beyond their immediate needs. Women are "slaves" and, owing to the "state of depression" in which they find themselves, are "far from being prolific"; children have little connection to their parents (153–55).

Indians' inability to associate with one another most importantly extends to their forms of government, their subsistence living determining their inability to form sustained political organizations. Indians form only "small, independent communities" because larger communities would make subsistence hunting "impossible" since each group must claim a great deal of land and drive out rivals (161). Although Indians' hunting communities are characterized by equality, this is not a positive attribute because "being strangers to property, they are unacquainted with what is the great object of laws and policy, as well as the chief motive which induced mankind to the various arrangements of regular government" (162). Thus, the inherent love of liberty attributed to Indians in this era and later is a defect of their character because it signifies that they cannot submit to a higher authority for the purpose of forming governments. Because no Indian is subservient to another, the "sentiment of independence is imprinted so deeply in their nature that no change of condition can eradicate it, and bend their minds to servitude," Robertson writes; "accustomed to be absolute masters of their own conduct, they disdain to execute the orders of another; and having never known control, they will not submit to correction" (162). Because Indians do not understand the concept of individual ownership of property, they cannot perceive the value of the rule of law, nor do they even need it, Robertson writes, because "there can hardly be any such subject of difference or discussion among the members of the same community, as will require the hand of authority to interpose an order to adjust it. Where the right of separate and exclusive possession is not introduced, the great object of law and jurisdiction does not exist" (162–63). Without the desire to own and improve property, therefore, Indians form governments only for relations with other groups. "The object of government among savages is rather foreign than domestic," Robertson observes; "they do not aim at maintaining order and police by public regulations, or the exertions of any permanent authority, but labour to preserve such union among the members of their tribe, that they may watch the motions of their enemies and act against them with concert and vigour" (163).

Warfare among Indians, then, is not carried on for glory, which is an abstract idea and therefore impossible for them to conceive, or the gain of property, of which they also have no conception, but for personal vengeance. Their arts—the objects they make, the houses they build—are performed with little attention or skill (167, 176–77). As far as their religious beliefs go, "unaccustomed to reflect either upon what they themselves are, or to inquire who is the author of their existence," Robertson writes, Indians "pass their days like the animals around them, without knowledge or veneration of any superior power" (180–81). At the end of his account of Indians in their permanent state of nature, Robertson observes that "a human being, as he comes originally from the hand of nature, is every where the same" and, further, that any change in condition depends on "the state of society in which he is placed" (189). Robertson has already explained that Indians exist, by reason of the hand of nature, in a society that by definition cannot produce individuals who possess the traits that inhere in the universal human, traits that, as Joan Scott points out, only European men can possess—reason and the recognition of individual ownership of property as the foundation of civil society being chief among them.[24] That Indians could somehow be equal to whites is theoretically impossible. Robertson appeals to the abstractions of Enlightenment philosophy rather than commenting on the practical possibilities for Native peoples here. Charles Mills writes that eighteenth-century philosophy held that theoretically "people have rights and duties even in the state of nature because of their nature as human beings," so that "the political contract simply *codifies* a morality that already exists"; the "objective moral foundation" of human society, then, is "*the freedom and equality of all men in the state of nature.*" But "this natural freedom and equality" is confined to "*white* men," Mills writes, because nonwhite subpersons cannot recognize "the duties of natural law" and are therefore "designated as born *un*free and *un*equal."[25] There would seem to be two states of nature in practice: one for whites, which is the starting point for progress, and one for Native peoples, which is permanent. Robertson shifts from one to the other in this passage. Relegating excluded groups of people to subperson status reconciles the contradiction between Enlightenment philosophical theory and colonial practice, Mills points out. Subpersons are permanently in a pre- or nonpolitical state of nature because of their inherent characteristics; subpersons do not have the moral capacity to be free.

Immediately after the Revolution, the U.S. government made a series of treaties with various Indian nations on its borders in which it declared its "conquest" of the nations and its control of their territory, in line with the belief in inherent European superiority and authority. By 1788, however, Congress recognized what was by then obvious: that the United States could not control that land and did not have control of Indian nations. Instead of continuing to assert its dominion when it obviously did not have it, the United States renegotiated the postwar treaties and instituted a policy of recognizing Native autonomy and purchasing Native land. This was "a major policy retreat," historian Dorothy Jones writes; "from the assertion of full political sovereignty over territory acquired from Great Britain, the United States was forced to an acknowledgement that it had only limited sovereignty and that the limitations were set by the rights of the Indians inhabiting the land."[26] In his 1789 report to George Washington and the Congress, Henry Knox points out that declaring war on Indians was a losing proposition: the United States had neither the troops nor the money to finance a campaign. Making treaties, on the other hand, was far cheaper and in keeping with the principles of natural law and the republic itself. "It is presumable, that a nation solicitous of establishing its character on the broad basis of justice, would not only hesitate at, but reject every proposition to benefit itself, by the injury of any neighboring community, however contemptible and weak it might be, either with respect to its manners or power," Knox writes; "the Indians being the prior occupants, possess the right of the soil. It cannot be taken from them unless by their free consent, or by the right of conquest in case of a just war. To dispossess them on any other principle, would be a gross violation of the fundamental laws of nature, and of that distributive justice which is the glory of a nation."[27] Knox suggests that a law be passed declaring that the Indian nations "possess the right of soil of all lands within their limits, respectively, and that they are not to be divested thereof, but in consequence of fair and bona fide purchases, made under the authority, or with the express approbation, of the United States" (53). The individual states would not "complain of the invasion of [their] territorial rights" because "the independent nations and tribes of Indians ought to be considered as foreign nations, not as subjects of any particular State. . . . The general sovereignty [that is, the federal government] must possess the right of making all treaties, on the execution or violation of which depend peace or war" (53). This statement essentially became federal policy. "In future, the obligations of policy, humanity, and justice," Knox writes, "together with the respect which every nation sacredly owes to its own reputation, unite in requiring a noble, liberal, and disinterested administration of Indian affairs" (53).

Although he allows for the probability that encroaching whites will inevitably affect the hunting on Indians' lands and make them more inclined to part with it, revealing his assumption that Indians only hunt, Knox muses on the possibility that "instead of exterminating a part of the human race by our modes of population, we had persevered, through all difficulties, and at last had imparted our knowledge of cultivation and the arts to the aboriginals of the country, by which the source of future life and happiness had been preserved and extended" (53). Knox observes that although "it has been conceived to be impracticable to civilize the Indians of North America," to deny the capacity of Indians for improvement is "a supposition entirely contradicted by the progress of society, from the barbarous ages to its present degree of perfection" (53). Perfection, however, is necessarily a EuroAmerican state, specifically the United States. Indians might come to understand the superiority of individual property ownership, Knox argues, if they received presents of domestic animals and instruction in farming techniques (54). He suggests that "silver medals and gorgets, uniform clothing, and a sort of military commission" be presented to Indians, as Britain had done previously, and that disinterested missionaries, involved in neither trade nor government activities, be introduced who would "be their friends and fathers" (54). "Such a plan," Knox continues, "although it might not fully effect the civilization of the Indians, would most probably be attended with the salutary effect of attaching them to the interest of the United States" (54). Knox argues, in effect, that Indians who can be induced to appreciate the value of property, along with Christianity and EuroAmerican farming techniques, can be persuaded to concede U.S. authority. As there are in effect two states of nature—a fully abstract one for Europeans and one that is both abstract and very real (according to European thinkers) for Native peoples—there are two kinds of progress. There is an endless trajectory toward greater perfection for Europeans, and for Native peoples there is a hypothetical trajectory (getting Indians to want to progress is a struggle in itself) toward the only perfection they can achieve, which is to recognize the superiority of European society and accede to its authority. Indians' hypothetical improvement—becoming more "like" EuroAmericans—is always embedded in the idea of their political incorporation and, with rare exceptions mainly confined to the response to the Cherokee resistance, is always a sign of their political subordination.

Thus, while Knox accepts the possibility that Indians can improve, a modern, Christian, autonomous Indian nation is still beyond the bounds of possibility. Charles Mills usefully calls attention to the elusive problem of what *cannot* be thought about subpersons, which he calls an "epistemology of ignorance." "To be constructed as 'white'" requires "a cognitive model that precludes self-transparency and genuine understanding of social realities," Mills argues; "as a general rule . . . *white misunderstanding, misrepresentation, evasion, and self-deception on matters related to race are* among the most pervasive mental phenomena of the past few hundred years, a cognitive and moral economy psychically required for conquest, colonization, and enslavement" (19; emphasis in original). One cannot, by definition, both be Indian and demonstrate civilized attributes or practices. Indians who become Christians, learn to read and write English, and so on can only be understood, in the abstract, as accepting submission to EuroAmerican authority because, being inherently inferior, Indians can only be subject to EuroAmerican authority. Knox's policy, then, is a necessary modification of EuroAmerican assertions of colonial authority and supremacy.

Conceptions of Indians' difference continued to coexist with insistence that the U.S. government's actions be in concert with its asserted principles and recognition of Native political claims through the early nineteenth century. In *Notes on the State of Virginia* (1787), for example, Thomas Jefferson confidently asserts, "That the lands of this country were taken from [Indians] by conquest, is not so general a truth as is supposed. I find in our historians and records, repeated proofs of purchase, which cover a considerable part of the lower country [of Virginia]; and many more would doubtless be found on further search."[28] By the 1830s, however, historical and political circumstances had changed such that Indians' racial difference became dominant in U.S. society generally; the need to make U.S. actions congruent with U.S. principles receded primarily to the legal system, where it affirmed the legitimacy of U.S. authority. By 1834, historian George Bancroft—himself a Jacksonian Democrat and sometime party functionary—in the first volume of his *History of the United States* argued that the racially superior Anglo-Saxon settlers effected a conquest of Indians, who were predestined to disappear anyway.[29] Historian James Brewer Stewart argues that the naturalization of racial difference over the period 1820–40 marks the emergence of what he calls "racial modernity" in the United States. The period saw increasing mob violence directed at African American and white abolitionists, slave insurrections, the expansion of the plantation economy as a result of the invention of the cotton gin, an influx of lower-class European immigrants, a shift from artisan to industrial production, the emergence of the two-party political system—and Indian removal. By

1830, Stewart argues, most white northerners accepted the concept of ontological racial difference, understanding the existence of "superior and inferior races as uniform, biologically determined, self-evident, naturalized, immutable 'truths,'" which was promulgated in emerging "integrated trans-regional systems of intellectual endeavor, popular culture, politics and state power that enforced uniform white supremacist norms as 'self-evident' social 'facts.'"[30] By the end of the 1830s, Stewart writes, "modern white supremacist culture" was in place (182). The Cherokee Nation cases record a transitional moment when Jefferson's position still held sway among the powerful, including the members of the Supreme Court, but before the complete naturalization of Bancroft's narrative of racial superiority.

EVADING INDIAN AUTONOMY

The three cases of Indian law decided by the Marshall Court—*Johnson v. M'Intosh* in 1823, *Cherokee Nation v. Georgia* in 1831, and *Worcester v. Georgia* in 1832—reveal the contradictions inherent in the practice of relying on the tradition of treaty-making to establish legitimate control of land while at the same time attempting to deny the political autonomy of Native peoples. The Cherokees demonstrated that Knox's policy could not solve that problem. Their spokesmen represented the Cherokees to the white public as literate, Christian, farming people who had formed a government based on republican principles that nevertheless retained traditional Cherokee structures and intended to remain autonomous, as it always had been. They had improved, but they did not recognize the superior authority of whites or the United States. They modernized an Indian nation but did not wish to become "amalgamated" into the United States; they wished to retain their historic political autonomy.

This position could not stand in relation to the United States' colonial and imperial power. The problem for John Marshall's Supreme Court was that it had to assert colonial authority—tyrannical, imperial authority, of the kind the United States had thrown off in the Revolution—while appearing not to. Marshall could not quite deny Native political autonomy by means of the idea of racial difference because that would imperil the treaty as a means of legitimating U.S. control of territory. Instead he conceded Native autonomy, but in the sense of it being almost momentary, lasting only long enough for Indians to enter into willing treaty agreements with U.S. officials in order to transfer land. After which, Native peoples would surely die off since they were an anachronistic early moment in the history of man confronted with the most modern and civilized and, to them, alien of societies. Marshall situates Native racial difference in a progressive history of human civilization. In order to retain the legitimacy conferred on the United States by the treaties, he also posited that the representative new Americans who made treaties with Native peoples acted ethically, in the best interests of the Indians. These U.S. citizens *sympathized* with the inevitable plight of the savage. In order to both concede Native autonomy and insist on racial difference, Marshall relied on the moral superiority of U.S. citizens and, by extension, the United States itself. Thus he made use of sympathy, another dominant discourse of the antebellum era, to further ensure the legitimacy of the United States' claim to authority over land.

In *Johnson v. M'Intosh* (1823), Chief Justice John Marshall somewhat tentatively supports what he would reject in the Cherokee Nation cases—that conquest is the foundation of the U.S. government's claim to ultimate control of Indian land. The problem is that the "conquest" of North America presents an unavoidable conflict between what Marshall calls "the actual state of things" and the philosophical principles on which the new state is founded. Representing land speculators in the Ohio River valley, Daniel Webster argued that since independent Indian nations had sold their land to the speculators, the speculators' title to the land superseded that of the state of Virginia, which claimed the land, as well as that of the federal government. Marshall rejected the land speculators' arguments and asserted federal authority instead based on the doctrine of discovery, in which European nations recognized their separate claims to North American land by reason of their representatives' discovery of it in order to "avoid conflicting settlements, and consequent war with each other." Discovery gave the European nations ultimate title to the land still held, by right of occupancy only, by Native tribes, which could sell land only to the European nation claiming the land by right of discovery. While Indian possession could not be denied, Marshall ruled, Europeans did deny Indians' right to "complete sovereignty," and thus Native peoples could not sell to whatever person or political entity they chose.[31]

Native peoples had been subjected to conquest, Marshall argues, but it was impossible for them to be either assimilated or "safely governed as a distinct people" (589). He maintains that Native peoples in North America constituted a different category altogether from other groups that had been subjected to conquest. Indians were "fierce savages, whose occupation was war, and whose subsistence was drawn chiefly from the forest"; they could not be governed "because they were as brave and as high spirited as they were fierce, and were ready to repel by arms every attempt on their independence," Marshall continues, sounding rather like the frontier romances of the day (590). "The Europeans were under the necessity of either abandoning the country, and relinquishing their pompous claims to it," Marshall writes, "or of enforcing those claims by the sword, and by the adoption of principles adapted to the condition of a people with whom it was impossible to mix" (590). Interestingly, Marshall notes that in "frequent and bloody wars, the whites were not always the aggressors" (590), which leads one to conclude that if whites were not always the aggressors, they must have been usually the aggressors—although they were driven to it by the savagery and recalcitrance of Indians who refused to give up.

These Indians formed governments that Europeans recognized, Marshall admits, because contention for control of territory among Europeans and the vulnerability of European settlements required the recognition of Indian nations that would defend their "property" and that EuroAmericans would seek out in "friendship" (596–97). Marshall writes,

> However extravagant the pretension of converting the discovery of an inhabited country into conquest may appear, if the principle has been asserted in the first instance, and afterwards sustained; if a country has been acquired and held under it; if the property of the great mass of the community originates in it, it becomes the law of the land, and cannot be questioned. . . . However [the doctrine of discovery] may be opposed to natural right, and to the usages of civilized nations, yet, if it be indispensable to that system under which the country has been settled, and be adapted to the actual condition of the two people, it may, *perhaps*, be supported by reason, and certainly cannot be rejected by Courts of justice. (591–92; emphasis added)

Marshall must admit that claiming that the mere discovery of North America amounted to a total conquest of the Indian nations inhabiting it was a shaky argument at best. The history of treaty-making appears to have given him pause. He hesitates over it and the conflict between the claim of conquest and U.S. founding ideology when he admits that he violates the natural rights of Native peoples as well as the law of nations by supporting a system of government ostensibly founded on those same principles.

That "perhaps" in *Johnson* is elaborated on in *Cherokee Nation v. Georgia* (1831), in which Marshall posits the compromise between "natural rights" and "the actual state of things" at the heart of the contradictory history of Indian law described by Deloria and Wilkins. The Cherokee Nation cases arose out of the state of Georgia's systematic efforts to destroy the Cherokee government in the early nineteenth century. These efforts culminated in Georgia's 1829 declaration that it had "full . . . jurisdiction, both civil and criminal," over the Cherokees.[32]

Led by Chief John Ross, the Cherokees hired William Wirt, John Quincy Adams's attorney general, to force the Court to come to a decision on their status. The Cherokees argued that the history of treaty-making between European colonial governments and the United States and the Cherokees demonstrated that the Cherokees formed an autonomous foreign state over which neither the individual states nor the U.S. government could claim dominion. Legal historian G. Edward White observes that the Cherokees' argument was based on natural law principles, which for the Marshall Court encompassed the natural rights principles of the revolutionary era—"the inalienable rights of life, liberty and property"—as well as the natural law "principles of justice, humanity, tolerance, and 'civilized' living that were 'beyond dispute' in any culture which considered itself enlightened."[33] Natural law, the Cherokees argued, established that Native political autonomy and sovereignty existed prior to the formation of the United States and the presence of British colonial authority in North America. But the Cherokees were not only making use of natural law theory; they were also, like Canassatego and the other Iroquois leaders at Lancaster in 1744, insisting on the validity of what they had always known—that they had formed and continued to form political entities not subordinate to European authority "from time immemorial."[34]

The Court held that treaties entered into between the United States and Native peoples confirmed that Native peoples formed sovereign nations over the internal affairs of which the United States could not claim dominion and that Native peoples were citizens of those Indian nations. It further held that land could be acquired from Indian nations only if they freely consented to the sale. The chief justice's concept of "domestic dependent nations," however, which is generally accepted as the principal legal holding of the case, attempted to reconcile the principles of the U.S. government with the necessity of colonial control. Indians formed *nations*, he posits, but because they were *Indian* nations and because Indians could be characterized by their essential difference from and inferiority to Europeans, they were in a permanent state of "pupilage" to the United States. Although their consent was necessary for the legitimate transfer of land, because they were Indians and could not long survive the onslaught of a superior civilization, their consent was only a matter of time.

The justices of the Court staged the conflict between conceding Native autonomy and maintaining U.S. authority in their separate opinions. In Justice Smith Thompson's dissenting opinion, which the chief justice requested that he write and which was later published by the Court's reporter and widely circulated, Thompson writes that the Cherokees' "progress made in civilization" (that is, endorsing Christianity, practicing EuroAmerican-style agriculture, and modeling aspects of their government on the United States) did nothing to destroy their "national or foreign character, so long as they are permitted to maintain a separate and distinct government: it is their political condition that constitutes their *foreign* character, and in that sense must the term *foreign* be understood as used in the constitution" (55; emphasis in original). Thompson reasons back from the fact that treaties had been made to conclude that Indians must therefore form legitimate political entities. As G. Edward White notes, it was not sympathy for Indians that led Thompson to his argument—and it is one that White and other legal scholars suspect that Marshall himself supported while serving up a more politically viable decision himself—but the fact that treaties had been made, ratified, and held to be law.[35] To argue that Indian nations were not autonomous political entities would put the United States in the position of mere conqueror; EuroAmerican practice and ideology thus superseded any consideration of Native peoples.

In his concurring opinion, Justice William Johnson focuses not on history and legal principles but on the exercise of colonial power that Thompson rejects. Johnson in fact extrapolates from actual conditions, in which Native peoples manifestly do not recede and magically disappear in the face of EuroAmerican encroachment, as they were theoretically supposed to do. Furthermore, Indians who became "like" Europeans did not consent to EuroAmerican authority—like the Cherokees, for example. If Indians changed their ways of living as a result of contact with Europeans, Johnson points out, they would probably decide *not* to give up their land. "Every advance, from the hunter state to a more fixed state of society, must have a tendency to impair that preemptive right [that is, the U.S. government's exclusive right to buy land from Native peoples claimed through the doctrine of discovery], and ultimately to destroy it altogether, both by increasing the Indian population, and by attaching them more firmly to the soil," he observes (23). While "the hunter state bore with it the promise of vacating the territory," Johnson continues, "a more fixed state of society would amount to a permanent destruction of the hope" of Indians disappearing to provide a clean slate for EuroAmerican settlement (23). Faced with Cherokees who *had* adopted "a more fixed state of society," Johnson exposes the high political stakes in the concept of Indians' inherent difference: it is the only available means of displacing and denying Native legal claims while retaining the notion of their consent to give up their land, which is still necessary to legitimate EuroAmerican control of territory.

Despite the importance of *Cherokee Nation* in succeeding years, the immediate effect of the ruling was only to delay a decision on the status of Native peoples. The Court held that it could not issue a ruling in the case because Cherokees were neither foreigners nor citizens and thus it had no jurisdiction. A year after *Cherokee Nation*, however, Marshall sought out *Worcester v. Georgia* (1832) in order to clarify the federal government's relation to Native peoples. It is regarded today, above the other two cases in the Marshall trilogy, as "the foundational case in federal Indian law."[36] One of Georgia's laws required non-Natives on Cherokee land to take an oath of allegiance to Georgia. Two missionaries from the American Board of Commissioners for Foreign Missions, Samuel Worcester and Elizur Butler, refused to comply. Because Worcester also held a federally appointed postmastership, Georgia's attempt to criminalize his presence in the Cherokee Nation without a state-issued license amounted to a violation of the federal government's authority (32–33). With the knowledge that President Andrew Jackson was on its side, Georgia did not bother to send a lawyer to defend itself. Nevertheless, Marshall found Georgia in violation of federal law based on his reading of a history of scrupulously legal land transfers in treaties first by European governments and then by the U.S. government, a history in which, surprisingly, Europeans are often weak and unable to assert their authority. Indeed, their very weakness and their reliance on treaties showed that EuroAmericans retained the land the United States claimed legitimately.

Marshall's history begins with the British royal charters given to the colonies, which, while they may have granted land from the Atlantic to the Pacific, did not grant control of Native inhabitants; they merely established Britain's preemptive right to buy land from Native peoples through its colonial agents. The "numerous and warlike nations" of Indians were "equally willing and able to defend their possessions," he writes, in similar fashion to his version of European-Native relations in *Johnson*. Here, however, the notion of conquest is nowhere to be found. "The extravagant and absurd idea, that the feeble settlements made on the sea coast, or the companies under whom they were made, acquired legitimate power by them to govern the people, or occupy the lands from sea to sea, did not enter the mind of any man," he maintains; "they were well understood to convey the title which, according to the common law of European sovereigns respecting America, they might rightfully convey, and no more."[37]

Recognizing the political authority of Indians, however, also required pointing out their difference and inferiority. "Fierce and warlike in their character, [Indians] might be formidable enemies, or effective friends," Marshall writes; "instead of rousing their resentments, by asserting claims to their lands, or to dominion over their persons, their alliance was sought by flattering professions, and purchased by rich presents" (546). This description serves as an elaboration of the concept of Indians' "pupilage" that Marshall posited in *Cherokee Nation*. Indians making treaties were "not well acquainted with the meaning of the words, nor [did they suppose] it to be material whether they were called the subjects, or the children of their father in Europe" (546). "So long as their actual independence was untouched, and their right to self government acknowledged, they were willing to profess dependence on the power which furnished supplies of which they were in absolute need, and restrained dangerous intruders from entering their country: and this was probably the sense in which the term was understood by them," Marshall writes (546–47). Like Robertson's savages, Marshall's Indians did not think any further than meeting their own physical needs at any one particular moment.

Given the competition for power in North America, the contending European nations were not in a position to claim Native land or control Native peoples. Nevertheless, the political alliance European nations sought could be acquired by offering flattery and presents, a means of persuasion suitable for appeasing "fierce and warlike" savages who could not understand the subtleties of diplomacy. These independent tribes could not keep themselves in "supplies" or police their own territories. They happily declared their dependence on Britain without knowing exactly what that meant. Marshall transforms Indians' necessary political autonomy into Indians' equally necessary subordination and dependence because of their inherent condition of "pupilage" to EuroAmerican society. Even so, the king remains scrupulously legal: he "purchased their lands when they were willing to sell, at a price they were willing to take; but never coerced a surrender of them. He also purchased their alliance and dependence by subsidies; but never intruded into the interior of their affairs, or interfered with their self government, as far as respected themselves only" (547).

The same relations existed between the Cherokee Nation and the U.S. government, although in this instance, Marshall goes out of his way to emphasize the weakness and pretense of the United States in its early dealings with the Cherokees. The language of the 1802 Treaty of Hopewell signed by the Cherokees and the United States shows that the United States attempted to "assume a higher tone . . . to impress on the Cherokees the same respect for congress which was before felt for the king of Great Britain" (551). But, Marshall points out, the treaty's language—"the commissioners plenipotentiary of the United States give peace to all the Cherokees, and receive them into the favour and protection of the United States of America, on the following conditions"—reveals instead the comparative weakness of the United States. "When the United States gave peace, did they not also receive it?" Marshall asks; "if we consult the history of the day, does it not inform us that the United States were at least as anxious to obtain it as the Cherokee?" (551). He continues in the same vein: "We may ask, further: did the Cherokees come to the seat of American government to solicit peace; or, did the American commissioners go to them to obtain it? The treaty was made at Hopewell, not at New York. The word 'give' then, has no real importance attached to it" (551).

It must be singular in the history of European colonialism for the colonizing authority to loudly proclaim its weakness before the colonized. In a striking departure from his narrative of conquest in *Johnson*, Marshall in *Worcester* seems to be going out of his way to argue that the citizens of the new United States, careful adherents of republican ideals, could not possibly have had a hand in coercion or violence. Surely the Indians freely consented to whatever agreements they were presented. Still, the Cherokees, being "fierce" savages, did not really understand what was going on. They probably did not perceive the "higher tone" of the language because they did not understand the language: "There is the more reason for supposing that the Cherokee chiefs were not very critical judges of the language, from the fact that every one makes his mark; no chief was capable of signing his name. It is probable that the treaty was interpreted to them" (551). Indians "who could not write, and most probably could not read [and] . . . certainly were not critical judges of our language" nevertheless signed treaties establishing their complete dependence on the United States (552). While their inability to understand English and to write marks Native peoples' perpetual state of pupilage, the representatives of the United States cannot, in this version of the story, be seen as taking advantage of the situation. Sympathy for Indians was a well-developed discourse by the early 1830s, the correct, moral position for U.S. elite intellectuals to espouse. In the opening paragraphs of the *Cherokee Nation* ruling, Marshall observed that

if the courts were permitted to indulge their sympathies, a case better calculated to excite them can scarcely be imagined. A people once numerous, powerful, and truly independent, found by our ancestors in the quiet and uncontrolled possession of an ample domain, gradually sinking beneath our superior policy, our arts and our arms, have yielded their lands by successive treaties, each of which contains a solemn guarantee of the residue, until they retain no more of their formerly extensive territory than is deemed necessary to their comfortable existence. (15)

Marshall's version of the discourse differs from the bulk of such writing only in his emphasis on treaties. At the height of the Cherokee resistance, invocations of the moral necessity of sympathy for Indians displace the contradiction between the dual ideological requirements of a legitimate contract on the one hand (there was no "conquest"; they willingly sold it to us) and the assertion of Indian difference on the other (but, unfortunately, Indians are so different that they did not understand what they were doing) through a fantasy of white benevolence (we must all feel badly about the inferiority and therefore the fate of the Indians).

As in *Cherokee Nation*, one of Marshall's colleagues on the Court provides a gloss on his reasoning. In a concurring opinion in *Worcester*, Justice John McLean admits the probable truth of Georgia's argument that "civilizing" Native peoples, "inducing them to assume the forms of a regular government and of civilized life," may also induce them *not* to cede land to EuroAmericans, as Justice William Johnson pointed out in *Cherokee Nation*. This is an impossible situation. "The exercise of the power of self-government by the Indians, within a state, is undoubtedly contemplated to be temporary," McLean insists; "this is shown by the settled policy of the government, in the extinguishment of their title. . . . It is a question, not of abstract right, but of public policy" (593). This does not mean that he advocates force, however: "I do not mean to say, that the same moral rule which should regulate the affairs of private life, should not be regarded by communities of nations. But, a sound national policy does require that the Indian tribes within our states should exchange their territories, upon equitable principles, or, eventually consent to be amalgamated in our political communities" (593). Autonomous Indian nations within the jurisdiction of a state, McLean writes, "may seriously embarrass or obstruct the operation of state laws," a situation he says is "inconsistent with the political welfare of the states, and the social advantage of their citizens"— although he does not specify exactly how the social advance of whites would be affected by Native political autonomy (594). One could guess though, that, like the Georgians, these citizens would be surrounded by good land that they could not legally take for themselves, despite their moral, intellectual, and political superiority.

As did Marshall in his *Johnson* ruling, McLean makes the distinction between "abstract right" and "public policy." In the abstract, according to the philosophical and legal foundations of the United States, one has to allow for Native political autonomy; as a matter of immediate political concern, however, such political autonomy can be only evanescent. While neither McLean nor the other justices of the Court can give up the notion of consent, even for

Indians, there is no question of the necessity of Native peoples disappearing politically, either by selling land willingly and on good terms and presumably moving west or by "amalgamation," a hypothetical situation that Associate Justice Joseph Story exposes in an 1828 oration on pilgrim history as just another ploy on the part of settlers—except for the New England pilgrims, in his opinion—to justify the acquisition of Native land.[38] That one justice in each of the Cherokee Nation decisions admits that when Native peoples acquire the practices and beliefs of EuroAmerican society they become more attached to their land rather than less—or better able to defend their interest in the land through the treaty relationship and public campaigns of the kind the Cherokees carried out—also reveals that the concept of inherent racial difference was not fully naturalized in the early 1830s. For all of their belief in racial difference, the justices of the Court could not yet completely deny what was obvious—that Native peoples live in time, not in a static state of nature.

CRITICISM AND THE POLITICAL STRUGGLES OF NATIVE PEOPLES

In the nineteenth century, the U.S. government sought to place Native lands under its jurisdiction and the theory of Indian difference held that Native peoples would disappear—but they did not. Twentieth-century developments in U.S. Indian policy might be seen as an attempt on the part of the United States to come to terms with this fact. After the allotment era divested Native peoples of millions of acres of land, they persisted in tribal communities. In 1924, Native peoples were made citizens of the United States; in 1934, in the Indian Reorganization Act, the federal government identified the kind of Native governments with which it would deal; from the late 1940s to the 1960s, the federal government attempted to forcibly "assimilate" Native peoples by "terminating" Indian nations—disestablishing the governments, as in the 1907 formation of the state of Oklahoma from what had been Indian Territory, and declaring the nations nonexistent. Most scholars mark a resurgence of Native political activity in the struggle against termination, in which Indian nations, like the Cherokees more than 100 years earlier, argued that the United States had made treaty agreements that it could not legally break. The discussion of Native "sovereignty" that is central to political struggles today began to take shape at this time; according to Vine Deloria, the term itself first emerged in the 1950s when Washington State tribes asserted their treaty rights to fish.[39]

The conventional wisdom on the political status of Native peoples in the contemporary United States is influenced more by post-1960s civil rights movements, however, in which Native peoples are counted, Deloria and Wilkins write, as one of the many "racial/ethnic groups who have suffered various and continuing measures of discrimination in their effort to gain full citizenship status" (vii). This position, they argue, holds that

> the passage of time and the ratification of assorted treaty provisions, as well as the enactment of specific laws that enfranchised individual Indians or targeted particular classes of Indians or specific tribes as American citizens, have negated or at least significantly diminished whatever distinctive status or rights Indians were thought to have retained. The best thing for tribal members to do, for those who support this logic, is to accept their present status as American citizens and work to make American society a better place in which to live. (vii–viii)

In reviewing the history of the U.S. government's interactions with Native peoples, Deloria and Wilkins argue instead that the only reasonable and ethical way for the U.S. government to conduct relations with Indian nations is to return "tribes to their political status as it existed prior to the prohibition against treaty making in 1871" (158–59). Putting forward such an argument, however, they point out, challenges the national "mythology" of the United States (vii).

The multicultural paradigm for the scholarship on Native writing and the representation of Indians—part of the national mythology that Wilkins and Deloria criticize—precludes an examination of the politics of the representation of Indians and the historicity of Native writing because it is largely driven by a fixation on determining, describing, and analyzing the cultural difference of Native peoples and Native writing.[40] Charles Mills's concept of the epistemology of ignorance is useful here: if the concepts of Native political autonomy and Native existence in time—or the concept of the modern Indian nation—are political problems that must be denied and made impossible for most EuroAmericans (and others) to even conceive of by the mid-nineteenth century, the scholarship, which generally began in the wake of the civil rights movements in the 1950s and 1960s, cannot recognize the concept of a modernizing, autonomous Indian nation or Native political struggle as being at all significant or having anything significant to do with Native writing, which is valued for its expression of cultural difference and therefore of Native cultural identity. Native political struggles can be subsumed under the general rubric of struggles for individual civil rights, as Deloria and Wilkins point out. It is not uncommon for a critic to either insist or imply that Native peoples thought of

Indian nations as cultural, not political, entities or that Indian nations are hybrids formed in the wake of colonization and so to be regretted as a diminution of authentic traditional culture.[41]

Culturalist scholarship on "Third World societies," Arif Dirlik writes, has the effect of "not only . . . legitimizing hegemonic relations between societies, but also . . . mystifying hegemonic relations of exploitation and oppression within societies" by opposing (here) Native culture to "the West."[42] In this setting Native peoples can either maintain a reified cultural difference or succumb to Eurocentrism. As Indians' difference has become cultural rather than racial in contemporary criticism, the sympathy that elite EuroAmerican intellectuals habitually produced for disappearing Indians has also shifted as scholars model an appreciation of Native cultural difference that, in their telling, will make the United States a better place and in part make up for the ethnocentric excesses of the past. To return to the Supreme Court's decisions on Indians in the 1830s, the two discursive means of denying Native peoples' political autonomy and squaring the fact of the history of treaty-making with U.S. (and white) authority, the difference of Indians on the one hand and whites' sympathy for Indians on the other, persist in a critical discourse that represents itself as liberal and even progressive. The effects of difference and sympathy today, as in the nineteenth century, are to displace Native peoples' political struggle—their struggle for history and autonomy—while maintaining the ideological coherence of the United States.

Literary scholarship begins by seeking to account for the cultural beliefs and practices through which Indians demonstrate their difference, a process that is somewhat impeded by the fact that writing itself is, as the criticism has it, not a culturally "Indian" practice. According to the literary criticism, the main difference between Native peoples and Europeans is that Native peoples are "oral" and white people write. In Native writing, then, evidence of "oral tradition," as the criticism defines it, is the standard of literary value.[43] Oral tradition can be marked in a number of traits that the literary work might evidence, narratives, forms, figures, or ideas that show evidence of authentic culture. While writing in English is itself a historic effect of European colonialism, culture is positioned as that which has not changed over time as a result of Eurocentrism, as Dirlik points out. Arnold Krupat sets out the oral versus written position in his often-cited book, *The Voice in the Margin: Native American Literature and the Canon* (1989), in which he argues two points that are widely accepted in the criticism. First, he claims that Native American literature derives from an authentic oral tradition, which anthropologists (and proto-anthropologists before them) began to write down in the nineteenth century. (Thus, the historical nature of white people writing about Indians is as invisible as that of Native peoples writing about themselves.) Since neither English nor writing is "native" to Native Americans, the fact that Native peoples write in English detracts from the Indianness of the literature. Krupat makes this implication clearer when he proposes two categories for Native literature: Native American literature, which derives from oral tradition identifiable as such to the scholar, and mixed-blood or hybrid literature, which combines elements of Native American and "Western" traditions and includes all Native writing in English.[44] Krupat is not clear on whether or not Native American literature can be written down by Native peoples, who seemingly would be violating their Native American–ness in doing so. Accounting for the difference of Native American writing leads directly to Krupat's second point, that Native American literature must be incorporated into the canon of American literature as an expression of American national identity. "Any national literary *canon*," Krupat writes, "may . . . be thought to stand as the heterodox, collective autobiography of any who would define themselves in relation to a particular *national* identity—literature as a kind of multivoiced record of the *American*, for example" (215; emphasis in original). Thus, since the value of Native literature depends on its congruence with an oral tradition that whites produce, without regard to the conditions of that production, the incorporation of the literature into the canon that represents the United States takes place without regard to the history or continuity of Native struggles for political autonomy.

Most recent literary criticism values Native writers of the nineteenth century for embracing both their culture and citizenship in the United States, although the right relation between endorsement of culture and endorsement of inclusion in the United States is seldom to be found.[45] In that absence, speculation on the state of Native writers' psychological identities abounds, and a writer who does not manifest a sufficient appreciation of his or her culture often suffers moral condemnation. The movement from attention to literature as an expression of cultural values to commentary on the psychological identity of individual writers is, as John Guillory and Adam Kuper point out, characteristic of multicultural criticism.[46] But the extent to which scholars feel free not only to speculate on the psychological lives of Native intellectuals for whom there is usually very little information but also to condemn those who do not measure up, culturally speaking, is remarkable. The writing itself is often treated as an occasion for psychological analysis.

Two recent books about several of the same writers included here illustrate the movement from culture to individual psychology, and thence to political incorporation, characteristic of critical writing on early Native literature, as well as the moral assessments levied against Native writers judged to be not in the right relation to their cultures. The objective of Bernd Peyers's *The Tutor'd Mind: Indian Missionary-Writers in Antebellum America* (1997) is to delineate "the evolution of a decolonized personality, or 'tutor'd mind,' and its authentic voice in postcolonial American Indian literature" through an "ethnohistory" of the works of Samson Occom, William Apess, Elias Boudinot, and George Copway.[47] Because "European cultural megalomania left American Indians with only two plausible routes of escape from the colonial situation: physical extinction or total assimilation," he argues, Native writers must be evaluated psychologically on how well they have managed to retain their cultures and cultural identities (4). That they might face ongoing political struggles Peyer dismisses as summarily as he does the complexity of Native life in the wake of colonialism; the "conquest" of Native peoples has been "complete and irreversible," he writes (4–5). His history of Native writers is an analysis of the development of the Native person he calls "transcultural," who, "rather than being incapacitated by a disturbed personality . . . can, given the right social conditions, develop a 'new multiracial consciousness' that is culturally complex and still psychologically sound" (19).[48] With his use of the term "multiracial consciousness" and his dismissal of the possibility of Native political struggle, Peyer situates the properly "transcultural" Native writer squarely within the confines of the properly multicultural United States.

Cheryl Walker reiterates Peyers's movement from cultural identity to psychological identity to political incorporation in *Indian Nation: Native American Literatures and Nineteenth-Century Nationalism* (1997), although her emphasis is on rhetoric in Native writing and Native writers' participation in what she calls the "National Symbolic." Walker writes that her book "focuses upon nineteenth-century Native American writing and its reflections upon nationhood"—but the only nation here is the United States, as Native writers, she asserts, argue for "Native American citizenship in the U.S."[49] Native peoples, Walker observes, "resisted attempts to impose an idea of nation that derived from European models on their native and essentially tribal structures of governance and knowledge, because such ideas obviously threatened many aspects of their cultures" (3). Culture is thus the primary thing that Native peoples have and wish to protect, and their governments are "tribal," that is, representative of an earlier form of human society that cannot be compared to EuroAmerican governments. "Native Americans had not traditionally understood nations as the West came to define them," Walker continues; "nor did race play much of a role in their thinking. In Indian oral traditions the nation originally meant simply the people and the environment they inhabited, an environment without legislated boundaries" (4–5). To support this assertion, Walker quotes William Least Heat-Moon in his travel book, *Prairyerth (a Deep Map)* (1991), as a Native source that demonstrates that "red" people do not think about "legislated boundaries." Least Heat-Moon writes: "The white man asked, where is your nation? The red man said, My nation is the grass and roots and the four-leggeds and the six leggeds and the belly wrigglers and swimmers and the winds and all things that grow and don't grow" (5).[50]

This aspect of Walker's argument requires a bit of elaboration because it reveals both the recurrent sentimentality of the writing on Native peoples and, perhaps in conjunction with that sentimentality, an almost aggressively ahistorical critical stance. Least Heat-Moon, despite his name, is not a Native person, although at one point in his career as a writer of popular travel narratives he claimed to be Native. In his first travel book, *Blue Highways: A Journey into America* (1982), he claimed to be Osage, but he subsequently abandoned that story and stated that his father was a (white) scoutmaster in Kansas City and that he adopted the name Least Heat-Moon as his nom de plume.[51] Since the publication of her book, Walker has noted that Least Heat-Moon is not in fact a Native person, but she maintains that his statement is representative of the fact that Native peoples thought of nations primarily as cultural rather than political entities.[52] It is an obvious fact, Walker asserts, quoting some particularly clichéd prose on the topic to support her contention, that not only do Indians not form political entities but they never have, because they are culturally incapable of doing it.

In that absence, "America"—the United States—is the only nation in which Native peoples can gain citizenship and rights. In *Indian Nation*, Walker argues that Indians can either reimagine the American nation as prototypically multicultural or they will end up psychologically damaged. She describes "two versions of the national allegory" in Native writing, "the egalitarian and the differential" (16). In the first, she writes, "the American nation was seen by indigenous people as essentially a mobile force field where groups might negotiate for particular rights and privileges but which would not inevitably mean the triumph of one and the extirpation of all others" (15). That is, Native peoples recognized the value of multiculturalism. In the second, Walker writes, Native writers who mimicked the discourse of whites rejected their own heritage and "as often as not began a process of national disestablishment [that is, they rejected their cultures] that resulted, in the lives of the Indian authors themselves, in an almost complete loss of psychic balance" (16). A successful Indian writer therefore manages both to claim citizenship in the United States and to retain some elements of his or her culture, at least enough to achieve psychological balance, although how this is measured remains unclear. An unsuccessful Indian writer crosses over to the other side, becomes too involved in "white culture," and loses his or her psychological balance and therefore literary credibility because to be an Indian writer one must demonstrate one's affiliation with Indian culture—like William Least Heat-Moon, one supposes.

Culturalist criticism confines Native writing to the expression of the critic's notion of the values or beliefs that constitute that culture and then incorporates Native peoples into the United States politically by making them representative of one of the many ethnic cultures that constitute the multicultural United States.[53] Employing concepts such as "cultural encounters," "contact," and even "sharing" (between cultures), recent scholarship on representations of Indians is remarkable for the extent to which it downplays violence and conflict.[54] It is perhaps inevitable that culturalist critical discourse would invoke ethnography in its analyses. Indeed, in his important book on images of Indians in U.S. history, *The White Man's Indian* (1978), Robert Berkhofer argues that scholars ought to "apply ethnography to separate White ideology from present and past White images to discover the real Native Americans."[55] Not only is the scholar an ethnographer now—or cultural interpreter, as Dirlik points out—but so are the objects of study, the Europeans who wrote about Indians. Tellingly, such criticism consistently returns, often in conclusion or summary, to the goal of what is often called "cross-cultural" understanding. At the end of his book, *Les Sauvages Americains: Representations of Native Americans in French and English Colonial Literature* (1997), for example, Gordon Sayre observes that despite the record of violence and conflict of the period, "explorer-ethnographers" had "interactions" with Native peoples, in which they gained "new perspectives on European culture."[56] These "explorer-ethnographers" learned that Indians were generous and humane, were receptive to outsiders, were respectful of wilderness living skills, were willing to instruct the English in how to live in the forest and the French to be honorable and to live independently, and even caused Europeans to question their vanity. Europeans' recognition of these useful and admirable traits sometimes led to greater intercultural harmony, although most of the time it did not. Americans, Sayre concludes, "continue to play Indian and to adapt, reject, assimilate, and evaluate native cultures in the midst of dispossessing them" (321). The implication here is that we need to know Indians better as Indians, as inhabitants of cultures, in order to enable them to continue to be Indians, as we understand this state, which would seem to follow Berkhofer's proscription. In so doing, we will be better people ourselves. The doomed Indian returns—we are still "dispossessing" Indians—only now he or she will be saved when we learn to appreciate Indian cultures, which we ourselves have discerned through close reading.

One of the most prevalent critical assertions about Native peoples and their historical relations with EuroAmericans, one that seems to appear in any discussion of Native peoples and the representation of Indians in the nineteenth century, is that EuroAmericans gave Native peoples a "choice" to "assimilate or become extinct." This formulation posits a radical difference between the "two cultures," assuming that Native peoples live a traditional, precolonization life or have lost their difference and have acceded to EuroAmerican culture. It also puts whites in the position of giving Native peoples a say in how they would live, thus making whites both omniscient (as if they could actually determine how Native peoples would live) and benevolent (they might have been ethnocentric, but some of them at least meant well). In this respect, it figures a political relationship as a personal relationship.

At least as common as references to "Manifest Destiny" and the "Vanishing American," the assimilate-or-become-extinct narrative, like those two figures of critical shorthand, is accepted as self-evident and therefore not in need of any sustained historical evidence or explanation. Lucy Maddox makes that narrative the central problematic of her book, *Removals: Nineteenth-Century American Literature and the Politics of Indian Affairs* (1991). She describes an ongoing "debate" about the "admission" of Native peoples to American society, arguing that nineteenth-century Americans' belief that Indians could be citizens if they would just be "like" white people is analogous to present-day critics' insistence that Native writers should write like white people if they want to be "included" in the canon of American literature. "Although the argument now focuses on the admission of Native American history and literature(s) into the canon and the curriculum, what was at issue in earlier phases of the debate was the admission of the Indian people themselves into the structures of American society," Maddox writes.[57] "Then as now," Maddox continues, "the voices that have dominated the discussion have begun with the assumption that accommodation really means the complete assimilation of the Indians into white institutions" (5). Maddox's position is that not allowing Native peoples to express their cultural difference as citizens of the United States is the only form of political subordination possible because there is no other political entity imaginable except for the United States. The only freedom Native peoples have is in the expression of their culture, and the only political position they have is as citizens of the United States.

In the nineteenth century, Maddox writes, "no matter where the writer begins, and no matter what his or her sympathies . . . analyses of 'the Indian question' almost always end . . . at the virtually impassible stone wall of the choice between civilization or extinction for the Indians" (8). It is true that it was argued that Native peoples must become "civilized" in order to, hypothetically, be "included" in civil (U.S.) society. It is also true that Native peoples were overwhelmingly represented as doomed to extinction. The problem is in simplistically linking these two historical facts in a binary opposition and assuming that a choice can be made by whites to think one or the other and by Native peoples to do one or the other when these representations are of a piece. Both the hypothetical civilization of Indians and the hypothetical extinction of Indians are part of the same discursive field. They both ultimately lead to the same thing: the denial of Native political autonomy, the naturalizing of the incorporation of Native land under U.S. jurisdiction, and the reinforcement of white superiority and Native subordination. No one gave Indians a "choice" to do anything. Native peoples could be in one of two positions: subordinate or dead. That's not a "choice"; it's political oppression. With regard to the representation of Indians, the main problem is that knowledge works to justify and maintain the *political* subordination of Native peoples, which is a larger and historically more important process than the psychological dilemmas of individual white people.

Recently, Native critics such as Elizabeth Cook-Lynn, Robert Allen Warrior, Craig Womack, and Jace Weaver have argued for the development of a specifically Native criticism of the literature, which they insist should examine the traditional knowledge of particular tribes, the history of their struggle against colonialism, and above all the future integrity of Indian nations and the role of literature and intellectual production in that future.[58] Arguing that much of the work by Native critics remains fixed on "parochial questions of identity and authenticity," Warrior urges the development among Native scholars of critical discourses based on the history of Native criticism and the struggles for political sovereignty, which he calls "intellectual sovereignty."[59] Womack, a Creek scholar, has described an approach to Creek literature, oral and written, founded on both traditional knowledge and political history in his *Red on Red: Native American Literary Separatism* (1999). Womack's invocation of "separatism" is pointed. His object is to outline a specifically Creek perspective on Creek literature, but, he points out, "my argument is not that this is the *only* way to understand Creek writing, but an important one given that literatures bear some kind of relationship to communities, both writing communities and the community of the primary culture, from which they originate."[60]

Established critics have characterized these initiatives on the part of Native scholars in rather dramatic terms that expose the political underpinnings of the conceptual structure of the criticism itself. In *The Turn to the Native: Studies in Criticism and Culture* (1996), Arnold Krupat characterizes Warrior's argument that Native literatures ought to be understood as national, tribal literatures as "cultural nationalism," to which Krupat opposes his own "humanist universalism."[61] Krupat warns against a "separatism" that he describes as essentially antidemocratic and anti-"progressive" (27–28). Similarly, Kenneth Lincoln argues in his book, *Sing with the Heart of a Bear: Fusions of Native and American Poetry, 1890–1999* (2000), that because "the Americas are fusional cultures, complexly translative," Native writers like Wendy Rose who criticize white academics' continued obsession with Indians' cultural and psychological identity and multicultural "inclusion" on those terms are exhibiting "xenophobic anger" and merely endorsing polarizing differences.[62]

The charge of separatism reads arguments about history and political relations as assertions of cultural autonomy and purity, which is logical only within the constricted conceptual field of culturalist analysis, where everything must be explained as culture, including political relations. At the same time, the separatism charge inadvertently betrays an anxiety about the *political* separatism of Native peoples that has been a threat in Native-European relations from the beginning of settlement in North America. Both Krupat and Lincoln position the United States as morally superior because it embodies the values of "progressive" democracy without addressing the particulars of U.S. history in relation to Native peoples. If sympathy in the nineteenth century demonstrated the moral superiority of white people and elided what white people—individually and institutionally—were actually doing to Native peoples, multicultural criticism of Native American literature insists that its appreciation for the cultural difference of Indians actually demonstrates the moral superiority of universalist U.S. political values, thereby eliding not just history but, in the case of the response to Native criticism, current Native political claims. In both cases, the good feelings of white people clean up the messy details of politics and history. Native scholars who argue that Native literature is intrinsic to ongoing political struggles for autonomy are refusing incorporation as U.S. citizens, a refusal that not surprisingly appears to be unfathomable to many scholars since the ideal of U.S. coherence is fundamental to this scholarship. One might suppose as well that critical anxiety arises from the problem that without a culturalist framework—without cultural difference and psychological identity as objects—there is simply no other way to conceive of how to read Native writing.

RECOGNITION, HISTORY, PLAYING INDIAN

Like other critics of multiculturalism, Nancy Fraser argues that the emphasis on matters of culture and identity in the criticism displaces attention to historic struggles over political and economic relations and that contemporary
"recognition struggles"—struggles for the recognition of identity—"often
serve . . . to drastically simplify and reify group identities."[63] Fraser argues that
recognition would be conceived more usefully in terms of social status than in
terms of cultural identity. In that case, "misrecognition . . . does not mean
the depreciation and deformation of group identity," she argues, "but social
subordination—in the sense of being prevented from participating as a peer in
social life" (113). "To redress this injustice still requires a politics of recognition," she continues, "but in the 'status model' this is no longer reduced to a
question of identity; rather, it means a politics aimed at overcoming subordination by establishing a misrecognized party as a full member of society,
capable of participating on a par with the rest" (113). Fraser provides a fairly
close approximation of what Native writers in the early nineteenth century
sought to achieve—the recognition of their political autonomy and their freedom from subordination to EuroAmericans. For the writers included here
who deal with EuroAmerican authority (U.S. and, in the case of Peter Jones,
British), recognition of their autonomy is the primary object of their struggle,
not definition of their static difference. History is essential in this struggle for
recognition. History inserts Native peoples into EuroAmerican time, into a
confrontation with those who would exclude them from it and deny their
political, not to mention biological, existence. Canassatego's speech at Lancaster is an early record of this necessary historiography: the confrontation is over
who has a legitimate claim to the land, which produces competing histories.

Arif Dirlik describes history as "the most fundamental location of Eurocentrism."[64] The modern conception of time—past, present, future—that emerges
in the eighteenth century, he points out, is not exclusive (as it is usually
construed with regard to the other) but rather radically inclusive; history
"takes entire societies and the whole world in all its aspects as its domain, and
seeks to classify and explain them holistically and systematically" (252). The
fact that the effects of Eurocentrism permeate societies around the world today
does not indicate a universal European supremacy, in which Native peoples are
mere victims of overwhelming force, Dirlik maintains; rather, those affected
societies "interpellate" the effects of Eurocentrism, such that "their political,
social, and economic relations" are transformed but not homogenized or
assimilated to "the structures and values of Eurocentrism."[65] These societies

are merely dislodged "from their historical trajectories before Europe onto new trajectories, without any implication of uniformity, for the very universalization of Eurocentrism has bred new kinds of struggles over history, which continue in the present," he writes (18). European history excludes Native peoples from time while radically including Native societies in the history of man; William Robertson's history of American Indians is an example of these all-encompassing histories that served as the foundation for ethnology and anthropology in the nineteenth century. Native writers disputed the terms of their inclusion in this history because the political effects of that inclusion were unmistakable to them. For Native writers, to claim modern time is to claim the history of European depredations on Native peoples and to refute EuroAmericans' insistence that racial difference is the explanation for everything that happened to Native peoples, as well as for their eventual doom. To claim to progress through time, to argue that Native peoples can and will persist into the future, is to claim political standing and to insist on recognition.

Rather than tell history as Europeans do—the rise and triumph of the nation, its providential destiny—Native writers, as Dirlik says, "interpellate" the effects of Eurocentrism by transforming the EuroAmerican march of progress into a different story. Native writers are quite clear on how EuroAmericans acquired Native land, and it was not through scrupulously legitimate treaties, as Thomas Jefferson and John Marshall would have it. Instead, EuroAmericans systematically assaulted Native governments in order to weaken and destroy their authority over land. The experiences of the Cherokees in Georgia were known to all of the early writers—the conflict, especially the cases in the Supreme Court; the fight over the passage of the Indian Removal Bill of 1830; and the details of Georgia's and other southern states' activities were well covered in the newspapers, thanks in no small measure to the Cherokees' efforts to publicize their fight.

As the writers themselves noted, however, it was not only the state or local governments that attempted to undermine Native governments but also missionaries and traders, who would not seem to have had explicitly political goals. William Apess observes in his *Eulogy on King Philip* (1836) that "the missionaries have injured us more than they have done us good, by degrading us as a people, in breaking up our governments and leaving us without any suffrages whatever, or a legal right among men."[66] If Native writers were sharp in their criticism of the EuroAmericans' efforts to destroy Native governments, they also insisted that those governments survived and adapted to new conditions, as did the Cherokees' government. George Copway's *Life, History, and Speeches* (1847), for example, ends with an accounting of all of the Christian

Ojibwe governments and their progress toward abandoning "the wigwam and the chase, and [resorting] to farming for a living," which emphasizes the degree of autonomy and self-sufficiency of those governments.[67] Tuscarora writer David Cusick's *Sketches of Ancient History of the Six Nations* (1827) ends with a chronology of Iroquois Confederacy leaders, or Atotarhos, before the arrival of Columbus, demonstrating that the Iroquois government preceded and by implication continued after European settlement. Cusick includes a prophesy of Atotarho XI, who reigned, he writes, 150 years before Columbus: "In a dream he foretells the whites would cross the Big Waters and bring some liquors, and buy up the red people's lands; he advised them not to comply with the wishes of the whites, lest they should ruin themselves and displease their Maker; they would destroy the tree of peace and extinguish the great Council Fire at Onondaga, which was long so preserved to promote their national sovereignty."[68] Dirlik writes that for indigenous and other colonized peoples, the past is both "legacy and project," a "dialectical interaction between past legacy and present circumstances."[69] The prophesy of Atotarho XI may serve as an illustration of the point—the coming of Columbus does not cancel out but rather is incorporated into the narrative of Atotarhos and the sovereignty of the Confederacy.

Native peoples were acting as best they could to preserve their political autonomy—their control of their lives—and their authority for their knowledge in the face of an invasion that would destroy their freedom, their political organization, and their knowledge in order to assert authority over their land. As a result of treaty relations and other historical factors (the loss of language as a result of colonization being predominant among them), it became crucial—a point agreed upon by Native leaders throughout history to the present moment—that Native peoples learn to use and manipulate English in order to preserve themselves. However, inserting themselves into Eurocentric time presents the problem of how to think about the past, the time before European colonization, and, most important, traditional knowledge, beliefs, and practices. Native writers differ in their thinking about these matters. Elias Boudinot wanted to stamp out all evidence of anything "primitive" from the Cherokee Nation; William Apess did not know much of Pequot history and had to get it from books; Seneca writer Nathaniel Thayer Strong points out that white contemporaries attempting to establish what Indians were like before white people appeared probably would not find out because even the elders among the tribes could not say for certain which practices and beliefs were extant before colonization since they had changed so much over time.

Just about every Native writer active in the nineteenth century remarked at one point or another that whites do not know what they are talking about when they talk about Indians, however. From early in the nineteenth century, Native writers maintained that white expertise about Indians' difference was essentially an assertion of political authority. The earliest Native writers in the nineteenth century were thus keenly aware of the problems they faced, of the power of EuroAmerican misrepresentation and the necessity of establishing authority for their own knowledge. Whatever their relation to tradition, each of these writers had to find a way to think about it since they were inundated with EuroAmerican misrepresentations. Copway writes in his *Life* that "the *traditions* handed down from father to son, were held very sacred; one half of these are not known by the white people, however far their researches may have extended. There is an unwillingness, on the part of the Indians to communicate many of their traditions. The only way to come at these is, to educate the Indians, so that they may be able to write out what they have heard, or may hear, and publish it" (43–44; emphasis in original). Twenty years before Copway, David Cusick, who, as he himself notes, did not have a perfect command of English, decided to write his *Sketches of Ancient History of the Six Nations* because no one of "my people" had come forward to write it themselves; thus he "endeavored to throw some light on the history of the original population of the country, which I believe never have been recorded" (34).

The historical differences of the writers across nations are most evident on the point of the EuroAmerican representation of their racial difference. In *Playing Indian* (1998), Philip Deloria points out that while white Americans have used their conceptions of Indians to fashion psychological identities for themselves as Americans—displacing the history of actual Native peoples by inhabiting representations of Indians—Native peoples "play" at being Indian as well. "It would be folly to imagine that white Americans blissfully used Indianness to tangle with their ideological dilemmas while native people stood idly by," he writes. "Throughout a long history of Indian play, native people have been present at the margins, insinuating their way into Euro-American discourse. . . . As the nineteenth and twentieth centuries unfolded, increasing numbers of Indians participated in white people's Indian play, assisting, confirming, co-opting, challenging, and legitimating the performative tradition of aboriginal American identity" (8). As the period 1827 to 1863 saw the rapid naturalizing of the epistemology of racial difference in regard to Native peoples, it also saw their manipulations of and interactions with that racial identity change perceptibly.

Writers' uses of "Indian play"—which seems too benign a term considering what is at stake—differed, especially depending on the time in which they wrote. While all of the writers included in this book faced the same political struggle and all recognized the assertion of Indians' racial difference as a mere justification for political and economic oppression, the periods before 1830, between 1830 and 1840, and after 1840 mark out the relative degrees of naturalization of racial difference achieved over time. Prior to 1830, the conception was so new that both David Cusick and Elias Boudinot set it aside completely, but in the period from 1830 to 1840, as the conception rapidly became the norm, writers like the Seneca Maris Bryant Pierce and Elias Boudinot in his later writing found the concept of racial difference so outrageous that they attacked it directly, affecting tones of utter disbelief at whites' stupidity for believing such things. William Apess, who wrote between 1829 and 1836, most completely charted the rise to normality of the knowledge about Indians' racial difference, from his initial rejection of the term "Indian" in his 1829 conversion narrative *A Son of the Forest* to his sophisticated manipulation of his audience's expectations of him and his critique of those expectations when he described himself as merely the "Indian Preacher" in the public notices for his oration, the *Eulogy on King Philip*, in 1836. After about 1840, however, in the writing of George Copway, Nicholson Parker, Ely Parker, and Nathaniel Thayer Strong, the normalizing of Indians' racial difference was complete. By the 1840s, it apparently became de rigueur for Native orators to appear before white audiences in costume, dressed for the part of the Indian. Native intellectuals displayed a range of responses to this situation: while Nicholson Parker willingly dressed as an Indian for his public appearances, and indeed along with his sister Caroline served as a model for depictions of traditional Seneca dress in Lewis Henry Morgan's *League of the Iroquois* (1851), Peter Jones, whose career spanned the 1820s through the 1850s mainly in Canada and Britain, wrote his wife in 1845 complaining of having to appear in an "*odious* Indian costume" while on a tour in Britain to raise money for a school for Ojibwe children.[70] Some writers, like Strong in his 1863 speech on Red Jacket, were prevented by the reification of their own difference and that of their ancestors from being able to complete their arguments about Native equality and historicity.

At the same time, writers such as Nicholson Parker, Ely Parker, and Copway manipulate the concept in increasingly sophisticated ways, as in Nicholson Parker's use in his lectures of the Vanishing American trope as a rebuke to his audience and a point of departure for an alternative history. As these writers collectively struggle with the problem of racial difference, they begin to define a Native intellectual life that reconciles past with present and envisions a future for Native peoples. That they do this at the moment when they are being written out of existence makes their achievement all the more remarkable.

These writers and their works do not offer a tidy conclusion, a single text that triumphs over adversity. Their texts taken together dramatize a continuous process among Native intellectuals of essentially thinking one's freedom into existence in a political and epistemological system that not only oppresses Native peoples but also renders them literally dead. That is not a problem that one writer can solve on his or her own; indeed, it is not useful to characterize it as a problem at all, which implies that there is a straightforward solution. It is rather a historical condition of existence. The writers included here show the emergence in English of this struggle to think through the effects of Euro-centrism. In the end, this work raises questions about and deepens our under-standing of the Native writing that follows and the representation of Indians in general.

CHAPTER ONE

The Cherokee Resistance

EVERYBODY'S INDIANS

When the Jeep Cherokee was introduced in 1974, it was the era of Red Power politics—the takeovers of Alcatraz, Wounded Knee, and the Bureau of Indian Affairs, when *Little Big Man* was a popular film and Cher had a number-one hit with "Half-breed."[1] It seems almost a given that a sporty, outdoorsy vehicle—the proto-suv—would have to have an Indian name. But why Cherokee? Why not Lakota or Sioux, since most popular representations of Native peoples since the late nineteenth century generally have been modeled on the Plains tribes? Why not Dakota or Comanche or Navajo? These all came later in the vehicular nomenclature, only after Cherokee was taken. This seems odd when one thinks that the Cherokees are almost universally described in the scholarship as the most "acculturated" of the Indian nations; after all, they have been counted one of the "five civilized tribes" since at least the late nineteenth century. On the face of it, they would seem the wrong candidates for the job of representing the stereotypical Indian, yet they seem always available and in the most peculiar and even intimate ways. It's a well-established joke in Native discourse that white people habitually claim Cherokee princesses for grandmothers.[2] At the same time, however, these claims of an Indian, specifically a Cherokee, in the family can be more complicated than they might at first appear. When former president Bill Clinton said that his grandmother on his mother's side was one-quarter Cherokee, he was mocked in the mainstream media for his sentimentality, possibly in part because that was one of the ways in which the mainstream media habitually portrayed him. Experts were consulted, but no one could attest to the authenticity of Clinton's claim.[3] But, given that his family is from Arkansas, it's entirely plausible that the story is true, however undocumented it is. A group of Cherokees settled in western Arkansas territory early in the nineteenth century; not all people who "removed" went to Indian Territory; and many Native peoples refused to be counted on government rolls—and this is to say nothing of the vicissitudes of individual lives.

While the Cherokees are persistently available as a type of ur-Indian, their history remains obscured in an especially resilient sentimentality, perhaps moreso than for other Indian nations. That sentiment is particularly available in the terms closely associated with the Cherokees in popular discourse and in scholarship; the Cherokees continue to be associated primarily with "removal" on the "Trail of Tears," terms that themselves could bear some investigation. My interest here is in the terms used to describe this history and what they might signify. In the 1820s and 1830s, "removal" often appeared in newspaper notices to describe a business's change in address—it "removed" to the new address. The concept has different valences in relation to Native peoples. On the one hand, proremoval discourse maintained that Indians would be much happier beyond the reach of the white civilization that was rapidly overtaking them, that removal was merely a matter of gathering up one's things and going, like moving across town to a shop in a better location—in the wilds beyond the boundaries of the civil state, where, as Charles Mills points out, wild people have always belonged.[4] On the other hand, the concept conveys a sense of the psychic as well as political necessity for whites to erase from consciousness an understanding of Native political struggles as such and of their arguments from the historical record. The "Trail of Tears" epitomizes how nineteenth-century sentimentalism works to do that. The emerging middle class of U.S. citizens in the early nineteenth century learned to feel badly for Indians, as their confrontation with a superior civilization would inevitably destroy them. According to this line of thinking, it wasn't that actual white people were wreaking such havoc in Native societies but rather that the havoc wrought was inevitable when inferior met superior. "Trail of Tears" sounds positively misty and romantic in these circumstances; the tears shed are those of *white* people at the sad disappearance of the doomed Indians. As John Marshall's comments in *Cherokee Nation* exemplify, sympathy for Indians has been the U.S. intellectual's pose ever since the early nineteenth century, helping to explain away as inevitable something that was not inevitable at all.

This chapter addresses the writing put forward by the Cherokee leadership in the most heated years of their struggle against removal, from about 1826 to 1837. One significant reason why the Cherokees remain so strangely and contradictorily present in U.S. discourse is that their spokesmen—Elias Boudinot, John Ridge, John Ross, and the not-always-identifiable writers of the Cherokee memorials to Congress—publicly claimed to be the same as whites, self-consciously, calculatedly, and persistently.[5] Specifically, they claimed to form a modern Indian nation, one that could not be characterized as representing a timeless prepolitical state of nature, but one that existed in time, as European nations did. In the Supreme Court, the Cherokees limited themselves to arguing that the treaties between themselves and the United States demonstrated that the United States and its predecessors had already recognized the autonomy of the Cherokee Nation, and that the actions of Georgia and other states, as well as of the United States itself, were in violation of its sovereignty. In an organized and diligent public campaign, which included sending Elias Boudinot and John Ridge out on speaking tours of northeastern cities, publishing the *Cherokee Phoenix*, submitting memorials to Congress, and drawing on the aid of missionary organizations, particularly the American Board of Commissioners for Foreign Missions, the Cherokees added the argument that they were becoming more and more civilized, and thus did form legitimate political entities. They claimed that the citizens of the Cherokee Nation could and did "improve" and change through their own will. Thus, they claimed what was both theoretically and politically impossible for EuroAmericans, and their arguments caused extensive public debate, even a crisis over defining what kind of political entity the United States was. Remarkably, some EuroAmericans, including members of Congress, admitted (momentarily, for the most part) that, based on the evidence of treaties, Native peoples formed civil governments and therefore were not naturally, providentially subordinate to whites.

The Cherokee spokesmen were a small group of men put forward by other Cherokees, although it's difficult to say how much support they had from the majority of Cherokees for their specific arguments, to represent Cherokees' interests to the white public. In recent scholarship, Theda Perdue, Gregory Evans Dowd, and Timothy Sweet have all argued that the spokesmen's representations of Cherokee advances in civilization cannot be assumed to be accurate as to actual practices, which, they point out, were a fluid mix of tradition and change as a result of EuroAmerican influence.[6] The spokesmen's comments present a political strategy that was put forward in a particular intellectual milieu; their espousal of civilization must therefore be understood in the context of both the practices of treaty relations and the theory of Indian difference represented by the likes of William Robertson. In that context, when the Cherokees argued for their treaty rights, EuroAmericans responded by saying that Indians cannot really form legitimate political entities because they are confined to a timeless, prepolitical state of nature in which they have neither the moral nor intellectual capacity to recognize the tenets of natural law in order to form legitimate governments. The Cherokee spokesmen's response to this line of reasoning was to argue that they did indeed exist in time, that they had historically formed governments that themselves had changed over time, whether or not whites recognized these as legitimate governments, and that they were indeed becoming more and more civilized as time passed. They respond to being positioned as outside of time by positioning themselves in time, and therefore representing themselves as natural equals to rather than natural subordinates of whites. In effect, they argue that if the Cherokees' earlier way of life could be characterized as "primitive," they were rapidly moving forward, progressing on a kind of parallel track to EuroAmericans, whom they might even surpass.

At first glance, the spokesmen's invoking civilization looks like a capitulation to EuroAmericans' ideas about their inherent superiority, and indeed some scholarship characterizes their position in that manner. For example, William G. McLoughlin, a prominent historian of the nineteenth-century Cherokees, maintains that in the early nineteenth century the Cherokees who wished to "acculturate"—that is, acquire EuroAmerican practices and beliefs— were also Cherokee "nationalists," whose ethnocentrism was a reaction to whites rejecting the idea of Native citizenship in the United States. In his *Cherokee Renascence in the New Republic* (1986), McLoughlin writes, "The Cherokees did not think of themselves as a nation in 1776 or in 1789. They were a people united by language, customs, and kinship"—that is, he argues, they may have had a distinctive culture, but they certainly didn't form political entities per se.[7] Reacting to the romantic nationalism that drove whites to exclude Indians as potential citizens of the United States, McLoughlin argues that the Cherokees themselves became romantic nationalists, "stressing their differences from other people." "With unerring logic," McLoughlin writes, "they concluded that national identity rested upon a cultural heritage imbedded in history, language, culture, and a distinct and identifiable 'homeland'" (xvii). According to McLoughlin, the Cherokees' "awareness of the racial and ethnocentric paternalism developing among even the most benevolent white philanthropists forced [them] to struggle to retain their sovereignty and their land" (xviii). He concludes, "By 1827, the Cherokees had learned so well the ideology of their conquerors that they were able to use it against them" (xviii). Thus, in McLoughlin's terms, Eurocentrism is itself responsible for the Native struggle for sovereignty.

The Cherokee spokesmen and the other "acculturated" Cherokees that they are taken to represent are often morally faulted for abandoning their cultures. For example, in a chapter on Sequoyah and the Cherokee syllabary he invented in 1821 in her recent *A Is for American*, the historian Jill Lepore observes that "by the early nineteenth century the Cherokee people had adopted many of the trappings of 'civilization'" and that "a census taken in 1835 revealed that the Cherokees' social and economic world was very little different from that of their white neighbors: they had hundreds of mills, schools, manufactories—and thousands of African slaves" (81). I want to consider Lepore's rhetoric here. The Cherokees she describes are the slavish imitators of whites, desiring the "trappings" of a society that we all know is not at all civilized, down to the worst of that society's practices, slavery. It's true that many of the "acculturated" Cherokees owned slaves—Ross and Ridge did, but Boudinot did not—and that, in the 1820s, the Cherokee Council began to pass laws, similar to those of the southern states, regulating slavery.[8] There is no defense for slavery; but what Lepore implies is that *any* adaptation of EuroAmerican practice or belief is in itself morally wrong. At the same time, there is an inevitable underlying assumption that Cherokees must be morally better than whites—because they're not contaminated by "civilization." It must be allowed, however, that Cherokees were just as prone to engaging in the reprehensible practices of the era and place in which they lived as anybody else was. To conflate slavery and "civilization" as Lepore appears to be doing, without accounting for the complexity of historic change, is to inadvertently evoke the position common in the nineteenth century that Indians who come into contact with EuroAmerican civilization will inevitably only pick up its worst vices. That contention was of course founded on the assertion that Indians are an inherently inferior earlier instance of human society for whom historic change can only be corruption. As Arif Dirlik points out, culturalist scholarship gives Native peoples no choice: they must produce their cultural difference in an acceptable fashion or be judged failures and reprobates.

As they were in the nineteenth century, the Cherokees remain difficult to explain. In the introduction to her edited collection of Elias Boudinot's writings, for example, Theda Perdue observes that Boudinot is "an ambiguous and puzzling figure in Cherokee history, because the 'Nation' he gave his life to save simply did not exist" (32). This is because, Perdue continues, "the Cherokee Nation was composed primarily of traditionalists who clung to the culture Boudinot dedicated his life to eradicating" (32). The Cherokees who endorsed "civilization" and progress are only puzzling when the Cherokee Nation can only be conceived of as a purely cultural entity rather than a political entity with a future autonomous existence the terms of which can be fought over by its citizens and inhabitants. It's impossible to understand the Cherokee spokesmen's use of the concept "civilization" without reference to the concept of a modernizing Indian nation that persists despite the existence of the United

States. It's not that the Cherokee position is incomprehensible; it's that the scholarship's categories are inadequate to the task of understanding it.

It's true, however, that apparently rejecting all aspects of Cherokee practices and belief, accepting the EuroAmerican definition of civilization as being essentially "like" whites, and insisting on natural equality with whites cause problems in the spokesmen's discourse. This doesn't make the spokesmen incomprehensible, however. Ridge and Boudinot rejected traditional practices outright, characterizing them as the primitive foundation from which the Cherokees were moving ever forward but not something to be retained in any manner whatsoever. Together they were the public face of the Cherokee Nation, particularly in their lecture tours in northeastern cities, where they often appeared together, and in the pages of the *Cherokee Phoenix*, which had both a Cherokee and EuroAmerican readership. Until 1832, both Ridge and Boudinot maintained that the Cherokees could not be separated from their land. After 1832, however, when it appeared that *Worcester v. Georgia* would not change Jackson administration policy, the Boudinot and Ridge families formed the core of a minority group, often called the Treaty Party, that began to advocate removal. Boudinot lost the editorship of the *Cherokee Phoenix* in 1832 in a battle with John Ross over the newspaper's position on removal.[9] Andrew Jackson and his commissioner, Reverend John F. Schermerhorn, a Dutch Reformed minister from New York, negotiated with the Ridge faction, producing the terms of a removal treaty in March 1835, which the Cherokees were then to ratify when in council. When the council met in October, the Cherokees rejected it. They were then summarily ordered to New Echota to make another treaty and told that anyone who wasn't in attendance would be counted in favor. When the council authorized John Ross to take a party to Washington to negotiate, the Georgia guard arrested Ross and held him without charge for twelve days, confiscating his papers and council records. In the meantime, accompanied by Boudinot's brother Stand Watie, the guard also seized the offices of the *Cherokee Phoenix*. On 29 December 1835, with none of the officers of the nation and a fraction of the population present, the Treaty of New Echota was signed in Tennessee.[10]

If land or geography is the foundation of culture and identity for Native peoples—Canassatego's statement that "we came out of this ground" isn't a metaphorical expression—Ridge and Boudinot can be seen to have paid for the transgression of having allowed for the separation of geography and identity with their lives when they were assassinated in 1839 for breaking Cherokee Nation laws against selling Cherokee land without the sanction of the nation.[11] John Ross had a more complex relation to traditional practices and beliefs than

Boudinot and Ridge. Although he is invariably described as "one-eighth Cherokee," Ross was elected principal chief of the Cherokee Nation from 1827 to his death in 1866, and historians agree that he represented the wishes of the more traditional Cherokees. Like other "acculturated" Native leaders, Ross would seem to have been placed in a leadership position by people more traditional that he precisely because he was better able to deal with whites since he knew them and was more "like" them. At the same time, however, Ross's wife, Quatie, was by most accounts a traditional Cherokee woman (she did not speak English), and Ross himself was distressed when members of his family announced that they were marrying white women.[12]

Ross wrote voluminous official correspondence and documents, but not much for public presentation under his own name, and there he for the most part sticks to the arguments about Cherokee civilization and progress. There is his involvement with John Howard Payne, however, who appeared in the Cherokee Nation at about the time of the struggle over the Treaty of New Echota. Payne was a recently returned expatriot, a friend of Washington Irving's who had made a not-very-successful living acting and writing melodramas for the London stage; he was famous for having composed "Home Sweet Home." When he returned to the United States, he decided to start a literary magazine; traveling through the South in 1834 ostensibly seeking material for his venture, he sought an introduction to Ross because, he said, he wanted to write a history of the Cherokees. Ross welcomed him; he gave Payne documents, laws, and correspondence to copy and invited him to attend the council in October 1835 where the Treaty of New Echota was rejected. He also introduced Payne to "Cherokee antiquarians" who could tell him the "traditionary history" of the nation. Payne gathered voluminous records, but he never published his history; Ross put him to work instead helping the Cherokees fight off the U.S. government, writing letters and helping to write memorials to Congress as they were negotiating the terms of their removal in 1838.[13] It appears that Ross understood traditional knowledge as *history* and, unlike Ridge and Boudinot, believed that it should not be rejected but rather written down and accounted for, and celebrated.

Treaty relations with EuroAmericans have both advantages and disadvantages. In this first sustained assault by Native peoples on colonial authority in EuroAmericans' own institutions, the Cherokees demonstrated both the principal advantages and, inadvertently, the principal disadvantages. The process of defining a modern Indian nation, reconciling traditional knowledge and practice with modernity, is ongoing in Native discourse. The Cherokee spokesmen presented the first systematic written Native engagement with Eurocentrism that addresses itself to the politics of knowledge about Native peoples. In this they set out the parameters and expose some of the recurring problems and concerns of Native discourse throughout the nineteenth century and beyond. The Cherokee spokesmen and their arguments are paradigmatic in that sense. Furthermore, the Cherokee struggle and its articulation by its spokesmen forced a political crisis in the United States, one of the results of which was the Supreme Court's Cherokee Nation rulings, which, paradoxical as they were, have continued to serve as a means for Native peoples to disrupt U.S. political authority and even, once the historical contradictions are taken into account, reject it altogether. These may not qualify as tidy "successes" over their oppressors, but they certainly are not failures either.

CIVILIZATION AND MISREPRESENTATION

In the early nineteenth century, the pressures on all Indian nations grew with the expanding population of whites, which disrupted and openly interfered with the operation of Indian nations economically and politically. In the South in particular, the spread of the plantation system after the invention of the cotton gin, which made it easier to cultivate more land with slave labor, brought Indian nations in Georgia, Alabama, and Mississippi into conflict with the state and federal governments. In response to these pressures, the Cherokees began systematically to take measures designed to stabilize their nation in the face of white encroachment. In 1794, the Cherokees formed a National Council with a principal and second principal chief. In 1802, Georgia surrendered its claims to land extending to the Pacific Ocean under its royal charter to the federal government, which in turn agreed to help to extinguish Indian title to land within Georgia's borders. The nature of this agreement would be a subject of debate during the removal crisis. In 1808, the Cherokees began writing down a legal code in English; in 1817, they declared themselves a republic; in 1826 they founded the capital city of New Echota; in 1827 they held a constitutional convention, which established a government consisting of a principal chief, a bicameral national council, and courts, and elected John Ross principal chief. The Cherokee Council eagerly sought missionaries in the early nineteenth century, all of whom started schools. In 1821, Sequoyah completed the syllabary, which allowed for printing the Cherokee language, and with the aid of missionaries from the American Board of Commissioners for Foreign Missions, the *Cherokee Phoenix* newspaper began publication in 1828.[14]

Elias Boudinot was born Gallegina or Buck Watie around 1804. He was the son of Oo-Watie, who sent his son to a Moravian mission school at the age of six and later to the school of the American Board of Commissioners for Foreign Missions (ABCFM) at Cornwall, Connecticut. On the way to that school, Buck Watie met the white man whose name he took, the president of the American Bible Society and author of the book *A Star in the West: Or, a Humble Attempt to Discover the Long Lost Ten Tribes of Israel, Preparatory to Their Return to Their Beloved City, Jerusalem* (1816), which makes the argument, common since at least the seventeenth century, that the Native peoples of North America are descended from the lost tribes of Israel. Boudinot the Cherokee became a dedicated evangelical Christian, but when he was clearly too sickly as a young man to attend theological seminary, he returned to the Cherokee Nation in 1822. The Cherokee Council sent him on a speaking tour of eastern towns and cities in the spring of 1826 to solicit donations to buy a printing press and type in both English and Sequoyah's newly invented Cherokee syllabary, as well as to found a Cherokee national school. That same spring, Boudinot married Harriet Gold, who was white, in Connecticut, after both he and his future wife had been burned in effigy in Cornwall when the townspeople found out what they intended to do.[15]

Boudinot envisioned, as his commentators have pointed out, Cherokees who are in practice and belief no different from whites—but still Cherokees who are distinguished by their government and their history, who are not subject to U.S. or EuroAmerican authority. The two main points that Boudinot as a Cherokee spokesman tried to get across to whites were, first, that the Cherokees formed a political entity that was separate from and not subordinate to U.S. authority and, second, that the Cherokees and other Native peoples had been misrepresented by whites as static primitives locked in time, when they in fact had changed over time like whites themselves. Furthermore, he insisted, white people would never understand that on their own; Native peoples must be understood as authoritative about their own knowledge, and they must produce that knowledge themselves if they are ever to hope to rectify the situation.

Although he's usually discussed as an isolated figure—by other Cherokees and Native peoples generally, because of his views—Boudinot must be understood in relation to other Native and African American writers active at the time, including David Cusick, the Tuscarora whose *Sketches of Ancient History of the Six Nations* appeared in 1827; William Apess, whose *A Son of the Forest* was first published in 1829; and the African American writer David Walker, whose *Appeal* was first published in 1829 as well. All of these writers, including Boudinot, produced analyses of the early uses of discourses of racial difference as the means of justifying the oppression of Native and African American people in both the Indian removal and African colonization schemes, and they all produced more or less the same critique: they reject racial difference, claim history and therefore political equality for themselves, and, often through the use of sustained textual analysis, refute whites' knowledge about them as politically self-interested misrepresentations. Boudinot, Apess, and Walker, who are more accomplished writers than Cusick, also all point out the psychological effects of such misrepresentations on both colonizer and colonized. While Boudinot was a Cherokee chauvinist and an unapologetic elitist, he is nonetheless also representative of an emerging oppositional critique in the antebellum United States on the part of African American and Native intellectuals and the whites who were allied with them.

Boudinot sets out his general perspective in his "Address to the Whites," which was given during his 1826 lecture tour. The first paragraph of the "Address" sets out the problem of being trapped in time by the knowledge about Indian difference; the second two paragraphs then claim historic time for Native peoples. Boudinot begins by talking about misrepresentation: "To those who are unacquainted with the manners, habits, and improvements of the Aborigenes of this country, the term *Indian* is pregnant with ideas the most repelling and degrading" (68). These "impressions" originate in "infant prejudices"—even though, in keeping with Boudinot's elitism, some of those repelling and degrading ideas might be accurate. Boudinot observes that "some there are, perhaps even in this enlightened assembly, who at the bare sight of an Indian, or at the mention of the name, would throw back their imaginations to ancient times, to the ravages of savage warfare, to the yells pronounced over the mangled bodies of women and children, thus creating an opinion, inapplicable and highly injurious to those for whose temporal interest and eternal welfare, I come to plead" (68–69). He describes the same effects of misrepresentation that David Walker and William Apess did at about the same time: the problem is that whites have consciously misrepresented Native peoples as savages, which causes most people in society to believe such misrepresentations, which makes his job, arguing for their "temporal interest and eternal welfare," much more difficult, "even in this enlightened assembly," which in context can be read as a subtle rebuke. As William Apess after him often noted, a Native person has to endure being responded to as a savage Indian, no matter how "civilized" his appearance. Boudinot attempts first to explain the irrationality of whites' perceptions about Indians.

Next, he claims historic time for Native peoples and inclusion in modern European history on equal terms, not the anachronistic embodiment of the theoretical, prepolitical state of nature provided by the likes of William

Oil portrait of Elias Boudinot, one of a companion pair made of himself and his wife, Harriet Gold Boudinot, probably at the time of their marriage. Reprinted with permission from Ralph Henry Gabriel, Elias Boudinot, Cherokee, and His America *(Norman: University of Oklahoma Press, 1941), frontispiece. Photograph courtesy of the Edward E. Ayer Collection, Newberry Library, Chicago.*

Robertson, but in relation to European time: "Though it is true that he is ignorant, that he is a heathen, that he is a savage; yet he is no more than all others have been under similar circumstances. Eighteen centuries ago what were the inhabitants of Great Britain?" (69). Making this argument requires addressing the discrepancy between white knowledge about Indians and Native reality:

> A period is fast approaching when the stale remark—"Do what you will, an Indian will still be an Indian," must be placed no more in speech. . . . With whatever plausibility this popular objection may have heretofore been made, every candid mind must now be sensible that it can no longer be uttered, except by those who are uninformed with respect to us, who are strongly prejudiced against us, or who are filled with vindictive feelings towards us; for the present history of the Indians, particularly of that nation to which I belong, most incontrovertibly establishes the fallacy of this remark. (69)

As if answering Robertson directly, he argues that "it needs not abstract reasoning to provide to the minds of good men, that Indians are susceptible of attainments necessary to the formation of polished society. It needs not the power of argument on the nature of man, to silence forever the remark that 'it is the purpose of the Almighty that the Indians should be exterminated'" (70). He bypasses the historians then and appeals to the common sense of the "good men" in his "enlightened audience," which, considering his own ardent beliefs and that this address is being given at a church, ultimately signifies those who are truly enlightened by Christianity. Like Apess after him, Boudinot uses Christianity as the means of a critique of scientific knowledge: "It needs only that the world should know what we have done in the last few years, to foresee what we may do with the assistance of our white brethren, and that of the common Parent of us all" (70).

The history that he tells is not the inexorable progress from savagery to civilization, but rather of conflict and Native struggle against the oppression of European colonizers. "However guilty these unhappy nations may have been," Boudinot writes, "yet many and unreasonable were the wrongs they suffered, many the hardships they endured, and many their wanderings through the trackless wilderness" (70). Like George Copway after him, Boudinot considers his own tribe different and better: other tribes "stand as monuments to the Indian's fate," but not the Cherokees, whose history and present conditions he proceeds to tell (70–71). He begins his history of the Cherokee Nation with a geographic description, noting first that "its extent . . . [is] defined by treaties"

(71). He describes it as both productive and beautiful; "these advantages, calculated to make the inhabitants healthy, vigorous, and intelligent, cannot fail to cause this country to become interesting" (71). He then reads the Cherokees within the historical framework of the environmentalism that Robertson rejects in the case of Native peoples in North America: the land itself is so productive that the people cannot fail to use that land and "improve" it, which EuroAmerican thinkers believe is a trait exclusive to themselves. Under these circumstances, Boudinot asserts, "the Cherokee Nation, however obscure and trifling it may now appear, will finally become, if not under its present occupants, one of the Garden spots of America" (71).

Boudinot describes the Cherokees' progress in agriculture, to which they turned, or returned, after the game was hunted out "by reason of the surrounding white population" (71), making the point that as the Cherokees progress through time, they also improve the land, as Europeans do. In *American Georgics*, the literary critic Timothy Sweet calls this the Cherokees' "counternarrative of progress," in which they demonstrated that they had a proper relationship to the land. In this, Sweet explains, they "drew on images which were familiar to whites through the discourse of rural virtue but which had roots in Cherokee agricultural traditions as well," both accurately representing some aspects of that tradition and "[eliding] other aspects, such as the persistence of communal labor practices and the conception of land as a national heritage rather than as individual, inalienable property" (122). Sweet points out that the Cherokees had in fact been mainly agricultural until becoming involved in the European fur trade in the eighteenth century; by the early nineteenth century, the men, who had largely left Cherokee women to tend to agricultural pursuits, returned to those pursuits themselves (122–33). While Boudinot articulates the counternarrative that Sweet describes, Sweet also points out that Boudinot chose not to tell the actual historical trajectory of Cherokee agricultural practices to a white audience, an audience that could conceive of progress only as a straightforward march from savagism to civilization (128). "It cannot be doubted," Boudinot wrote in his "Address to the Whites," "that the nation is improving, rapidly improving in those particulars which must finally constitute the inhabitants an industrious and intelligent people" (72).

The nation's progress can be ensured, finally, only by Christianity, literacy, a strengthened government, and, most importantly, control of knowledge about the Cherokees by the Cherokees themselves. Boudinot's Christianity is inescapable; but in this address, he emphasizes the Cherokees' authority for knowledge about themselves as much as, if not more than, Christianity. After describing the improvements in agriculture, Boudinot observes that "there are yet powerful obstacles, both within and without," including "prejudices in regard to them in the general community" and the influences of "their immediate white neighbors, who differ from them chiefly in name" (72). Combating these obstacles requires that the Cherokees be educated to communicate knowledge both to each other and to whites. Sequoyah's syllabary, Boudinot writes, now enables all Cherokees to read the New Testament, which leads to an apostrophe of praise: "The shrill sound of the Savage yell shall die away as the roaring of far distant thunder; and the Heaven wrought music will gladden the affrighted wilderness" (74). The bulk of his attention, however, is focused on the government. Although the government needs improvement, he writes, as the people "rise in information and refinement, changes in it must follow, until they arrive at that state of advancement, when I trust they will be admitted into all the privileges of the American family" (74–75). Here Boudinot appears to be referring to the "privileges" of civilization in the sense of the political structure of the U.S. government, as the Cherokees form their government on the U.S. model, rather than their being incorporated as U.S. citizens. Boudinot goes on to discuss the structure of the Cherokee government—its districts, judicial system, legislature, National Council, and principal chiefs (75).

To ensure the progress of the nation, "ignorance" both within and without the nation must be combated, and here Boudinot appeals for aid to establish "a Seminary of respectable character" and to purchase the type in English and Cherokee to publish a newspaper (75–76). Boudinot envisions the newspaper as a vehicle for discussing the politics, history, and progress of the nation, a role in addition to and more prominent than its religious purposes:

> Such a paper, comprising a summary of religious and political events, &c. on the one hand; and on the other, exhibiting the feelings, disposition, improvements, and prospects of the Indians; their traditions, their true character, as it once was and as it now is; the ways and means most likely to throw the mantle of civilization over all tribes, and such other matters as will tend to diffuse proper and correct impressions in regard to their condition— such a paper could not fail to create much interest in the American community, favourable to the aborigines, and to have a powerful influence on the advancement of the Indians themselves. (76)

He describes a running documentation of the operation of government, along with a running history of the nation's march toward improvement, which is precisely the information that counters EuroAmerican assertions that Indians cannot form real governments and do not participate in history. To that end, the newspaper is also to be produced by Cherokee people, in order to be authoritative about Cherokee people:

> I am inclined to think, after all that has been said of the aborigenes, after all that has been written in narratives, professedly to elucidate the leading traits of their character, that the public knows little of that character. To obtain correct and complete knowledge of these people, there must exist a vehicle of Indian intelligence, altogether different from those which have heretofore been employed. Will not a paper published in an Indian country, under proper and judicious regulations, have the desired effect? I do not say that Indians will produce learned and elaborate dissertations in explanation and vindication of their own character; but they may exhibit specimens of their intellectual efforts, of their eloquence, or their moral, civil, and physical advancement, which will do quite as much to remove prejudice and to give profitable information. (77)

If the problem is that whites grievously misrepresent Native peoples, with disastrous personal and political results for Native peoples, then knowledge has to be produced by Native peoples for it to be accurate about Native peoples. This is the main, ongoing argument made by all of the Native writers included in this book, and it matters not that the most "acculturated" of the writers is the one who makes the argument first (at least in print), as misrepresentation is a condition of all Native existence, regardless of the stand any particular Native writer takes on what scholars construe as culture.

Thus, even as Boudinot envisions the Cherokee Nation as a phoenix, the ashes from which the phoenix rises are the figurative product of whites' actions toward the Cherokees, which are products of how they think about the Cherokees, not the result of anything the Cherokees themselves had done or what they supposedly were. When Boudinot deploys the civilization-or-extinction rhetoric at the end of the address, extinction is a possibility, not an inevitability, and the result of the actions of EuroAmericans, not the nature of Indians. "There is, in Indian history, something very melancholy, and which seems to establish a mournful precedent for the future events of the few sons of the forest, now scattered over this vast continent," he writes (79). "The poor aborigines [have melted] away before the white population," he continues, and then adds: "I merely speak of the fact, without at all referring to the cause" (79). The cause is white rapacity fueled by willful ignorance, and his point is that that destruction can be stopped and the Cherokee Nation can continue unimpeded by white oppression, separate from U.S. authority.

Portrait of John Ridge, which appeared in the second volume of McKenney and Hall's Indian Tribes of North America *in 1842, after Ridge's death. McKenney wrote that Ridge "successfully cultivated the arts of peace, and the literature of the white man, and had exhibited the mildness and benevolence of character, peculiarly interesting in the descendant of a wild and ferocious race" (182). Photograph courtesy of the Edward E. Ayer Collection, Newberry Library, Chicago.*

Boudinot's cousin John Ridge makes essentially the same points that Boudinot does in an essay he wrote in 1826 for Albert Gallatin, future founder (in 1842) of the American Ethnological Society, who was at the time collecting information about Native languages with the help of Thomas McKenney, commissioner for Indian affairs in the War Department. Ridge was at the time a twenty-two-year-old lawyer working for the Creeks to renegotiate the Treaty of Indian Springs of 1825. As a young man, Ridge was too ill to even complete his education at the ABCFM school in Connecticut. However, he returned to the Cherokee Nation to become a successful lawyer. Like his father, John Ridge was also a successful farmer—and a slaveowner. Like Elias Boudinot, Ridge married a white woman, Sarah Bird Northrup, whom he met in 1824 while at the ABCFM school in Connecticut. Their union, like Boudinot and Gold's marriage two years later, caused public outrage in the town, although Ridge and his wife were not burned in effigy.[16] While Boudinot was the more prolific of the two spokesmen, Ridge also wrote a good deal, for the *Cherokee Phoenix* and for regional and religious newspapers, although not much of that writing has survived. Ridge was also well known and well regarded as an orator and was frequently called upon to negotiate with the U.S. government during this period.[17]

Ridge follows Gallatin's questionnaire form, noting the state of population, agriculture, manufactures, commerce, government and laws, religion, and knowledge in the Cherokee Nation. Like Boudinot, he starts with boundaries and the division of the territory into districts. Ridge's argument of Cherokee equality with whites extends to a similar superiority to Africans; he insists that the people farm and that "there are a few instances of African Mixture with Cherokee blood & wherever it is seen is considered in the light of misfortune & disgrace."[18] Intermarriage with whites, he notes, "has been increasing in proportion to the march of civilization" (81). He spends a good deal of time describing "the nature of our Government," so that "you will be better able to ascertain the State of our improvement" (82). What he describes, however, is a mixture of traditional practices and EuroAmerican influences. He also describes traditional governmental forms as susceptible to EuroAmerican depredation in pursuit of land. The council is made up of "a standing body of Chieftains, who are first in the social Circle, and foremost in the deadly fight":

> They possess within themselves Legislative judicial and executive powers. The first law of Nature and of Indians is against the victim belongs [without trial], and the friends and relatives of the aggressor are compelled by law to remain neuter. This was a principle of Government in the worst of Shapes of our people. Our Chiefs were numerous and their accountability was small [= their responsibility was trifling]. Lands could then be obtained [of them] at a price most convenient to the United States as their Commissioners with the assistance of the Agent could always procure a majority for a Cession, and when this was done the patriotic Chiefs yielded to secure their shares for the trifling equivalent, Savage ignorance saw its own folly by the effect

which presented itself in a shape not to be misunderstood. The tide of white population was advancing on all sides & the Indians poor in goods, but well supplied with the vices of their neighbors were retreating to a given point where they would eventually be crushed in the folds of the encroaching Serpent! The Remedy was within themselves and this could only be supplied successfully in the amendment of their Government. (82)

Ridge advances the argument that Cherokee government existed before white people arrived but that the traditional structures in place were inadequate to the task of dealing with white people's rapacity. He continues with a detailed account of the laws governing the Cherokee Nation at that time, noting that "we have not as yet many written laws, it being the . . . policy of our Government to regulate itself to the capacity and state of improvement of our Citizens" (83). "Most of the adjudications are founded in the Spirit of Natural Law or Common Sense," he adds (83).

Despite Boudinot's emphasis on Cherokee government and autonomy, a review of the address published in the *North American Review* reads the sameness of Indians only in terms of their hypothetical political incorporation into the United States. After excerpting a long passage of Boudinot's, the reviewer observes that it "[savors] a little of the marvelous" that the Cherokees "have written laws, and a representative government, though not, as far as we can learn, of a very republican cast."[19] Although the Cherokees present the "novel spectacle" of improvement, the reviewer insists that "a community of *civilized* Indians is an anomaly that never has existed, nor do we believe it ever will exist," and warns: "Bring the Indians up to this mark, and you put them on a level with whites; they will then intermarry, and the smaller mass will be swallowed up by the larger; the red skin will become white, and the Indian will be remembered only as the tenant of the forest, which have likewise disappeared before the march of civilization" (474). The presumptions of Euro-American discourse reveal themselves here. The abstract individual that is the model citizen of the civil state is in effect only a European abstract individual, and that civil state is in effect only a European civil state. When Native peoples claim to be the same, to be civilized, and to inhabit civil states, they cannot be understood to be inhabiting separate, autonomous states, because a civilized state that isn't European by definition cannot exist. The only way that Indians can be understood as civil is if they literally, physically, become white people through intermarriage—which, again, has the ancillary effect of incorporating their land into the United States, which is the only thing that really matters where Native peoples are concerned. It's an ironic assumption in relation to

Boudinot's personal life: Harriet Gold was made a citizen of the Cherokee Nation, and laws were passed to extend automatic citizenship to the children of white women married to Cherokee men, a departure from Cherokee traditional matrilineal practices.

Disputing such misrepresentation was the better part of Elias Boudinot's job. In an essay published on 21 April 1830 in the *Cherokee Phoenix*, Boudinot responds to a report of the House of Representatives Committee on Indian Affairs on removal. The report makes the familiar argument that, because Indians are a "hunting" people, they are inevitably doomed. Boudinot cites a passage from the report: "When the game is all gone, as it soon must be, and [Indians'] physical as well as moral energies shall have undergone farther decline, which the entire failure of the resources of the chase has never failed to remark in their downward career, the hideous features of their prospects will become more manifest" (114). To which Boudinot replies:

> Whoever really believes that the Cherokees subsist on game, is most wretchedly deceived, and is grossly ignorant of existing facts. *The Cherokees do not live upon the chase*, but upon the fruits of the earth produced by their labour. We should like to see any person point to a single family in this nation who obtain their clothing and provisions by hunting. *We* know of no one. (114)

Of course Cherokee people hunt, he notes,

> about as much as white people do in new counties, but they no more depend upon this occupation for living than new settlers do. . . . Cut off the last vestige of game in these woods, and you cannot starve the Cherokees—they have plenty of corn, and domestic animals, and they raise their own cotton, and manufacture their own clothing. (114–15)

The House committee report, produced during the debates over the Removal Bill, in effect summarizes the Jackson administration's position. Boudinot quotes this disingenuous proviso in the report: " 'The committee do not mean to exaggerate, either in the state of facts, as they are believed to exist, or in the deductions which they make from them, as to the future prospects of the Indians' " (115). To which Boudinot responds: "The Committee have, nevertheless, greatly exaggerated—all their statements, of what they call *facts*, are nothing but unfounded assertions" (115). He quotes the committee again, to the effect that it is still true " 'that an Indian cannot work' "; that "the same improvidence and thirst for spirituous liquors attend them, that have been the foes of their happiness elsewhere"; and therefore "the condition of the common Indian is perceptibly declining, both in the means of subsistence and the habits necessary to procure them" (115). Therefore, the committee contends, "the mass of the population of the Southern Indian tribes are a less respectable order of human beings now, than they were ten years ago" (115).

These "naked assertions," Boudinot indicates, are patently absurd: "Who labors for the Cherokee and builds his house, clears his farm, makes his fences, attends to his hogs, cattle and horses; who raises his corn, his cotton and manufacturers his clothing? Can the committee tell? Yes they have an answer at hand. He has no house, no farm, no hogs, cattle, no corn to save him from starvation, and clothing to cover him from nakedness. We know not what to say to such assertions" (115–16). "The above maxim," he writes, "has been received by many as truth, but not by the intelligent observers of their character, but by their enemies and such as have not had the means of knowing facts" (116). There are those who will make such assertions when they know them to be false in order to justify their oppressive actions, and then there are those, a much larger and more dangerous group, one might argue, who merely repeat what is already "known" without investigating whether or not that knowledge is accurate. In Boudinot's words: "[The committee notes that] they have sought information from every proper source within their reach and do not fear that the general correctness of their statements will be confirmed by the most rigid scrutiny. Here then, is the great mystery—*the committee feel sensibly the want of* STATISTICAL *and* ACCURATE *information!*," which, he notes, could be had from the Cherokee Nation (the government) itself. "But such a course would not possibly answer," Boudinot concludes, because the committee "seek information from somewhere else, not from documents, and resident whitemen, but from the enemies of the Indians, who are looking with eager expectation to their removal, that they may take possession of the spoil, obtained by means the most unmanly and iniquitous" (117).

DEBATING REMOVAL

For a short period of time, the arguments that Indians formed autonomous states over which the United States could not claim authority, that Native peoples by extension had always formed autonomous states, whatever the details of their form, and that Native peoples were historical and could change in time all held the attention of quite a few members of Congress and the general public. That a group of people so different from EuroAmericans, so distant from them in human time (as far as most EuroAmericans were concerned), so thoroughly known and endlessly studied by EuroAmericans, and so obviously impeding the free exercise of EuroAmerican political authority were represented by some whites as free, equal, and politically autonomous is due mainly, if not entirely, to the existence of treaties. Most who advocated Native sovereignty reasoned back from the historical fact of treaties having been made with Indian nations to conclude that Native peoples did indeed form civil governments, that they therefore must have the capacity to recognize natural rights, and that they therefore must be fully human, not justifiably subordinated subpersons. It was clear to the Cherokees' supporters that the legitimacy of the republic itself was at stake. The treaties were contracts agreed to by all who entered into them, approved by the president and members of the Senate; consent was a requirement that went to the essence of the republic itself. One of the Cherokees' supporters in Philadelphia asked:

> But shall a government founded on that celebrated exposition of the rights of man, which accompanied our declaration of independence, grossly violate those rights in others, for which they then contended? If *dependent nations* have a right to *declare themselves independent*, ought not *independent nations* be permitted to *remain independent*? Can a people be viewed as the friends of liberty at home, who are ready to avail themselves of superior strength to exercise tyranny abroad? and would it not be tyranny to drive a nation from their own comparatively cultivated fields, and comfortable dwellings, to create, if under such disheartening circumstances they should have energy for the undertaking, a new abode in the wilderness, when, judging of the future by the past, they may expect to be expelled again by our unprincipled cupidity?[20]

The use of force to "remove" Indians was not just unconscionable, but anti-American. It is sometimes argued or pointed out that the supporters of the Cherokees were more interested in legal abstractions than in the Cherokees themselves, but that is exactly why the conflict is significant.[21] The actual history of treaties forced EuroAmericans, at least some of them, to set aside common knowledge about Indians' inferiority and savagery and contemplate the political legitimacy of "others." In the long history of modern European colonialism, that would seem to be a radical break. Here I want to discuss how the concept of "civilization" operates in the "debate" over removal in the principal works advocating these positions, Jeremiah Evarts's William Penn letters advocating Cherokee treaty rights and Lewis Cass's *North American Review* essay setting out the theoretical and philosophical position of the Jackson administration. What I want to show here is, first, how the fact of treaties allows at least a certain kind of EuroAmerican thinker to concede that

Native peoples must be "civilized" and, second, how the advocates of Euro-American authority attempt to argue their way out of that position. What I think the contrast shows is the precariousness of the removal position: it's balanced on the assertion of the unchanging nature of Indians, as well as their always impending disappearance. No one can ever deny the fact of treaties or their necessity.

The main force behind white support for the Cherokees, Jeremiah Evarts, was trained as a lawyer but never worked as one because of illness; instead he served with the American Board of Commissioners for Foreign Missions, which was headquartered in Boston and sent missionaries out around the world, including to the Cherokee Nation and other Indian nations in the United States. Boudinot, Ridge, and another Cherokee leader, David Brown, all attended the ABCFM school in Connecticut. Evarts was editor of the ABCFM's journal, the *Panoplist*, later the *Missionary Herald*, and a member of the organization's administration, first as corresponding secretary and then as treasurer. Throughout the 1820s, Evarts became more involved in missions to Indian nations. As the removal controversy began taking shape after the election of Andrew Jackson, Evarts began writing a series of essays in the *National Intelligencer*, a politically important Washington, D.C., newspaper, under the pseudonym William Penn. The first proprietor of Pennsylvania, Penn was celebrated for having made the first treaty with Indians to purchase land that had already been deeded to him by the king.[22] Through at least the mid-nineteenth century, Penn was a popular signifier of the right relation with Native peoples, one that was at once Christian and politically legitimate and in keeping with the expressed ideals of the republic.[23] The twenty-four essays, published between August and December 1829, were widely circulated and reprinted in newspapers and in pamphlet form, and after Jackson's first message to Congress in December 1829, they were the motivation for public meetings held throughout the United States, but particularly in the Northeast, at which petitions against removal were drafted and sent to Congress.[24]

Evarts's commentators emphasize his Christian beliefs in relation to his work on behalf of Indians, but even these commentators often note that the bulk of his arguments on behalf of the Cherokees are based on the history and analysis of treaties. Evarts deduces the existence of Indians' natural rights—therefore their sovereignty, therefore their freedom—from the undeniable historical fact of treaties having been made in which the Cherokees were understood to be autonomous political entities. Over the course of the twenty-four essays, Evarts systematically examines, one by one, the sixteen different treaties made by the Cherokee Nation and the United States and then the six colonial treaties between the Cherokees and Britain, before turning to dismantling Georgia's argument (all are reprinted in Evarts, *Cherokee Removal: The "William Penn" Essays and Other Writings*). He regards his presentation as a legal case: in the fourteenth essay, he submits an "apology for the long discussion" but maintains that "the people of the United States are jurymen in the case, and must hear it" (120). The second essay establishes what is in effect the thesis of his argument over the course of the essays. Evarts writes that the Cherokees have a "perfect title" to their land:

> The Cherokees are human beings, endowed by their Creator with the same natural rights as other men. They are in peaceable possession of a territory which they have always regarded as their own. This territory was in the possession of their ancestors, through an unknown series of generations, and has come down to them with a title *absolutely unincumbered in every respect.* (53)

He disputes the description of the Cherokees as "mere wanderers" who cannot possess the land, noting that "at the earliest period of our becoming acquainted with their condition, they had fixed habitations, and were in undisputed possession of a widely extended country" (54). Further, the fact that the Cherokees do not have written history to demonstrate their possession of the land, but only "tradition," does not matter. "We might as well ask the Chinese, what right *they* have to the territory which they occupy," Evarts writes; "to such a question they would answer, 'God gave this land to our ancestors. Our nation has *always* been in possession of it. . . . The nations of Europe are comparatively of recent origins; the commencement of ours is lost in remote antiquity'" (54). "What can be said to such a statement as this?" Evarts asks; "Who can argue so plain a case?" (54).

Evarts's examination of the relevant treaties made with the Cherokees in the late eighteenth and early nineteenth centuries demonstrates the inevitability of these conclusions. He cites treaty texts extensively to show that the United States and the state of Georgia have always (until recently, in Georgia's case) recognized that Indians formed nations, that those nations were sovereign, and that neither the United States nor the state of Georgia could force the Cherokees to sell land without their consent. He notes that in many of the treaties it is clear that the United States is not superior to and does not presume to dictate the actions of Indian nations. On the contrary, the 1785 Treaty of Hopewell, Evarts points out, recognizes the Cherokee Nation's right to declare war, noting that "to declare war and make peace are enumerated, in our own declaration of independence as among the highest attributes of national sovereignty. The other attributes there enumerated are to form alliances and to establish commerce. It is a curious fact, that every one of these attributes was exercised by the Cherokees, in the negotiation of the Treaty of Hopewell." This fact, he notes, contradicts Georgia's assertion that the Cherokees were a mere race of hunters, "a sort of non-descript tenants at will" (68). These supposed tenants at will, Evarts points out, were "solemnly admitted to have the right of declaring war upon their landlords" and "are also strangely allowed to possess the right of punishing, according to their pleasure, any of their landlords, who would 'attempt to settle' upon any lands, which, it is now contended, were then the absolute property of said landlords" (68–69).

Like the Cherokee memorialists, Evarts turns to the language of the treaties themselves, in which the Cherokees are described as a "nation" with "citizens" by the president of the United States, George Washington, the Senate, and the "commissioners plenipotentiary" of the United States. "It will not be pretended that the *Cherokees* reduced the treaty to writing," Evarts points out; and if the father of the country, a Senate composed of men who were legal scholars and had participated in the constitutional convention, two of whom became Supreme Court justices, one of them chief justice, used such language, it would be absurd to think, he argues, that they did not really mean it (71). "The document in question is not a jumble of words, thrown together without meaning, having no objects, and easily explained away, as a pompous nullity," Evarts writes; "on the contrary, it was composed with great care, executed with uncommon solemnity, and doubtless ratified with ample consideration. It has, therefore, a solid basis, and a substantial meaning" (71). Whether the Cherokee Nation is a weak state or not, Evarts writes, "so long as it has distinct rights and interests, and manages its own concerns, it is a substantive power; and should be respected as such" (73). Georgia's denial of the import of the plain language of the treaties effectively makes the treaties negotiated by the president and approved by the Senate "frauds" of a "barefaced and most disgraceful character," Evarts writes, "the effect of which is to dispossess a 'nation' of its hereditary land and government, and to drive the individuals of which it is composed (who are called in the preamble already cited, the '*citizens and members thereof*')—to drive away these '*citizens*' as outcasts and vagabonds" (77).

Thus the textual analysis of treaties leads Evarts to the conclusion that Georgia's insistence on the difference of Indians is a self-interested assertion made in order to justify the use of force to acquire Indian land. In his essays, Evarts refers to the same treaty and the same passage that Marshall later would in *Worcester*, and, as with the memorialists' reference to this passage, comparison of the two reveals how fragile and politically necessary racial difference is. Where Evarts and the memorialists proceed from written text, Marshall must fabricate a scenario that attempts to both keep the legitimacy of treaties intact and reinforce the notion of Native inferiority. Marshall surmises that the Indians didn't really understand what they were doing and that the U.S. commissioners, not being in a position to assert their military superiority, were instead driven to make such agreements because of their moral superiority. Marshall's reading of this passage from an eighteenth-century treaty, which must be seen as a response to the two previous readings (those of Evarts and the memorialists), demonstrates the political utility of sympathy for Indians in the United States. Justifications for the oppression of Native peoples in a republic, given the circumstances of the treaties and the ideology of the republic itself, are a little trickier than in other forms of colonialism. The United States is not a monarchy the authority of which is providentially ordained. At this point in history, it is not yet an "empire"—although that would soon become, by the 1840s, a common concept—the supremacy of which would be unquestioned. The good republicans who formed the United States in rebellion against tyranny, to protect individual rights, are themselves individuals who have deep feelings, kind impulses, and sincere desires to do right. Marshall's comments in *Worcester* demonstrate that republican benevolence is a necessary political strategy in the United States when faced with political conflicts that go to its ideological foundations.

After considering each of the treaties entered into between the United States and the Cherokee Nation, as well as examples of treaties with other southern tribes, Evarts begins a systematic dismantling of Georgia's position. Georgia's argument that Indians are wandering savages and white people are civilized cultivators of the soil, Evarts points out, is not founded in fact. The Cherokees are manifestly *not* a "wandering people," he writes, but rather have farms, a government, a legislature, a judicial system, schools, and churches. "Judge ye," Evarts has the Cherokees say to Georgia, "whether we are such a sort of people, as the writers on the laws of nations had in their minds, when they talked of vagrants, hunters, and savages" (126–27). Georgia's rejoinder to such arguments is to baldly state that "civilized" Indians become *more* attached to their land and therefore more difficult to "remove" from it, and therefore Georgia can't get the land that it wants, which reveals that the abstract idea of the superiority of the civilized to rule the savage is merely the justification for taking land and acquiring power. In his imagined debate in the fifteenth essay, Evarts has the Georgians reply to the Cherokees as follows:

[You] had no business to betake yourselves to an agricultural life. It is a downright imposition upon us. This is the very thing that we complain of. The more you work on land, the more unwilling you are to leave it. Just so it is with your schools; they only serve to attach you the more strongly to your country. It is all designed to keep us, the people of a sovereign and independent State, from the enjoyment of our just rights. We must refer you to the law of nations again, which declares that populous countries, whose inhabitants live by agriculture, have a right to take the lands of hunters and apply them to a better use. (127)

Thus, Evarts recognizes that the *only* means Georgia has to assert its authority over Indians is its insistence on their essential difference from whites and the inability of Indians to change over time, as whites do.

That this assertion is not founded in plain fact is revealed in Georgia's ("very recently argued") current argument that Indians cannot form real nations. Again, turning to written text, Evarts maintains that this argument "cannot be entitled to the least degree of credit," as "communities of Indians have been called nations, in every book of travels, geography, and history, in which they have been mentioned at all, from the discovery of America to the present day" (148). Furthermore, "treaties have been made with them, (uniformly under the *name* of treaties,) during this whole period" by both Georgia as a British colony and the United States under the Articles of Confederation and the Constitution, the validity of which Georgia recognized until only very recently:

It would seem, according to the present doctrine of Georgia politicians, that civilized people may be called nations and make treaties; but uncivilized people are to be called savages, and public engagements with them are to be denominated—*what* such engagements are to be denominated, we are not as yet informed. There must be a new code of national law, and a new set of writers upon it, in order to help Georgia out of her present imagined difficulties:—I say *imagined*, because there is no real difficulty; not the slightest. What are the distinctive marks of a civilized people, and who is to decide whether these marks are found in a given case, are matters unexplained. Nor are we told in what respects treaties between civilized nations are to be interpreted differently from public engagements with an uncivilized people. (148–49)

Thus it is that the inescapable fact of treaties allows some EuroAmerican thinkers to accept the notion that Native peoples could be "civilized," which most importantly means that they could form legitimate, autonomous governments. At the very least, Evarts's arguments should demonstrate why "civilization" is such an imperative concept in the Cherokee spokesmen's arguments for treaty rights. Indeed, the proremoval opposition had to demonstrate that Native peoples could not possibly be civilized, despite the treaties, and still keep the legitimating authority of treaties intact, which causes, as Evarts points out, reliance on precarious assertions about the nature of Native peoples.

Andrew Jackson's main spokesman in the public discourse on removal was Lewis Cass, the governor of Michigan Territory from 1813 to 1830, after which he became Jackson's secretary of war. Cass published a long article in the *North American Review* in January 1830, just after Jackson's December 1829 speech to Congress and as the Removal Bill was introduced by committees in both the House and Senate—and after the William Penn essays had become popular and indeed fomented an organized protest movement to support the Cherokee cause. The article, titled "Review of *Documents and Proceedings Relating to the Formation and Progress of a Board in the City of New York, for the Emigration, Preservation, and Improvement of the Aborigenes of America*," came to be viewed as the authoritative statement of the administration's point of view and was excoriated in detail in articles published in reply and in congressional speeches given in the spring of 1830. Drawing on Robertson's *History of America*, Cass argues that Indians inherently are morally incapable of forming civil governments, but to keep the treaties intact, he claims that they are anomalous and, as would be the case in the Marshall Court's rulings in the coming two years, that the superior morality of EuroAmericans keeps the treaties intact as legal agreements long enough for Indians to consent to give up their land.

In the article, Cass complains that Indians had absolutely refused to change: "Distress could not teach them providence, nor want industry. . . . Their habits were stationary and unbending; never changing with the change of circumstances" (67). As evidence of their obtuseness, he points out that they remain hunters even when the game is gone; that missionaries have no effect, regardless what efforts they might make. This is essentially Robertson's account of the Indians of North America, which Cass cites in detail in the essay. In Cass's view, the Cherokees who seem to be the exception are only "some of the *half-breeds* and their immediate connexions," who have managed because of their geographic location on the main slave-trading route to acquire slaves to work the land. Indian men, he claims, refuse to do agricultural labor and leave it to their women, who are "drudges." By their participation in the slave trade, a few have managed to acquire some property, while "the great body of the [Cherokee] people are in a state of helpless and hopeless poverty" through their "improvidence and habitual indolence" (71). Civil government belongs only to white people; the "half-breeds" who formed the republican government in 1827, claimed Cass, demanded the recognition of sovereignty "for the first time, since the discovery of the continent" (102).

Following Robertson, Cass contends that Indians are morally incapable of forming governments. He observes that

> government is unknown among them; certainly, that government which prescribes general rules and enforces or vindicates them. . . . The tribes seem to be held together by a kind of family ligament; by the ties of blood, which in the infancy of society are stronger as other associations are weaker. They have no criminal code, no courts, no officers, no punishments. They have no relative duties to enforce, no debts to collect, no property to restore. They are in a state of nature, as much so as it is possible for any people to be. Injuries are redressed by revenge, and strength is the security for right. (74)

Constrained in their permanent state of nature because of their inherent moral failings, Indians cannot be understood to have a title to the land that supersedes that of morally superior Christians, Cass claims. He quotes Chancellor James Kent's *Commentaries on American Law*, in which Kent argues that "agricultural settlers" have a "sounder claim" to the continent than that of "wandering savages" who have a "loose and frail, if not absurd title . . . to an immense continent, evidently designed by Providence to be subdued and cultivated, and to become the residence of civilized nations" (77).

The problem of actual treaty documents remains, however. According to Cass, Indians occupy a position that is an "anomaly in the political world, and the questions connected with it are eminently practical, depending upon peculiar circumstances, and changing with them" (78–79).[25] Treaties may have been made with Indians, and some version of "title" to the land may have been conceded to them, but because they themselves are different, *peculiar*, those treaties and titles do not have the same meaning as the same agreements made between whites. Treaties made between Indians and whites, Cass argues, do not represent agreements made between two autonomous political entities but rather a meeting of superior and inferior with, as in Marshall's account in *Worcester*, the sympathy of whites for Indians being the main cause for any "stipulations" in the treaties that may appear to be in Indians' favor. "As the representatives of a powerful and intelligent nation, negotiating with a feeble, depressed, and ignorant remnant of the people, who once held the whole, and yet hold a portion of the country," Cass observes, "they cannot disregard the just claims of such a people for protection and kindness" (81). Those who argue that Indian nations are sovereigns with "absolute dominion of the soil" (83) are laboring "in the ardor of a mistaken benevolence," Cass writes (82). Benevolence can go only so far.

There are "apparent inconsistencies" in Indian relations, Cass admits; the United States has "introduced a system difficult to reconcile with our preconceived notions" (83). That is to say, it is undeniable that treaties *were* made, and some people deduce that Indians must possess natural rights because of the very existence of treaties. But the apparent inconsistency between insisting that Indians cannot form nations when many documents ratified by the U.S. Senate appear to be predicated on recognition of Indian nations' sovereignty does not really have to be explained. The fact is that Indian treaties are an "anomaly," as are Indians themselves: "The Indians themselves are an anomaly upon the face of the earth; and the relations, which have been established between them and the nations of Christendom, are equally anomalous. Their intercourse is regulated by practical principles, arising out of peculiar circumstances" (83). Anomalies do not have to be *explained*: they just *are*. The "reservations and guarantees" made in treaties with Indians, which might be interpreted to signify their political autonomy, "were designed to secure to the Indians their preexisting rights, as they had enjoyed and we had acknowledged them; to secure to them the possession of their lands; that right of occupancy, which is compatible with their habits and pursuits, and with our immediate jurisdiction and ultimate domain" (83).

At one point Cass reveals the political ramifications of recognizing the validity of Indian treaties and admits the danger of *not* maintaining that Indians and treaties with them are "peculiar":

> If the peculiar relations subsisting between us and the Indians are not to control and regulate the construction of our compacts with them, every Indian treaty is a virtual acknowledgment of their independence, and its conclusion with them a practical recognition of their right to all the attributes of sovereignty. If their claims to establish and maintain a government, and to possess the absolute title of the land, are deducible from the course of these negotiations, or from the general nature of the instruments [the treaties] themselves, we have in fact abandoned all just right to restrain or coerce them. They are as independent as we are, and come forward and take their stations among the nations of the earth. (87)

If Indians are not peculiar, then they must be the same, and civilized. Quoting Chief Justice Spencer of the Supreme Court of New York, Cass adds, " 'I know of no half-way doctrine on this subject. We have either an exclusive jurisdiction, pervading every part of the state, including the territory held by [the] Indians, or we have no jurisdiction over them whilst acting within our reservations' " (87–88). Such a situation cannot be: the free "consent" that many argue must be obtained from Indians is, again, not a real problem, because the treaty of which it is a feature is itself anomalous, and it is obvious (at least to Cass and other Jacksonians) that "a just regard to the safety of both [Indians and whites] requires, that we should govern and they obey" (94).

In 1831 and 1832, John Marshall came up with the "half-way doctrine" that Cass had found impossible to imagine, explaining the textual evidence of the treaties as the benevolence of white people and pinning his hopes for the future on the disappearance of Indians. Legally, this has turned out to be an extremely precarious position for U.S. authority. While the legal system retained the trace of Native autonomy that even Marshall's compromise allowed, Cass's position soon became common knowledge. In May 1831, Jeremiah Evarts—who had orchestrated responses to Cass's essay in various periodicals, monitored congressional debates on the Removal Bill for the ABCFM, and advised congressional and other supporters of the Cherokees—died of consumption. After it appeared that Andrew Jackson would not enforce the Supreme Court's March 1832 ruling in *Worcester v. Georgia* that Georgia's extension of its laws over the Cherokees was unconstitutional, the Cherokee Nation's principal white supporters began to advise them to make the best of a bad situation and begin removal.

It is often noted that support for the Cherokees dissipated rapidly, especially after the passage of the Removal Act, or was supplanted by white support for the nascent antislavery movement. The demands of African Americans held as slaves are in some respects easier to assimilate and easier to subvert: African Americans couldn't demand political autonomy, as they had no land; they could only claim inclusion in the political system, which allows for a benevolence that essentially keeps the oppression of African Americans in place. The fact that Native peoples had a well-known, well-discussed, and to many whites highly convincing argument for political autonomy (and therefore equality) leads to the disappearance of their conflict as a political issue. It disappears because the only way it can truly be solved, at least from the perspective of EuroAmerican authority, is if Indians themselves disappear.

TIME IMMEMORIAL

A series of memorials that the Cherokee Council submitted to the U.S. Congress from 1830 to 1832 lay out the Cherokees' position and document the increasing assaults on their autonomy by the government and people of Georgia. The principles set out in the written texts of the treaties, they argue, validate their understanding of themselves and the existence of their nation, in which they have existed since "time immemorial." That phrase becomes a refrain in these memorials, in the cases presented to the Supreme Court, and in Cherokee writing generally. In *American Georgics*, his discussion of the Cherokee spokesmen's arguments for their improvement of the land, Timothy Sweet writes that, despite the Cherokees' insistence on being the same as whites and their claims of "improving" the land in the same way that whites claimed that they did, they consistently represented the land not as the right of individuals to own and exploit for their own purposes, but rather as a "national heritage" that must be held collectively, by the Cherokee Nation (122). This national heritage is also historical: as with Canassatego at Lancaster, Cherokee history is bound up in the place, literally, as an origin and as a means of understanding the world. "Time immemorial" describes how long the Cherokees had been on the land, and it inevitably contrasts with the timeless, prepolitical state of nature that Indians were supposed to inhabit. These accounts of Cherokee memory before Congress radically interrupt modern European notions of time and progress, both by insisting on the validity of tradition (the land is a national heritage, not a thing for individual expropriation) and by countering the narrative of U.S. history. Rather than having abandoned traditional identity, the memorialists—the circumstances of the writing of these documents and their authors remain unknown, although they were submitted under the auspices of the national council—can be seen as having stripped their identity down to its bare bones: existing on particular land, with a particular group of people, over time.

In 1828, the election of Andrew Jackson—a southerner, former military officer, and well-known advocate of removing Native peoples—encouraged southern states, Georgia most notoriously, but also Alabama and Mississippi, to take action against the Indian nations within their boundaries. In response to the Cherokees' 1827 declaration of sovereignty, on 19 December 1828, after Jackson's election, the state of Georgia extended its own laws over Cherokee territory and people, effective 3 June 1830, officially reducing the Cherokees to subperson status. Georgia declared the Cherokees subject to state law; declared null and void all acts of the Cherokee Council; made criminal any Cherokee's influencing another not to "remove"; and declared that neither Creek nor Cherokee Indians could be witnesses in court cases involving whites. On the same day, the governor of Georgia also issued a proclamation that gold had been discovered in Cherokee territory, that all of that territory belonged to the state of Georgia, and that any person not authorized by the state to mine for gold was to leave immediately.[26] Jackson provided Georgia public encouragement in his December 1829 annual message to Congress, given before the Removal Act was introduced in both houses of Congress in January 1830. In it, he described the *imperium in imperio* argument made by Georgia and the advocates of removal, which essentially held that, because Indians are morally and intellectually incapable of forming true civil governments, the Cherokee government was a strange hybrid of white and Indian and not truly Indian at all and that the Cherokee government formed in recent years was an illegal pretender state formed within the boundaries of a true, preexisting sovereign state. "The fate of the Mohegan, the Narragansett, and the Delaware is fast overtaking the Choctaw, the Cherokee, and the Creek," Jackson declared; "that this fate surely awaits them if they remain within the limits of the States does not admit of a doubt."[27] Here Jackson transfers the conflict between inherently inferior Indians and inherently superior EuroAmericans specifically to conflicts between governments, real and pretended. "A portion . . . of the Southern tribes," he argues, "having mingled much with the whites and made some progress in the arts of civilized life, have lately attempted to erect an independent government within the limits of Georgia and Alabama. These States, claiming to be the only sovereigns within their territories, extended their laws over the Indians, which induced the latter to call upon the United States for protection" (47). The threatening term "mingling" indicates the racial logic underlying Jackson's position. The reviewer of Boudinot's "Address to the Whites" reads the prospect of Indians forming a republican government as their desire to intermarry with whites, after which they disappear biologically as well as politically. Jackson, less sanguine than the reviewer, describes the prospect of Indians forming republican governments as miscegenation, which carries with it white degradation and Indian violation of the natural order.

A modern Indian nation is a political and moral abomination in this line of thought. But for the Cherokees, a modern Indian nation was exactly what they were trying to describe. In a memorial presented to the House of Representatives in February 1830 and to the House Committee on Removal in March 1830, submitted after Jackson's election and Georgia's declaration of the extension of its laws over the Cherokees, to be effective the following year, the Cherokees countered Georgia's arguments for extending its jurisdiction with invocations of "time immemorial" and the history of treaties. Although the memorial begins with a kind of ritualized submission—"As weak and poor children are accustomed to look to their guardians and patrons for protection, so we would come and make our grievances known. Will you listen to us?" (7)—it quickly gets to the specifics of the conflict at hand. First, they point out that they have possessed the land "from time immemorial, as a gift from our common Father in Heaven," and give this account of their history:

> We have already said, that, when the white man came to the shores of America, our ancestors were found in peaceable possession of this very land. They bequeathed it to us as their children, and we have sacredly kept it, as containing the remains of our beloved men. This right of inheritance we have *never ceded*, nor ever *forfeited*. Permit us to ask, what better right can the people have to a country, than the right of *inheritance* and *immemorial peaceable possession*? (7–8)

In a manner reminiscent of Canassatego at Lancaster in 1744, they insist that their memory of themselves counters EuroAmerican assertions of their inherent inability to form legitimate governments.

Moreover, they argue, EuroAmerican documentation supplements rather than supersedes that tradition. The treaties show, they assert, that "our rights as a separate people are distinctly acknowledged, and guaranties given that they shall be secured and protected" (8). The Cherokees, the memorial continues, have "always understood" the treaties in that way, and "the conduct of the Government towards us from its organization until very lately, the talks given to our beloved men by the Presidents of the United States, and the speeches of the Agents and Commissioners, all concur to show that we are not mistaken in our interpretation" (8). Furthermore, they add, "some of our beloved men who signed the treaties are still living, and their testimony tends to the same conclusion" (8). Finally, they bring up the problem of the role of consent in legitimating a contract: "If we were but tenants at will, why was it necessary that our consent must first be obtained, before these Governments [Georgia and the United States] could take lawful possession of our lands? The answer is obvious. These Governments perfectly understood our rights—our right to the country, and our right to self Government" (8). Thus it is not just the memory of Cherokees but the written documents of whites that prove that whites recognize the autonomy of Indian nations, and therefore the full humanity of Native peoples.

In a section of the memorial over the signature of Lewis Ross, the Cherokees add the term "known history" and European political philosophy to the proof of their memory and signed treaties, shifting the focus somewhat from Cherokee tradition to European history. Georgia's claim of "sovereignty over this nation" and its "threatened and decreed . . . extension of . . . jurisdictional

limits over our people" is assailed as "utterly at variance with the laws of nations, of the United States, and of the subsisting treaties between us, and the
known history of said State, of this nation, and of the United States" (2). They
review the history of the Cherokees' relationship with the United States, pointing out that "it is evident from facts deducible from known history, that the
Indians were found here by the white man, in the enjoyment of plenty and
peace, and all the rights of soil and domain, inherited from their ancestors,
from time immemorial, well furnished with kings, chiefs, and warriors, the
bulwarks of liberty, and the pride of their race" (3). Here in a more acute fashion, the Cherokees articulate "known history"—known by both EuroAmericans and Cherokees, verifiable in EuroAmericans' records and Cherokees'
counternarratives of that record, largely oral—and the "time immemorial"
before colonization. The United States concluded the Treaty of Hopewell in
1785 after the peace with Great Britain, and, the memorialists continue, "it
remains to be proved, under a view of all these circumstances, and the knowledge we have of history, how our right to self-government was affected and
destroyed by the Declaration of Independence, which never notices the subject
of Cherokee sovereignty" (3).

Following Jeremiah Evarts's William Penn essays, the memorialists call attention to the language of the Treaty of Hopewell, the same one that Chief
Justice John Marshall discusses at length in his *Worcester* ruling two years later.
They argue that the United States has clearly indicated that it views the Cherokee Nation as an autonomous nation:

> If, as it is stated by the Hon. Secretary of War, that the Cherokees were mere
> tenants at will, and only permitted to enjoy possession of the soil to pursue
> game; and if the States of North Carolina and Georgia were sovereigns in
> truth and right over us; why did President Washington send "Commis-
> sioners Plenipotentiaries" to treat with the subjects of those States? Why did
> they permit the chiefs and warriors to enter into treaty, when, if they were
> subjects, they had grossly rebelled and revolted from their allegiance? And
> why did not those sovereigns make their lives pay the forfeit of their guilt,
> agreeably to the laws of said States? The answer must be plain—they were
> not subjects, but a distinct nation, and in that light viewed by Washington,
> and by all the people of the Union, at that period. (3)

Perhaps the strength of the argument presented here is what caused Marshall
to attend to this particular passage himself, insisting that although the Euro-
Americans may have been politically weak at the time, they were also still
intellectually superior to Indians, and that the seemingly incontrovertible evi-

dence of the treaty's language—that they did understand the Cherokee Nation as a sovereign nation like any other—can be explained by insisting as well that it was their civility and benevolent interest in the welfare of the poor Indians that caused the U.S. negotiators to use such language.

But the memorialists maintain that "the jurisdiction . . . of our nation over its soil is settled by the laws, treaties, and constitution of the United States, and has been exercised from time out of memory" (4). They argue that they always have been a nation and if the form of the nation's government changes, that does not mean that the sovereignty itself is a new thing: "As a distinct nation, we had a right to improve our Government, suitable to the moral, civil, and intellectual advancement of our people; and had we anticipated any notice of it, it was the voice of encouragement by an approving world" (4). They employ a certain degree of understatement in rejecting the idea of their inherent incapacity to maintain themselves in the wake of contact with EuroAmericans:

> Arguments to effect the emigration of our people, and to escape the troubles and disquietudes incident to a residence contiguous to the whites, have been urged upon us, and the arm of protection has been withheld, that we may experience still deeper and ampler proofs of the correctness of the doctrine; but we will adhere to what is right and agreeable to ourselves; and our attachment to the soil of our ancestors is too strong to be shaken. (5)

EuroAmerican accounts of "known history" they reject out of hand, commenting,

> We have been invited to a retrospective view of the past history of Indians, who have melted away before the light of civilization, and the mountains of difficulties that have opposed our race in their advancement in civilized life. We have done so; and, while we deplore the fate of thousands of our complexion and kind, we rejoice that our nation stands and grows a lasting monument of God's mercy, and a durable contradiction to the misconceived opinion that the aborigines are incapable of civilization. The opposing mountains, that cast fearful shadows in the road of Cherokee improvement, have dispersed into vernal clouds; and our people stand adorned with the flowers of achievement flourishing around them, and are encouraged to secure the attainment of all that is useful in science and Christian knowledge. (5)

The claim to "civilization" and "progress" must be understood in context—as a material but also temporal claim, a claim to history on their own terms. They are not Indians who wish to be white people, but Native peoples who have a range of experiences with and relations to Eurocentrism, which might be marked in the names of the signatures on this particular memorial, which include English names, like Thomas Foeman, James Hamilton, and John Timson; translated Cherokee names, like Sleeping Rabbit, Laugh at Musk, Deer in Water, and White Path; and transliterated Cherokee names, like Situaka, Choo-wa-loo-ca, Nah-hoo-lar, and Tor-yes-kee. The speaker of the Cherokee Council is Going Snake, who signs with a mark (6).

In the memorials of 1831 and 1832—submitted after the passage of the Removal Act in May 1830, as Georgia's declared jurisdiction officially began, and as the Cherokee Nation cases were before the Supreme Court—the memorialists dispense with arguments about their own civilized improvements and instead describe the uncivilized behavior of whites and Georgia's use of force, which, like the concept of consent, has special meaning: a republican government built on natural law is supposed to adhere to the rule of law rather than indulge in the use of force. "It is deemed useless to detail the present state of their advancement in the arts of civilization," they write in the 1831 memorial (over the signatures of Richard Taylor, John Ridge, and William Shorey Coodey), when the "question is one of *justice*—one which does not depend upon domestic changes to govern its decision" (5). They contrast the words of Thomas Jefferson on the sovereignty of Indian nations with testimony about murder, false imprisonment, robbery, and kidnapping committed by Georgians in the Cherokee Nation. In the 1832 memorial, over the signatures of John Morton, John Ridge, and William Shorey Coodey, they tell of an invasion by the Georgia militia to enforce Georgia's jurisdiction over Cherokee land:

[A] *military force* has been organized and stationed in the country, armed as though they had to combat with a foe hostile in disposition and fearful in strength. The country is patrolled by them in every direction, often traveling thirty miles by night to strike terror and dismay wherever it is believed the slightest degree of unwillingness prevails to acknowledge and bow in submission to the "sovereignty" of the State. The gold mines have been seized upon by them, and the benefits of their mother earth, where, from immemorial ages, the Cherokees have dwelt, denied them, at the hazard of bloodshed, or four years' imprisonment, at hard labor, in the walls of a penitentiary! The *robber* has entered many of their dwellings at the meridian sun, and securely enjoyed the fruits of his calling—"Indian testimony" not being allowed in the courts of *justice*. False accounts have been alleged, and judgments obtained, and the innocent made to suffer by the wicked artifices and *advantages* of the white man. (2; emphasis in original)

In this absurd and impossible situation then, they appeal to Congress to take action against the injustices done them, because, they implore, "in vain has appeal after appeal been made to the present Executive of the United States" and because it is apparent that the "treaties and legislative acts" on which they had been relying for some protection "present but trifling obstacles to the march of Indian oppression" (1).

The memorials are testimony, a public accounting of the violence done to the Cherokee Nation and people—as in many of the narrative colonial treaty documents of the seventeenth and eighteenth centuries. In the 1832 memorial, they warn, "Some hundreds of privileged intruders are already seated upon the choicest lands belonging to the Cherokees, [intruders] who annoy and disturb the peace of the country, by the most wanton acts of plunder and cruelty, and yet are the means in operation by which another influx of this species of population is to be accomplished" (4). The Cherokees, they state emphatically, "cannot view it as a *peaceable* extinguishment, upon *fair*, or *reasonable* terms, that title which they possess to their lands, recognized by your honorable bodies to be in, and have *guarantied* to, the '*Cherokee Nation*,'—the *individuals* having no separate ownership to any part or portion of the country" (4).

SEQUOYAH, THE CHEROKEE ANTIQUARIANS, AND PROGRESS

In a January 1829 *Cherokee Phoenix* editorial, Boudinot described the difference between the present state of the Cherokee Nation and its state thirty years previously:

[Then, in the villages in the spring and summer] were assembled . . . men and women, old and young, to dance their *bear dance, buffalo dance, eagle dance, green-corn dance* &c. &c. &c. and when the day appeared, instead of going to their farms, and labouring for the support of their families, the young and middle aged of the males were seen to leave their houses, their faces fantastically painted, and their heads decorated with feathers, and step off with a merry whoop, which indicated that they were *real men*, to a ball play, or a meeting of a similar nature. . . . In those days of ignorance and heathenism, prejudices against the customs of the whites were inveterate, so much so that white men, who came along the Cherokees, had to throw away their costume and adopt the *leggings*. (103)

Although he said he personally believed that "in a moral and intellectual point of view the scenery was dark & gloomy," nevertheless, he insisted that the Cherokees were capable of change. "The introduction of light and intelligence has struck a mortal blow to the superstitious practices of the Cherokees," he wrote, "and by the aid of that light a new order of things is introduced, and it is to be hoped will now eradicate the vestiges of older days" (103).

Neither Boudinot nor the other "elite" and "acculturated" Cherokees who made such statements or voiced such opinions ever denied being Cherokee, abandoned the nation, or accepted subordination to whites. They counter EuroAmericans' removing them from time to deny them political autonomy and equality by insisting that they have always been in time and are rapidly moving forward and becoming a modern Indian nation. The object of being understood to be in time is not to be white—not political and cultural assimilation—but rather to continue as an autonomous Indian nation. It's true that claiming Eurocentric time leads to intellectual and political impasses, in particular, on the point of the value of traditional knowledge and history. In Ridge and Boudinot's writing, as Boudinot indicates above, traditional life is an earlier moment in the history of the tribe that must be put behind them in order to progress and advance in civilization. John Ross represents a different position, where traditional knowledge and beliefs represent the history of the nation, which is not to be rejected, but rather to be collected and preserved before the people who have that knowledge are gone. The question of how to think about traditional knowledge in the modern world motivates Native discourse to the present day; the Cherokee spokesmen are among the earliest Native intellectuals to articulate this concern in English.

Sequoyah is a pivotal figure for Cherokees who make arguments about their advances in civilization: both Ridge and Boudinot retold the story of Sequoyah and the Cherokee syllabary in their travels across the Northeast and in their published writing. Sequoyah represents the advances made in civilization by Cherokee people, and, again, the Cherokees are on something like a parallel track to EuroAmerican society, not seeking admission to it by virtue of having demonstrated themselves to be civilized enough, but rather demonstrating that they had formed and would form a government and ought to be left to their own devices. As Timothy Sweet points out in *American Georgics* in his discussion of the spokesmen's discourse on their improvement of agricultural practices, "the Cherokee spokesmen were not assimilationists . . . for they insisted on separate nationhood and national sovereignty."[28] "In the Cherokee counternarrative," he continues, "much of what looked to whites like accession to civilization, such as the development of letters, was, from another perspective, an assertion of continuity, a maintenance of national identity" (125). Sequoyah's syllabary would seem to be a particularly powerful example of what Dirlik calls interpellation, and on different levels. The syllabary itself was an adaptation of European literacy; it was used in every way printed alphabets were used—for mundane accounting, correspondence, religious tracts, the newspaper, laws passed by the Cherokee Council, and also history, including the history of Sequoyah himself. Use of the syllabary quickly became widespread; Willard Walker and James Sarbaugh write that "Cherokee literacy was widely diffused and virtually every non-literate Cherokee had access to Cherokee readers in his own settlement, if not in his own household."[29] White men came to write down Sequoyah's account of his invention; according to Walker and Sarbaugh, Sequoyah became an "international celebrity" (72).

The syllabary was, as Timothy Sweet indicates, an "assertion of continuity." John Ross recognized this in a letter to Sequoyah ("George Gist") in January 1832, in which he transmitted a medal the Cherokee Nation had made to honor his accomplishment. Ross calls Sequoyah "a man of more than ordinary genius" whose "incomparable system" benefited all Cherokees.[30]

> The old & the youth find no difficulty in learning to read & write in their native language and to correspond with their distant friends with the same facility that the whites do. Types have been made and a printing press established in this nation. The scriptures have been translated & printed in Cherokee; and whilst posterity continues to be benefited by the discovery, your name will exist in grateful remembrance. (234–35)

If within the Cherokee Nation the syllabary allowed for record keeping, communication, and education, outside the Cherokee Nation, it demonstrated the progress of the Cherokee people. Politically, the syllabary became the strongest evidence of the civilized status of the Cherokee people. "It will also serve as an index for the aboriginal tribes, or nations, similarly to advance in science and respectability," Ross writes; "in short, the great good designed by the author of human existence in directing your genius in this happy discovery, cannot be fully estimated, it is incalculable" (235).

In Boudinot's and Ridge's speaking tours and in their writing, Sequoyah's invention was almost always present as the incontrovertible proof of the Cherokees' progress in civilization. In the 1 April 1832 issue of the *American Annals of Education*, Boudinot contributed a long letter on the Cherokee syllabary that addresses itself to Samuel L. Knapp's comments on Sequoyah in his *Lectures on American Literature* (1829), a book in which Sequoyah represents at the same time the exceptionality of the United States against Europe and the outer limits to which an Indian could aspire within the state of nature.[31] After an introduction in which the editor of the journal pauses to consider the impossibility of knowledge without writing—"let us suppose ourselves unable to communicate our thoughts to the absent, or to keep a record of the past, or to preserve our knowledge for the future, with no other evidence of our rights and property but beads, and wampum"—and in which he notes that the essay was "*prepared* and *corrected*" by Boudinot himself, Boudinot relates that story of how the Cherokees have been "raised . . . to an elevation unattained by any other Indian nation" to become "a reading and intellectual people" (49). Even when Boudinot quotes Knapp's book, he notes that "the facts stated by him can be relied on, as they were derived from Sequoyah himself, through the interpretation of intelligent Cherokees" (50). Thus Boudinot's use of what is ostensibly a white man's account of Cherokee learning becomes validated by having been produced, essentially, by Cherokees themselves. After quoting Knapp's report of how he came to meet Sequoyah, Boudinot adds: "The appearance and habits of Sequoyah are those of a full-blooded Cherokee, though his grandfather, on the father's side, was a white man. He was educated in all the customs of his nation, and, as Mr. K says, was and is to this day ignorant of any language but his own" (51). Sequoyah thus demonstrates the ability of the Cherokees to become "civilized" without becoming *white*.

Knapp relates how Sequoyah, stricken by a "swelling on his knee" that eventually "made him a cripple for life," began to ponder "the mystery of the power of *speaking by letters*," as he could no longer partake in "the excitements of war, and the pleasures of the chase" (51). Boudinot adds, however, that the real story requires more detail. "The *immediate* circumstances which induced [Sequoyah] to the great undertaking" had to do with a conversation among a group of young men "which took place at a certain town called Sauta" (51). The men were marveling at the ability of whites to send a message over a great distance by writing it down. "All admitted that this was indeed an art far beyond the reach of the Indian," Boudinot writes, "and they were utterly at a loss to conceive in what way it was done" (52). Sequoyah, however, insisted that "the thing is very easy; I can do it myself," and from that point began work on his syllabary, although he notes that "it would seem from the narrative of Mr. K that he had thought on the subject long before" (52).

Boudinot also recounts how Sequoyah had to resist the beliefs of some of his tribe, "who believed that the knowledge of letters belonged only to the white man," and who "attempted to convince him that God had made that great distinction between the white and red man, by relating to him the following tradition":

In the beginning God created Yv* we yah e, a term applied to an Indian, signifying a *real* or *genuine man*; and the *yv* we na *gv*, or *white man*. The Indian was the elder, and in his hands the Creator placed a *book*; in the hands of the other he placed a *bow* and *arrow*, with a command that they should both make a good use of them. The Indian was very slow in receiving the book and appeared so indifferent about it that the white man came and stole it from him when his attention was directed another way. He was then compelled to take the bow and arrow, and gain his subsistence by pursuing the chase. He had thus forfeited the book which his Creator had placed in his hands, and which now of right belonged to his white brother. (52)

That the white man—not the real or genuine man—stole the book away from the Indian while he wasn't paying attention is a narrative laden with irony when one considers, for example, the notorious uses to which writing was put in treaties. Whatever the source of the story, writing itself had been the means of stealing the land, and, given the actions of the Cherokees and the implications of Boudinot's narrative, writing is the means of keeping the land. After excerpting Knapp's account of how Sequoyah developed a system of syllabic representation using eighty-six English letters (from a spelling book Sequoyah possessed) and other symbols, Boudinot recounts again how many Cherokees thought Sequoyah was "a delirious person, or an idiot," an assessment apparently shared by John Ross, whom Boudinot describes as "an intelligent Cherokee, who is now the principal Chief of the nation" (54). Boudinot seems to indicate that while all Indians are capable of civilization, only some Indians are willing to try.

Knapp describes how Sequoyah proved his system to the Cherokees by submitting it to a test, how he attempted to develop a representation of the Cherokee number system, and how he even had "a great taste for painting": "He mixes his colors with skill; taking all the art and science of his tribe upon the subject" (57). Knapp notes Sequoyah's intuitive sense of perspective, a kind of primitive's understanding of the essence of artistic expression: "His resemblances of the human form, it is true, are coarse, but often spirited and correct; and he gave action, and sometimes grace, to his representations of animals" (57). According to Knapp, then, Sequoyah still exists in "a rude state of nature," and his heroic accomplishments arise from his own sense of Indians' backwardness. Sequoyah "reasoned correctly," wrote Knapp, that advances in whites' civilization were caused by having writing—so they did not have to rely on "an uncertain tradition" (57). Boudinot, on the other hand, emphasized the speed with which the Cherokees took up writing in their own language and were becoming "a reading people" and the fact that, contrary to Knapp's account, it was not the U.S. government that had Cherokee press type cast but rather the Cherokee government, with the aid of contributions (57).

At about the same time that Boudinot's article appeared, John Ridge used the story of Sequoyah in a speech he gave in Boston in March 1832 after the *Cherokee Nation v. Georgia* decision of March 1831 seemed to give them no means of negotiating with the administration. News of the *Worcester v. Georgia* decision reached Boston and Ridge and his audience, dramatically, only two hours before he and Boudinot were scheduled to speak on 7 March. In his speech, Ridge warned prophetically that although the Supreme Court had "decided the Missionary case in favor of the rights of the Cherokees . . . it remains to be seen if the decision of the Court can be sustained."[32]

In the *Liberator*'s account of the speech on 10 March 1832, Ridge dramatized how far the Cherokees had progressed:

The Cherokees, he said, were once a nation of savages; of warriors and hunters. He could himself remember that period. They lived in towns of wigwams, with a common fence around the dancing ground and council fire. There was no individuality of property. The warriors joined in the war dance, and went to the chase or the battle, and when they returned from the latter, the war-whoop gave notice of their approach, and the number of scalps they brought from the enemy. The scalps were held between a man and woman, who danced in triumph; and so rude were their women then, that they would put these scalps into their mouths, and exult and mock over the miseries of the relatives of the slain!

Following the advice of George Washington, however, the Cherokees became "a civilized and a christianized community." Ridge recounted how the women "were now employed in useful industry, at the wheel or the needle, instructing their children, or attending to their domestic duties." The men, "instead of going out against their oppressions with the war song and the tomahawk to wreak vengeance on their enemies, and die fighting in the last ditch, . . . were now *battling with the weapons of intellectual argument!*" The writer of the account continues: "This fact alone, he should think, ought to satisfy any one, that they had become a civilized nation. He felt a pride in tracing the improvement of his people. They were proud to be Cherokees, and would scorn to be compared to the character of Georgia!—[great applause]." It seems not to be other Indians that the Cherokees had been fighting before they became literate, but their "oppressors," and it seems that the "weapons of intellectual argument" are more effective than the tomahawk.

That implication becomes even more pronounced in Ridge's story of Sequoyah. Ridge tells the same story of Cherokee progress as does Boudinot, including the "tradition" of the stolen book, although he emphasizes the resistance from his own people, and in particular from his own wife, that Sequoyah had to overcome. Ridge also tells the story of Sequoyah as proof of Cherokee progress, and indeed, in his telling, the Cherokees leaped from the state of nature to the modern world in one man's actions. Like Boudinot, Ridge tells the story of the Great Spirit and the red boy and the white boy. Sequoyah "was a poor man, living in a retired part of the nation, and he told the head men one day, that he could make a book." Then the "chiefs" told him the story of the Great Spirit making a red boy and a white boy and giving the red boy a book and the white boy a bow and arrow. The white boy stole the red boy's book "and went off, leaving him the bow and arrow, and therefore an Indian could not make a book." Sequoyah—here George Guess—"shut himself up to study; his corn was left to the weeds, and he was pronounced a crazy man, by the tribe. His wife thought so too, and burnt up his manuscripts, whenever she could find them; but he persevered." Finally he settled on the characters in his alphabet and then taught others to read: "And from this invention of this great man, the Cherokees have become a reading people."

Some indication of the complexity of the syllabary's use can be seen in an account by John Howard Payne in "Notable Persons in Cherokee History" of a reading of the story of Sequoyah's invention of the alphabet written in Cherokee by Major George Lowrey, the second principal chief. The story was read in Cherokee to a large group gathered at John Ross's cabin in October 1835, where they were attending the council meeting at which they rejected the Treaty of New Echota. The story was then translated into English, apparently for Payne's benefit. This account is remarkable for several reasons. Contrary to the assumption prevalent in the literary criticism, it shows that oral tradition and literacy cannot be separated from each other historically or chronologically; they coexist. As many contemporary Native writers maintain, "oral tradition" is constantly reinvented. The story of Sequoyah becomes a different kind of traditional story—and this is especially evident in Payne's account of the reading because he records interjections and kibitzing from the audience, their reactions to the events in the story, and so on. Sequoyah is presented as a supremely inventive man who is undaunted by writing, the skill that Euro-Americans insist demonstrates their inherent superiority. Even though his own people—his own wife—find his ambitions absurd, he succeeds. If traditional stories are in part supposed to tell people how to be in the world, how to behave, what to do, the story of Sequoyah is instructive, especially at the moment it was read. By the October 1835 council meeting, the Cherokees had been told they had to sign the New Echota removal treaty since March of that year. They had been collectively under assault for years, an assault that included, for individuals, all the daily means of degradation that the council's memorials described. And certainly the misrepresentation that the writers describe was a daily fact of life. The story of Sequoyah's invention, and his inventiveness, shows that Cherokees can rise above these assaults, go whites one better, and still remain Cherokees.

Lowrey's account begins with the fact that "George Gist [*sic*] was forsaken by his father," who was white, "when an infant and brought up by his mother" (386). As a small boy, "it was his amusement to construct small houses with sticks," which leads to his building a house over a spring for the milk from his mother's cows; then, "of his own accord, [he] . . . became a cow-milker" (386). He does this, which would not be something Cherokee men would traditionally do, because "he was lured by his pride and the pleasure in the dairy he had built" (386). Then he herds horses in the woods, becomes a good rider, and learns to "break them for us" (386). He helps his mother in the garden and cornfield; then he helps her in her small fur trading business by collecting furs from hunters (386). His mother, of course, "was very much pleased with her son's conduct and thought him most promising"; he also "had a great many friends, not only among the young, but also among the aged" (386). "At that time it was the fashion of the Cherokee to decorate themselves with ornaments of silver, such as ear-rings, nose bobs, armlets, bracelets, gorgets, and fine chains," and so Sequoyah becomes interested in silverwork. After he "grew very perfect" in silverwork, however, he gets tired of it and takes up drawing. "His success in this new undertaking got his name up still higher among his countrymen," Payne, quoting Lowrey, writes, "and they thought him a man of genius, capable of anything he should choose to undertake" (386–87).

At this point, Payne describes what was going on as the story was being read:

Here a part of the manuscript was missing. We sought for it on all sides— under the table—among the bedding, it was no where to be found. "No matter," said Major Lowry [*sic*],—It was only what the Bark told me and the Bark is hereabout.

We will go fetch him, exclaimed half a dozen voices, and presently the Bark appeared.

It is remarkable that when the fragment was afterwards found, it was almost verbatim what the Bark repeated and no correction was thought necessary on comparison. (387)

Sequoyah taught the Bark how to "sketch horses, cows, sheep, and even men; and often, when thus employed, they would enter into conversation about the works of white men" (387). The Bark was very much impressed with "the writing down of what was passing in their minds so that it would keep upon paper after it had gone out of their minds" (387). This does not impress Sequoyah, who "went so far as to declare that he was of opinion that he could detain and communicate their ideas just as well as the white people could" (387).

Once again, Payne observes the audience:

> The Indians were very much excited while the Bark was repeating this. In some of the pauses, for the interpreter to explain, one would exclaim—
> "Oh—Yes—that happened that way-yonder" and another,
> "Ha! Now you're going to tell"—and then he would nod his head for the Bark to proceed, and seemed delighted—
> I asked if the invention of the Alphabet immediately followed this—
> Oh, no, was the reply. That occurred a great many years later. Listen. You will perceive when that happened. (387)

The story does not get to the alphabet immediately. Instead, Lowrey relates that because Sequoyah was so talented, "he also became greatly considered among all the handsome women" (387). "Here there was a general smile among the Indians," Payne writes. Sequoyah began to neglect all of his silverwork and drawing and instead "went about visiting one another; and every day he had more and more friends" (387). This socializing also involved drinking, but in this setting, drinking is not an occasion for condemnation. Sequoyah, who didn't drink at first, would get whiskey for his friends and soon became even more popular. "Here the Indians gave a sort-of-joyous, but-silent smile," Payne writes. "His friends increased upon him so fast, that instead of a bottle, he would have to give a three gallon keg for their supply," Lowrey continues, "and he would make them all drink with him, until the keg was empty" (387). "The Indians were greatly amused with this paragraph," Payne adds (387).

Sequoyah was very congenial when drinking. "He would very good naturedly enter into huge discourses with his friends; and urge upon them they should love one another; and treat one another as brother; and then he would sit himself down and sing songs for their amusement, until, with much drinking, he would sing himself to sleep" (387–88). "Here the Indians broke into a general laugh," Payne writes. Eventually, however, Sequoyah realized that he wasn't taking care of his mother properly and he sought different means of supporting her before settling on becoming a blacksmith. One day in 1820, while visiting Archibald Campbell, who was apparently a white man, Sequoyah announces again that he can make a system for writing Cherokee. This scene parallels the earlier scene with the Bark. He and some friends are discussing "the ingenuity of the white men in contriving ways to communicate on paper":

> Some of the party remarked how wonderful it was to think that simply by making marks on paper, and sending the paper to another; two persons could understand as well as if talking together face to face; and how these things were done, it was impossible to conceive. Gist then remarked "I can see no impossibility in conceiving how it is done. The white man is no magician. It is said in ancient times when writing first began, a man named Moses—made marks upon a stone. I, too, can make marks upon a stone. I can agree with you by what name to call those marks and that will be writing and can be understood." He then took up a small whetstone and with a pin from his sleeve, scratched marks upon the whetstone and said, "There can I make characters, as Moses did, which every one of you will understand." (388)

His friends thought this was hilarious:

> They bantered him upon his scheme to make stones converse; told him he would find those stones very unentertaining company when he had nothing else for bread; and advised him to get his reason back, and settle down to regular and rational occupations, like other men. (388)

Many aspects of this narrative reject the entire range of EuroAmerican thinking about Indians. Notably, Sequoyah works constantly; he's inventive, logical, persistent, all qualities that Indians weren't supposed to possess. He lives in a farming community and he hunts, as Elias Boudinot pointed out, like other people of whatever color would if they were living in the same place. Also, the representation of drinking is not an occasion for announcing the inevitable decline of the red man, but rather something that is a part of Native society, like it or not, but, importantly, something that Sequoyah rejects before it gets out of hand. And finally, Sequoyah is very much a part of the society in which he lives, where he's appreciated and loved, even when his plans to invent a writing system seem crazy to the people around him.

Finally, Lowrey gets to the part of the story in which Sequoyah invents the alphabet and in which he himself plays a part. Sequoyah returns to his home and begins working on his alphabet, and "after vast-labor and study he had completed eighty-six characters and with these began to frame sentences"

(388). People still worry about Sequoyah, however. A friend named Turtle Fields visits Sequoyah and tells him that "our people are much concerned about you. They think you are wasting your life. They think, my friend, that you are making a fool of yourself, and will no longer be respected" (388). To which Sequoyah replies:

> It is not our people that have advised me to this and it is not therefore our people who can be blamed if I am wrong. What I have done I have done from myself. If our people think I am making a fool of myself, you may tell our people that what I am doing will not make fools of them. They did not cause me to begin and they shall not cause me to give up. If I am no longer respected, what I am doing will not make our people any less respected, either by themselves or others; and so I shall go on and so you may tell our people. (388–89)

The community is worried about Sequoyah's strangeness and the fact that he may no longer be respected and, by extension, that the people themselves would not be respected. Sequoyah finishes his alphabet and then teaches several people how to use it, including his own daughter. Then he visits George Lowrey, and they have a conversation about the nature of the alphabet. Sequoyah insists that "when I have heard any thing, I can write it down, and lay it by, and take it up again at some future day. And there find all that I have heard exactly as I heard it" (389). Lowrey thinks the alphabet is a mnemonic device. "It may be that you are not forgetful," he says. "The marks you have made bring up certain associations, as poles or heaps of stone call back all the events connected with particular places, or as a knot in a handkerchief reminds you of an engagement. You understand, not from the marks you invented, but from what these marks lead you to remember" (389). But Sequoyah insists that "the same marks will make me remember very different things, according to the way in which I place them; and things which I had forgotten. When I write any thing, I lay it by; I think of it no more; I do not remember what I have written: but at any time afterwards when I take up the paper, all I have written is brought back to my recollection by the reading on the paper" (389). Still, Lowrey isn't convinced until Sequoyah's small daughter demonstrates reading—although at first he insists that the individual sounds are too much like Creek sounds. "And George Lowry left George Gist, very much surprised and he was convinced there was something in it, and that George Gist had succeeded. This was in 1821" (389).

Sequoyah's story as Lowrey tells it is about adapting to and prevailing over the effects of Eurocentrism. It is about the power of writing to improve

Portrait of John Ross holding the September 1836 memorial from the Cherokee Nation protesting the Treaty of New Echota. It appeared in the final volume of Indian Tribes of North America *in 1844, the text of which was devoted to James Hall's "Essay on the History of the North American Indians." Hall represented Ross as the ideal civilized Indian who could serve as leader of a separate, Native-governed state. Ross was not a warrior, Hall noted, but rather a civilian, "plain and unassuming in his appearance, of calm and quiet deportment . . . a man of great sagacity and untiring energy" (3:176). From McKenney and Hall,* Indian Tribes of North America, *3:176. Photograph courtesy of the Edward E. Ayer Collection, Newberry Library, Chicago.*

Cherokees' lives rather than misrepresent them; it is written down but read aloud, repeated over time, assented to and participated in by a group of people, not solitary readers. If the story of Sequoyah is an adaptation of older practices of oral storytelling used to great effect by Cherokee leaders, they—the ones associated with Ross, that is—also remained committed to producing a record of Cherokee traditional knowledge. In his efforts to write down Cherokee traditions, Payne received information and advice from Daniel S. Butrick, a missionary to the Cherokees who collected information from them about their history, beliefs, and practices. Butrick appears to have been singular in the care with which he went about his investigations, and his efforts show that the "elite" leaders of the Cherokees—Ross, Lowrey, and others—did not (all) reject traditional knowledge, and even understood it as having possible political utility. Butrick wrote to Payne that in order to persuade Cherokees of his good intentions, he obtained letters from their "beloved chiefs," first Charles Hicks and then, "finding the aged antiquarians still rather retired," John Ross, "one of their most beloved chiefs."[33] Butrick enclosed the letter, which Ross addressed "To Cherokee Antiquarians." In the letter, Ross endorses Butrick's effort to "research into the *original customs & manners* of our Nation" and assures the antiquarians that his plan "will not in sleightest [*sic*] degree affect the private or political rights of the Cherokee people, but on the other hand his work will be interesting and useful"; indeed, it "may be of advantage to us."[34] Ross also tells the antiquarians that Butrick's work would not be published until George Lowrey, Ross himself, and a convocation of "all the wise antiquarians of the nation" had reviewed it, evaluating it for errors (354). This was imperative, Ross writes, because "the aged men who have been correctly instructed in the traditions of our ancestors and now living, are comparatively few, and unless this knowledge was speedily obtained for preservation, it must be lost to posterity, after your exit from the stage of action" (354). Like Lowrey's story of Sequoyah, the history that Ross and other Cherokee leaders planned to have written is not the production of a single individual, but rather a representation of the Cherokee Nation itself, as a political entity.

But getting information from the antiquarians was not at all a straightforward process. In a letter to Payne in 1840, Butrick lists the problems of collecting information in what amounts to a comprehensive critique of how whites try and fail to find out what Indians know because they refuse to recognize the humanity or intelligence of Native peoples:

> First, [their traditions] are known to but few among themselves. The mass of the people are entirely ignorant of them, not only of the youth and

middle aged, but even among the aged but few can be found instructed in the learning of the ancients.

Second. Those who have the knowledge requisite, have received this knowledge as a sacred deposit, and would rather die than betray their trust, by making known this sacred knowledge in an improper manner, or to persons not worthier to receive it.

Third. Some of their ancient customs were not to be made known to any except sons designed for, and trained up for sacred officers, on pain of death, to be inflicted by the invisible powers above. . . . Such information, of course cannot be obtained in any tribe where there are no Christians, nor from any individuals who are not experimentally convinced of the superior efficacy of the Christian religion, that is, experimental Christians.

Fourth. The Indians are almost unbounded in their desire to please their fellows, and their own people generally. They study, and practice among themselves the rules of native politeness to an unexampled degree. Therefore you cannot by any means persuade an Indian, not influenced by the Christian religion, to say anything which will tend to render him unpopular among his people. And, suppose he commences conversation on most important subjects, yet on perceiving a sneer, or a look of contempt, his mouth is perfectly closed, and all attempts afterwards to open it are vain.

Fifth. Indians not only hold white men in contempt, but consider them irreligious, unprincipled & cruel, and therefore all intimate connection with them is interdicted by common consent, and is unpopular. Of course a whiteman [sic] must be clothed with extraordinary credential indeed, who would not be himself a reproach among the Indians, and a disgrace to such as he might gain over in his friendship. Some Indians of dissipated habits, will associate with white men of the same character in order to obtain a portion of the inebriating cup, yet in their sober moments hold them in contempt.

Sixth. There is yet another difficulty, arising, not only from the disposition of Indians to tantalize but also from the principle that they are not bound always to tell the truth to white men. Of course the narrator may invent his own story as he proceeds, offering it to his inquisitive white guest, as among their important antiquities.

There is yet another reason why no important information is ever obtained by white men from Indians relative to their antiquities. It is this, people are slow to believe what they do not wish to be true. Now almost all United States citizens, missionaries as well as others, have a most degraded opinion of the Indians; and when they solicit information concerning them, it is to establish this opinion. Thus, for instance, one enquires of some ignoramus what the old Indians used to say about Noah's flood. The reply, perhaps, is, "that on a certain occasion when all the people were assembled at an all night dance, a dog commenced howling in a most astonishing manner; and when his master commanded silence, the dog spoke and told him the cause of his distress, viz. that the world was to be drowned," or, On hearing this the inquisitive mind is satisfied, and ever after when the subject of Indian antiquities is introduced, the above story is brought forward with a sarcastic laugh, in order to put to the blush every one who would speak honorably of the ancient Indians. I need not say that such persons may spend all their days among the Indians and yet die as ignorant of their true character almost as if they had never been born. There are others who live among the Indians too indifferent to make enquiries; and, to excuse this indifference, will readily assert that there is nothing relative to Indian antiquities worthy of investigation, when the fact is, if there had been ten thousand diamonds, shaded by the least possible obscurity their sluggish minds would never have discovered them. (8–10)

Payne was copying manuscripts in Ross's home when the Georgia Guard descended on them, confiscating his papers as well as Ross's.[35] He spent thirteen days chained in a log cabin jail with Ross, the son of the speaker of the Cherokee Council, and "the odiferous decomposing corpse of a Cherokee who had been executed several weeks before."[36] Despite his close connection with the Cherokees, and having published a long account of his arrest and a defense of the Cherokees in a Knoxville, Tennessee, newspaper on his release from prison, Payne never published his intended book on the Cherokees.[37] He apparently thought Cherokee traditions would be suitable for inclusion in a genteel literary magazine—quaint, amusing, and romantic Indian traditions were common in such publications—but ended up with a voluminous collection of complicated history, tradition, and political struggle that he possibly, although one can't say for sure, didn't know what to do with. The material that he collected certainly exceeded the conventions, both sentimental and scientific, of EuroAmericans' representation of Indians' knowledge. One might speculate that the harrowing experience of spending thirteen days in jail chained up with the principal chief of the Cherokee Nation, the corpse of an executed Cherokee man rotting in the rafters of the jail where it was tied up, threatened by the Georgia authorities when they discovered Payne had described the guard as "banditti" in his papers, would have made it very difficult to produce the kinds of sentimental stories that the refined and refining classes liked to read in their weekly papers. Indeed, Payne never did start his literary magazine. Ross called on him in the spring of 1838 to come to Washington and help write letters and memorials to Congress as the Cherokees were fighting out the terms of removal, which he did through the summer of that year. In 1840, Payne accompanied Ross and a party of Cherokees to Indian Territory and remained there for several months, publishing a long newspaper account of a murder trial in the Cherokee Nation's new capital of Tahlequah.[38] But he gave up his literary pursuits. In 1842, he was appointed U.S. consul in Tunisia, where he died in 1852.[39]

In October 1832, Boudinot resigned the editorship of the *Cherokee Phoenix* because Ross and the council refused to allow discussion of removal in the newspaper. The "resolutions" that the Treaty Party put forward at that time included the following:

> *Resolved*, That it is our decided opinion, founded upon the melancholy experience of the Cherokees within the last two years, and upon facts which history has furnished us in regard to other Indian nations, that our people cannot exist amidst a white population, subject to laws which they have no hand in making, and which they do not understand; that the suppression of the Cherokee Government, which connected this people in a distinct community, will not only check their progress in improvement and advancement in knowledge, but, by means of numerous influences and temptations which this new state of things has created, will completely destroy every thing like civilization among them, and ultimately reduce them to poverty, misery, and wretchedness.[40]

The primary argument given for advocating removal is the political oppression of the Cherokee government by whites. In the view of the Treaty Party, it is the actions of whites themselves that are preventing the Cherokees from becoming "civilized." Identifying themselves as "friends of free discussion," the Treaty Party members wrote: "[Although we] should leave the place of our nativity with as much regret as any of our citizens, we consider the lot of the *Exile* immeasurably more to be preferred than a submission to the laws of the States, and thus becoming witnesses of the ruin and degradation of the Cherokee people."[41]

In response to the schism, Ross and the council publicly repudiated the members of the Treaty Party and protested their actions to U.S. officials (who were not inclined to be sympathetic) in private meetings, when they could get them, and in memorials submitted to Congress. After the Treaty of New Echota was signed in December 1835 at the home of John Ridge, Ross himself published two pamphlets in 1836 and 1837 setting out the majority Cherokee position once again in an attempt to raise a public outcry against a treaty that was widely recognized as fraudulent by both whites and Native peoples. In his 1837 pamphlet, Ross points out that the "pretended Treaty" would grant the western land to the Cherokees "on the proviso, 'that such land shall *revert* to the United States, if the Indians become extinct, or abandon the same.'" He argues that "the use of this very phrase, *revert*, is an evidence that the United States do not consider that there is an absolute property given in the soil allotted to the Indians, in payment for their valuable country; the United States retains the absolute property in her own hands, only allowing to the Indians a far inferior right of occupancy to that which they have ever been admitted to possess where they now are, and there they were born." He points out that the Indian title to the land "is to be subject, not only to . . . laws already existing, but to such laws as may be made hereafter; and to which laws, present and prospective, the Indian regulations for self-government must be equally subordinate." He complains that the treaty then "makes the Indians blindly promise submission" to the United States, which "may entirely extinguish, not only the right of occupancy, but of self-government." Ross then essentially predicts the events of the late nineteenth century, when the United States systematically dismantled the Indian nations of Indian Territory in order to form the state of Oklahoma in 1907. "Suppose it should suit the policy of the United States," he writes, "to pass a law organizing a territorial government upon the Cherokee lands, west? That law necessarily destroys the character of the Cherokee nation as a distinct community; the nation becomes legally extinct; the lands revert to the United States, and the Cherokee people are bound, by assenting to the conditions of the pretended Treaty, to acquiesce in this law providing a plausible pretext for their annihilation."[42]

In response, Boudinot published a pamphlet in 1837 that was also submitted to Congress; in it he refutes the accusations against his motivations for advocating removal, pointing out, "It is enough to say that our parties have been similar to other political parties found among the whites. They have been characterized by high feeling, and not unfrequently, by undue asperity."[43] He makes no excuses for the fact that it was only "a portion of our people" who decided that, faced with white depredations and "instead of contending uselessly against superior power, the only course left, was, to yield to circumstances over which they had no control" and negotiate for removal (160). He accuses Ross of having "deluded" the majority of the Cherokees "with expectations incompatible with, and injurious to, their interest" (161). As Theda Perdue notes, Boudinot at this point had come to the conclusion that the Chero-kees could either remove or, if they stayed in the East, become extinct; the reason he gives for this dichotomy, however, is not that the Cherokees cannot, because of their inherent moral and intellectual inferiority, live in proximity to whites, as was argued by Lewis Cass and other advocates for removal, but because of the actions of "our oppressor," as he called Georgia, and by exten-sion the United States and their citizens (157, 168).

What separates Boudinot from Ross, as scholars writing about Boudinot have observed, is that Boudinot assumes that he, as an educated, Christian man, knows what's best for the majority of the Cherokee population. Bernd Peyer in fact argues that "in claiming the unorthodox right for himself to make political decisions over the heads of the Cherokee populace, Boudinot was acting in accordance not only with the elitist Anglo-Protestant social standards taught to him by his Presbyterian mentors but also with the patronizing stance of the Cherokee mixed-blood proto-elite as savants of a new and better way of life."[44] Accusing Ross of having a pecuniary interest in his efforts to at least secure more money for the land that the Cherokees were being forced to leave, Boudinot concludes the pamphlet by returning to his argument that the Cher-okee people themselves are in such dire straits that they must escape the influence of whites. Boudinot has abandoned his pre-1832 optimism about the state of Cherokee society for an (entirely understandable) apocalyptic despair. Addressing Ross directly, Boudinot writes:

> Look at the mass—look at the entire population as it now is, and say, can you see any indication of a progressing improvement—anything that can en-courage a philanthropist? You know that it is almost a dreary waste. I care not if I am accounted a slanderer of my country's reputation—every observ-ing man in this nation know that I speak the words of truth and soberness. In the light that I consider my countrymen, not as mere animals, and to judge of their happiness by their condition as such, which to be sure is bad enough, but as moral beings, to be affected for better or for worse, by moral circumstances, I say their condition is wretched. (223–24)

"Vice and immorality," he laments, intemperance and its associated "wretch-edness and misery," assault the Cherokee Nation (224). Whether or not Boudi-not's appointment of himself as the moral compass for the Cherokees is a habit of thought he acquired from whites and is therefore not "culturally" Cherokee, as Peyer's comments imply, his despair at the effects of colonialism on the Cherokee people does not indicate that he believes the Cherokees are inherently inferior but that they are in a great deal of trouble, being subjected to white assaults in every aspect of their society, and that their last hope of survival is to escape the influence of whites entirely.

It is a mistake to condemn Boudinot for passages such as this, for his denial of his own past. What his writing demonstrates at the very least is that there were and are many perspectives among Native intellectuals and political leaders about how to best deal with the effects of U.S. colonialism.

CHAPTER TWO

William Apess, Racial Difference, and Native History

A REAL WILD INDIAN

After receiving word in Boston in March 1832 of the Supreme Court's *Worcester v. Georgia* decision, John Ridge traveled to Washington, where he wrote on 6 April to his cousin Stand Watie, "The Union pauses and stands still to look upon the crisis our intellectual warfare has brought them. . . . The Cherokee question as it now stands is the greatest that has ever presented itself to the consideration of the American People." In this early reaction to the Court's ruling that Georgia had no authority over Cherokee land or people, Ridge knew that the legal victory was not enough, because, as he put it, "the Chicken Snake General Jackson" would have "time to crawl and hide in the luxuriant grass of his nefarious hypocracy [*sic*]" before any actions could be taken to restore the Cherokee government.[1] Ridge had left Elias Boudinot in Boston, where the two had been since February, giving lectures in the area to raise money and support for the Cherokee resistance.[2] White antiremoval sentiment was reaching its peak at this time, soon after the *Worcester* decision but before it became apparent, as it did especially after his reelection in 1832, that Jackson would disregard the Supreme Court ruling and force the Cherokees and other southern tribes to move west of the Mississippi. Boudinot was still drawing crowds in late April, when a thirty-year-old spinster named Louisa Jane Park described in a letter to her stepmother an evening of oratory on behalf of the Cherokees, which included, in addition to Boudinot, the Massachusetts congressman Edward Everett, the conservative Congregational minister Lyman Beecher (father of Harriet, Catharine, and Henry Ward), and an unnamed Native orator, who was William Apess.

This was an interesting group, not only because the Federal Street church where they gathered was that of William Ellery Channing, leader of Boston's Unitarians and Lyman Beecher's liberal rival at a time when the conflict between the two groups was ongoing. That these two appeared together might give some indication of the popularity of the Cherokee cause in Boston at the time.[3] Beecher also had had previous dealings with Elias Boudinot as an agent of the American Board of Commissioners for Foreign Missions school in Cornwall, Connecticut. In 1825, when news of Boudinot's engagement to Harriet Gold became public, Beecher and his fellow agents issued a public condemnation, denouncing the impending marriage as an "outrage," an "evil," and an "insult to the known feelings of the Christian community."[4] This effective call to arms helped whip up the frenzy in the town that led to Boudinot and Gold being burned in effigy on the village green.

Louisa Park, who in a few years would publish the first of several romantic novels in verse, observed that Everett "at first . . . set all my teeth on edge, for he hissed like a serpent; every *S* was told." Still, she "soon became interested in what he had to say," despite "the ungracefulness and sameness of his gesticulation," reporting that "he perpetually waved his right arm on high, and brought it down with a rat-tat-tat upon the paper he held in his left hand." The broad sentimental style that had made Everett a famous orator was even then losing favor among Boston's literati. Park conceded that Everett "was now and then eloquent":

> He gave us the *substance* of the communications which have passed between the Cherokee nation and our government, with great conciseness, spirit, and at times in a tone of irony which amounted to a severe invective; and wound up with the "permission" for the poor Indians to quit their comfortable farms and "wander across the swamp and prairie, brake and fen, mountain and stream—across the great Mississippi, to the banks of the Red River." Then after a pause, he added in a lower and most impressive tone— "Before the poor Indians reach those banks of the Red River—they will arrive in a land where 'the wicked cease from troubling and the weary are at rest.'"—The house was still as a tomb, and no doubt many eyes were as mine filled with tears, so simple and unexpected was this touch of pathos. The *manner*, you know, is a great deal in these things; and then our feelings had been gradually wrought up by the statements he had been making.[5]

Park's account of Everett's oratorical effectiveness exemplifies what would soon become the dominant manner in which whites think about Native peoples; the momentary recognition of Native political struggles will soon enough give way to the doomed Indian narrative that evokes such pleasurable emotional responses in the audience Park describes. Four years hence, in his *Eulogy on King Philip*, Apess would demand that his Boston audience recognize the explicitly political struggles of Native peoples in New England and the United States, mocking white sympathy, in an oration that was very likely at least in part a response to Everett's own oratorical version of King Philip's war given some months previously, in which his elaborate sympathy for Indians served only to justify political oppression.

Louisa Park was accompanied to the church by a number of young girls, as well as two servants. According to her letter, the girls found Elias Boudinot himself inconceivable, let alone the content of his speech. "A swarthy independent-looking gentleman," Park wrote, Boudinot was "drest [sic] like *other people*, to the great astonishment and disappointment of Caroline Knowles and her companions; I could scarcely persuade them that this was one of the Indians they came to see; little Charlotte Coolidge seemed to think she had been imposed upon, and declared she 'would not have stirred a step if she had known'; mighty was her wrath at not beholding a 'real wild Indian with his hair streaming down his back, a tomahawk in his hand, and a wampum belt, making a speech to us in Cherokee.'" Park remained cool to that idea. "What especial edification they thought of deriving from such a harangue, I know not," she added. Boudinot, she reported, "talked like a man of sense and education," but she observed disappointedly that "there was nothing figurative in his style; and his address was very long, sometimes dry and uninteresting." If the girls wanted an Indian, Louisa Park remained interested in oratorical talent.

The last of the evening's speakers gained both the audience's and Park's approval:

> The other of our "red brethren" mounted the pulpit stairs as [Boudinot] descended, and his "palaver" seemed to hit the taste of the audience more decidedly. He was dressed like his companion, and at the distance I was, both resembled Mr. Sam. Houston!—begging his pardon for comparing him to savages.[6] We now had a few tropes and metaphors, which never failed of applause; some of them were manifestly claptraps; but on the whole I was both surprised and pleased. This man was evidently not quite so well educated, had not the same familiarity with choice language, and was not so *civilized* as his companion, but there was more native eloquence in his address; his earnestness was evidently sincere, and I felt the difference between hearing an actor on the stage, or even a lawyer defending a client— and listening to a patriot engaged bona fide, with all his heart and soul, in stating the wrongs and pleading the cause of his oppressed country. He was sometimes vehement—and Gen. Jackson had one or two side-knocks, to my great satisfaction.

Three days before this night of oratory on behalf of the Cherokees, the *Boston Evening Transcript* printed a notice announcing that the "Rev. Wm Apess of the Pequot tribe of Indians" would give a lecture at Boylston Hall, one of Boston's largest, which seated one thousand.[7] An itinerant Methodist preacher since 1829, Apess had been traveling in Massachusetts, New York, Connecticut, and Rhode Island; he had published his autobiography, *A Son of the Forest*, in 1829 and a revised version in 1831. As John Ridge, who was known as the better orator of himself and Boudinot, was gone from Boston on Cherokee business, it appears likely that Apess replaced him on the program as the closing speaker. It also appears that this oration introduced Apess to Boston's reformers and reform-minded white audiences; in May, June, and July several notices appeared in the *Liberator* for sermons or lectures Apess would give on "the purity of the gospel" and "the judgment of the great day" in addition to "an Address on the subject of Slavery."[8] Editor William Lloyd Garrison, who in April 1831 (immediately after the March 1831 *Cherokee Nation* decision) had included in the *Liberator*'s masthead a vignette of Indian treaties trampled underfoot, met with and endorsed Apess. On 19 May 1832, Garrison printed a notice for a lecture by the "missionary of the Pequod tribe of Indians," adding, "We intend to be among his hearers. A short interview with him has given us a very favorable opinion of his talents and piety."[9]

Also in May 1832, the Boston antiquarian Samuel Gardner Drake took note of Apess's presence in town in his book *Indian Biography*, an alphabetically arranged account of Indians "conspicuous in the history of North America." In the entry on King Philip, Drake, who was prone to making personal asides in all of his books, waspishly observes:

> If Indian tradition do not err, some of the blood of the immortal Philip, now circulates in this city. The Rev. Wm. Apes, of the Independent Methodist order, a Pequot, is preaching occasionally among us. He has seen a chequered and various life, as appears by a book which he has published, entitled, "A Son of the Forest." He contemplates giving the traditionary, as well as the real history and antiquities, of the Pequots; which must be a work desired by every one. Mr. Apes is thirty-four years of age, very active and intelligent. He makes a wide mistake in his life, by calling Philip king of the Pequots; for Philip was not born when that tribe was destroyed. And there is no tradition that Wampanoag chiefs ever claimed dominion over the Pequots, but on the contrary the latter were "a terror to all their neighbors."[10]

Drake, who was the same age as Apess, had had a checkered life of his own until he became a bookseller with a particular interest in Indians and the

Drawing of William Apess, in which his countenance is in marked contrast to the pointedly ironic rhetoric of his writing. This lithograph may have been based on the painting listed in an inventory of collateral Apess put up for a loan in 1836; the painting was valued at fifteen dollars, making it one of his most valuable possessions. From William Apess, A Son of the Forest, *rev. ed. (New York, 1831), frontispiece. Photograph courtesy of the Edward E. Ayer Collection, Newberry Library, Chicago.*

history of New England. In 1825, he had annotated and reprinted Benjamin Church's 1716 account of King Philip's War, which he reprinted numerous times over the next ten years. In 1830, he opened the Antiquarian Bookstore in Boston. After publishing the first edition of *Indian Biography* in 1832, he changed its title to *The Book of the Indians of North America* in 1833 and its format to a straightforward, if obsessively detailed, antiquarian history of Indians and Europeans in North America from the earliest European accounts to the contemporary moment, revising and adding material to the book's many editions until 1851.[11] Drake was an expert on the history of King Philip's

War, and Apess's mistake apparently bothered him so much that he seems to have published another public correction in a review of Apess's *A Son of the Forest* (1831) in the August 1832 *American Monthly Review*. The anonymous reviewer makes the same observation there as in *Indian Biography*—that Apess was planning to write "the traditionary as well as the real history and antiquities of the Pequots"—which, considering that Apess does not mention such a plan in any of his published works, points to the possibility that Apess told Drake this himself or that he spoke of it publicly in 1832. The reviewer advises Apess to "enlarge the boundaries of his knowledge of Indian history, and not allow himself to be carried away by every slight and imperfect tradition. In this way we trust, from the other advantages of his situation, being *native to the question*, he will make an authentic and valuable book."[12]

Drake could have and may have provided Apess source materials for his writings; at his bookstore—or "Institute of Miscellaneous Literature," as he called it—he sold a range of historiography, including local history and school books, new and second-hand.[13] At a time when preoccupation with New England's colonial history and its relations with Native peoples permeated Boston society, Drake's bookstore became a gathering place for historians and the historically inclined, including George Bancroft, whose first volume of *The History of the United States* was published in Boston in 1834; Jared Sparks, editor of the *Library of American Biography* and former editor of the *North American Review*, who published Lewis Cass on Indian removal; and Edward Everett.[14] Perhaps William Apess, who worked at least occasionally as a book vendor, was also among the group. Drake sold tickets to both performances of Apess's *Eulogy on King Philip*, in which Apess cites Drake directly and from whose *Book of the Indians* Apess takes many of the details of his account of King Philip's War—with a great deal of rearrangement and reinterpretation.

There may also have been a specific reason for Apess's interest in Massachusetts at that time, given his activities in Mashpee a year later. A short article from the *Taunton Sun*, reprinted in The *Boston Investigator* the day before the speeches on behalf of the Cherokees, suggests a possible focus of his interest:

> It is rumored that the miserable *Aborigenes* now residing in *Massachusetts*, intend to bring their case before the Supreme Court of the United States, in order to obtain exemption from the State laws by which they are degraded and oppressed, and deprived of all those rights which are considered as belonging to human beings. What will Massachusetts say to this interference on the part of those she has so long considered under her guardianship, and whom she has reduced by *her* laws to a condition worse than that of slavery?[15]

Although this newspaper item is not specific, by 1832 there was growing discontent among the Mashpee people on Cape Cod. (The standard spelling of the tribe's name was "Marshpee" at that time.) Like the Pequots in Connecticut, the Mashpees were ruled by white "overseers" who were appointed by the Massachusetts government, controlled what income the tribe had, and served as the rule of law on the "plantation," which had been formed in the seventeenth century when traditional Wampanoag leaders deeded land to a group of Christian Wampanoags.[16] In the early 1830s, the Mashpees and their overseers were at odds over the sale of the plantation's timber, an important—and relatively rare—natural resource on Cape Cod.[17] There were other conflicts as well. In 1831, the Mashpees petitioned the legislature for two schoolhouses, which the Commonwealth built, although neither the overseers nor the Commonwealth made any effort to secure schoolteachers to teach in the schoolhouses.[18] Even more insulting to the Mashpees, Harvard College continued to use an eighteenth-century bequest to support missionaries to Indians to fund a Congregational minister named Phineas Fish, who disdained to minister to Indians, occupied and derived income from 400 acres of the plantation, and refused to budge from his sinecure despite the Mashpees' vocal dissatisfaction. Local whites supported Fish's intransigence at least in part because in Fish they had a "free" minister, one for whose upkeep they did not have to pay. Like the Pequots, the Mashpees had a long and continuous history of conflict with whites over what their relation to state government was and how they would be governed. When whites in Boston and elsewhere began taking up the cause of Cherokee treaty rights, the irony probably wasn't lost on the Mashpees. By the time William Apess visited the plantation in the spring of 1833, he and the Mashpees appear to have been perfectly suited to each other.

For a short period of time, William Apess became notorious in Boston—known as an orator, a political operative, and a writer. The journals of Boston's literary and political elite noticed him and his books and the Massachusetts governor and legislature and the administrators of Harvard College (who were often legislators themselves) faced him in political controversy. He became associated with the leaders of the newly organized antislavery movement and was championed by Boston's antimasonic newspaper at the height of the antimasonic movement and defended by its editor, who himself was something of a political provocateur.[19] In retrospect, Apess seems to have been someone who was in the right place at the right time. A man who did not know the history of his own tribe, he spent his most productive years in a city where the history of relations between Native peoples and white settlers was social pastime and political obsession. Coming from a tribe that was barely holding on in the early nineteenth century, that had an ambiguous relation to white government and no treaties with it, he ended up in what was the center of white involvement in the antiremoval effort, the hometown of Jeremiah Evarts and Joseph Story, a place where the case against removal was promulgated in all its philosophic detail in newspapers and journals. Apess must have found an intellectual community as well. Samuel Gardner Drake, prickly though he apparently could be, at the very least took Apess seriously as a writer. That Apess gave antislavery lectures indicates that he was known to the abolitionist community, white and African American, which included, after the death of David Walker in 1830, at least two active African American writers: Maria Stewart and Hosea Easton. Easton, whose grandfather was Native, was, like Apess, a Methodist minister. Apess also found the Mashpees, who needed a leader equipped to engage in sustained political battle with whites, in order that they should "rule themselves," as they said.

This chapter follows Apess's developing critique of racial difference in his works, published from 1829 to 1836, at the moment when that concept was becoming naturalized. Without tribal responsibilities, probably at least in part because his tribe was in such disarray, Apess wrote more than any other Native writer until the turn of the nineteenth century. Unlike Elias Boudinot, who knew Cherokee history and tradition and wanted to change them both, Apess, whose tribe the English settlers had declared no longer existent in the official documents that ended the Pequot War of 1637–38, had to find his history, which he did largely by reading against EuroAmerican accounts. All of the Native and African American writers in this period address the problem of racial difference, but Apess is the one who carried the analysis the farthest. Of the other Native writers active at the same time, besides Boudinot and Ridge, David Cusick published only his *Sketches of Ancient History of the Six Nations*, and while the Seneca writers Maris Bryant Pierce and Nathaniel Thayer Strong published essays when the Senecas were fighting removal in the 1830s, they then turned to work for their tribe for the rest of their lives and did not publish again. Of the African American writers, David Walker died under mysterious circumstances in 1830. Maria Stewart published a book of her orations in defense of equality but left Boston in 1833 to teach in New York, and although she lived a long life, she did not publish again until the late nineteenth century. Hosea Easton left Boston for Connecticut in 1833, where he accepted the pastorate of a church that was regularly attacked by white mobs. He died in 1837, the same year that saw the publication of his book *Treatise on the Intellectual Character and Civil and Political Condition of the Colored People of the U. States and the Prejudice Exercised Towards them: With a Sermon on the Duty of the Church to Them*, a book that arguably shows William Apess's influence.[20]

Apess's thinking bears traces of the intellectual movements with which he came into contact: Elias Boudinot's critique of white knowledge in his "Address" and in the pages of the *Cherokee Phoenix*; the similar critique of white knowledge put forward by the antislavery writers, both African American and white, especially William Lloyd Garrison, who published his refutation of the African colonization movement, *Thoughts on Colonization*, in the summer of 1832; and what Apess calls "the history of New England writers"—antiquarians, politicos, the Harvard-educated gentlemen who populated historical societies—whose ruminations proliferated in Boston. Historiography is essential to Apess's political struggle. In his first two books, books that pit his "experience"—a term Apess uses repeatedly in these works—and that of other Native peoples against white misrepresentation, Apess describes the political and psychological effects of misrepresentation but cannot quite explain why whites, especially professing Christians, think the way they do about Native peoples. After his exposure to the antislavery movement in Boston, however, Apess produces in the essay "An Indian's Looking-glass for the White Man" a critique of the politics of EuroAmerican knowledge about Indians in which he lays bare the motivations behind the apparently disinterested assertions of Native peoples' racial difference. In his last two works, *Indian Nullification of the Unconstitutional Laws of Massachusetts Relative to the Marshpee Tribe; or, The Pretended Riot Explained* (1835) and *Eulogy on King Philip* (1836), Apess puts that analysis to use in relation to both the contemporaneous political struggle of the Mashpees for their rights and to the most sacrosanct of New England narratives, the story of the Wampanoag King Philip, who led an uprising against the Puritans in the late seventeenth century. In these last two works, Apess interrupts—or, to use Dirlik's term, interpellates—EuroAmerican history through Native experience, ultimately producing counterhistories that hinge not on Native disappearance but rather continuity, that of the Native peoples who were at that moment rapidly being disappeared from U.S. history by its EuroAmerican writers. In the space of only a few years, Apess left a record of thinking his way through to an understanding of himself and other New England Native peoples as having both historical and political identity, at the very moment when whites were defining that identity out of existence.

There is more critical writing on William Apess than on any other Native writer of the nineteenth century, and possibly of the twentieth as well. Most of that criticism easily incorporates Apess into the narrative of multicultural inclusion in American literature, figuring him as demanding U.S. citizenship for himself and African Americans, although he is just as often (in seeming contradiction but not surprisingly) positioned as the tragic Indian "caught between two cultures." Apess's critics almost always comment on the persistent irony evident throughout his works, as well as his habit of employing "reversals"—savage for civilized being his obvious favorite.[21] The "reversals" *are* ironic, and their effect is usually to show that whites and Native peoples are equals. Apess's historiography is a necessarily ironic historiography: he must demonstrate to an audience largely composed of whites that what they think they know about Indians is not only inaccurate but also absurd. He must dislodge the foundation of white knowledge—the notion of Indians' ontological difference—in order to open up space for a different history. Apess's deployment of irony is a means of calling attention to the discrepancy between white knowledge and Native experience, and it dramatizes the frustration of being in an absurd position on a daily basis, mocks the discrepancy between what's known about him and how he and other Native peoples perceive themselves.

EXPERIENCES

That discrepancy applies to the Pequots as a tribe in a fairly dramatic fashion: they were written out of existence at the end of Pequot War in 1638, which was reported as fact by every historian who followed, despite the Pequots being very much still around. At the end of the war, the Pequots agreed, according to settlers in Connecticut, "they should no more inhabit their Native Countrey; nor should any of them be called Pequots but Moheags and Narrangansets for ever."[22] The Pequot War was the first Puritan war against the Indians, and the immigrants viewed it as God having demonstrated their righteousness. As one historian notes, "even the most prosaic of the Puritan writers" who took up the narrative, and most of them did, were "inspired [to] rhetorical heights" by their triumph over the forces of evil.[23] The most well known event of that war was a massacre at the Pequot fort in Mystic, where settlers and their Narragansett allies torched a palisade full of women, children, and old people, in which an estimated 300 to 700 were killed. Later, the Puritans' graphic accounts of it were cause for some embarrassment and half-hearted justification on the part of their nineteenth-century descendants, but the import of the story remained: the Pequots were all gone. In 1655, however, after having paid a yearly tribute since the end of the war, the Pequots petitioned Connecticut for a reservation, a governor, and a code of laws. The colony then established four towns, separated the tribe between the two eastern towns (the present-day Mashantucket

Pequots) and the two western ones (the present-day Paucatuck and Eastern Pequots), and appointed two Native governors, although by the eighteenth century white overseers were in place. Like other New England tribes, the Pequots fought a continual battle over white encroachment on their land: by 1800 they had lost much of their population; many men were killed fighting for the colonists in the Revolution; some left to join the Brothertown Indians on Oneida land in New York; and many had moved out of the towns in search of work as indentured servants, day laborers, or mariners. Still, despite the fact that by 1800 there were only thirty to forty tribal members living in the Mashantucket towns, the tribe had an income from land leases, the sale of firewood, and interest on its bank account. They chose two men to serve as tribal spokesmen, and they actively voiced their dissatisfaction with those who governed them, petitioning to remove overseers who were unresponsive or who misappropriated their income, and often suggested replacement over-seers.[24] Apess's parents left the towns looking for work, but when he was a child, his extended family was still living near the Pequot reservation, and even after he was taken from his grandparents' house and bound out as an inden-tured servant, he never was very far from where his family lived.[25]

Apess's people were supposed to be extinct, literally, and yet they persisted. The way whites got around the obvious was by maintaining that these people living in towns were not really Pequots because they didn't live as Indians were supposed to live; they were just the remnants, waiting for actual, biological extinction to arrive, as it surely would. Much of the criticism of Apess's works, especially the first two, which are generally considered his "autobiographical" works, A Son of the Forest and Experiences of Five Christian Indians of the Pequod Tribe (1833), devotes itself to determining how Apess could think of himself as Pequot when he did not speak the language, embraced Christianity, and did not write about his "oral tradition." As Apess never equivocates about being a Pequot Native person, this leads to certain mental gymnastics on the part of his critics. One of the accepted arguments (as evidenced by its repeti-tion) is that it was his evangelical Methodism that allowed Apess to finally come to think of himself as Pequot, which is based on the idea that the "orality" of Methodism allowed Apess to make a connection to the "orality" of traditional Pequot life.[26] This assertion makes sense only if one accepts the notion that "orality" is an ahistorical, detachable category, where one instance of it is equivalent to another, in ways that remain undefined. Looking for evidence of Apess's "culture" is misguided at the very least, because, as Robert Warrior points out, Apess lived in a society in "chronic crisis."[27] Moreover, as Scott Manning Stevens points out, the precontact culture had undergone such change that the people themselves couldn't account for it. Instead, Stevens writes, Apess's experience can be taken as representative of that of many Native peoples in the eastern United States, whose precontact practices had been lost or changed radically.[28]

This is exactly Apess's point. Apess himself returns again and again to his "experience" in his first two books. In *A Son of the Forest*, the subtitle of which is *The Experience of William Apess, a Native of the Forest*, he observes, "The reader knows full well that experience is the best schoolmaster, for what we have experienced, that we know, and all the world cannot possibly beat it out of us" (8–9). Apess brings his experience and that of other Native peoples to bear against white misrepresentation in order to explain why whites think what they do, no matter how counterintuitive and absurd. He does this for himself and for Native peoples as much as for his largely white readers in order to free himself from that misrepresentation and to represent his own experience and by extension that of other Native peoples. His daily life, as he represents it, is a near-constant barrage of misperception and misrecognition, and he is quite clear on the psychological and material damage that that assault produces. Both of his first two books incorporate a narrative of Native experience on the one hand and a reflection on the representation of that experience by whites on the other. By the time Apess gets to the "Indian's Looking-glass" essay at the end of *Experiences of Five Christian Indians*, he understands that misrepresentation is the means for whites of both justifying political and economic oppression and remaining unable to recognize the humanity of other human beings. That misrepresentation may be ignorant, but it is not unmotivated, on a deep level. Ultimately, whites' inhumane treatment of Native peoples who are obviously human beings—people "at least apparently human," as Charles Mills puts it— demonstrates that they are choosing to participate in this system for the advantages, real or imagined, that it affords them. Moreover, the practice of writing is integral to the operation of this system of systematic, institutionalized oppression. Thus the importance for Native peoples of representing themselves in writing, of having authority for the representation of their own experience, and the intellectual and material means to accomplish it.

There are two scenes in *A Son of the Forest* where Apess dramatizes the effects of misrepresentation in the daily lives of Native peoples. In one, he describes how, when he was four years old, his drunken grandmother, home from having peddled baskets and spent the money on drink, confronted him "without any provocation whatever on my part, [and] began to belabor me most unmercifully with a club; she asked me if I hated her, and I very innocently answered in the affirmative as I did not then know what the word meant and thought all of the while that I was answering aright; and so she continued asking me the same question, and I as often answered her in the same way, whereupon she continued beating me, by which means one of my arms was broken in three places" (6). An uncle who was living in the house rescued him, and the next morning, "when it was discovered that I had been most dangerously injured," a friendly neighbor who would later take Apess in, Mr. Furman, went to the selectmen of the town, who arranged to have Apess taken from his grandparents and bound out (6). Apess was well aware of how whites would perceive such a story: they would be ready to attribute his grandmother's violence to the degradation of Indians, the inevitable result of their living in too close proximity to "civilized" society and being unable, because of their inherently savage natures, to adjust to it. Instead, Apess attributes his grandmother's despair and violence to whites' actions and offers a concise assessment of the relation between political oppression and the psychology of the colonized. "I attribute [her violence] in a great measure to the whites," he writes, "inasmuch as they introduced among my countrymen that bane of comfort and happiness, ardent spirits—seduced them into a love of it and, when under its unhappy influence, wronged them out of their lawful possession—that land, where reposed the ashes of their sires." (7). This is the familiar, and historically accurate, accusation that whites often used alcohol to coerce Native peoples to give up land "legally," in treaties and other agreements.

Apess goes further, however, when he introduces the relatively uncommon accusation of "violence of the most revolting kind" done to Native women (7). As a result of such violence and the legalized theft of their land, Apess writes, Native peoples "were scattered abroad," as his parents had been, away from their people and in constant search of work to support themselves—like his grandmother, having to travel to sell what she could make (7). Whereas before whites arrived, Native peoples had "roamed over their goodly possessions," able to provide for themselves, after whites' theft of their land, they were forced to again "roam," with little or no hope of supporting themselves, being interlopers on the margins of white society. "Now many of them were seen reeling about intoxicated with liquor, neglecting to provide for themselves and families, who before were assiduously engaged in supplying the necessities of those depending on them for support," Apess writes (7). Whites' effective theft of Native land—again, through "legal" agreements coerced through the introduction of alcohol, is the cause, as far as Apess is concerned, for his grandmother's despair and violence.

This scene is followed almost immediately by another, in which he describes how, while berry-picking in the woods as a child, he is terrified by white women whom he mistakes for Indians because of their dark skin color. As a very young child, he writes, he "thought it disgraceful to be called an Indian," because "it was considered as a slur upon an oppressed and scattered nation" (10)—making the same point as does Elias Boudinot in his "Address to the Whites," published three years previously. "The proper term which ought to be applied to our nation, to distinguish it from the rest of the human family," he continues, "is that of '*Natives*'—and I humbly conceive that the natives of this country are the only people under heaven who have a just title to the name, inasmuch as we are the only people who retain the original complexion of our father Adam" (10). O'Connell notes that this is a reference to Apess's interest in the theory that Native peoples were one of the lost tribes of Israel, but it can also be pointed out that to be "native" is to be native to the land occupied and claimed by whites.[29] He is also, certainly, invoking the trope of the Indians who are more truly Christian than Christians themselves. But at the same time that Apess rejects and mocks whites' knowledge about Indians, he also shows how far away he is from the tribe itself and how much he could be affected by whites' misrepresentation of Indians. Apess writes that despite his rejection of the term "Indian" and what it stood for, "so completely was I weaned from the interests and affections of my brethren that a mere threat of being sent away among the Indians into the dreary woods had a much better effect in making me obedient to the commands of my superiors than any corporal punishment that they ever inflicted" (10). His own fantasies of Indians were conflated with his personal experiences. He writes, "I thought that, if those who should have loved and protected me treated me with such unkindness, surely I had not reason to expect mercy or favor at the hands of those who knew me in no other relation than that of cast-off member of the tribe" (10). He goes to the woods to pick berries with members of the Furman family and encounters there "a company of white females, on the same errand—their complexion was, to say the least, as *dark* as that of the natives" (10). "This circumstance filled my mind with terror," Apess writes, "and I broke from the party with my utmost speed, and I could not muster courage enough to look behind until I had reached home. By this time my imagination had pictured out a tale of blood" (10–11). Even Mr. Furman is convinced that the boy had encountered bloodthirsty savages in the woods, "notwithstanding the manifest incredibility of my tale of terror" (11). Apess addresses the discrepancy in his conclusion to this story, observing:

> The great fear I entertained of my brethren was occasioned by the many stories I had heard of their cruelty toward the whites—how they were in the

habit of killing and scalping men, women, and children. . . . But the whites did not tell me that they were in a great majority of instances the aggressors. . . . If the whites had told me how cruel they had been to the "poor Indian," I should have apprehended as much harm from them. (11)

As most critics have noted, evangelical Methodism was Apess's means of establishing equality with whites—as it was for many disenfranchised people in the early nineteenth century.[30] But as Apess himself notes in A Son of the Forest, while God is no respecter of persons, white people are, as evidenced by the fact that they often come to his sermons "to see the 'Indian' " (51). The problem is that all Methodists and all Christians do not put their abstract theological beliefs into practice. Each of the narratives in Experiences of Five Christian Indians is in fact an indictment of that discrepancy, told through the experiences of Native women. For example, after her husband and all of her children die, Hannah Caleb sinks into despair that Christianity at first cannot alleviate: "The anguish of my soul . . . no tongue can tell—for it was keen and pungent; and withal I felt a great enmity to the Christian religion, often wishing, in the depravity of my heart, I had been left like the rest of my kindred, ignorant and unknown." The reason, she explains, is that "I saw such a great inconsistency in their precepts and examples that I could not believe them" (145). What Christianity offers, but white Christians do not, is the assurance that Indians are not inherently different and inferior. As Caleb puts it:

> How must I feel, possessing the same powers of mind, with the same flesh and blood, and all we differed was merely in looks? [Or] how would you feel? Judge ye, though you never have been thrust out of society, and set at naught, and placed beyond the notice of all and hissed at as we have been— and I pray God you never may be. These pictures of distress and shame were enough to make me cry out, Oh horrid inconsistency—who would be a Christian? (145)

Part of the power of Apess's writing is his ability to dramatize the psychological distress that whites' knowledge about Indians causes Native peoples. He relentlessly insists that whites see Native peoples as they do themselves, as individuals and as equals. But he cannot explain why it is that whites believe what they do—why they cannot listen to reason. Though the appendix makes up almost half of A Son of the Forest, most critics either ignore it or dismiss it as only material that Apess lifted from the white minister Elias Boudinot's A Star in the West (1816), itself a compilation of miscellaneous historical materials purporting to establish the Native peoples of North America as descendants of one of the ten lost tribes of Israel. But if Boudinot's object is to prove that argument, Apess's extracts, as Scott Stevens observes, are "sympathetic" and "divided into historical narrative and observations on Indian character." Of the fact that most of the material is copied from other sources, principally if not entirely from Boudinot, Stevens's hypothesis is that "Apess may have felt that quotation would add to its 'objectivity' or at least its authority among his white readers."[31] The appendix is where Apess's analysis of whites' knowledge about Indians has not quite caught up with his arguments for the moral and political equality of Native peoples, or rather, where he hasn't yet made the explicit connection between the racial differentiation of Native peoples and their political oppression; he still accepts the notion of a unitary Indian "character" that differentiates Indians from whites. As both Stevens and Laura Murray note, he cites the "positive" or "sympathetic" modes of representing that Indian character. But in the details of the excerpts he chooses, Apess's tacit acceptance of a different, inherently Indian "character" ultimately contradicts his arguments for Native equality. Because he needs to write a history for Native peoples, and because of his circumstances, he must make use of what whites have written, and he must therefore develop an analysis of what whites "know" about Indians and why they know it.

Apess introduces the appendix, for example, by noting that he thinks "some general observations on the origin and character of the Indians, as a nation, would be acceptable to the numerous and highly respectable persons who have lent their patronage to his work" (52).[32] Here, Indians form one nation in the sense of forming a separate race. Even so, in the next two introductory paragraphs, before he begins excerpting Boudinot, Apess disputes whites' representations of Indians' inherent savagery; his implicit injection of Native history belies the notion of inherent difference.

> Ever since the discovery of America, the "civilized" or enlightened natives of the Old World regarded its inhabitants as an extensive race of "savages"! Of course, they were treated as barbarians, and for nearly two centuries they suffered without intermission, as the Europeans acted on the principle that *might* makes *right*—and if they could succeed in defrauding the natives out of their lands and drive them from the seaboard, they were satisfied for a time. (53)

While Apess implies that the positions of savage and civilized are reversed, as so many critics have noted, his solution at this point is to put Indians in the position of having the truly "civilized" character, rather than criticizing the concept of racial character itself.

This approach still forces Apess to evaluate and edit the white historiography he uses. Although, as Laura Murray notes, it is difficult to come to any conclusion about what Apess includes in the appendix, and Apess himself writes that the excerpts "are thrown together without that order that an accomplished scholar would observe" (52), there are still aspects of Boudinot's text that Apess rejects without rejecting Boudinot himself. Boudinot, for example, in his chapter entitled "Their General Character and Established Customs and Habits," repeats the usual observation, in keeping with William Robertson, that Indians are inherently disinterested in anything but the pursuit of war and that they are "cruel and revengeful."[33] Apess disputes this account, however: "It is often said of the '*savages*' that their mode of carrying on war, and the method of treating their prisoners, is cruel and barbarous in the extreme," he writes, "but did not the whites set them the brutal example?" (53). When he returns to the behavior of Indians in war, later in the appendix, he notes that although "the warlike ability of the Indians has been very generally despised by European officers—and this opinion has cost many thousands of men their lives," it is not Indians' inherent savagery that makes them warriors to be feared, but rather their military discipline. He again quotes Boudinot's *Star in the West*, which is citing yet another text, an account of eighteenth-century conflicts in the Ohio River Valley, in which resistant Indians "put the government to immense expense of blood and treasure" (70). The Indians' success is attributable, the unnamed writer continues, to the fact that "the Indians are the best disciplined troops in the world, especially when we consider that the ammunition and arms that they are obliged to use are of the worst sort, without bayonets or cartouch boxes" (70).

At this point then, Apess revises white knowledge by leaving out what he finds most offensive about it. But, again, he has not quite yet dealt with whites' knowledge as a *system*, in which what might appear to be "positive" or sympathetic knowledge about Indians nevertheless still serves to differentiate Native peoples from whites and ultimately to justify their oppression. Murray notes this in Apess's inclusion—again from Boudinot—of Washington Irving's essay "Traits of Indian Character." Irving's is the standard romantic portrait of noble savages: he sympathizes with their suffering; he praises the inherent qualities they possessed before they came into contact with settlers; he comments on how their different inherent qualities doom them to extinction with the advent of civilization. Murray points out that although Apess left out information that Irving included on the Creek War, he retained "some particularly racist material that Irving himself left out from later editions" of the essay, including the following observation: "It has pleased heaven to give [Indians] but limited powers of mind and feeble lights to guide their judgments: it becomes us who are blessed with higher intellects to think for them, and set them an example of humanity."[34] Part of the problem is that Native peoples themselves have not written the accounts of their own experiences and history. In introducing the excerpt from Irving, Apess writes:

> The Indian character, I have observed before, has been greatly misrepresented. Justice has not and, I may add, justice cannot be fully done to them by the historian. My people have had no press to record their sufferings or to make known their grievances; on this account many a tale of blood and woe has never been known to the public. (60)

The difficulty of Apess's position might be marked by his mistaken description of the Wampanoag King Philip as a Pequot. Although critics have speculated on whether Apess meant to do this or not, it appears, at least from the appendix, that his misattribution comes from Boudinot's *Star of the West*, which describes King Philip as "an independent sovereign of the Pequots," who "disdained to submit, but died fighting at the head of his men" (58).[35] One might be tempted at this point to say that Apess is sadly alienated from Pequot traditions, but that is the condition under which he writes at that moment in time. His apparent lack of knowledge about his own history, if he has to get some of it from books, does not bespeak how Apess works to change the conditions under which he and other Native peoples live nor of how those conditions came about in the first place. Much of his writing is focused on articulating those two problems. As Stevens observes, Apess's experiences are probably representative of a great many Native peoples in the East, who had been subjected to colonization for two hundred years at that point.[36]

At the end of *A Son of the Forest*, Apess has not solved the problem of Indians' "character" or the notion of their inherent difference. In the 1830s, that notion was signified increasingly in the concept of color, which Apess took up in "An Indian's Looking-glass for the White Man," an essay he appended to *Experiences of Five Christian Indians*. It was published sometime before May 1833, as he was handing out copies of the book and reading from it in his meetings when he arrived at Mashpee. The essay bears evidence of his contact with African American and white antislavery writers in his refutation of color as the signifier of difference and inferiority, as well as in his reference to the contemporary controversy over "amalgamation" between the races that had arisen from abolitionists' uncompromising demands for full African American political equality in the early years of their struggle (159).[37] David Walker's

Appeal addressed these same issues and was extraordinarily well known, given the hysteria it provoked in whites, and Garrison devoted much coverage to the essay in the *Liberator*.[38] Apess mentions the Cherokee resistance at the end of "Indian's Looking-glass" when he refers to "a Webster, an Everett, and a Wirt, and many others who are distinguished characters . . . who advocate our cause daily" (160). There is some possible influence of the Cherokees' use of natural law arguments in their Supreme Court cases in Apess's description of himself as a "naturalist" who is better able to describe his own experience than whites and in his observation that whites deprive Indians "of their lawful rights, that nature and God require them to have" (156, 157). There is even an indication that Apess was familiar with events at Mashpee when he remarks that whites "think it no crime to go upon Indian lands and cut and carry off their most valuable timber, or anything else they chose" (156).

Critics often describe Apess as one who prefigures or endorses a multicultural vision of the United States, and he is sometimes even described as partly African American (on little or no evidence), which apparently strengthens the case for his multicultural endorsements.[39] The connections between Apess and African Americans—specifically, the writers and writing readily available in Boston in the early 1830s—are instead political, epistemological, and strategic. Many activists—white, African American, and Native alike—observed at the time that the similarity between plans to colonize African Americans and to remove Indians from the East was obvious and that the supporters of removal and colonization justified both plans in the same way: African Americans and Native peoples were ontologically different from whites and therefore must be "removed." Garrison observed in 1832 in *Thoughts on Colonization* that African Americans "are as unanimously opposed to removal to Africa, as the Cherokees from the council-fires and graves of their fathers."[40] Antiremoval and antislavery activists often also came out of the same, broad-based "benevolent community" that publicized the Cherokee resistance in widely circulated magazines and newspapers at the same time that they began to attack slavery—the same community to which Jeremiah Evarts belonged.[41] Antislavery writers argued that African Americans were morally equal to whites and must be *citizens* of the United States and that therefore they cannot be understood to be different from whites in any significant way. In order to make those arguments, the antislavery writers pointed out how whites' assertions of African American difference were entirely politically motivated. This is the critique that begins to appear in Apess's writing only after he goes to Boston and becomes associated with the antislavery movement. That Apess has not really addressed the political position of Native peoples prior to that point can be understood in relation to his circumstances, which would seem to indicate indistinct political connections. At the same time, Apess's inability to reject the notion of racial character or difference in A Son of the Forest can be seen in a political light. It is more difficult to produce a critique of difference as regards groups of people when historically they have always inhabited different political entities—the difference has to be differentiated. In any case, "Indian's Looking-glass" is a breakthrough in Apess's thinking, where he both recognizes the political ground of whites' knowledge about Indian difference and rejects the notion of any kind of essential or inherent difference, thus detaching difference from biology, which allows him to move toward a repoliticized understanding of Native experience.

"Indian's Looking-glass" is in some respects an elaboration on the berry-picking scene in A Son of the Forest, but, in keeping with the antislavery writers, Apess pushes his analysis further than he does in his first book, to what is in effect a meditation on the politics of skin color as a signifier of ontological difference and inferiority—for Native peoples and for all "people of color," a term that does not appear in A Son of the Forest.[42] The opening paragraph of "Looking-glass" is quite similar to the opening paragraph of the preamble to David Walker's Appeal. Like Walker, who describes African Americans as "the most degraded, wretched, and abject set of beings that ever lived since the world began" thanks to the actions of "Christian Americans,"[43] Apess describes Native peoples as "the most mean, abject, miserable race of beings in the world" and the reservations in New England as "a complete place of prodigality and prostitution" (155). Throughout "Looking-glass," he describes both the material and psychological conditions on those reservations. As implied in his comments on his grandmother, Apess writes that women "left without protection . . . are seduced by white men, and finally left to be common prostitutes for them and to be destroyed by that burning, fiery curse . . . rum" (155). He lists reasons for these conditions: many of the men are away at sea; they are also "made to believe they are minors and have not the abilities given them from God to take care of themselves"; many of their "Agents"—their "overseers" and "guardians"—"are unfaithful and care not whether the Indians live or die"; and they "have no education to take care of themselves" (155–56).

Like the African American and white antislavery writers active at the time, Apess indicts Christians for failing to act in accordance with their own theology. The conditions on reservations are the result of Christians' actions, he reiterates, actions that whites make on the pretext of Native difference, on the evidence of the color of their skin. Apess points out that white Christians' invocation of color as the signifier of difference reveals the hypocrisy of their professed interest in improving Indians' lives. Given the conditions under which Native peoples live, Apess writes,

> I would take the liberty to ask why they are not brought forward and pains taken to educate them . . . and those of the brightest and first-rate talents put forward and held up to office. Perhaps some unholy, unprincipled men would cry out, "The skin is not good enough"; but stop, friends—I am not talking about skin but about principles. I would ask if there cannot be as good feelings and principles under a red skin as there can be under a white. (156)

By "principle" Apess means knowledge that justifies actions, which, he says, "I have heard repeatedly, from the most respectable gentlemen and ladies." He asks,

> Why are we not protected in our persons and property throughout the Union? Is it not because there reigns in the breast of many who are leaders a most unrighteous, unbecoming, and impure black principle, and as corrupt and unholy as it can be—while these very same unfeeling, self-esteemed characters pretend to take the skin as a pretext to keep us from our unalienable and lawful rights? I would ask you if you would like to be disfranchised from all your rights, merely because your skin is white, and for no other crime. (156)

This is another of Apess's ironic reversals: what lies beneath whites' insistence on the inferiority of black or red people is the "impure black principle," which is the desire to keep Native and African American people from that which is their "unalienable and lawful [right]." The use of the figure of the looking-glass to represent the necessity of looking carefully at one's own moral failings was popular in the eighteenth and early nineteenth centuries, in both the United States and Britain. Mason Lock (Parson) Weems, for example, wrote both *The Drunkard's Looking-glass* (Philadelphia, 1808) and *God's Revenge Against Dueling, or, the Duelist's Looking-glass* (Philadelphia, 1827).[44] The implications of Apess's use of the metaphor go somewhat further than a Dorian Gray–like revelation of the white man's interior moral corruption. He holds up an *Indian's* looking-glass for the white man: the Indian—maintained by whites to be without reason and who can be read here as Apess himself—provides the means of unmasking the motivations of the white man's knowledge. What the white man sees in the mirror are ultimately his own moral failings, but more immediately the political motivations of his misrepresentation of Native peoples.

Apess further elaborates on that analysis in another, surreal metaphor, where he considers the power of writing to produce false knowledge about Indian difference:

> Assemble all nations together in your imagination, and let the whites be seated among them, and then let us look for the whites, and I doubt not it would be hard finding them; for to the rest of the nations, they are still but a handful. Now suppose these skins were put together, and each skin had its national crimes written upon it—which skin do you think would have the greatest? I will ask one question more. Can you charge the Indians with robbing a nation almost of their whole continent, and murdering their women and children, and then depriving the remainder of their lawful rights, that nature and God require them to have? And to cap the climax, rob another nation to till their grounds and welter out their days under the lash with hunger and fatigue under the scorching rays of a burning sun? I should look at all the skins, and I know what when I cast my eye upon that white skin, and if I saw those crimes written upon it, I should enter my protest against it immediately and cleave to that which is more honorable. And I can tell you that I am satisfied with the manner of my creation, fully— whether others are or not. (157)

In the image of writing on white skin, Apess not only refers to the history of writing itself—done on animal skins—but also his own work as a reader and a critic. The image is certainly complex. White writing reveals the national crimes of whites, both in terms of their own account of their history—on which Apess himself had to rely—and the knowledge about black/red difference through which whites attempt to justify their inescapable history of violence and oppression. Whites' knowledge about racial difference is only knowledge about themselves, ultimately revealing their own moral failings. At the same time, however, someone has to see, read, and counter that writing, and that would be William Apess, who declares, "I should enter my protest against it immediately and cleave to that which is more honorable." The surreal image of white skin with national crimes written on it returns then, through an ironic reversal, to the imperative of Native writing to denounce misrepresentation and define "that which is more honorable" in the face of whites' increasing insistence upon self-evident knowledge of Native difference and inferiority. This is the task that Apess takes up in his last two works, in which he extends this insight about the power of knowledge about Indians and of writing to both oppress and liberate Native peoples to the more complex task of describing how that power works in society and how Native peoples must claim it for themselves.

NULLIFYING ACTS

Apess's reputation preceded him when he arrived on Cape Cod in the late spring of 1833 distributing a "small pamphlet," which, according to Sylvannus Bourne Phinney, editor of the *Barnstable Patriot*, turns out to have been *Experiences of Five Christian Indians of the Pequot Tribe*. Pointedly comparing Apess to Black Hawk (the defeated Sauk and Fox leader who was then in the midst of a widely publicized tour of eastern cities before being returned to prison in St. Louis), Phinney notes that Apess had met with "a rather cool reception in this village." In Phinney's view, Apess's presence at Mashpee was cause for alarm: "If the style of this 'prophets' preaching to the heterogeneous population of Marshpee is what we learn it is, we hope a little of the spirit shown by the authorities of Georgia in a somewhat similar instance will be exercised towards him," Phinney wrote threateningly. The plantation, he observed, was in no need of "public teachers in both a religious and moral respect":

> If we are not misinformed, the teachings of this man are calculated to excite the distrust and jealousy of the inhabitants towards their present guardians and minister; and with his pretensions to elevate them to what we all wish they might be, he will make them, in their present ill-prepared state for such preaching, ten times more turbulent, uncomfortable, unmanageable and unhappy than they now are.[45]

For his part, Apess wrote that he had second thoughts about the Mashpees after first visiting them, thinking there were too many factions, and that in any case they were in the care of their minister, Phineas Fish. He returned, however, and gave a lecture in the meetinghouse, which he judged "wrought well," and recounted:

> A small pamphlet that contained a sketch of the history of the Indians of New England had had a good effect. As I was reading from it, an individual among the assembly took occasion to clap his hands and, with a loud shout, to cry, "Truth, truth!" This gave rise to a general conversation, and it was truly heartrending to me to hear what my kindred people had suffered at the hands of the whites.[46]

Apess's *Indian Nullification of the Unconstitutional Laws of Massachusetts; or, the Pretended Riot Explained* (Boston, 1835) was the end result of a battle for political control of Mashpee land, a battle in which Apess orchestrated a systematic assault on white authority through various forms of writing. The ways in which writing played a part in that conflict are myriad. When he first arrived on Cape Cod, Apess *read* his own account of Native experience to the Mashpees in an effort to show them that they could find their own voices, as he had done. In *Indian Nullification*, he describes how he insisted, when the Mashpees asked for his help, that they draw up a document declaring that he and his descendants were "to be considered as belonging to the Marshpee tribe of Indians" (174). With his assistance, the Mashpees then drew up two written notices—one to the governor of Massachusetts, another to the president of Harvard University—detailing their complaints and informing each official that the Mashpees were independent and could "rule [their] own tribe" and choose their own preacher. Furthermore, they write, "We will publish this to the world" (177). They formed a government with a president and officers and drew up a document for proprietors to sign to make it official. They posted written notices around the borders of the plantation informing any and all of the following: "We have determined to make our own laws and govern ourselves. . . . This is to give notice that we have resolved if any person is seen on our plantation after the first of July carting or cutting wood, without our leave, or in any way trespassing upon our lands, they shall be bound hand and foot, and thrown off."[47] They cultivated a relationship with Benjamin Franklin Hallett, the lawyer-editor of the antimasonic *Boston Daily Advocate*, a native of Cape Cod who soon became their lawyer. Hallett provided Apess a forum through both the newspaper and the printer Jonathan Howe. It was Howe who published both Hallett's argument on behalf of the Mashpees and Apess's *Indian Nullification*, the only one of Apess's works that was not self-published.[48] One also has to wonder to what extent the Cherokee model was on Apess's mind— that is, the combined efforts of their newspaper, their spokesmen, and their political operatives in the struggle with the Georgia and U.S. governments. Their fight and that of the Mashpees were concurrent. Finally, when the Mashpees were frustrated with both the Commonwealth's undermining of the autonomy that it supposedly granted them as a result of the "revolt" and its plan to return to the legislature in yet another effort to remove the tenacious Phineas Fish, Apess published *Indian Nullification*, which, like Garrison's *Thoughts on Colonization*, is a compendium of different written accounts from which Apess proceeds to shape a critique of white thinking about Indians.

Although nothing had happened in the month since Apess and Blind Joe

Amos, the young Baptist minister at Mashpee, had delivered their notices to Harvard and the Commonwealth, the declaration of autonomy produced in late June 1833, effective 1 July, provoked a response from the governor on the same day. Gideon Hawley, who was the son of the Mashpees' minister in the late eighteenth century, rode immediately to Governor Levi Lincoln at his residence in Worcester with a letter from Phineas Fish detailing the revolt. In *Nullification*, Apess recounts what happened next:

> He stated that the Indians were in open rebellion and that blood was likely to be shed. . . . It was reported and believed among us that he said we had armed ourselves and were prepared to carry all before us with tomahawk and scalping knife; that death and destruction, and all the horrors of a savage war, were impending; that of the white inhabitants some were already dead and the rest dreadfully alarmed! An awful picture indeed. (180–81)

Two days after Gideon Hawley's desperate ride, Lincoln appointed Josiah Fiske to "represent to [the Mashpees], the parental feelings and regard of the Government of the Commonwealth towards them." "Parental feelings" became the state's theme in this conflict, and it demonstrates what might be called the strong arm of sympathy for Indians in the nineteenth century. Moreover, when Apess was assembling *Indian Nullification*, the government's documentation of the conflict at Mashpee—in particular, the governor's correspondence with his representative —was available to him as part of the official record submitted to the legislature in the winter of 1834. In this correspondence, Lincoln tells Fiske to admonish the Mashpees that they themselves had requested the state's "guardianship," which was only for their protection, and besides, could only be changed by the legislature (which was not in session again until January 1834).[49] Hawley's arrival caused Lincoln to write more urgently to Fiske that "the Indians must be made to understand their relation to the Government of the State" and to direct,

> If there should be any seditious or riotous proceedings, let the ringleaders be arrested and delivered over to the civil power, under the ordinary processes of Law, and if more serious consequences than are now apprehended are like to ensue, advise me by express, if necessary, or otherwise, as the urgency of the case may require.[50]

On the first of July the "riot" for which the governor had made plans occurred. According to Josiah Fiske, who had not as yet arrived on the scene himself, Apess and the Mashpees waited for whites to come onto the plantation to load wood and then stopped them from doing so.[51] In *Nullification*, Apess represents a more accidental confrontation: he was walking in the woods, he maintains, when he came upon a group of four white men who were taking wood from the plantation, including two brothers named Sampson, who were known to have vowed to disregard the Mashpees' declarations. Then a group of Mashpee men arrive: "I then," Apess writes, "having previously cautioned the Indians to do no bodily injury to any man, unless in their own defense, but to stand for their rights and nothing else, desired them to unload the teams, which they did very promptly" (181). In a letter that did not appear in the public documents, written before he went to the meeting on 4 July, Fiske informed Armstrong that he intended to arrest Apess and the eight Mashpee men who were with him at the "riot":

> Apess is unquestionably a false and dangerous man & ought not to be permitted to have a resting place any longer upon the plantation. I have a desire . . . to . . . give them some testimonials of the parental regard and feelings which the Executive entertains for them and after that if it shall not have a salutary effect upon them they must take the consequences.[52]

A more straightforward demonstration of the exercise of power that sympathy for Indians occludes is difficult to imagine: be duped by my sympathy or I'll throw you in jail, which is exactly what happened to William Apess.

When Fiske arrived at Mashpee on the second of July, he called a meeting for the third, but no one showed up. On the fourth, Fiske received a letter from Daniel Amos, the Mashpee president, who wrote that the Mashpees "would wait with pleasure upon the Commissioner July 4th, at nine of the clock, in *their* meeting house, their [*sic*] being no other place in which it would be desirable for them to see him." The Mashpees had to break into the meeting-house because Phineas Fish would not surrender the key; Apess presided at the meeting. When Fiske arrived alone, the Mashpees demanded that the overseers be called to the meeting as well, which they were, and, as Fiske wrote, "the residue of the day, till nearly sunset, was spent in hearing their complaints and in attending to the numerous grievances, real or supposed, which had been experienced by any of the men, women or children belonging to the declining race of the Marshpee Indians."[53] Fiske's situating Mashpee grievances and political demands in the discourse of Native disappearance is telling: if only they would just disappear. According to Apess, the truth of the Mashpee experience made the white audience "uneasy." They were "often getting up, going out, and returning, as if apprehensive of some danger," the cause of which apprehension, Apess writes, was that three or four Mashpee men who had been out hunting came to the meeting with their guns. "This circumstance was thought, or pretended to be thought, by a few of our neighbors to portend violence and murder," he observes (183).

The word "pretended" makes an essential point: whites' ideas about Indian savagery are neither true nor logical, but mere justification—and whites know it, a circumstance that becomes clear as the meeting continues. The suspicion circulating in the meeting was exacerbated when the governor's most recent missive to Fiske was read aloud. Lincoln wrote to Fiske that he should confine his actions "to the application of the *civil power*," but that if things got out of hand, "the Sheriff will, with your advice, call out the *posse comitatus*, and should there be reason to fear the efficiency of this resort, I will be present personally, to direct any *military* requisitions" (183).[54] The Mashpees felt this "a provocation and a stimulus," Apess writes, that the governor "should think they had put him in mind of his oath of office, to secure the Commonwealth from danger, and given him cause to call out perhaps fifty or sixty thousand militia; especially when the great strength and power of the Marshpee tribe was considered" (183). Governor Lincoln's threat to call out the militia soon became a matter for public mockery on the part of local newspapers.

Late in the day, at Fiske's request, John Reed, the sheriff of Barnstable County, whom the overseers had insisted accompany them to the meeting, explained the laws governing the Mashpees. Apess describes the explanation:

> He told us that merely declaring a law to be oppressive could not abrogate it; and that it would become us, as good citizens whom the government was disposed to treat well, to wait for the session of the Legislature and then apply for relief. (Surely it was either insult or wrong to call the Marshpees citizens, for such they never were, from the Declaration of Independence up to the session of the Legislature in 1834.) (183)

Fiske, Apess continues, "then pathetically stated his opinions concerning the awful consequences which would result from a violation of the laws, and spoke much at large of the parental feeling of [the] government for the remnant of a once mighty and distinguished race" (183–84). Apess's mocking reference to Fiske's sympathy for doomed Indians makes clear the connection between whites' representations of Indians' difference and their subordination of Native peoples. He insists that Mashpee self-government be recognized immediately:

> Wm. Apess replied that the laws ought to be altered without delay; that it was perfectly manifest that they were unconstitutional; and that, even if they were not so, there was nothing in them to authorize the white inhabitants to act as they had done. (184)

In this Apess indicates the political limbo in which the Mashpees found themselves; without the guarantee of autonomy and implied equality in treaties, the Mashpees can only appeal to the high moral ground invoked in the Constitution—even if, as was the case for African Americans, Native peoples were excluded from its terms.

His tone, Apess admits, "alarmed some of the whites present considerably" (184). At this point, Sheriff Reed questioned Apess's right to be involved; Apess said the tribe had adopted him. Reed answered that the Indians had no right to adopt Apess. "I replied that, if the plantation belonged to them, they undoubtedly had a right to give me leave to dwell upon it" (184), thereby making the point that who counts as an Indian is the *political* domain of Indian people. The exchange deteriorated further, and then Reed arrested Apess (184). Reed "was not very desirous to execute" the arrest warrant, Apess writes. "With some apprehension" the sheriff told Apess that he must go with him "peaceably" or "he could have out the whole county of Barnstable" (184). "I was not conscious of giving any cause for this perturbation of mind," Apess remarks somewhat disingenuously, "but I suppose others saw my conduct in a different light" (184). Although, he adds, "if I had refused to obey the warrant the sheriff would not have been able to enforce it." Wishing, however, "to have the truth appear, viz., that it was not the intention or wish of the Marshpees to do violence or shed blood," Apess went with Sheriff Reed (184). That night Josiah Fiske wrote the governor that Apess's arrest had had the desired effect: "The Indians seemed to have forgotten for a moment that they had muskets with them and looked with perfect amazement at the sheriff when he had taken their Champion from the Moderators [sic] seat in the meetinghouse and conducted him with great dignity to a seat in his carriage at the door."[55]

Apess was arraigned on riot and trespass charges and then released after a former overseer posted the bond and fine.[56] Most of the white habitants of the area were not at all pleased with Apess's release. In Apess's words,

> Truth had been shot to their hearts, and if I should say that they bellowed like mad bulls and spouted like whales gored mortally by the harpoon, I do not think the figure of speech would be too strong. . . . There was a great deal of loose talk and a pretty considerable uproar. (185)[57]

Convinced by Fiske's arguments, the Mashpees' leaders met on 6 July to rescind the former resolutions and wait to petition the legislature in January 1834 (189). In September, Apess was convicted of riot and sentenced to thirty days in jail.[58]

While Apess points out that calling the Mashpees' "citizens" of Massachusetts is a misrepresentation, as they never had been citizens, Josiah Fiske, instead of figuring the Mashpees as actual citizens, figured them as *analogous* to citizens. In a December 1833 account of the conflict, Fiske writes that "it was the settled purpose of Apes to establish in the minds of the natives a belief that each generation has a right to act for itself, and that guardianship laws which had been imposed by the consent of one generation, should not be enforced against the will of another."[59] Fiske seems to construe the original agreement between the Christian Mashpees and the Massachusetts colony as a contract to which the Mashpees had agreed and by so doing essentially gave Massachusetts complete authority over the Mashpees, such that they had no redress when they found the relationship unsatisfactory. Newspaper writers also described the Mashpees in vague terms of citizenship, although the only status the Mashpees had was that of consenting subordinate. Sylvannus Phinney, for example, editor of the *Barnstable Patriot*, wrote that Apess told the Mashpees

> that they ought to govern themselves, throw off their guardianship imposed upon them by the State, manage and dispose of their own property as they please: that they are sacrificing their plantation to enrich their masters, whose only ambition is to keep them in ignorance and want, that they may the better despoil them of their estate: that if they will shake off the yoke, many of them may become as great as "their brother," Daniel Webster, &c. &c.—After this manner, [Apess] wro't them up to a high pitch of PATRIOTISM, and they concluded to "secede."[60]

Despite his relatively accurate account of the Mashpees' demands, which are based on their argument that they have no political rights whatsoever, Phinney implies that the Mashpees are included in the political system already. Like Fiske, Phinney incorporates the Mashpees into contemporary political rhetoric without regard to the actual state of political relations.

The argument presented before a legislative committee on behalf of the Mashpees by their lawyer, Benjamin Franklin Hallett, was printed and sold for the delegation's benefit.[61] In the pamphlet, *Rights of the Marshpee Indians*, Hallett outlines in detail the history of the Mashpee Indians' relation to European authority and their current demand for self-government.[62] Like Jeremiah Evarts in the "William Penn" letters, Hallett proceeds from one legal agreement or act of the legislature to another to demonstrate that the Mashpees never consented to be governed by the guardianship system imposed upon them and argues that, because they were human beings fully capable of governing themselves, the laws of the Commonwealth of Massachusetts and the United States itself demanded that they be restored that capacity. Like Evarts,

Hallett addresses the problem of Native title to the land and finds that the settlers themselves, from the beginning of their contact with Native peoples, recognized "that the title of the Indians was superior to their own" (5). Unlike Evarts and unlike the Cherokees, however, Hallett argues that the Mashpees are already citizens of the United States. Since at that point they weren't legally citizens—that is, they could not vote or be taxed—Hallett uses the term broadly to indicate the inhabitants of a society, maintaining that Indians are citizens by default. Because the Mashpees are not "*aliens*" or a "domestic nation" with "rights secured by treaty" like the Cherokees, nor are they "hereditary vassals or servants" made so through "conquest" (as were African Americans), nor "public enemies," nor "paupers," Hallett argues, they could only be citizens (16). The constitution of the Commonwealth of Massachusetts, Hallett notes, defines an "inhabitant" of the state as "every person . . . in that town, district or *plantation* where he dwelleth or hath his home" (16; emphasis in original).

The object in the conflict, however, was for the Mashpees to secure collective control of and authority over the land that they had inherited from that seventeenth-century transaction. As Hallett points out, though, Native peoples without a specific treaty relationship with the United States are not legally defined as one thing or another. In their petition for self-government, the Mashpees both recognize and reject their political subordination to Massachusetts and the United States. They recognize the state's ultimate authority over the Mashpees as citizen-inhabitants, but they also reject the state's claim of authority over Mashpee land and their internal affairs. They petition to be "incorporated into a town, under the general laws of the state . . . with certain exceptions adapted to the condition of that people, and desired by them" (35). Those exceptions included limiting voters to men who were descendants of the seventeenth-century proprietors or who had been admitted to the voting rolls by a vote of the hereditary proprietors and a government composed of Native town selectmen. While the selectmen would have control of the government— how common land was used, how money to support the government was raised—the proposed act provided for a white-controlled political entity that would oversee how Mashpee land was used by individuals and to ensure that that land would not go out of the hands of those individuals, and into the hands, presumably, of the surrounding whites. They do not petition for the right to vote in Massachusetts, and the proposed act specifically exempts them from being taxed by the state.[63]

In a public appearance at the Massachusetts House of Representatives, the Mashpee spokesmen—Apess, Joseph Amos, and Isaac Combs, Phineas Fish's former deacon—were well received by members of the Massachusetts legislature, who, the *Liberator* wrote, were particularly appreciative of William Apess's oratorical skills. An audience composed mainly of members of the Massachusetts house "listened . . . most respectfully and attentively" to "a fearless, comprehensive and eloquent speech," which "endeavored to prove that under such laws and Overseers, no people could rise from their degradation" and applauded the speakers' "dextrous and pointed thrusts at the whites, for their treatment of the sons of the forest since the time of the pilgrims" (221). In late March, the act was passed unanimously by the Senate and opposed in the House only by a Mr. Lucas of Plymouth.[64] A single commissioner appointed by the governor replaced the board of overseers, and the commonwealth reserved the right to "alter, succeed or repeal" the act forming the Indian District "at their pleasure."[65]

The legislature declined to rule on the status of Phineas Fish, insisting that he was Harvard's problem to solve. Harvard had begun soliciting information on his ministry from Fish, who replied in December 1833 in a long, heavily underscored letter justifying his activities, or lack of activities, and excoriating Apess as a troublemaker. Ordained as a Harvard-trained Unitarian, Fish had become more conservative fairly early in his career and declared himself an orthodox Congregational soon after graduation. Harvard—its administrators, professors, and students—was the center of Unitarianism at a time when Boston's white population was much preoccupied by the religious conflicts between the two.[66] Fish seems to have been singularly unable to perceive how other whites might perceive him; in his conflict with the legislature and Harvard, it appears that the benevolent elites running both institutions were somewhat taken aback by Fish's unabashed small-mindedness. No one was able to justify him as a minister to the Indians—or even as a good minister. Although one of his defenders described Fish as having a "strong mind" and being "one of the best ethical writers this country," he also could not help but note that Fish was "a feeble speaker in the pulpit."[67] In his letter to Josiah Quincy and the Harvard Board of Fellows, Fish insists, "My sermons have been practical, rather than controversial. Persons of simpler mind have repeatedly assured me, that they understood me without difficulty." He writes that he faces many "discouragements" at Mashpee, for which he cannot be blamed. Apess, he charges, is a "rapacious" power monger who "flatters them [the Mashpees] that he can enlighten & enrich them—that he can break their chains & in a moment exalt them to happiness & distinction." Fish also claims that Apess covets the meetinghouse, "[declaring] he will occupy it at a certain time—that he will exclude myself—church & congregation, & *no white man shall have any connection with Indian affairs*" (emphasis in original).[68]

Fish was more circumspect in discussing his ministry and the threats upon it when he submitted a memorial to the legislature in January 1834. In it, he speaks only of a mysterious "Stranger" who appeared among the Mashpees to stir them up.[69] But he cannot stop from revealing himself when it comes to the matter of the meetinghouse. Referring to the Mashpee petitions for control of it, Fish writes, " 'Our meeting House,' say they, 'is almost worn out by white people, and is not fit for respectable people to meet.' As it was built by a *White* Missionary Society, and as it was thoroughly repaired at the expense of the *White* Legislature of the State, perhaps the *whites* may think themselves entitled to some wear of it, & being no way 'fit for *respectable* people,' the Church and Congregation hope they may the more readily be left unmolested in their accustomed use of it."[70]

William Apess's encounter with Fish starts innocently enough. In *Indian Nullification*, Apess reports that Fish treats him "with proper kindness" and invites him to preach in the meetinghouse (170). Once at the meetinghouse, Apess describes a "charming landscape": the "sacred edifice in the midst of a noble forest," the Indian burial ground "overgrown with pines, in which the graves were all ranged north and south," a "delightful brook" (170). There were no Indians in the church, though, a point Apess makes by elaborating on the notion of skin color that he so excoriates in "Indian's Looking-glass."

> I turned to meet my Indian brethren and give them the hand of friendship; but I was greatly disappointed in the appearance of those who advanced. All the Indians I had ever seen were of a reddish color, sometimes approaching a yellow, but now, look to what quarter I would, most of those who were coming were pale faces, and, in my disappointment, it seemed to me that the hue of death sat upon their countenances. It seemed very strange to me that my brethren should have changed their natural color and become in every respect like white men. (170)

If the white parishioners who are supposedly Indian have the hue of death, that death is the death to Native peoples of the benefits of Christianity, and at the same time, the "theft" of Christianity is as the theft of land. "The pale men were certainly stealing from the Indians their portion in the Gospel," he writes, "by leaving their own houses of worship and crowding [the Indians] out of theirs" (171).

Finding that "plain dealing was disagreeable to my white auditory," with Fish at his side Apess seeks out the Mashpees themselves. "I addressed them upon temperance and education, subjects which I thought very needful to be discussed, and plainly told them what I had heard from their missionary, viz., that it was their general disposition to be idle, not to hoe the cornfields they had planted, to take no care of their hay after mowing it, and to lie drunken under their fences" (171)—that is, he told them that according to Fish (and other whites), it was well known that Indians are inherently lazy, irresponsible drunks. The solution, Apess tells the Mashpees, is education. Finally, he writes, "addressing the throne of grace, I besought the Lord to have mercy on them and relieve them from the oppressions under which they labored" (171–72). Fish intervened at this point. "Here Mr. Fish cautioned me not to say anything about oppression," Apess writes, "that being, he said, the very thing that made them discontented. They thought themselves oppressed, he observed, but such was not the case. They already had liberty enough" (172). Their problem, Fish says, is not what whites are doing to them, but rather what the Mashpees themselves inherently *are*. Apess presses Fish: he asks why the Indians are not "[granted] . . . the privileges enjoyed by the whites about them," and Fish maintains that "that would never do, as [the Mashpees] would immediately part with all their lands" (172). This gets at the issue at hand, although obliquely. Under the guise of benevolent concern for childlike Indians—their "parental feelings"—whites control Native land and other property for their own benefit. Apess calls Fish on his duty as a missionary, telling Fish that "if [the Mashpees'] improvement was his aim, he ought to go among them and inquire into their affairs." Fish replies, Apess writes, "that he did go at times [to them] but did not say much to them about their worldly concerns," thinking it not "proper" to do so (172).

That Fish and other missionaries disregard their role as educators is Apess's main charge against them. When the misrepresentation of the Mashpees in English is endemic, their ability to communicate the truth of their experience in English is imperative. The white missionaries to the Mashpees have failed miserably, however. Rev. Gideon Hawley, Fish's predecessor, "*did not teach one* Indian to read during his [fifty years'] residence among them," Apess writes (186; emphasis in original). According to Apess, neither Fish nor Hawley organized schools. "When the Marshpee children were put out to service, it was with the express understanding, as their parents all agree, that they should not be schooled. Many of those who held them in servitude used them more like dogs than human beings, feeding them scantily, lodging them hard, and clothing them with rags" (187). The Mashpee children remain ignorant of Christianity and grow up unable to dispute their own misrepresentation and oppression. Both Hawley and Fish, Apess writes, "were willing to have the use of the property of the Marshpees, I fear, under a mere pretext of doing them good; and, therefore, the owners were constantly proclaimed to be savages."

That is, knowledge about Indians being inferior savages *justifies* the political relation—in this case, the control of Mashpee land. Benevolence is a pretext for material gain. "I wonder what the whites would say, should the Indians take possession of any part of their property," Apess asks; "many and many a red man has been butchered for a less wrong than the Marshpees complain of" (187).

Apess represents missionaries as a means of securing a future for Native peoples insofar as the missionary is the means of acquiring Christianity and literacy, which in turn are the means through which Indians demand their equality with whites. White missionaries, he charges, have failed in this. "I greatly doubt that any missionary has ever thought of making the Indian or African his equal," Apess writes; "as soon as we begin to talk about equal rights, the cry of amalgamation is set up, as if men of color could not enjoy their natural rights without any necessity for intermarriage between the sons and daughters of the two races" (230). This Apess dismisses as mere obfuscation on the part of whites and protests, "I should not have mentioned [amalgamation] at all, but that it has been rung in my ears by almost every white lecturer I ever had the misfortune to meet" (231). Instead of offering religion and literacy, Apess sees missionaries rather as determined to destroy Native political organization. "It seems to have been usually the object to seat the Indians between two stools, in order that they might fall to the ground, by breaking up their government and forms of society, without giving them any others in their place," Apess writes (230). "It does not appear to be the aim of the missionaries to improve the Indians by making citizens of them," he continues; "hence, in most cases, anarchy and confusion are the results" (230). No missionary, Apess insists, "from the days of Eliot to the year 1834," has made one Indian a citizen. "That latter date marks the first instance of such an experiment," he adds. "Is it not strange that free men should thus have been held in bondage more than two hundred years, and that setting them at liberty at this late date should be called *an experiment* now?" (230).

Indian Nullification received at least several reviews, all positive in their different ways and often noting the similarity of the Mashpees' cause to that of the Cherokees.[71] Sylvannus Phinney seems to have enjoyed the controversy. "Parson Apes deals severely with his opponents," Phinney observes, "and shows up some of our *big folks* in fine style; and we feel *ourselves* quite honored, that the *Patriot* should have been thought worthy to come under his notice, and have two or three pages of his book devoted to it in connection with Gov. Lincoln and many other *dignitaries*." There is also a jab at Apess himself, however: "Of us, he says, among other things, we and our correspondents have rendered ourselves liable to a suit for defamation, *but he thinks it best to let us go!* He 'will forgive and pray for us!'—How kind—how christian like!" In fact, Phinney informs his readers, Apess, "this *pious* historian," had sent Phinney a letter "threatening a *'legal investigation,'*" but, as Phinney took no notice, "we were soon visited by the Rev. gentleman, when he blustered most awfully— Nothing said about *forgiving* or *praying for* us then. But we suppose he gets satisfaction in *booking* us."[72] The *New England Magazine*, one of Boston's most prestigious literary journals, noting that Apess made his living as a day laborer and book vendor, observed that *Indian Nullification* "is written far better than could have been expected from an Indian, and is well worth reading." How- ever, it complained, "The only fault we find is, that the author has suffered himself to be exasperated by the persecution he has endured."[73]

The public attention to Apess's book was evidently noted at Harvard. In September 1835, President Quincy dispatched Rev. James Walker, a member of the Board of Fellows—who was also known as the "Unitarian Warrior"—to investigate Mashpee.[74] Walker left a list of queries to be made at Mashpee, including this one: "Apes? What has he done? What is he doing now? & with what success?"[75] Fish responded with another of his long justificatory letters. Hallett reported to Walker that many Indians would not attend any church, as they disliked Fish, were not Baptists, and were "dissatisfied with Apes."[76] By January 1834 Apess had left Methodism to form his own "Free and United Church," which may have been in response to the Cherokees' abandonment of Methodism when the church, which had been successful in converting many Cherokees, withdrew its missionaries during the removal crisis.[77] Accounts of congregants in the two Native churches at Mashpee conflict. In the spring of 1835, Apess in *Indian Nullification* gives the membership of his church as decidedly larger than that of Blind Joe's (254–55); Walker's report to Harvard, entitled "Facts in Regard to the Difficulties at Marshpee," however, reverses the figures and adds that Apess was "now understood to be rapidly loosing [*sic*] [the Indians'] confidence, & not without good reason." Fish reported to Walker on 3 October that Apess was "very frequently absent" from Mashpee in the fall of 1835.[78]

DENOMINATED INDIAN

Apess could not have chosen a more pointed day on which to deliver his *Eulogy on King Philip* for the first time, given his subject matter and politics. The eighth of January was the widely celebrated anniversary of Andrew Jackson's 1815 defeat of the British in the Battle of New Orleans—a victory that made

Jackson's political career and secured U.S. claims to western territory; it was a date forever associated with Jackson.[79] Although by then Apess had fallen out of favor at Mashpee for reasons that remain mysterious, the *Eulogy* can be seen in light of local concerns as well: the disposition of the meetinghouse, and with it, Phineas Fish, remained unsettled after James Walker's fact-finding mission in late 1835.[80] Harvard records include a "Petition of Sundry Indians of Marshpee for the Preservation of the Parsonage" addressed to the Massachusetts legislature and dated January 1836 that appears to be a preemptive strike on Fish's part, as he never took action in the legislature.[81] Finally, Edward Everett, who was a well-known sympathizer with Indians, certainly influential at Harvard, and the brother of Alexander Hill Everett, a state legislator and proven friend of the Mashpees, had been sworn in as governor of Massachusetts on 4 January.[82]

The newspaper announcements for the *Eulogy* bespeak a certain calculated indirection, however. The notice reads: "THE INDIAN KING PHILIP.—An Eulogy will be pronounced upon him by an Indian Preacher at the Odeon on Friday Evening next, at 7 o'clock—doors open at 6." Apess charged 25 cents admission for a gentleman and lady, the standard rate, and at least five different bookstores sold tickets, including those of Samuel Gardner Drake and of William Ticknor, who would later achieve prominence as half of the publishing firm of Ticknor and Fields.[83] Apess advertised in at least four newspapers: the *Liberator*, the *Advocate*, the Whig *Morning Post*, and the *Evening Transcript*, a newspaper favored by the immigrant Irish working classes.[84] Since a recent refurbishment, the Odeon had become one of Boston's finest halls, seating 1,500 on red moreen settees under gas lights and hosting the likes of Daniel Webster. On the same day that Apess delivered the *Eulogy*, the Massachusetts House selected a "Mr. Rodgers of the Odeon" (a church also occupied the building) as one of its chaplains.[85] Apess caused a stir at the first performance, due to his criticism of missionaries. The second announcement for the *Eulogy*, to be given on 26 January at Boylston Hall, where he had appeared in 1832, noted that the "Indian Preacher" had "been invited to repeat his Eulogy upon Philip," and that he had "consented to give an Abridgement of it and his full view of the Mission cause—as there was some dissatisfaction with the previous one at the Odeon. Any gentleman wishing to reply, can do so."[86]

If the missionary cause links the *Eulogy* to Phineas Fish, there are also more specific connections to be made to Edward Everett, who was a talented practitioner of these types of orations. In December 1835, Everett's oration, "An Address Delivered at Bloody-Brook," originally given in September 1835, was published "by request" to high praise in Boston in December, as Everett's orations usually were. It commemorated a battle that took place during King Philip's War (1675–76) but also rehearsed the narrative of pilgrim piety and Indian doom, one in which Everett encouraged his audience to pause and "drop a compassionate tear . . . for . . . the benighted children of the forest—the Orphans of Providence."[87] Although Everett's speeches on behalf of the Cherokees made him a celebrated friend of the Indian as far as whites were concerned for ever afterward, by December 1832, eight months after he and Apess shared a stage on behalf of Cherokee rights, Everett was advising them to accept the inevitability of removal and go quietly west. While it is impossible to say for sure whether Apess knew of this oration, it seems highly likely that he did, given the timing and the subject matter. Apess would surely have received Everett's lachrymose sympathy for Indians in light of his relations with the Cherokees, who were at that moment fighting off the Treaty of New Echota. The conflict was well covered in newspapers, including *Niles' Weekly Register*, a Baltimore paper whose editor had an interest in Indians and which had published a notice about one of Apess's lectures on Mashpee Indian rights that fall.[88] Considering Apess's disdain for the "parental feelings" of the previous governor of Massachusetts for the poor doomed Mashpees, and his analysis of such regard as mere justification for oppression, it seems plausible that Everett is a target in the *Eulogy*.

When it was first given, the *Eulogy* in its historical moment, form, and subject matter was as complex and layered as Apess's metaphor of written-on skin in the "Looking-glass" essay. He chose to deliver it on the day most identified with Andrew Jackson, at the moment when Jackson's oppression of Native peoples had reached a sort of political climax in the signing of the Treaty of New Echota only a few weeks earlier. He addressed the hypocrisy of missionaries when the Mashpees were still maneuvering to rid themselves of their own hypocritical missionary.[89] The new governor of the commonwealth was probably the most celebrated white person who sympathized with the plight of the poor savages of America at the time. Apess used a form, the eulogy, and a narrative, that of King Philip's War, that even in the early nineteenth century were venerable means for U.S. intellectuals to tell the story of the nation's noble origins. Important people gave important eulogies on Adams, Jefferson, Washington, and Lafayette, rehearsing the character traits of republican leaders and citizens; historians, ministers, and politicians endlessly recited the narrative of New Englanders' direct descent from upright Christians who beat back Indian savagery to form a society, as Daniel Webster put it, founded "in the principles of the fullest liberty, and the purest religion."[90]

Apess tells the story of how one gets from the Puritans to New Echota. He tells the story of the people whose existence those origin stories attempt to erase; he demonstrates the political autonomy of Native peoples rather than their natural subordination; he reads against the historical record from the perspective of Native experience; through analysis, mockery, satire, and invective, he exposes the material underpinnings of apparently disinterested white benevolence. Much of the scholarship on Apess congratulates him for criticizing white people, but it's not at all remarkable that a Native writer, when given the opportunity, should criticize EuroAmericans for their misrepresentation of Native peoples—this has been present in the historical record from the beginning. What's interesting is how Apess makes that critique, and why he does it.

Considering his notoriety, the fact that Apess advertised himself as the "Indian Preacher" lecturing on the "Indian King Philip"—as if people needed to be reminded—situates the *Eulogy* as an especially nuanced instance of "playing Indian." He had written in detail of the frustration of being the object of curiosity as an Indian preacher and even rejected the term "Indian" entirely in his first book, yet in the *Eulogy* he presents himself as an Indian lecturing on a fellow Indian, despite the fact that one is an enlightened Christian and the other a savage. He certainly could have guessed how his audience would be prepared to hear him. One might assume that at least some of the members of his audience were reeled in by the promise of seeing an Indian speak, expecting, perhaps, an evening of Christian piety and yet another recital of their own exemplary origins, or, like Louisa Park's young charges, a real wild Indian with a tomahawk in his hand, haranguing them in an Indian language. They might have been expecting to enjoy indulging themselves in getting "wrought up," as Louisa Park put it, in their feelings of sympathy for the doomed savages of America. Then again, during the Mashpee controversy, Apess set his audience of members of the Massachusetts House cheering at his pointed attacks on their own pilgrim ancestors, although there is no record of what he actually said. Part of his attraction certainly was that in an era when oratory was practically a spectator sport, Apess was by all accounts very good at it. To his audience that in itself may have outweighed at least momentarily what it was that he was actually saying. Perhaps he expected that sort of reception for the *Eulogy* as well. Thus, in front of an audience that he very consciously solicited, that readily absorbed as truth patently false knowledge about Native peoples, in the form and the narrative most common in the production of that false knowledge, Apess attacks the center of that false knowledge, the concept of racial difference, and shows how that knowledge about racial difference is the foundation of the knowledge deployed to oppress Native peoples. Everything else—the critique of Christian piety, sympathy, and history—follows from that basic insight.[91]

While most critics recite a list of mainly literary antecedents for Apess's *Eulogy on King Philip*, there are versions of the narrative from the settings in which Apess participated, history and political oratory, that are more germane for comparison.[92] Political orations and public lectures on Puritan themes were common in the 1820s and 1830s in the Boston area; indeed, on the night of the second presentation of the *Eulogy* Francis Calley Gray, a colleague of Joseph Story's on Harvard's Board of Fellows, lectured on "The Pilgrims of Plymouth" for the Massachusetts Historical Society at the Masonic Temple, which was a few blocks away from Boylston Hall where Apess held forth on— more or less—the same topic.[93] Dominant in most recitations of Puritan history from about 1820—Webster's 1820 "Forefather's Day" address at Plymouth is usually given as the starting point—is "the idea that Puritan New England was the republic in embryo."[94] The rise of the pilgrim-republican narrative in early U.S. historiography is also concurrent with the normalizing of racial difference, the era of widespread racial violence, Indian removal, and tightening legal regulation of African Americans, free and slave. That narrative can be seen as not merely the expression of ideas of national belonging in an abstract psychological sense, as it has been most recently read by historians and literary critics, but rather as politically necessary for U.S. intellectuals to justify and explain the existence of a state the actions of which are in deep conflict with its professed ideals—as antislavery and antiremoval writers pointed out at the time, over and over again.[95]

Puritan history was not without its difficulties, however, and particularly in regard to Native peoples. Puritan historiography of the 1820s and 1830s in Boston—reprinted and newly edited seventeenth-century texts, political orations, historical works—are striking for their unease with the pilgrims' historical record, and they often very consciously attempt to explain away the obvious violence their ancestors unapologetically—unsympathetically—directed at Native peoples.[96] One has to wonder at the extent to which the Cherokee conflict influenced these writers: Boston's intellectual classes were generally pro-Cherokee, and at the very least most of them condemned the oppressive and tyrannical behavior of the Georgians, if not out of sympathy for Indians, then out of a belief in sectional differences between the civilized North and the slaveholding South.

Samuel Gardner Drake couldn't stop himself from condemning pilgrims' behavior toward Indians, at least in the 1830s. By its second edition, his history of the North American Indians included blunt assessments of the pilgrims throughout. Singling out Increase Mather's comments on King Philip's War, Drake observes that "the philosophic mind will be shocked at the expression of some, very eminent in that day for piety and excellence of moral life." Nevertheless, he writes, "The low and vulgar epithets sneeringly cast upon the Indians by their English contemporaries are not to be attributed to a single individual but to the English in general. It is too obvious that the early historians viewed the Indians as inferior beings, and some went so far as to hardly to allow them *to be* human."[97] Drake reprinted his book almost every year from 1832 to 1840, sometimes more than once (usually with additional information and sometimes a revised title) and maintained his highly critical stance toward the Puritans throughout the 1830s. He included four separate chapters on King Philip's War as well as several engravings related to it; Apess refers to the book in the text of his *Eulogy* and in fact takes his narrative of King Philip's War largely from Drake, with extensive modifications.

Those who engaged in political oratory on Puritan themes were more circumspect than Drake about Puritan behavior, and while Drake certainly doesn't abandon the notion of racial difference in his defense of the Indians, the political orators rely on it to a much larger extent both to explain the violence (Indians are inherently savage and cruel) and to elide the implications of that violence, so that Puritans can still be republicans in essence. In his oration "History and Influence of the Puritans" (1828), for example, Joseph Story is quite concerned with the Puritans' historical record with regard to Native peoples. Nevertheless, any violence done Indians in the record was justifiable violence, Story maintains, because the pilgrims settled only to spread Christianity and when Indians reacted violently, it was because of their inherent character. That said, however, one still ought to feel badly for Indians, he expostulates: "Humanity must continue to sigh at the constant sacrifices of this bloody, but wasting race. And Religion, if she may not blush at the deed, must, as she sees the successive victims depart, cling to the altar with a drooping heart, and mourn over a destiny without hope and without example."[98]

It was Story's friend Edward Everett who really knew how to tell the story of Indians in New England. In the fall of 1835, Everett was at the height of his reputation as an orator, well known for "[explicating] the meaning of republicanism and union for citizens of the new nation" in orations on all manner of topics.[99] In his "Address at Bloody-Brook," Everett writes that the fate of the New England Indians is "deplorable" but "an unavoidable consequence" because Indians "[belong] to a different variety of the species" and "[suffer] all the disadvantages of social and intellectual inferiority" (590). The Indian could never "maintain his place, by the side of the swelling, pressing population, the diligence and dexterity,—the superior thrift, arts, and arms,—the seductive vices, of the civilized race" (590–91). Treaties are a product of Anglo-Saxon moral superiority, but eventually their existence is a moot point, because "as the civilized race rapidly multiplies, the native tribes will recede, sink into the wilderness, and disappear" (590). Even more so than Story, however, Everett returns again and again to pilgrims' possible involvement in "wars of extermination" to refute the notion of settler violence. "No general and indiscriminate slaughter took place," he contends, and "unless we deny altogether the rightfulness of settling the continent . . . I am not sure, that any different result could have taken place" (594).

Having dispensed with fate, Everett concludes with the elaborate set pieces for which he was known and admired. King Philip's story ends with the Puritans' sale of his wife and child into slavery, a fact that gave pause to some New England historians. The passage received praise in a review of the pamphlet published in *New England Magazine* for December 1835; the reviewer notes that the address presents "a picture of the past—a highly-wrought and poetical description"; one of the most stirring passages is "a beautiful extract, which succeeds a thrilling account of the death of King Philip."[100] "And what was the fate of Philip's wife and son?," Everett asks. "This is a tale for husbands and wives, for parents and children. . . . They were sold into slavery—West-Indian slavery!—an Indian princess and her child, sold from the cool breezes of Mount Hope, from the wild freedom of the New-England forest, to gasp under the lash, beneath the blazing sun of the tropics! 'Bitter as death!' aye, bitter as hell! Is there anything—I do not say in the range of humanity—is there anything animated, that would not struggle against this?" (611). In contrast to the bathetic scene of the suffering mother and child, Everett concludes the address with a vision of the triumph prefigured in the Puritans' struggles against the Indians. "If we turn our thoughts to the grand design with which America was colonized, and the success with which, under providence, that design has been crowned, I own I find it difficult to express myself in terms of moderation," Everett begins, winding up for the peroration, "when I see the intellectual, moral and religious growth of the community,—its establishments, its institutions, its social action . . . my heart melts within me for grief, that they, the high-souled and long-suffering fathers,—they, the pioneers of the mighty enterprise,—they, the founders of the glorious temple, must die before the sight of all these blessings" (618–19).

Although there is no way to prove that Apess knew these orations or had them in mind when he wrote his *Eulogy*, the weaknesses that they reveal in what he calls the "history of New England writers" are certainly germane to his arguments. Those weaknesses are egregious from Apess's perspective. The narrative of American triumph over Indians rests on the shaky ground of pilgrim piety on the one hand and Indian inherent difference on the other, both of which are subject to not only reinterpretation of historical texts but also the critique presented by Native experience.

Apess's first step is to rehistoricize and repoliticize the state of nature to which whites confine Indians in demonstrating their inherent difference. At the beginning of the *Eulogy*, he writes that his purpose is "to bring before you beings made by the God of Nature, and in whose hearts and heads he has planted sympathies that shall live forever in the memory of the world, whose brilliant talents shown in the display of natural things, so that the most culti-vated, whose powers shown with equal luster, were not able to prepare mantles to cover the burning elements of an uncivilized world" (277). The state of nature Apess describes is a historical, not a permanent, condition. In compar-ing Indian and European methods of warfare, Apess maintains that "if we have common sense and ability to allow the difference between the civilized and the uncivilized, we cannot but see that one mode of warfare is as just as the other; for while one is sanctioned by the authority of enlightened and cultivated men, the other is an agreement according to the pure laws of nature, growing out of natural consequences" (278). "My image is of God," Apess writes; "I am not a beast" (278). The state of nature also inevitably returns to natural law, the repository of the universal human through which both Native peoples and African Americans argued for political equality; King Philip is then representa-tive of the "natural sons of an Almighty Being" who are historically different and politically equal at the same time (279).

White knowledge—white misrepresentation—is the problem that Apess must address. He must "vindicate" Philip's character on behalf of the "remain-ing few" Indians who consider Philip a hero; and "if possible," he writes, he would "melt the prejudice that exists in the hearts of those who are in the possession of his soil, and only by the right of conquest" (277). Whites' violent acquisition of land is motivated by prejudice or false knowledge; moreover, violence's link to knowledge is indicated in Apess's reference to himself as one "who proudly tells you, the blood of a denominated savage runs in his veins" (277). "Denominated" speaks to Indians having been named "savage," and the succeeding arguments of the *Eulogy* show how that naming takes place and why whites need to do it. The "true character of Philip," as with all Native peoples, is not one that can be distinguished because of race but rather one that is individual and specific to the conditions faced—which, in Philip's case, was the violent and aggressive behavior of whites.

In his history of early New England settlement, Apess argues that the Indians bore the assaults and insults of pilgrims with fortitude, until the abuse became too much, too insulting, at which point they were completely justified in striking back. Indians' hospitality and friendliness is returned by pilgrims' stealing food, kidnapping children and relatives, occupying land in violation of treaties and other agreements. And for all of this, Apess writes, they receive "the applause of being savages" and whites represent them as "made by God on purpose for them to destroy" (281). His reversal of savage and civilized returns to the fact that Indians are "denominated" savage: white knowledge about Indians is not disinterested fact but rather self-interested assertion. If pilgrims can tell themselves that they are morally superior Christians who have a right and a duty to destroy the people they have named savages, what is left after that destruction is Native land. Even in the era of early settlement, Apess represents the root of the conflict between Native peoples and pilgrims as control of the land, and pilgrims' means of violating that control include misrepresentation of Native peoples and disregard of Native governments. From the beginning of settlement, Apess maintains, pilgrims were violating treaties: in December 1620, he writes, "the Pilgrims landed at Plymouth, and without asking liberty from anyone possessed themselves of a portion of the country, and built themselves houses, and then made a treaty, and commanded them to accede to it" (280). Whites, according to Chicataubut, the leader of a Massachusetts band, are a "wild people" who "[disdain] our ancient antiquities and honorable customs"—which include laws and boundaries (282). When pilgrims make treaties recognizing the jurisdiction of Native tribes, they then break those agreements when it suits them. Such agreements were made only out of necessity. "It does not appear," Apess writes, "that Massasoit or his sons were respected because they were human beings but because [pilgrims] feared him; and we are led to believe that, if it had been in the power of the Pilgrims, they would have butchered them out and out, notwithstanding the piety they professed" (283).

Rather than the narrative of Indians' inherent inability to survive in coexistence with civilization, Apess argues that it was not only false Christians' misrepresentations to themselves but also to Native peoples through which Native peoples themselves were destroyed. He notes that the "history of New England writers" has held that "our tribes were large and respectable." The question then becomes, how was it that "they have been destroyed?" (285). Indians were "duped and flattered" by "hypocritical proceedings," he writes, flattered by informing the Indians that their God was a going to speak to them, and then place them before the cannon's mouth in a line, and then putting the match to it and kill thousands of them. . . . Let us again review their weapons to civilize the nations of this soil. What were they? Rum and powder and ball, together with all the diseases, such as the smallpox and every other disease imaginable, and in this way sweep off thousands and tens of thousands. (285–86)

What Christians represent as the signs of God's will, Apess maintains was their own willful behavior, even to the point of introducing disease: "These diseases were carried among them," he writes, "on purpose to destroy" Indians (286). He makes an oblique reference to the sympathy that white writers called upon when narrating the disappearance and destruction of Indians, when he writes, "Let the children of the Pilgrims blush, while the son of the forest drops a tear and groans over the fate of his murdered and departed fathers" (286). It is perhaps a specific reference to Edward Everett's eloquent tears dropped on account of the departed Indians in the "Address at Bloody-Brook"; in any case, Apess shifts the representation of feeling from sympathizing whites to Indians mourning the effects of whites' willful violence.

Apess then drives home his point: white Christians' behavior reveals that they are not at all interested in Indians' welfare but rather in what land can be got out of them, that the knowledge they profess about Indians is based on that objective, and that their present-day descendants are the inheritors of that false knowledge.

Although in words they deny it, yet in the works they approve of the iniquities of their fathers. And as the seed of iniquity and prejudice was sown in that day, so it still remains; and there is a deep-rooted popular opinion in the hearts of many that Indians were made, etc. on purpose for destruction, to be driven out by white Christians, and they to take their places; and that God had decreed it from all eternity. If such theologians would only study the works of nature more, they would understand the purposes of good better than they do; that the favor of the Almighty was good and holy, and all his nobler works were made to adorn his image, by being his grateful servants and admiring each other as angels, and not, as they say, to drive and devour each other. (287)

Taking Indians' land is the main objective; and here Apess cites the "words of a humble divine of the Far West," which he takes from the pages of the *New York Evangelist*:

"The savage has left the ground for civilized man; the rich prairie, from bringing forth all its strengths to be burned, is now receiving numerous enclosures, and brings a harvest of corn and wheat to feed the church. . . . This is now God's vineyard; he has gathered the vine . . . and drove the red Canaanites from trampling it down, or in any way hindering its increase." (287)

These are the "very pious" missionaries, Apess continues—those who supported Cherokee removal, for instance—who insist that they would convert Indians "but must first drive them out" and off of their land (287). These missionaries then would destroy Native government to get Native land under the guise of Christian conversion and sympathy for Indians: "Must I say, and shall I say it, that missionaries have injured us more than they have done us good, by degrading us as a people, in breaking up our governments, and leaving us without any suffrages whatever, or a legal right among men" (287).

If the reason behind whites' false knowledge about Indians is what David Walker and other anticolonial writers called their "avarice," the question remains how and why whites who are somewhat removed from the material gains to be had at the expense of Indians continue to think what they do about Indians, despite evidence to the contrary. Apess tells the story of an Indian at Kennebunk, who lived on land granted him by the colony in a township settled by whites. Although "he himself did all that lay in his power to comfort his white neighbors, in case of sickness and death," his neighbors still subjected him to "the common prejudices against Indians" that "[prevented] any sympathy with him" (289). Despite the fact that "this poor Indian . . . had nourished and waited to aid the Pilgrims in their trouble," when his own child dies, no one comes to his aid (289). The man then "gave up his farm, dug up the body of his child, and carried it 200 miles, through the wilderness, to join the Canadian Indians" (289). Unlike the many Indians in historical fiction of the era who disappear into the western woods, this particular Indian's going west to join Canadian Indians signifies not the workings of inevitable doom, but rather the result of whites' willful behavior and patently false knowledge. Apess explains:

This was as [whites] were taught by their haughty divines and orators of the day. But nevertheless, the people were to blame, for they might have read for themselves; and they doubtless would have found that we were not made to be vessels of wrath, as they say we were. And had the whites found it out, perhaps they would not have rejoiced at a poor Indian's death or, when they were swept off, would not have called it the Lord killing Indians to make room for them upon their lands. This is something like many people wishing for their friends to die, that they might get their property. I am astonished when I look at people's absurd blindness—when all are liable to die, and all subject to all kinds of diseases. (289)

The providential "extinction" of Indians—they just fall away and disappear, helpfully—is not providential at all, but rather the result of whites' desire for Indian land, the things that they tell themselves in order to justify taking that land, and the dissemination of that knowledge to the point where it becomes common and widely accepted, determining peoples' behavior and what they are *able* to think about Indians, even when exposed to information obviously to the contrary. Somewhat anachronistically, Apess blames the behavior of whites on the false knowledge that is easily refuted if only they would *read* more carefully—although they will not because they want Indians' "property," not the truth. As for the "haughty divines and orators," one might think of Increase Mather, William Hubbard, and their contemporaries, but also Daniel Webster, Joseph Story, and Edward Everett himself, who themselves participated in a rewriting of history that, Apess maintains here, misrepresents Indians and only justifies present oppressive relations.

Apess then proceeds to the story of King Philip, who serves an Indian nation violated by settlers, fighting for the recognition of Native government, and prefiguring the political struggles of both the Cherokees and the Mashpees. Although Apess cannot point to specific treaties entered into by King Philip, Drake's *Book of the Indians* does provide him with records of Philip's land sales that establish government and territorial boundaries. However, there is a distinct difference in emphasis between Drake's and Apess's accounts of land transactions.[101] Drake writes that the record of land sales shows that the Indians voluntarily sold off their lands in order to "obtain such things as their neighbors possessed."[102] In Apess's version, the land sale record provides evidence of Philip's political authority and its violation by settlers. Philip has a "throne," he "comes into office," he has "counselors and interpreters"; like the Cherokees, he sells the land he feels he must in order to maintain relations with "those rude intruders around him" (290). Where Drake merely lists, among other legal transactions, a suit against Philip for land and monetary compensation for a promise made by Philip's dead older brother, Alexander, Apess stops to consider it. He notes that the court decided in favor of "Talmon, the young Pilgrim," who received "a large tract of land" from Philip to settle the matter (291). "Now let us review this a little," Apess continues: "The man who bought this land made the contract, he says, with Alexander, ten or twelve years before;

then why did he not bring forward his contract before the court? It is easy to understand why he did not. Their object was to cheat, or get the whole back again this way. Only look at the sum demanded, and it is enough to satisfy the critical observer" (291). Apess may be said here to be participating in a tradition of Native discourse that appears in the earliest records, in which Indians recite detailed accounts of various "legal" swindles perpetrated on them.

The object of settler duplicity is always the acquisition of land in a way that may be construed as legitimate. Apess refers to land, the ultimate prize, but also the extent of systematic oppression, including the particular case of the Mashpees and their struggle with Fish impending in the legislature that January. "Indeed, it would be a strange thing for the poor unfortunate Indians to find justice in those courts of the pretended pious in those days," he continues, "or ever since; and for a proof of my assertion I will refer the reader or hearer to the records of legislature and courts throughout New England, and also to my book, *Indian Nullification*" (291).

Apess's emphasis on Philip's legal transactions is significant in light of the conditions faced by many New England tribes, including the Mashpees and the Pequots, who had no or not as many of the formal treaties through which the arguments for Native autonomy and sovereignty were commonly made. There were instead largely a range of legal agreements, most of them local, that would seem to make the argument for the existence of a previously recognized Native sovereignty more difficult, given that formal treaties with Indian nations recognized the Indian nations as nations in the text itself, and then in Congress, as treaties had to be ratified by the Senate. New England Indians were therefore in a more ambiguous position than the Cherokees or the Iroquois. In Apess's first several books, then, the political context of white knowledge is much more elusive to him than it is for someone for whom the political stakes are quite clear, such as Elias Boudinot or Maris Bryant Pierce. In his account of King Philip's legal conflicts, Apess elevates those contracts to the status of treaties that unequivocally signify Native sovereignty.

The pilgrims, not content to exasperate Philip by harassing him and treating him as their vassal, refusing to recognize his authority, must go further, Apess writes, and send Sassamon—"an Indian and a traitor"—ostensibly to convert Philip's people to Christianity, an act that is clearly politically motivated. "I would appeal to this audience," Apess writes; "Is it not certain that the Plymouth people strove to pick a quarrel with Philip and his men? What could have been more insulting than to send a man to them who was false, and looked upon as such? For it is most certain that a traitor was, above all others, the more to be detested than any other" (293). Sassamon becomes the occasion for a struggle over Native sovereignty. While Edward Everett represents Sassamon as being killed "within the jurisdiction of Plymouth, and those concerned in it, three in number, were immediately brought to justice," Apess writes that, by Indian law, Sassamon must be put to death for his treason—and that treason is against the *state* (600). But when Sassamon was put to death, the pilgrims claimed jurisdiction, charging three of King Philip's men with murder—only one of whom, Apess points out, actually had anything to do with Sassamon's death—and subsequently hanging them. Sassamon's case, as Apess tells it, is in fact quite similar to a dispute over Cherokee sovereignty in Georgia that precipitated the Cherokee Nation cases. In *State v. George Tassels* (1830), Georgia declared its jurisdiction over a murder committed on Cherokee land by one Cherokee against another. Although William Wirt, the Cherokees' lawyer, petitioned for and got a writ of error from the Supreme Court, which required a stay of execution and Georgia's appearance before the Court, Georgia ignored it and executed Tassels. Wirt's next test case was *Cherokee Nation v. Georgia*.[103]

In Apess's *Eulogy*, King Philip himself, rather than being the noble but doomed savage of the narratives told by the likes of Edward Everett, is instead not at all different from whites, except to be more intelligent and more inventive than most. Apess is at pains to show that Philip is both exemplary and ordinary at the same time. His opening paragraphs set out different nations with different heroes—King Philip and George Washington—but his King Philip contrasts oddly with the usual exemplary figures of the period, whose less than exemplary characteristics were seldom discussed in public. Brave, resourceful, intelligent, and generous, King Philip is also ordinary, understandably exasperated by settler duplicity, and driven even to cruel acts. Although the eulogy form invites the audience to identify with King Philip, even against their own ancestors, Philip has no specifically "Indian" characteristics that they may idealize. Philip has "more manly nobility in him than . . . all the head Pilgrims put together"; he is more courageous than Washington crossing the Delaware when he and his men escape the pilgrims by canoe; he treats settler captives with "a great deal more Christian-like spirit" than the settlers treat Natives, accepting even the prisoner Mary Rowlandson as an equal (296, 297, 300). While King Philip may be more humane than his American contemporaries, he is not inherently different from them. When Philip kills Mohawks and blames settlers in order to gain the Mohawks' alliance against them, a story Apess takes from Drake, even this act is evidence of Philip's lack of difference from whites. Apess writes that Philip "was so exasperated that nothing but revenge could satisfy him," and comments, "This act was no worse than our political men do in our day, of their strife to wrong each other, who profess to be enlightened" (299). Indeed, Apess notes, "If [the pious settlers] were like my people, professing no purity at all, then their crimes would not appear to have such magnitude, but while they appear to be by profession more virtuous, their crimes still blacken" (300).

Like Edward Everett, Apess closes the narrative of King Philip with an account of the pilgrims' selling Philip's wife and son into slavery and, like Everett, prompts his audience with his own feelings. In a manner recalling David Walker's direct address, Apess writes, "I can hardly restrain my feelings, to think a people calling themselves Christians should conduct so scandalous, so outrageous, making themselves appear so despicable in the eyes of the Indians. . . . And surely none but such as believe they did right will ever go and undertake to celebrate that day of their landing, the 22nd of December" (301). It's not just that whites are incurably evil, it's that they willfully delude themselves—in order, ultimately, to get Native land. "Only look at it; then stop and pause," he continues, recalling pilgrim-republican narrative: "My fathers came here for liberty themselves, and then they must go and chain that mind they professed to serve, not content to rob and cheat the poor ignorant Indians but must take one of the king's sons and make a slave of him. Gentlemen and ladies, I blush at these tales, if you do not, especially when they professed to be a free and humane people" (301). "On the Sabbath day," Apess continues, "these people would gather themselves together and say that God is no respecter of persons; while the divines would pour forth, 'He says that he loves God and hates his brother is a liar, and the truth is not in him'—at the same time they hating and selling their fellow men in bondage" (301). As practiced by whites, who misrepresent its tenets to themselves as well as to Indians, Christianity has led only to the destruction of Native peoples, Apess complains: "Through the prayers, preaching, and example of those pretended pious has been the foundation of all the slavery and degradation in the American colonies toward colored people" (304). It is not the actions themselves on which Apess focuses, but rather the *knowledge* that justifies those actions. In this—and it can be seen as yet another "reversal"—Apess overturns the pilgrim-republican historiography, which conflates Christianity and republicanism in its attempt to establish the moral superiority of settlers in the face of the difficulties of the record. Christianity is merely a cover for oppression.

In closing, Apess returns to his own experience and the present moment, reminding his audience that "the doctrines of the Pilgrims has [*sic*] grown up with the people" (305). He assails the false knowledge of Indian difference that infuses the psychology of all whites, but which they cling to despite obvious information to the contrary. Despite the fact that "every white that knows their own history knows that there was not a whit of difference between them and the Indians of their days" (305), they insist on the falsehood. That false knowledge, he concludes, has its explanation in whites' desire for the land to be taken from Native peoples:

> Look at the disgraceful laws, disfranchising us as citizens. Look at the treaties made by Congress, all broken. Look at the deep-rooted plans made, when a territory becomes a state, that after so many years the laws shall be extended over the Indians that live within their boundaries. Yea, every charter that has been given was given with the view of driving the Indians out of the states, or dooming them to become chained under desperate laws, that would make them drag out a miserable life as one chained to the galley; and this is the course that has been pursued for nearly two hundred years. (306)

Apess uses "citizen" here, as elsewhere, in the general sense of human rights, to indicate human freedom and equality. The purpose of white government, he reminds his audience one more time, is to destroy Native governments in order to get land, and then to justify that destruction by insisting that Indians are too different to be treated as equal human beings. Whites insist on the ontological difference of Native peoples, he points out mockingly, as merely the justification for political power: "Even the president of the United States tells the Indians they cannot live among civilized people, and we want your lands and must have them and will have them. As if he had said to them, 'We want your land for our use to speculate upon; it aids us in paying off our national debt and supporting us in Congress to drive you off'" (307). Apess is correct in this assertion: the federal government's main source of income in the nineteenth century was the sale of federal land, much of it confiscated or otherwise acquired from Indians.[104] Thus the entire narrative of American progress and prosperity, the spread of American power about which Edward Everett rhapsodizes, reduces to greed, false knowledge, and systematic oppression.

APESS'S EFFECTS

The Massachusetts legislature ruled that Harvard had to settle the matter of the meetinghouse; in July 1836, a Harvard committee that included Joseph Story concluded that the best thing to do was not to dismiss Phineas Fish but instead to give some of the bequest that supported him to the Mashpees. The Mashpees persisted, however, and finally, in 1840, the legislature ruled that they controlled the meetinghouse. But before they could claim it, Fish had to be "actually and forcibly ejected."[105]

Apess died of apoplexy, or a cerebral hemorrhage in modern medicine, in New York City in April 1839, and as far as anyone has yet discovered, he published nothing more after he reprinted the *Eulogy on King Philip* and *Experiences of Five Christian Indians*, without "An Indian's Looking-glass for the White Man," in 1837. Apess has gained the attention of scholars only recently. Before an obituary and coroner's inquest for him were found, Barry O'Connell surmised that death as the result of alcoholism would explain Apess's abrupt disappearance from public life. In his introduction to Apess's collected works, O'Connell wrote: "It is only speculation that he may have turned to rum, in bitterness or for consolation, after his great success at Mashpee and thus begun a brief or long slide into anonymity" (xxxviii). Despite the fact that O'Connell later modified this position after the details of Apess's death were discovered in an essay in which he noted that the new information does not prove his initial "too conclusive judgment" of death by alcoholism, the story that Apess died in alcoholic despair has persisted.[106] The reason why the story of Apess's alcoholic slide into anonymity sticks is because it is utterly familiar: that's what psychologically damaged Indians who are caught between two cultures do, after all. Being poor and having high blood pressure are apparently not explanation enough.

The pathetic story of Apess's alcoholic death tells us that the parameters of the criticism are remarkably narrow and that, even in the scholarship, the thinking about Native peoples is infused with a sentimentality that is difficult to dislodge. The historical circumstances of the end of Apess's life can be explored, however, in order to dislodge that sentimentality a little and broaden the scope of the criticism. Apess was a Native intellectual in the antebellum United States, and his intellectual and political relationships were with other people of color, as well as with like-minded whites such as William Lloyd Garrison. The end of his life throws those facts into relief; what is of interest here is what Apess seemed to be working toward at the end of his life and whom he had significant relationships with.

It is relatively clear that Apess lost followers at Mashpee after the legislative battles of 1834. At least according to his correspondence with Harvard, Benjamin Hallett cooled toward Apess, who after 1834 is no longer mentioned in the Harvard records by either Harvard or the Mashpees. Hallett was a native of Barnstable and maintained his ties there; by 1836 he also had turned Jackson Democrat, giving an oration on the fourth of July that consisted mainly of a lengthy personal attack on Daniel Webster.[107] One might guess that Bostonians' interest in Apess—who was inevitably linked with the Mashpees— waned along with their interest in the Cherokees because the moment when Indians' rights were interesting to white audiences had passed. The Mashpees got their Indian district, and the Cherokees were to be removed and nothing could be done about it. Besides local concerns, the lack of interest in Apess can also be seen as indicative of the rapidly increasing naturalization of racial difference in the 1830s, which can itself be exemplified in Drake's shift in publishing ventures in the late 1830s. In 1839, Drake added to his other two regularly reprinted books, Benjamin Church's *History of Philip's War* and his own history of Indians in North America, a collection of Indian captivities, the titles of the first two editions of which promised to describe "surprising escapes from [Indians'] cruel hand" and Indians' "various methods of torture."[108] The 1838 Cherokee removal can be seen to mark the effective end of the period in which discussion of Native political rights appeared in mainstream U.S. discourse, both popular and elite.

Apess's fall from the favor of his former white supporters may have a more personal context, however. Drake dedicated his 1836 reprinting of his history of North American Indians to the lachrymose Edward Everett. Thanking Everett "for all former kind attentions," Drake writes that Everett was not only "the most ardent friend of the young men of his own race" but also "the most prominent assertor of the red man's rights in his country's councils."[109] This book was surely published after Apess gave the *Eulogy*—in which Apess took his account of King Philip's War from Drake's history, a point that would not have been lost on Drake. In the context of the *Eulogy*, Drake's fawning dedication to Everett would seem to be a rebuke of Apess, or perhaps an official abandonment.

There is also the strange instance of Drake's lying about who wrote *Indian Nullification*, which he did carefully, by attributing the authorship of the book to William Joseph Snelling, editor of the *New England Galaxy* during the Mashpee conflict, in his copy of the book and in a collection of autographs he assembled beginning in the late 1830s. Drake wrote on the flyleaf of his copy of *Indian Nullification* that Snelling wrote the book at Apess's "request" and that he "often consulted me during the progress of it."[110] Like his histories of Indians, Drake's collection of autographs is the work of a loosely organized packrat. His "autographical biography," as he called it, of notable persons, historical and contemporary, consisted of signatures harvested from letters, receipts, envelopes, lottery tickets, and bank notes, which were then pasted into a scrapbook.[111] Apess is represented by his signature on a ticket to the *Eulogy on King Philip*, and Drake has this to say about him:

Mr. William Apes says he is the author of the Son of the Forest. He is a Mohegan; told me he was a soldier in the war of 1812. He came to me begging money to build a church for his tribe. Sometime later he went & lived among the Marshpees, & became a leader among them, stirring them up to make certain demands on the State; & hence originated what was termed the Marshpee war, a history of which was published by W. J. Snelling. As the war was a bloodless one, it required the talents of Snelling to make it interesting. This he did not fail to do.[112]

Snelling appears early in the autographical biography, with a long note describing his troubles as of 1837, mainly having to do with his drinking. Snelling, Drake writes, "never could steer clear of all kinds of troubles," the worst being alcohol, and in 1837 he was "sent to the house of correction (at his own request) as a common drunkard!!" After Snelling's release, and despite his protestations that he wanted to stop drinking, Drake notes, "his presence disgusted with the odor of liquor." In a few months, Drake writes, his wife, who was "the sister of F. P. Leverett, the editor of the Latin Lexicon, & many other approved works," died, having "too freely [indulged] in the use of liquor." Snelling reported to Drake that he planned to write about his experiences in the house of correction, and he was editing the *Morning News*. "His talents would have gained him competence in any country where literature is valued, but our communities are so much like the merciless ocean, that a man of the best abilities, if, like a ship, one small thing is wanting, he is sure to founder & become a total loss," Drake concluded.[113]

The son of a prominent Boston family, Snelling was expelled from West Point, after which, in 1821, he joined his father in Minnesota Territory, where Colonel Josiah Snelling was commander of a fort at the confluence of the Minnesota and Mississippi Rivers. He circulated among the traders and the Dakota and Ojibwe people who gathered at the fort and, in 1830, returned to Boston to publish an account of his experiences called *Tales of the Northwest*. This was the beginning of his literary career. In 1831, he published a mocking biography of Andrew Jackson, as well as four pseudonymous edited collections for the juvenile market on the polar regions, central Africa, northern Europe, and the U.S. West. He became associated with the nascent antislavery movement. In January 1832, along with William Lloyd Garrison, he was one of the founders of the New England Anti-Slavery Society; he wrote and published a hymn to be sung at the society's meetings.[114] He seems to have come into contact with Apess in 1832 as well, when Apess brought a libel suit in Boston against John Reynolds, a former Methodist circuit rider and sometime inmate of the Vermont State Prison whose ordination in the Methodist church Apess opposed. Apess writes about the episode at the end of *Indian Nullification*. Reynolds had made defamatory remarks about Apess in the *Boston Daily Commercial Gazette* in August 1832, then called on Joseph Snelling, as well as someone named Norris, to attest to Apess's bad behavior to defend his actions. Reynolds's petition to the court (which Apess reprinted in *Indian Nullification*), however, states that Apess's "friends [stood] by him" (244), and Apess won his case. Snelling became editor of the *Galaxy*, a weekly, in 1833, which led to his publication of *Exposé of the Vice of Gambling*, which was reprinted from the *Galaxy*, and, in 1834, to his being brought to trial for libel himself, against a senior judge of the Boston Police Court. In 1837, he published *The Rat-Trap, or, Cogitations of a Convict in the House of Correction* on his experiences in prison.

Most interesting in light of his association with Apess is a remark Snelling made in a review of Black Hawk's *Life* that he published in the *North American Review* in January 1835. Snelling observes that Black Hawk's autobiography

> is the only autobiography of an Indian extant, for we do not consider Mr. Apes and a few other persons of unmixed Indian blood, who have written books, to be Indians. They were indeed born of aboriginal parents, but their tastes, feelings and train of ideas, were derived from the whites, and they were and are, in all essential particulars, civilized men. . . . But here is the autobiography of a wild, unadulterated savage, gall yet fermenting in his veins, his heart still burning with the sense of wrong, the words of wrath and scorn yet scarce cold upon his lips . . . and his hands still reeking with recent slaughter.[115]

One can guess how Apess received this observation. Although further on in the review and in his *Tales of the Northwest* Snelling shows himself to be familiar with conflicts between settlers and Native peoples in border settlements, his thinking about Native peoples is well within the conventional narrative of timeless savages in a state of nature, inherently unable to rule themselves, in providential and doomed conflict with oncoming civilization.[116] While it is possible—O'Connell thinks it "probable"—that Snelling helped assemble the many different documents that went into *Indian Nullification* (newspaper clippings, petitions, court documents, and correspondence), it doesn't appear that the writing of the principal author of the book is that of anyone other than Apess. O'Connell also thinks it possible that Snelling wrote the introduction to *Indian Nullification* because it is "in the third person and unlike anything else in style or tone, by [Apess]" (165). I don't see the stark difference between the introduction and the rest the book, however, and Apess refers to himself in the third person in *Nullification* several times, which is not beyond his capacity, given his notoriety and his understanding of himself as a public figure.

The odd thing is that Drake took the time to have Apess sign two tickets to the *Eulogy*, the second of which he pasted in a scrapbook he began to keep in the mid-1830s that he called "Indian Miscellany," a haphazard collection of newspaper articles on Indians that included reports of savagery, dispatches from various military confrontations, "humorous" anecdotes, scenes of Indians visiting civilization, sentimental narratives about star-crossed lovers and the rock from which a distraught Indian maiden leapt to her death, and the like.[117] The ticket is a square card of expensive-looking heavy stock; at the top is written, "Admit the bearer / to the / EULOGY ON PHILIP," and underneath, in faded brown ink, "Apes," signed in the same manner as the signature on the ticket in the autographical biography. Perhaps Drake had both of his scrapbooks in mind when he asked Apess for two signatures; the signatures suggest that he must have had at least a cordial relationship with Apess in January 1836.

The question remains why Drake would lie. There is enough evidence to suggest that, in addition to the fact that the time had passed when white audiences in Boston were interested in Indian rights and would tolerate unmitigated criticism of their pilgrim forebears, on a personal level, Drake was anxious to preserve his authority for New England history and his connections with Boston's historically minded elites—which would help explain the dedication to Everett. Drake was publicly identified with Apess: he mentioned Apess in his 1832 book *Indian Biography*, probably wrote the only review of *A Son of the Forest* (admonishing Apess to get his facts straight about the difference between Pequots and Wampanoags), and sold tickets to the *Eulogy* at his Antiquarian Bookstore. Apess refers to him by name in the printed text of the *Eulogy*. Clearly, Drake knew how Apess presented himself, and yet, in his autographical biography, he insinuates that Apess didn't write *A Son of the Forest* and that he was Mohegan, not Pequot. That makes no sense—except for the fact that, after the Pequot War ended in 1638, the English settlers famously denied the existence of the Pequots as a tribe, dividing the survivors between their Mohegan and Narragansett allies and ruling that the Pequots be called "Moheags and Narragansets for ever," a story that EuroAmerican historians have repeated forever afterward, even though by 1655 the Pequots had regrouped in four towns on land for which they petitioned Connecticut.[118] Insisting on Apess being a Mohegan erased him from history and denied the truth of what he had to say. Apess couldn't be what he said he was: it was a historical fact that Pequots had long ago disappeared. After the aside in the first edition of his history of the Indians, Drake never mentioned Apess publicly again. Even though Drake wrote about contemporary events like the Seminole Wars in his history of Indians, he never mentioned the Mashpee revolt, and he told the story of the Pequots the way every other white historian did. *Indian Nullification* directly addresses New England local history, Drake's purview, and a sizable white audience read it; it was even reviewed favorably in Boston's newspapers and journals. Drake dealt in books and printed ephemera; he scoured sources for every obscure detail about historical figures of New England, famous or not. He could have just ignored Apess—nearly everyone else did after 1836. But instead Drake took the time to lie about Apess in such a way that the false information would come to be taken as valid by other dealers in books like himself.[119] Once a story starts, it's difficult to stop, especially if it fits the preconceived narrative—witness the story of Apess's pathetic death by alcoholism.

Apess should not be reduced to being a victim of his former white supporters' disapproval and abandonment, however. I think he had his own plans for himself as a writer, and those plans were complicated by a severe economic depression, which had a major impact on the lives of poor people from 1836 to 1839. The Panic of 1837 hit Boston in the spring of 1836; from the spring to the fall of that year, for example, banks' interest rates on short-term loans increased from 18 percent to 45–50 percent.[120] For Apess, who made his living by bookselling and various forms of day labor, and others like him, any economic disruption could wipe out what little they possessed and send them looking for work elsewhere—as did Apess and his parents before him.[121] One can trace Apess's literary career in the record of his financial troubles.

Three debt actions were lodged against Apess from 1835 to 1837—for small amounts of debt but large amounts of damages; it's impossible to tell whether these cases were frivolous or valid. In the first, initiated in 1835, Ezra Tobey loaned Apess first $50 and then $100 in January 1835, on which Apess did not begin to make payment until September 1836. Tobey pursued the case in the April 1837 and 1838 court terms, but Apess never appeared in court.[122] In the second case, Phebe Ann Weden, a Mashpee proprietor, accused Apess of taking $20 worth of timber from land she claimed on the plantation and selling it on 1 January 1836. In July 1836, with Isaac Combs, Apess's ally in the legislative fight for Mashpee independence, serving as Phebe's representative because she was underage, a Barnstable judge found Apess guilty of trespass. In September 1836, however, Levi Scudder submitted an affidavit attesting to the fact that Phebe was the illegitimate daughter of Richard Weeton of Nantucket, which would seem to indicate that Apess received permission to take the timber from him. Still, Phebe Weden pursued her case in the court's April 1837 term.[123]

Finally, Enos Ames filed a petition in September 1837 for the payment of $25.75 for work he had done for Apess, whose property by that time was in the care of Sampson Alvis, another Mashpee proprietor. A writ for Apess's appearance in court filed at the time notes that Apess was not then in Massachusetts. This case continued—although neither Apess nor Alvis appeared in court—until April 1838.[124] None of these cases was ever resolved, at least in court.

In the midst of these disputes over money, in September 1836, Apess took out a mortgage for $1,500 with Richard Johnson of New Bedford.[125] The collateral that Apess put up for the loan included, besides the house, valued at $50, a barn, two wagons, furniture, dishes, silverware, tools, and a portrait of himself, valued at $15. The most expensive listing, however, was his library, valued at over $100, which included commentaries on and concordances of the Bible, bound tracts, the *Drunkard's Progress*, "Drake on the Indians," Parson Weems's "Life of Franklin," "Memoirs of Eliot," Webster's unabridged *Dictionary*, maps of the United States and the world, and Baptist, Episcopal, and Methodist religious works.[126] It is possible to speculate on Apess's financial problems in relation to this library. When Apess legally or illegally took the $20 worth of timber from the land that Phebe Weden claimed, it was right before he gave the *Eulogy on King Philip*. He would have needed money to rent the Odeon, print the tickets, and advertise, and then do the same for the second presentation of the oration, at Boylston Hall. Perhaps banking on his notoriety, he reprinted the second editions of *Experiences of Five Christian Indians* and *Eulogy on King Philip* in 1837, for which he would have needed to pay up front. Apess's decision to sell books during an economic depression was not fortunate, however. The economic depression affected the book trade so much that even William Ticknor, a successful publisher of mainly medical books at the time, ceased publishing new books entirely in 1836.[127] Judging from his nonappearance at the Barnstable Court of Common Pleas, Apess may have been gone from Mashpee by the latter part of 1837, possibly looking for work, although he didn't take up residence in New York City until January 1839.

Apess behaved like an intellectual: he had a substantial library; he gave lectures; he published books. He was an independent operator: he rented halls, had tickets printed, advertised in newspapers. For anyone not of the elite, let alone a Native person, an independent writing life was a difficult proposition in the 1830s. Still, Apess wrote at the moment when it was beginning to be possible to write as a profession, and he had both Snelling and Drake as models, one a newspaperman, the other a book dealer. Both Snelling and Drake began their careers in the 1830s and sustained themselves by regularly putting out new books, sometimes several a year, edited and authored, that they hoped would catch the reading public's attention. They did this in addition to keeping their day jobs; neither seems to have made much money from their ventures. While the shift in the white public's interest in Indians is readily discernible and even striking from the vantage point of the present, at the time, Apess would have known that he was a highly popular public speaker, that whites bought books on Indians like Drake's works, and that whites bought his own books. His reprinting of his last two books, and especially his exclusion of the incendiary "Looking-glass" essay from *Experiences of Five Christian Indians,* can be seen in this light. The fact that Apess was a serious historian and critic, not a sensationalist, however, made his position even more difficult. It's unlikely that history and criticism sold any better in the 1830s than they do today; the elite writers who produced such works—among Apess's contemporaries, George Bancroft, Ralph Waldo Emerson, and Alexander Hill Everett—didn't write for a living. (It's also interesting to note that, like some prominent New England intellectuals of the time, including Emerson and Edward Everett himself, Apess started out as a minister, only from the opposite end of society.) While the white public would always be interested in Indians, it was no longer interested in *critical* Indians who didn't play the part. It can be said that Apess sought to make a living from his thinking and writing, and at what turned out to be the end of his life, this struggle was made much more difficult by a depressed economy. If he was caught in or between anything, it was in the economics, not to mention the audacity, of deciding to be a working Native intellectual in the 1830s or between poverty and his own desires.

According to the New York City coroner's inquest, Apess's wife of three years, Elizabeth, testified that they had arrived in New York in January 1839. Elizabeth apparently married Apess sometime in 1836, which indicates that sometime between the inclusion of Apess and his wife Mary in an 1834 record of nonproprietors at Mashpee and 1836, Mary died and he married Elizabeth, although no listing in the extant records of Mashpee has been found of Mary's death.[128] The coroner's inquest transcribes Elizabeth's story of Apess's death:

> I, the wife of [decedent] have been married three years his name was William Apes he was born in Massachusetts was 41 years old he has been formerly a preacher of the Methodist society we have been boarding in this house 4 months he wrote some books which he sold and lectured on the history of the Indians he has lately been somewhat intemperate we have always lived on good terms never had any words with him On Friday he complained and on Saturday he went to Doctor Veers and got some medicine and came home and took the medicine and went to tea at his usual

hour on Saturday night the medicine operated very powerfully during the night on Sunday he attempted to get up and dress himself but was obliged to go back to bed the physic continued to operate as often as every half hour until he died on Sunday evening he sent for Doctor Atkinson he gave him some drops which he said would turn his sickness downwards on Monday he came again and gave him a black powder he said it made him feel worse afterwards he seemed to be better and walked to the glass and took a tooth brush and cleaned his teeth made him some toast and he eat a few mouth-fuls of and said he felt better he died in about 2 hours after he eat the toast Dr. Atkinson directed a mustard plaster to be put on his breast which was done.[129]

Another boarder, John Wight, and the boardinghouse owner's daughter, Catherine Garlick, endorsed Elizabeth's version of events. According to Catherine, Apess "had been some days on a Frolic" and then returned home and became ill; according to Wight, Apess would "sometimes get on a Frolic and continue a few days and then would abstain from liquor altogether."

Despite these references to "frolics," which suggest that like a lot of people Apess binged on alcohol, the cause of his death is given as apoplexy. Apess's botanic physician gives this account: after two days, Apess called for a doctor, who first gave him a combination of herbs and then at Apess's request two doses of lobelia, the main herb in the botanic medical practice systematized by Samuel Thomson in the early nineteenth century that was popular at the time.[130] The next morning, Dr. Atkinson administered another medicine "composed of charcoal mandrake white root and dogwood bark" and directed that a mustard plaster be applied. That was the last Dr. Atkinson saw of Apess. Dr. J. S. Hurd performed the autopsy—at the boardinghouse, apparently, and probably limited to examining the brain—and found "an inflammation of the membranes . . . and an effusion of water" in the brain, "which would be sufficient to cause death."[131] Nineteenth-century medicine attributed apoplexy to a wide range of causes, including both chronic intemperate habits (which Apess apparently did not have) and "softening of the brain."[132]

The 1830s were a time of great conflict over the professionalization of medicine, particularly in New York; even a coroner's inquest with a proper autopsy could not be assured.[133] Apess's death appeared in the newspapers as evidence of the danger of unregulated and unscientific medical practices: the *New York Sun*'s account, reprinted in the *Observer*, reports the details of the medicine the botanic physician administered to Apess, as well as Dr. Hurd's conclusion.[134] No evidence has yet turned up suggesting that Apess was known in

New York in the same way that he was known in Boston; rather, it seems that, at least in New York, in death he was more interesting as a medical case than as an Indian.

Boston and Cape Cod newspapers immediately picked up the news of Apess's death. In Boston, the *Evening Transcript* and the *Morning Post* published short notices that disagreed over whether Apess was married to a white woman or a Native woman. While the *Transcript* noted Apess's "frolics," the *Post* reported that "he was a man of remarkable talent, and contributed materially toward procuring the freedom of the Marshpee Indians in 1834, but his integrity was not equal to his ability. The Indians withdrew their confidence from him, and for several years he has been a wanderer."[135] The *Yarmouth Register* on Cape Cod, noting that the *New York Star* had attributed Apess's death to "the combined effects of intemperate habits, and, it is supposed, the administration of lobelia," added that he lived for several years at Mashpee, "most of the time . . . traveling the country urging contributions under the pretense that the avails would be applied to the melioration of the Indians of that plantation."[136] The *New Bedford Mercury* announced that "a Narragansett Indian named William Apes, better known by the name of 'Apes the Missionary Preacher,' . . . was found dead at his lodgings . . . from apoplexy."[137] Farther west, the *Greenfield (Mass.) Gazette and Mercury* reprinted the *Sun* report, noting that the "Indian Preacher," whose "conduct had been quite irregular" and who "had lost the confidence of the best portions of the community," had nevertheless "acquitted himself respectably" in Greenfield when he preached there a few years before.[138]

Sylvannus Phinney at the *Barnstable Patriot* was also kind to Apess in death. Attributing Apess's death to apoplexy, not intemperate habits, Phinney observed that he "was a man of strong natural abilities, and considerable information, which he often employed in planning and executing some favorite project either for himself or his Indian brethren." The "change in [Mashpee] government and the protection of [Mashpee] civil rights," Phinney wrote, changing his tune on the idea of Mashpee rights from the time of the conflict itself, "was mainly owing to the exertions of William Apess." Phinney also observed that Apess fell out of favor with the Mashpees "from the suspicion, we believe, that his interest in their welfare was not from the most disinterested and patriotic motives, and for the last two or three years he has been an itinerant preacher."[139]

Apess pursued a literary career, even if the world around him was not conducive to such an undertaking. The maps of the United States and the world that were listed in the inventory of his library reinforce an understanding of Apess as an intellectual, as someone who thought of himself and other Native peoples in relation to the rest of the world and in relation to other histories in the wake of European colonialism and imperialism. He had to understand those relations in order to understand what had happened to Native peoples and how they were supposed to go forward from where they were, politically, economically, even geographically. This was not just an intellectual or imaginative exercise; Apess was also tied to new economic and political relations that arose as a result of European imperialism, which were not confined by the boundaries of the United States. While notions of the Black Atlantic are firmly ensconced in U.S. history and literary studies, there is as yet little understanding of the political, economic, and intellectual relations of Native peoples in the United States with the rest of the world.[140] Apess's connections to the New England whale fishery provide some insight into those relationships.

Richard Johnson, who loaned Apess $1,500 in September 1836, was a leader of New Bedford's free African American community, a successful merchant of many years' standing; that fall, he was outfitting the first whaling expedition with an international "all-colored" crew on the brig *Rising States*, of which he was sole owner. The ship left New Bedford in November 1836.[141] Johnson was a friend of the celebrated African American merchant and sailor Paul Cuffe. According to Cuffe, even though Johnson was not enthusiastic about Cuffe's plan to colonize African Americans in Sierra Leone, in 1814 Johnson gave Cuffe $100 to support the venture.[142] Johnson was an agent for the *Liberator* from its inception; a distributor of Garrison's *Thoughts on Colonization* in 1832; one of the founders of the New-Bedford Union Society, an African American antislavery society, in 1833; and a delegate to conventions of free people of color in 1833 and 1834.[143] He was also an agent for the *Weekly Advocate* and the *Colored American*, both African American newspapers in New York City.[144]

While his reliance on Johnson for help reinforces Apess's connections to the antislavery movement, which began on his arrival in Boston in the spring of 1832, other connections point to the complexity of social and political affiliations among people of color in the early nineteenth century. In 1825, Johnson, then widowed, married the widowed daughter of Paul Cuffe, Ruth Cuffe Howard, and she joined him in his efforts on behalf of the African American community. Paul Cuffe's mother was Wampanoag and his father was African; Paul married a Wampanoag woman, and thus Ruth Johnson was three-quarters Wampanoag, although she married two African American men.[145] This is significant for reasons of contrast. Ruth Johnson acted on behalf of African American causes: she helped to found the African Christian Church in New

Bedford in the 1820s and was active in the antislavery movement; along with her husband and grown children, she protested "policies that directly and specifically impinged on the rights of people of color" in the Massachusetts legislature in 1837.[146] Despite her blood quantum, she identified herself as colored or African American. On the other hand, while he allied himself and other Native peoples with people of color generally, Apess identified himself as Native and, specifically, Pequot. This is important to bear in mind as scholars freely assume that because Apess argued for the rights of people of color in the antebellum United States, he must have been at least partly African American, or that because he drew attention to the oppression suffered by both Native and African American people, he must somehow be representative of a kind of multicultural political inclusion in the United States. His connections to the liberation movements of people of color in the antebellum United States and elsewhere are better understood as economic, political, and intellectual rather than vaguely cultural.

At the same time, however, Apess's connection to the whale fishery bespeaks international, or perhaps diasporic, relationships. Apess's son, his oldest child, went to sea on a whaler, which was in keeping with the practices of the Mashpees and other New England Indians in the early nineteenth century. New England Native peoples were well-known participants in the seafaring trades, especially whaling. As the Mashpee conflict was beginning in the Massachusetts legislature, the *North American Review* published an article in January 1834 on the whale fishery, the author of which observed that, despite the fact that "a large portion of the crew of a whaleman are the hardy, intelligent sons of our soil," the remaining crew members "are a motley collection":

> They are often found on the same deck the lingering remnants of the aborigines of this State, in specimens of the Gayhead and Marshpee tribes,—the runaway slave,—a renegade tar from the British navy,—the Irish,—the Dutch,—the mongrel Portuguese from the Azores, and the natives of the Sandwich Islands, from which captains make up the complements of crews diminished by accident or disease, or scanty by design.[147]

Possibly Apess's map of the world was a way to keep track of his son. After Barry O'Connell's publication of Apess's collected works, one of Apess's descendants contacted O'Connell from New Zealand. Erwin Apes told O'Connell that he was the grandson of William Elisha Apes, William Apess's son. In 1838, on the whaling ship *Ajax*, William Elisha and another sailor mutinied, Erwin Apes wrote, "over the inhumane treatment of the ship's boy. They took charge of the firearms and the ship and ordered it put into Port Otago where they loaded a whaleboat and deserted."[148] William Elisha married a Maori woman named Mata Punahere in 1844, shipped out in whalers from the United States as late as 1851 from Portland, Maine, had seven children, and died in 1891.[149] Apess mentions his son in the 1829 edition of *A Son of the Forest* in a passage that was excised from the revised edition of 1831. He describes how he left his "wife and . . . little son" boarding with a Methodist family while he traveled.[150] But the wife of the Methodist household turns out to be "very unkind, if not cruel." Apess returns to find his wife and son in lodgings "not fit for a dog" (320). The lady of the house "was even so cruel as to refuse a light in [Apess's wife's] room, and when medicines were ordered, [his wife] had to take them without sweetening, or anything whatsoever to make them palatable" (320). Although the family had to stay on because it was winter, they finally moved to Troy, Apess writes, after which "my wife was extremely rejoiced to get out of their fangs" (320).

Some of the information on William Elisha Apes comes from the memoir of Thomas Kennard, *The First White Boy on Otago*, which was first published in 1939. Kennard was a friend of William Elisha Apes and Mata Punahere's, and he mentions them in his book:

> I knew Mr. and Mrs. Apes well. He was said to have American Indian blood in him and when in a passion his eyes were red as fire. He was a six-footer and powerfully made, but his eldest son was short and broad, although the next son was very tall. Once my father-in-law (D. McNicol) and I were out on a wet evening and saw a light in an unoccupied hut at Goodwood, and found Mr. and Mrs. Apes there. They had lit a fire and were trying to dry their clothes, having nearly stripped off. Mr. McNicol said, "When I was taking the census you were good to me, so come to my house." They gladly accepted the offer and he gave them a good bed. That was over 80 years ago and there was no colour line then—the Maori was as good as the white man. They had been up as far as Waimate for a tangi or some celebration, and there returning when the storm overtook them and they sought refuge in the empty hut. Some of their descendants are still at Karitane and are well respected. (48)

This raises the question of whether William Apess's son became a Maori. It may be impossible to say, but at the very least these connections among Native peoples ought to be investigated further.

CHAPTER THREE

Traditionary History in Ojibwe Writing

GETTING INSIDE INDIANS' HEADS

In the early nineteenth century, EuroAmericans of seemingly every literary or scientific bent were keen to know and write down the stories and beliefs of Indians. Missionaries, lady travelers, and even Andrew Jackson's man Lewis Cass himself all wanted to know how Indians lived and what they thought. As territorial governor of Michigan from 1813 to 1831 before his promotion to secretary of war, Cass sent out elaborate questionnaires—nearly 300 separate queries—to his Indian agents, questionnaires that were seldom answered to his satisfaction.[1] (This type of quasi-scientific curiosity was not unusual for a government official with responsibility for Indians. Cass's colleague Thomas L. McKenney, the first commissioner for Indian affairs, collected Native artifacts as well as manuscripts and books related to Native peoples; in 1826, on his way back from attending the Treaty of Fond du Lac with Cass, he bought moccasins and several drawings from David Cusick.)[2] Writing about Indian traditions, as the beliefs and practices of Native peoples before the advent of European colonization were called, proliferated in the second quarter of the nineteenth century in discourses that often overlapped with one another before becoming clearly defined by the 1850s. As the discipline of ethnology took shape in periodical essays by men with an interest in science and philology, romantic Indian stories suffused the daily and weekly newspapers, periodicals, gift books and annuals, and books that constituted the explosion of print culture in the period, romantic stories that were often but not exclusively directed at women. In both venues, the sentimental and the proto-ethnological, Native traditions were represented as idealized, romanticized stories that described Native peoples as inhabitants of the distant past, as, indeed, ultimately the prehistory of the United States itself.

Native writers did exactly the opposite of what white writers did when they wrote about their traditions, and histories, in the period. They not only explained traditions but also explained their experience of whites and that of their tribes generally; they wrote about treaties and broken agreements; they wrote about the progress of Indian nations as they understood it—usually all in the same book. There are accounts of planned but unwritten histories in the period that exemplify this type of writing, indicating that it was, if not widespread, at least fairly common for Native peoples to wish to record their knowledge—and set the record straight—about themselves. William Apess apparently told Samuel Gardner Drake in 1832 that he planned to write a "traditionary history" of the Pequots, as Drake called it. He may have known more about Pequot history and tradition than is evident from his extant writing, or he may have known whom to ask. A missionary named Timothy Alden who was traveling through New York visited the aged Seneca leader Cornplanter, Red Jacket's rival, at the Allegheny reservation, where he found that Cornplanter had received instruction "by the instrumentality of an audible voice," which was written down by an interpreter from the Cattaraugus reservation named Henry York.[3] Cornplanter's "communications from the Great Spirit" were never published, Alden writes, because his friends discouraged him. Nevertheless Alden read the manuscript and reported that it included an account of the origins of the world and the story of the woman who fell from the sky, as well as "notices of what the voice has declared, confusedly intermixed with an historical account of some of the incidents in his life, his reflections on the ill treatment the Indians received from the British and the people of the United States, and certain other matters" (143–44). Alden was by no means a sympathetic reader. "Among the things recorded," Alden writes, "this is probably worthy of belief; that, in the course of his life, he has killed, with his own hand, seven men, and taken three prisoners, whom he did not destroy" (143–44).

Other Native peoples allowed white writers to take down and publish their stories, but they had no control over the end product. James Seaver's account of Mary Jemison's life, *Narrative of the Life of Mrs. Mary Jemison*, was first published in Canandaigua, New York, in 1824. Jemison, a white woman taken captive by a French and Shawnee raiding party during the Seven Years' War who was then adopted by and married into the Senecas, was around eighty years old at the time. She told her story because "many gentlemen of respectability, felt anxious that her narrative might be laid before the public, with a view not only to perpetuate the remembrance of the atrocities of the savages in former times, but to preserve some historical facts which they supposed to be intimately connected with her life, and which otherwise must be lost."[4] Mary

Jemison recounted her story for three days, after which Seaver made a book of it. James B. Patterson's *Life of Ma-ka-tai-me-she-kia-kiak or Black Hawk* was first published in Cincinnati in 1833, after Black Hawk returned to his home on the completion of his strange tour of the East at the conclusion of the war that bears his name. Whatever traces of Native agency remain in these accounts, both are versions of conventional forms—captivity narrative and frontier war story—and both close off their subjects by reiterating the narrative of Indians' providential doom.[5]

Ironically, the record of the white man John Howard Payne's unfinished history of the Cherokees may best illustrate why Native writers weren't able to write much in the period: people with writing skills had to be put to work for more immediate political ends. Payne may also demonstrate, obliquely, the incompatibility of the use of the sentimental style for representing Native traditions with the political struggles of Native peoples. Whereas sentiment radically dehistoricizes Native peoples, their political struggles require that they be represented in the past, present, and future, as all of the writers who wrote down histories were at pains to insist. In a similar way to Frederick Douglass in his 1847 autobiography, while Native writers adopted the dominant modes of writing favored by the U.S. middle classes at least in part in order to gain a hearing from them, in larger part they exceeded, conflicted with, criticized, and rejected the conventions for representing Indians. This chapter therefore describes the collision of EuroAmerican form and Native narratives in the case of Ojibwe writers active from the 1820s to the 1850s, who produced the largest body of Native histories and stories published in the first half of the nineteenth century.

The Ojibwes lived predominantly around Lake Superior and on the north shore of Lake Huron, in present-day southern Ontario and northern Michigan, Wisconsin, and Minnesota. Their lives were changed radically by the fur trade, and, especially after the close of the War of 1812, they were split between British and U.S. authority. Unlike the other writers included in this book, none of the Ojibwe writers deals with U.S. authority as a tribal person. Two of the writers discussed here, Jane Johnston Schoolcraft and William Whipple Warren, were from fur-trading families; their fathers were traders in the Lake Superior fur trade, and their mothers were Ojibwes who taught them the language and traditions. Both considered themselves neither completely Ojibwe nor entirely white, which in early-nineteenth-century Upper Northwest fur-trading societies was not a disadvantage; both of their families came under U.S. jurisdiction, and both of their fathers, John Johnston and Lyman Warren, came to the aid of the U.S. government in gaining alliances with Ojibwes and negotiating land cessions. The other three writers—Peter Jones, Jones's half-brother George Henry or Maungwudaus, and Jones's one-time protégé George Copway—were from Ojibwe bands on the north shore of Lake Ontario who were often called Mississaugas by Europeans.[6] Jones was a Methodist missionary, the first to establish churches and schools among the Ojibwes in southern Ontario; Maungwudaus and Copway converted to Methodism too, but to Jones's consternation, both abandoned the church.[7] While the Cherokee spokesmen, William Apess, and the Iroquois writers write within specific political struggles in the United States—the removal crisis; the Mashpee revolt; and, for the Iroquois, post–Revolutionary War conflicts over land and treaties in New York—the Ojibwe writers aren't connected by a particular political struggle but instead are bound together by the ongoing problems of misrepresentation and oppression. They have the language in common, the understanding of Ojibwe history and knowledge, and the willingness to represent these to a white public.

   The lack of direct involvement with U.S. authority might be a clue as to why the Ojibwe writers were able to write as much as they did, especially in the cases of Jones and Copway. Sidney Harring points out in *White Man's Law: Native People in Nineteenth-Century Canadian Jurisprudence* that British officials in Canada distinguished their policy of "liberal treatment" of Native peoples—of payment for land, reservations, and ceremonial presents—from the violence that they thought characterized the U.S. government's relations with Native peoples.[8] "After the passage of the early Indian Acts beginning in Upper Canada in 1837," Harring writes, "a policy of paternalism and protection was imposed over this 'liberal treatment' framework and in contradiction with it" (11). "For example," he states, "a policy protecting indigenous people from exploitation also kept Indian farmers from selling their produce and stopped Indians who had been voting from exercising that right of citizenship" (11). The official policy of paternalistic liberalism didn't prevent Native peoples in Canada from suffering the same consequences of colonization—denial of political status, denial of history and culture, destruction of their governmental structures—that Native peoples in the United States suffered, Harring points out; but describing the British relationship with Native peoples in Canada as "liberal"—a word that Harring notes was constantly used in government documents—was also a means of distinguishing British colonial rule from the violence of colonial rule in the United States.

   In comparison with Native writers dealing with the United States, it's striking that both Jones, who worked on behalf of Ojibwes all his life, and Copway, who began lecturing on his own plan for an Indian Territory in the United

States in 1848, which he eventually presented to Congress (where no one was interested in it), were comfortable advocating a paternalistic relationship with EuroAmerican government. This possibly has more to do with the kind of European government they were used to dealing with than with a willingness to subordinate themselves and Native peoples to EuroAmericans in Canada or the United States. Although Copway spends most of his writing life in the United States and offers his plan for an Indian Territory on the Northern Plains in lectures and eventually to Congress, he's not especially engaged in political disputes, and certainly not in the United States, where at the time he was writing and offering his plan, the Ojibwes were fighting a heated battle against removal—removal to which William Warren, acting as a U.S. interpreter in Minnesota at the time, objected.[9] Copway's plan for an Indian Territory called for the removal, by force if necessary, of Native tribes in the Northwest to what is now eastern South Dakota (at the time, Dakota territory; the Dakotas were hereditary enemies of the Ojibwes, and Copway has unkind words for them in his own work). The Native tribes would establish farming communities governed initially by both white and Native officials, although eventually Native officials would take over and the territory would become eligible for admission as a state.[10] Jones's biographer, Donald B. Smith, points out that a plan to resettle Christian Ojibwe people in a self-governing territory was broached by Canadian Ojibwes and rejected by the governor-general in 1845; Smith also writes that James Duane Doty, the territorial governor of Wisconsin, proposed a similar plan in 1841, which Congress rejected in 1842 (36–37). When Copway describes his plan in an article published in the *American Whig Review* in 1849, he calls for less land for Native peoples so they would not backslide by hunting. Further, only the "meritorious" Native peoples should rule—that is, those who have succeeded at farming, are sincere Christians, and so on—which would encourage traditional people to "study hard to improve in general information, and fit themselves for statesmen and divines."[11] He argues that such an Indian Territory would simplify relations with Indians and make them less expensive, and he is somewhat cavalier about U.S. authority: "Establish a court of justice in the Indian territory, and no trouble will be had with them, as the difficulties would be legally settled" (637). Whether this last bespeaks strategy or naiveté is impossible to determine, but such faith in the fairness of U.S. courts is not something that any U.S.-born Native writer would have endorsed at the time (or likely ever since).

In his *History of the Ojebway Indians*, Peter Jones also argued (before Copway did) that Native peoples should be forced if necessary to live on less land so they would have to farm and would not be tempted—an operative word for

Jones, who could be quite harsh about what he understood as his own peoples' moral turpitude—to return to hunting (172).[12] While Native leaders in the United States might make ceremonial reference to the "Great Father," the "Great Father" was not invited to take control of their governments, and few if any Native leaders argued that they should have less land so they would be better able to become civilized. The superior attitude of British administrators in Canada also seems to have some validity, however, at least in terms of the charge that U.S. relations with Native peoples appear to have been more overtly violent. While the British monarch has a symbolically benign relationship with his or her subjects, treaty relationships in the United States are contracts, the meaning of which must be negotiated, contested, and fought out. The peculiar necessity of these contracts, along with the peculiar—if momentary—ability of Native peoples to resist making them, even when most whites are convinced of their inherent superiority and Indians' impending providential disappearance, would seem to be fertile ground for violence, fraud, and deception.

In any case, as these writers were not consumed by defending their tribes and the misrepresentation of their people in confrontations with U.S. authority, they seem to have been able to devote more of their time to explicating their history and traditions than the Cherokees, William Apess, and the Iroquois writers were able to do. Even so, Peter Jones's life was occupied with his missionary duties, and his journals and *History of the Ojebway Indians* were published posthumously by his wife. William Warren finished his one book, traveled to New York to find a publisher (and also to find a doctor because he was ill), which he couldn't, and then died at the age of twenty-eight on returning to St. Paul. Jane Johnston Schoolcraft produced literary fairy tales based on her mother's stories in the 1820s; she was often ill, however, and especially after 1830 appears to have been preoccupied with her children, her estranged relationship with her husband, and her increasingly debilitating illnesses; she died addicted to laudanum in 1841. Maungwudaus, once a promising Methodist convert, abandoned Christianity, gathered a group of fellow Ojibwes, and went to Europe to perform in the company of George Catlin, who was then touring the European capitals with his enormous Indian Gallery of portraits. Maungwudaus published two pamphlets in association with his performing troupe. After he returned to North America and toured in the United States, he went back to Canada and never, as far as anyone knows, wrote again. George Copway enjoyed a brief literary celebrity that he seems to have done his best to exploit in the manner of mid-nineteenth-century literary entrepreneurs, producing an autobiography, a history, a narrative poem that someone else wrote, a travel book, and a newspaper between 1847 and 1851. But his behavior was erratic; he experienced a fitful decline through the 1850s, during which he still traveled giving lectures, and by the 1860s he was listed as an "Indian doctor" along with the seamstresses, grocers, undertakers, and insurance agents in Geneva, New York, a small town on Lake Cayuga.

Despite the disparity of their individual stories, however, the Ojibwe writers make the same arguments that other Native writers make in the period: they write to counter misrepresentation, they reject the notion of inherent differ- ence, they insist on Native authority for traditional knowledge, and they de- nounce EuroAmericans' claims to know their own knowledge better than they themselves do. Because of the nature of their writing, the Ojibwe writers emphasize traditional knowledge. In the works of most of these writers, tradi- tional knowledge is a broad and heterogeneous body of knowledge, not con- fined to the past, that is adaptable to the Eurocentric forms of literature and historiography. These writers—with the exception of Peter Jones—present tra- ditional knowledge as capable of beauty in the literary-aesthetic realm and as representative of the truth in history. They maintain this position at a moment when Native peoples' traditional knowledge was being refracted, rewritten, and effaced in the invention of ethnology and reified in sentimental and popu- lar entertainment.

ETHNOLOGY AND EFFACEMENT

Henry Rowe Schoolcraft began his career as a geologist in a Northwest Terri- tory expedition led by Lewis Cass, then territorial governor of Michigan, who later appointed Schoolcraft agent at Sault Sainte Marie on Lake Superior in 1822. There he met the Johnston family and married Jane Johnston the follow- ing year. Jane's father, John Johnston, was a Scotch-Irish immigrant fur trader from an aristocratic family of "declining fortunes" who married Oshaguaco- daywaygwa, whose father was a prominent Ojibwe leader, Waub Ojeeg.[13] As with other Native women married to white men in the fur trade, Mrs. John- ston's contacts, extended family, and influence were indispensable to her hus- band's business.[14] The Johnstons had four sons and four daughters; because there was no school at Sault Sainte Marie, Johnston educated the children at home, tutoring them "in literature, history, and the classics, and procured a large private library with a variety of source material for their studies."[15] Mrs. Johnston educated the children in their Ojibwe heritage; besides her political acumen, she was also celebrated as an important storyteller. While her brothers and sisters eventually attended boarding school in Canada, Jane was instead educated at home, except for a few months spent with relatives in Ireland when she accompanied her father on a business trip to Europe in 1809. Jane often traveled with her father to Detroit, Montreal, and Quebec on business and seems to have been her father's interpreter. Johnston wrote to Cass in 1822, apologizing for not getting back to him on the questionnaire he had sent with Henry Schoolcraft; he explained that he couldn't complete it without the help of Jane, who was ill, "on whose superior knowledge of the language I must chiefly rely for correct information."[16]

Jane and her mother, who was also called Susan, along with her mother's family, provided Schoolcraft with much of the information on Ojibwe life and language that he later used in his many books.[17] Henry Schoolcraft's first book, *Algic Researches* (1839), consisted of stories told to him by his wife's Ojibwe family and contacts, rewritten by himself, as well as a long theoretical introduction in which Schoolcraft delineates the evidence of the "Indian mind" found in Ojibwe stories, which demonstrated what everyone already thought about Indians: that they were childlike, incapable of reason, improvident, and unable to form true governments. There's a kind of symmetry in the biographies of Jane Johnston's husband and father and in the roles of Jane and her mother: whereas white men like her father had come into the country looking to gain Native peoples' furs, then their land, later those like her husband wanted Indians' knowledge. Schoolcraft used that knowledge to fashion a career first as an administrator of Indians, then as an ethnologist and Indian expert. EuroAmericans required Native peoples' knowledge in order to develop their theories of Indian difference, but that knowledge had to be separated from its historical and political contexts, including the people who supplied it. Like the story of John Howard Payne's unwritten history, the story of Jane Johnston Schoolcraft's effacement sheds some light on the difficulty that even educated Native peoples faced in getting their accounts of themselves written and published in the early nineteenth century.

Schoolcraft's transformation of the knowledge provided by his wife's family into evidence of Indians' difference, inferiority, and impending disappearance quite literally supported colonial control. Cass used Schoolcraft's work to write articles about the necessity of removal, including an essay published in the *North American Review* in 1830, the year before Andrew Jackson promoted him to secretary of war.[18] Cass was quite happy to discover that Schoolcraft was a boarder in the Johnstons' home when Schoolcraft first arrived in Sault Sainte Marie. He wrote to Schoolcraft:

I am anxious that Mr. Johnston and his family furnish full and detailed answers to my queries, more particularly upon all subjects connected with the language, and, if I may so speak, the polite literature of the Chippewa. . . . There is no quarter from which I can expect such full information, upon these topics as from this. I must beg you to aid me in this pursuit. Urge them during the long winter evenings to the task. The time cannot be more profitably or pleasantly spent, and, as I am told you are somewhat of an aboriginophile, you can assist. A perfect analysis of the language is a great desideratum. I pray you, in the spring, to let me have the fruits of your exertions.[19]

Cass used the information Schoolcraft supplied in a number of articles arguing, as in the 1830 *North American Review* article, that Native peoples' inherent inferiority made removal not only inevitable but also humane. Cass's "ethnological theories," Bieder writes in *Science Encounters the Indian*, were entirely dependent on the information Schoolcraft gathered, as Cass's questionnaires turned out to be a not entirely useful means of securing information since few people could answer them to Cass's satisfaction or even understand them.[20]

The Johnston family was well known and even celebrated in the fur trade, the Indian service, and beyond. In an account of his travels to and from the signing of the Treaty of Fond du Lac, Thomas McKenney describes the Johnston family as a kind of ideal combination of the natural gentility of Europeans and Native peoples. His description of the family epitomizes genteel discourse, which valorized the aristocratic virtues of "polish," manners, taste, good breeding, and "mental culture."[21] Both Mr. and Mrs. Johnston, McKenney observes, were descended from "nobility."[22] Mrs. Johnston was "the daughter of the famous *Wa-ba-jick*, the great chief formerly of *Le point* [sic], of Lake Superior, a man of renown, and one who ruled both in wisdom and valour, and proved himself, in every emergency, to have been worthy of the station he held as chief of his band" (181). John Johnston, though currently infirm, was a gentleman of the highest order; "his education and intercourse with polished society, in early life, indeed up to his thirtieth year, have given him many striking advantages over the inhabitants of those distant regions, and indeed fit him to shine any where" (182).

Jane was very much the picture of the genteel lady, and indeed, every account of Jane describes her in essentially the same way—as refined, intelligent, retiring, and extraordinarily well mannered. McKenney writes:

Her voice is feeble, and tremulous. Her utterance is slow and distinct. There is something silvery in it. Mildness of expression, and softness, and delicacy of manner, as well as of voice, characterize her. She dresses with great taste, and in all respects in the costume of our fashionables, but wears leggins of black silk, drawn and ruffled around the ankles, resembling those worn by our little girls. I think them ornamental. You would never judge, either from her complexion, or language, or from any other circumstance, that her mother was a Chippeway, except that her moderately high cheek bones, her dark and fine eye, and breadth of the jaw, slightly indicate it—and you would never believe it, except on her own confession, or upon some equally responsible testimony, were you to hear her converse, or see her beautiful, and some of them highly finished compositions, in both prose and poetry. You would not believe it, not because such attainments might not be universal, but because, from the lack of the means necessary for their accomplishment, such cases are so rare. (184)

This description of a woman who in later years would be called a "half-breed" is peculiar to its place and time, the early nineteenth-century fur trade and the era before racial difference became naturalized, when the idea of civilized Indians was not so far-fetched, even to the commissioner of Indian affairs. Jane Schoolcraft represents the female counterpart of the civilized Indian that can be imagined in the brief period in the 1820s and early 1830s when the Cherokees were fighting removal. The key aspect of the idea of civilized Indians, however, is represented by Jane's mother, who, McKenney writes, "has never been known in a single instance, to council her people but in accordance with her conceptions of what was best for them, and never in opposition to the views of the government" (183–84).

The *Literary Voyager*, a manuscript magazine begun by Henry Schoolcraft in an effort to amuse himself during the winter of 1826–27, fit into the genteel frontier world that McKenney describes, but it also demonstrates the conflicts beneath the surface. Schoolcraft, who disapproved of the drinking and card playing of many of the other white people at the agency and nearby fort during the winter, began a reading society in December for local people and some of the officers from the fort and their wives.[23] The magazine included bits of information from newspapers, sentimental poems, and notes on topics of interest submitted by members of the reading society, but the bulk of the material had to do with Native peoples and their traditions. The conflict between Jane Schoolcraft's and Henry Schoolcraft's understandings of Ojibwe knowledge is somewhat submerged in the *Voyager* but still present.

Henry sets the tone with his brief essay, "The Unchangeable Character of the Indian Mind," the title of which serves as a summary of his remarks. He

Jane Johnston Schoolcraft as a young woman, probably in the 1820s, about the time she contributed stories and poems to the Literary Voyager. *She was visited by Commissioner for Indian Affairs Thomas L. McKenney, who praised her gentility and "polish" as evidence that Indians could improve when exposed to education and Christianity. Photograph courtesy of the Bentley Historical Library, University of Michigan.*

observes that missionary activity has made no discernible improvement in the lives of Indians: "Philanthropy cannot console itself that its efforts to meliorate their condition have produced any important changes in their mental habits— that it has led them to adopt any new trains of thought, or more refined and methodical modes of action," he opines; "religion has no cause to exult in the extent of its achievements."[24] Attempting to civilize Indians is, in the end, useless: "Doomed to extinguishment by some inscrutable fiat," Indians will fall "before their invaders like grain beneath the scythe, and leaving their rich inheritance to 'men of other minds' " (110–11). Despite the fact that he has just argued that philanthropic efforts at civilizing Indians have failed because of the moral failures of Indians themselves, Schoolcraft leaves open the question of "whether we have acquitted ourselves of our duty towards our aboriginal population" (111). It seems, then, that even if whites have so far failed to civilize Indians, the Christian duty of whites should compel them to at least continue to try. In the meantime, however, Indians ought to be studied. "In the interim of continued experiment [in civilizing Indians], while opinions are forming and renewed efforts making, it is the dictate of a humane and liberal spirit to improve every opportunity for acquiring fresh information, and eliciting new and authentic traits of their character and history" (111). That job is particularly difficult, however, because Indians have no written history, and thus it helps to have an entrée into the community, such as that provided by Schoolcraft's in-laws.

Knowledge that Native peoples themselves might contribute is suppressed in this exercise in literary gentility. The *Voyager* includes an ostensible contribution by Mrs. Johnston, translated by Jane, titled "Character of Aboriginal Historical Tradition," which begins:

> I have learnt from a correspondent of yours, a very distant relation of mine, your intention of publishing a Paper; the utility and true meaning of which, has been fully explained to me by my friend. And as you are willing to admit contributors from amongst my countrymen and women, it has induced me to take the liberty of addressing you, and by this means I hope you will be able to form a more correct opinion of the ideas peculiar to the Ojibways.[25]

The apparent capitulation to the superiority of white knowledge makes the authorship of this essay suspect, especially since it was allegedly written by a woman who refused to speak English her entire life and never abandoned her own people. "My father was descended from one of the most ancient and respected leaders of the Ojibway bands—long before the white people had it in the power to distinguish an Indian by placing a piece of silver, in the shape of a medal on his breast," Mrs. Johnston says through Jane (and perhaps through Henry). She goes on to relate that the medal represented an alliance with whites to her father, not subordination. The medal also gives rise to commentary on the superiority of white knowledge. "That medal my father used to wear, and it is the only relic I still retain in memory of him, who first taught me how to esteem and appreciate white people. He often told me that you had a right knowledge of every thing, and that you knew the truth, because you had things past and present written down in books and were able to relate, from them, the great and noble actions of your forefathers, without variation" (6).

This is exactly what Henry Rowe Schoolcraft believed: Indians couldn't write, therefore they had no sense of past and present. The comments in this essay are too much in line with the conventional ideas about the moral differences between civilized writing societies and uncivilized "traditionary" societies to be entirely believable as the thoughts of Mrs. Johnston herself. In the essay, Mrs. Johnston goes on to lament that the stories told in her nation can't be true because the people who tell them are always forgetting things and adding new parts, so that "the history of my country has become almost wholly fabulous" (6). She pleads for "a man in black to come and instruct us poor Indians, and if we are to dwell in that house . . . when the man in black comes to teach us poor young ignorant people the right way, I shall know better; and when I can write, I shall not forget to send you all the pretty songs and stories my mother used to teach me—to be put in your paper" (7).

Jane's name—or her pseudonyms, Rosa and Leelinau, or her Ojibwe name, Bamewawagezhikaquay—appears on several poems and four stories in the magazine, and her writing does not entirely fit the sentimental model that the *Literary Voyager* invoked. Four of the poems—"Resignation," "To Sisters on a Walk in the Garden, After a Shower," "To a Friend Asleep," and "Lines Written Under Affliction"—are about Christian resignation to loss and suffering and declarations of faith. "To a Friend Asleep" concludes:

Awake! The sweet refreshing scene,
Invites us forth to tread the green,
With joyful hearts, and pious lays,
To join the glorious Maker's praise,
The wond'rous works—the paschal lamb,
the holy high, and just I am.[26]

These poems make plausible the likelihood of Jane's editorializing in the piece attributed to her mother. But there is also a long narrative poem on her grandfather, Waub Ojeeg, in which Jane makes modifications to the conventional image of the vengeful Indian warrior similar to those that William Apess makes in the material he includes in the appendix to *A Son of the Forest*—published only two years after Jane Schoolcraft's participation in the manuscript magazine. "Otagamiad" is presented as a dramatic dialogue among warriors contemplating going to war—a reasonable if passionate discussion in which the thoughtless, vengeful savage is nowhere to be found. Moreover, the "enemies" in this poem are defined vaguely enough to figure as much for whites as for other Native peoples. In this poem, Ojeeg, "a chief of fame" at La Pointe, addresses a council, pointing out that

> Long have our lands been hem'd around by foes,
> Whose secret ire, no check or limit knows,
> Whose public faith, so often pledg'd in vain,
> 'Twere base for freemen e'er to trust again.[27]

While these enemies are Native, the actions Jane describes are peculiarly like those of whites. "No treaty binds them, & no stream confines," Ojeeg says, and thus "War—war or slavery is our only choice" (61).

Other warriors disagree. Camudwa, "fam'd for eloquence of tongue / Whose breast resolv'd the coming strife with pain, / And peace still hop'd, by peaceful arts to gain," counsels that "The foe may yet, be reason'd into right" (62, 63). This in itself is a departure from EuroAmerican convention but not from the thinking of Native intellectuals. Indians only want revenge, according to whites, and they cannot possibly reason. Moreover, to return to William Robertson, Indians are not supposed to be able to think abstractly, which precludes them from acting from higher motivations than revenge. Camudwa, however, offers to deliver a message of peace to the enemies:

> And if we fail in speech—we still may fight.
> At least, one further effort, be our care,
> I will myself, the daring message bear,
> I give my body, to the mission free,
> And if I fall, my country, 'tis for thee! (62)

Next, Baimwawa endorses the idea of talking to these enemies, remembering that they had once not been enemies:

> The deeds of other days before my eyes,
> In all their friendship, love and faith arise,
> When hand in hand with him we rov'd the wood,
> Swept the long vale, or stem'd the boiling flood.
> In the same war path, match'd with ready blade,
> And liv'd, and fought, and triumph'd with his aid.
> When the same tongue, express'd our joys and pains,
> And the same blood ran freely thro' our veins? (62)

But Keewadin rejects this nostalgia, pointing out that these enemies have allied themselves with the French and colluded with the Dakotas:

They sunder'd name, league, language, rites and all.
They, with our firm allies, the Gallic race,
First broke the league, by secret arts and base,
Then play'd the warrior—call'd our bands a clog,
And earn'd their proper title, Fox and Dog.
Next to the false Dacota [*sic*] gave the land,
And leagued in war, our own destruction plan'd. (62)

Then "the sage Canowekeed" adds his view, which is to accept the fact that war is inevitable, but in a philosophical way: "If harsher fires, in ardent bosoms glow, / At least restrain them, till we meet the foe, / Calm judgment here, demands the care of all" (63). Jane doesn't offer any resolution to this range of voices, and perhaps that's the main point of the poem. "By causes new or old," Jane writes,

Each for himself, both knows & feels & sees,
The growing evils of a heartless peace,
And the sole question, of this high debate,
Is—shall we longer suffer—longer wait,
Or, with heroic will, for strife prepare,
And try the hazard of a gen'ral war! (63)

These Indian warriors are too philosophical to murderously take up the tomahawk and scalping knife.

Jane Schoolcraft's stories don't present history or historical relations or for the most part reproduce the conventions for sentimental stories about Indians; rather they appear to be modeled on literary fairy tales. Given her father's background and library, it is likely that Jane had been exposed to these kinds of fairy tales. While Jacob Grimm's *German Popular Stories* did not appear in English translation until 1825, the Mother Goose stories written by Charles Perrault were widely available in English beginning in the late eighteenth century, and it is certainly possible that John Johnston, being an aristocrat, would have purchased a copy for his children. Jane's stories are about transformation and wonder, which Jack Zipes describes as the key requirements of literary fairy tales; only one of the stories fits the sentimental model.[28] That story, "Origin of the Miscodeed, or the Maid of Tacquimenon," grafts a historical reference to Jane's maternal great-grandfather and a sentimental ending onto a traditional story about the origin of the miscodeed, a white flower that blooms early in the spring.

"The Origin of the Robin: An Oral Allegory," "The Forsaken Brother: A

Chippewa Tale," and "Mishosha, or the Magician and His Daughters: A Chippewa Tale or Legend" describe the abandonment of parents by children and the childrens' subsequent magical transformation. "The Origin of the Robin" is about how a father's unrealistic ambitions for his son destroy the son's life. The boy's father, an "old man," wishes his only son to "surpass all others in whatever was deemed most wise and great amongst his tribe."[29] The boy prepares to fast in order to find his guardian spirit. The old man "thought it necessary that his son must fast a much longer time than any of those persons known for their great power or wisdom, whose fame he envied" (66). The father insists that the son continue longer than others in his fast and isolation; even when the son has dreams "ominous of evil," the father won't let him stop. On the twelfth and final day, the father approaches the lodge and sees his son applying vermilion to himself and saying, "My father has ruined me, as a man; he would not listen to my request; he will now be the loser. I shall be forever happy in my new state, for I have been obedient to my parent; he alone will be the sufferer; for the Spirit is a just one, though not propitious to me. He has shown me pity, and now I must go"; then he becomes a robin (66). In "The Forsaken Brother," a boy is abandoned by his brother and sister after their parents' deaths and against their warnings, out of their own selfishness. The boy goes farther and farther into the woods and is turned into a wolf; the brother and sister feel the "bitterness of remorse" for the rest of their lives.[30] "Mishosha" begins with a married couple who want to kill each other because the wife is in love with a "young man whom she accidentally met in the woods," but instead they abandon their two sons.[31] The boys, as in "The Forsaken Brother," go into the woods, where the older boy is kidnapped by a magician in a canoe on a lake. After a series of trials in which the magician attempts to kill the older boy, the boy prevails; the two boys marry the daughters of the evil magician, and the magician is turned into a sycamore tree.

Henry Schoolcraft published "Origin of the Robin," "The Forsaken Brother," and "Mishosha" in *Algic Researches* in 1839, but he left out the last of the four stories that appeared in the *Literary Voyager* under Jane's name, "Moowis," a term that Philip Mason notes is "highly derogative" and "derives from the term for filth or excrement."[32] While the other stories are in a recognizably idealized literary style, both the narrative and the language make the story appear closer to traditional sources. In this story, an Ojibwe "belle" rejects a "beau," who in retaliation makes a man out of "dirt" and brings it to life. When the belle accepts this "image" in her suitor's place, the image is revealed as essentially excrement, and it disintegrates and disappears, after which the girl is heartbroken. The story begins, "There was a village full of Indians, and a noted belle or *muh-muh daw go qua* was living there. A noted beau or *muh muh daw go, ninnie* was there also."³³ When the "handsome beau," along with another young man whose presence isn't explained, "went to court this young woman, and laid down beside her," the belle "scratched the face of the handsome beau" (67). The young man was ashamed, went home, and refused to show himself, even after his rival, who was his cousin, tried to persuade him to emerge. Eventually, the village "decamped," and the scorned beau refused to go with them. Instead, he stayed in the abandoned camp and built a man of "dirt." The beau "rose and gathered all the bits of clothing, and ornaments of beads and other things, that had been left. He then made a coat and leggings of the same, nicely trimmed with the beads, and the suit was fine and complete. After making a pair of moccasins, nicely trimmed, he also made a bow and arrows. He then collected the dirt of the village, and filled the garments he had made, so as to appear as a man, and put the bow and arrows in his hands, and it came to life" (67).

Then the scorned beau and his dirt image go to the new camp, where they are happily received, and when the belle sees the dirt image, she falls in love. In one scene, the dirt image is invited to sit by the fire because it's winter, but he asks a child to sit between himself and the fire because it is too hot. Then he begins to stink: "All smelt the dirt. Some said, 'some one has trod on, and brought in dirt' " (67). The belle is not affected by the smell; she "wished the stranger would visit her" (67).

> The image went to his master, and they went out to different lodges, the image going as directed to the belle's. Towards morning, the image said to the young woman (as he had succeeded) "I must now go away," but she said, "I will go with you." He said "it is too far." She answered, "it is not so far but I can go with you." He first went to the lodge where he was entertained, and then to his master, and told him all of what had happened, and now he was going off with her. The young man thought it a pity that she had treated him so, and how sadly she would be punished. (67)

So the young man lets the dirt image go off, followed by the girl. The image gets far ahead of her and begins to disintegrate.

> When the sun rose high, she found one of his mittens and picked it up, but to her astonishment, found it full of dirt. She, however took it and wiped it, and going on further, she found the other mitten in the same condition. She thought, "fie!! Why does he do so," thinking he dirtied in them. She kept finding different articles of his dress, on the way all day, in the same condi-

tion. He kept ahead of her till towards evening, when the snow was like water, having melted by the heat of the day. No signs of her husband appearing, after having collected all the cloths that held him together, she began to cry, not knowing where to go, as their track was lost, on account of the snow's melting. She kept crying *Moowis* has led me astray and she kept singing and crying Moowis nin ge won e win ig, ne won e win ig. (67)

When Henry Schoolcraft finally published "Moowis" in the *Columbian Lady's and Gentleman's Magazine* in 1844, he made certain changes that are instructive. Schoolcraft takes out the scatological and sexual overtones of the story and presents it as his own—as he did all of the identifiable stories by his wife that he published. Moreover, he insists that this particular story is the truth: "This curious specimen of Indian story-telling is genuine. It was taken down, verbatim, from the lips of an aboriginal narrator, and the tradition is as literal as it can be made."[34] Schoolcraft added stilted language, touches of ethnological information, and psychological explanation. The "coquette" is heartless, but she doesn't seek out a sexual encounter any longer; rather, the story is about her coquettishness:

> When the handsome young man rallied from the coldness of her air and made an effort to overcome her indifference, she put together her thumb and three fingers, and raising her hand gracefully toward him, deliberately opened them in his face. This gesticulatory mode of rejection is one of the highest contempt, and the young hunter retired confused and abashed. (90)

Perhaps in keeping with the requirements of sentimental narrative in genteel magazines, the "beau-man" has a more detailed psychological life: "He was a very sensitive man, and the thing so preyed upon him that he became moody, and at last took to his bed" (90). The "rag-man" is described as a magical creation: the beau-man creates him from "bits of soiled cloth, clippings of finery, cast-off clothing and ornaments which had either been left or lost" after the village decamped (90). He is dirty, but not in the sexual or scatological sense. The beau-man himself is made of animal bones, "pieces of skins, clippings of dried meat, and even dirt," and he is held together with snow, an addition to the story (90). This circumstance saves Schoolcraft from having to mention the stink of the beau-man. The sexual encounter between the rag-man and the coquette also takes place within marriage, which happens the very night that the rag-man and his maker go to the lodge. "Marriage, in the forest race," Schoolcraft observes, "is a simple ceremony, and where the impediments of custom are small there is but little time demanded for their execution" (91). There's some confusion on the next day: the rag-man goes back to tell his maker "the events we have described," but the maker had been present when it was clear the rag-man would marry the girl, which suggests that the rag-man goes to tell his maker about the night spent with the coquette. It appears to be something that is left in the story that isn't supposed to be there, a trace of Jane's story that her husband didn't quite erase.

The *Literary Voyager* didn't last beyond March 1827; that month, the Schoolcrafts' only child, William Henry, died suddenly of scarlet fever, and the last issues of the magazine are devoted to elegies for the dead boy by his parents and others. By all accounts, William's death devastated both of his parents, but especially Jane. Though they had two more children, Jane Susan, born in the fall of 1828, and John, born in the fall of 1829, the couple became estranged. Henry, always a moralizer, had a kind of epiphany and made a public confession of faith while traveling in 1830. He convinced himself, Bremer writes, that his son's death was "an act of divine retribution upon himself and his wife for their sin in idolizing their boy above Jehovah Himself."[35] He wrote a letter to Jane, telling her that it was her Christian duty to give up her attachments to everyone but him:

> Nothing is more clearly scriptural, than that a woman should forsake "father & mother" & cleave to her husband, & that she should look up to him with a full confidence, as next to God, her "guide, philosopher & friend." Brought up in a remote place, without any thing which deserves the name of a regular education, without the salutary influence of society to form your mind, without a mother, in many things, to direct & with an over kind father, who saw everything in the fairest light, & made even your sisters & brothers & all about you bow to you as their superior in every mental and worldly thing. You must indeed have possessed a strength of intellect above the common order, not to have taken up some manners & opinions & feelings, as false & foolish, as flattery & self deceit can be.[36]

Bremer notes: "Although her subsequent correspondence would display ritual self-abasement in obedience to his instructions, she found it quite impossible to satisfy his demands, and the distance between them widened with the passing years" (112).

Henry Schoolcraft's description of his proper relation to his wife—that he be her "guide, philosopher & friend"—is quite interesting in light of his description of the Johnston family, particularly Mrs. Johnston, when he first came to the Sault. Writing in his journal on 28 July 1822, Schoolcraft observed that "Mrs. Johnston is a woman of excellent judgment and good sense; she is referred to on abstruse points of the Indian ceremonies and usages, so that I have in fact stumbled, as it were, on the only family in North West America who could, in Indian lore, have acted as my 'guide, philosopher, and friend.' "[37] Bieder has surmised that Henry Schoolcraft reasserted himself in 1830 at least in part because he felt overshadowed by the Johnston family. That may or may not be true; what is of interest here is how Schoolcraft effaces the knowledge he sought from the Johnstons and depended on in his career as an Indian agent— being indispensable to Cass was an important career move—and then as a self-styled ethnologist. Scholars who comment on Schoolcraft's work tend to represent Jane as a drag on Henry, useful in providing the raw material for his researches but sickly and sentimental and not worth thinking about. Jane Schoolcraft is elusive, but she doesn't quite disappear; indeed, it appears that in the wake of Thomas McKenney's comments on the family in his 1827 *Tour to the Lakes*, Jane was publicly known and even celebrated. These traces of Jane's biography in relation to Henry Schoolcraft's use of her knowledge reveal not only how Native peoples' authority for their knowledge is effaced in Euro-American writing but also how Native historicity is effaced and, in particular, how the fact of Native writing itself is denied, which has been and continues to be a problem in the criticism of Native literature.

Besides Thomas McKenney, the celebrated British writers Harriet Martineau and Anna Brownell Jameson visited the Schoolcrafts. Anna Jameson was one of the best-known critics, male or female, of the day when she visited the Schoolcrafts in 1837. She wrote books about Shakespeare's female characters, female sovereigns, loves of the poets, travel, and art criticism. One of her closest friends was Elizabeth Barrett Browning, and she was associated with (and sniped upon by, for what they regarded as excessive sentimentality) Harriet Martineau and Margaret Fuller. Though she began publishing works in London in 1826, her works were beginning to be reprinted—and would be, again and again—in New York by 1836. In 1837, Jameson traveled to Canada in part to attempt a reconciliation with her husband, Robert Jameson, who held a government post in Toronto. A formal separation resulted, along with her travel book, *Winter Studies and Summer Rambles in Canada* (1838).[38] Jane Schoolcraft gave Anna Jameson her own stories, the ones that have been associated with her only because of the survival of the *Literary Voyager* manuscript, to publish in Jameson's book, significantly, under Jane's own name. These were "The Forsaken Brother," "The Origin of the Robin," "Mishosha," and a story that she said her mother told her, "The Allegory of Winter and Summer." Henry Schoolcraft never acknowledged publicly Jane's contribution to—or authorship of—the work that he published under his own name. He informed her that she had to subordinate herself to his will. Yet she gave her stories to other people who published them. Anna Jameson wasn't the only writer who published Jane's stories. Chandler Robbins Gilman, another traveler, included two of her stories, "Origin of the Robin" and "The Forsaken Boy," in his *Life on the Lakes* in 1836, although he doesn't identify Jane as the author of the stories.[39]

Anna Jameson writes that Jane was as refined as European ladies, but with a difference:

> Her genuine refinement and simplicity, and native taste for literature, are charming. . . . She is proud of her Indian origin; she takes an enthusiastic and enlightened interest in the welfare of her people, and in their conversion to Christianity, being herself most unaffectedly pious. But there is a melancholy and pity in her voice, when speaking of them, as if she did indeed consider them a doomed race. We were conversing to-day of her grandfather Waub-Ojeeb, (the White-fisher,) a distinguished Chippewa chief and warrior, of those life and exploits she has promised to give me some connected particulars. Of her mother, O,she,gush,ko,da,wa,qua, she speaks with fond and even longing affection, as if the very sight of this beloved mother would be sufficient to restore her to health and strength. "I should be well if I could see my mother," seems to be the predominant feeling. Nowhere is the instinctive affection between parent and child so strong, so deep, so sacred, as among these people.[40]

Jameson's comments on the stories Jane gives her are not entirely encouraging. "The stories I have for you from Mrs. Schoolcraft's translation have at least the merit of being genuine," she writes to her imagined correspondent; "their very wildness and childishness, and dissimilarity to all other fictions, will recommend them to you" (87–88). The first story, "The Forsaken Brother," she writes, is "evidently intended to inculcate domestic union and brotherly love" (88). The moral of the second, "Mishosha," however, is more "difficult" to determine, "unless it be that courage, and perseverance, and cunning, are sure at length to triumph over even magical art; but it is surely very picturesque, and peculiar, and fanciful" (88).

Algic Researches is a collection of literary fairy tales with heavy-handed ethnological intrusions and a preface describing how the stories ought to be interpreted—that is, as evidence of "the unchangeable nature of the Indian mind."[41] Schoolcraft made his career on his wife's stories. Despite the fact that, like other literary entrepreneurs of the period, he published voluminously, he had no new stories to publish after 1844; he asked Jane's brother for more stories, but he never got any.[42] As the profession of ethnology was taking shape, Indian stories were taken less seriously because they were considered too fanciful. Ethnologists wanted the kind of knowledge represented by Cass's 300 questions, which could be organized into a systematic structure. At mid-century, Native peoples could be authenticators, but they could not control the narrative; it wasn't until the late nineteenth century, with the writing of such anthropologists as Daniel G. Brinton, that scientific writing about Indian stories—not written down by Native peoples, however—came to be taken seriously by the intellectually inclined. In the 1840s, it was impossible for the "traditionary" stories of Indians to be anything other than entertainment.

CHAOS, CONVERSION, AND PROGRESS

Like Jane Schoolcraft, Peter Jones had an Ojibwe mother who, although she had children with a white man, chose not to enter into white society. Jones's father was a U.S. citizen named Augustus Jones who came north to work as a surveyor; his mother, Tuhbenaheequay, had a relationship with Jones in the Ojibwe country when he worked there. Smith reports that Augustus Jones tried to persuade Tuhbenaheequay to convert to Christianity and live in a town, but she refused. Jones then married a Christian Mohawk woman named Sarah Tekarihogen. He maintained relationships with both women for several years before he eventually chose to stay with Sarah exclusively. Peter Jones was born in 1802, after his father had married Sarah; at fourteen, he and his older brother John went to live on his father's farm in Upper Canada with his half brothers and sisters, where they were sent to school. Tuhbenaheequay later married an Ojibwe man, Mesquacosy, with whom she had Maungwudaus, also known by his English name, George Henry, in 1811 at the Credit River reserve in Upper Canada. Peter Jones's father and stepmother were already Methodists when Jones went to live with them; he converted in 1823. Methodist missionaries also converted Maungwudaus, who had been raised as a traditional Ojibwe, about 1825. For a time he was a very highly respected teacher and put forward as a possible minister, but by 1844 he had left the church, formed a troupe of Ojibwes, and left for Europe to perform.[43]

Peter Jones wrote his *History of the Ojebways* in the 1830s but stopped working on it by 1845, apparently too ill and too busy to finish it. In 1861, five years after his death, his widow, Eliza, assembled and edited the book for publication.[44] As Jace Weaver notes in *That the People Might Live*, Jones is "still widely regarded as a fully assimilated Christian Indian, thoroughly absorbed into dominant cultural structures" (59). Nevertheless, Weaver maintains, Jones's criticism of whites is clear, and he worked for the autonomy of Ojibwe people within the British government of Canada all of his life. Weaver writes that Jones's work exemplifies what he calls "communitism" in Native writing, writing that "has a proactive commitment to Native community, including . . . the 'wider community' of Creation itself" (xiii). Jones's criticism of whites is indeed straightforward, and he unequivocally refuses the narrative of Indians' providential disappearance, writing in his *History*, "I cannot suppose for a moment that the Supreme Disposer has decreed that the doom of the red man is to fall and gradually disappear, like the mighty wilderness, before the axe of the European settler" (29). The problem for Jones is that the Indians must be converted to Christianity in order to survive; he sees everything within the framework of a superior and monolithic Christianity. Unlike Apess, for example, he cannot bring himself—or, perhaps, his wife and editor cannot bring herself—to include any criticism of Christians or the agents of Christianity for their behavior toward Indians. He views the Ojibwes as being on a path to spiritual progress, and there is no redeeming value whatsoever in any element of their pagan past, at least in what he writes explicitly. He dismisses Ojibwe traditional knowledge, writing, "From all that can be gathered from the wise old Sachems and their traditions [on the matter of Ojibwe origins], it appears that their notions as to their origins are little better than a mass of confusion" (36). Every element of their traditional practice evidences their inferiority. In contradistinction to comments of William Warren and George Copway on the topic, Jones maintains that the Ojibwes are only hunters who have "no settled home" (71). Their ideas on death and the soul, he concludes, are "confused and absurd" (102). As to their religion, "the poor dark-minded Indian ignorantly worships the creatures of his own imagination" (84). His people, he writes, are "deluded" (85).

Jones takes a scorched-earth attitude toward the improvement of Ojibwe people—he writes that he wished "for the time when the game and fur shall be so destroyed as to leave no inducement for [Christian Indians] to abandon their farms and houses" (172). He may not have been a subtle thinker, but he provides an example of why the common characterization of such writers as "assimilationist" is not exactly subtle either. Jones was an admirer of the Cherokees and followed closely their struggle against removal. Like Boudinot in particular, Jones believed that for Indians to move forward in time as Indians, they must be brought up to speed morally and intellectually; his rejection of the political subordination of Indians makes "assimilationist" an inaccurate characterization of his position. At the same time, Jones's *History* bespeaks the possibility that his understanding of the Ojibwe past, and his attachment to it,

Rev. Peter Jones, an accomplished fundraiser for Methodist missionary causes. This portrait was probably made during a British lecture tour in 1837–38. From Peter Jones, History of the Ojebway Indians, *frontispiece. Photograph courtesy of the Edward E. Ayer Collection, Newberry Library, Chicago.*

was more complicated than simple rejection because the book equivocates on the matter of tradition and his relation to it. Unlike Boudinot and Ridge, Jones lived a traditional life until he was an adolescent. This at least raises the possibility that he could not complete his book because he could not reconcile arguing for Native humanity and equality while rejecting wholesale everything the Ojibwes had ever thought or believed. Nevertheless, he provides an illustration of the struggle with radical change that characterizes all of the Ojibwe historians and provides some indication that his connection to traditional knowledge and practices is more complicated than might be perceived at first glance.

Jones shares with Elias Boudinot a certain inflexibility of thought, an apparently complete rejection of anything that departs from the norm of Christianity. At least as far as Jones is willing to state explicitly, there is no redeeming value in Indian beliefs; from there, there is nowhere to go but up, to Christianity. Indians ought not be understood as "far happier in [their] barbarous state than [they] would be as . . . civilized [Christians]," he observes, for those who might want to indulge in romance (91–92). However, Jones argues not that Indians are inherently different but rather that they are morally depraved, which he attributes to their willful behavior. The Indian "certainly knows that it is wrong to commit murder, quarrel, fight, steal, and commit fornication and adultery; but I ask, where is the Indian who ever lived in accordance with this intuitive knowledge of truth?" (92). Education in Christianity, he insists, is the only thing that will save Indian people. "It cannot be expected that the poor untutored Indian can follow the light, when we consider that 'the *light* that is in him is *darkness*,'" he writes, "and that he is under the power and control of the evil spirit, who worketh in the hearts of all the pagan nations of the earth" (92). Everyone, white and Indian alike, needs "the direct aid of the Holy Spirit of God" to resist evil: "If it be difficult for the Christian to follow the good he knows, what must be the utter helplessness of the pagan Indian, who is destitute of all Christian privileges?" (92). Again, even in Jones, the differences between Indians and non-Indians are historical, not essential or inherent. Even when he rejects—apparently—all that can be said to be "Indian" in his past, he has not accepted the notion of Indians' inherent inferiority, as much as he might be exasperated with what he sees as their bad behavior.

Jones's attitude toward Indian government is similarly divided: traditional government is "patriarchal, after the manner of the ancients," but it still exists (108). It is, however, inferior to governments formed by Christians. Chiefs lose power when they lose consensus: "They scarcely have any executive power, and can do but little without the concurrence of the subordinate chiefs and principal men. They have no written code of laws, nor any power to put their people to death by their own will" (109). Nevertheless, he reports, the Ojibwes "are taught by their chiefs and wise men to observe a certain line of conduct, such as to be kind and hospitable. They are also encouraged to be good hunters and warriors, and great pow-wows, or medicine men" (109). Indian governments, though they are still governments, are pagan governments, and it is up to the British to introduce true Christian government. Like William Warren, Jones notes that

Native governments suffered when whites intruded. But, unlike Warren, Jones insists that that disruption was part of the necessary move toward Christian righteousness: "The British Government have taken them under their paternal care; they have been taught to look up with reverence to their great Father, the governor, and the Indian agents. As a consequence, the chiefs have yielded their authority into the hands of more wise and powerful guardians" (110).

As Weaver points out, Jones worked all his life for Ojibwe rights and political autonomy, although within the British government of Canada: the chiefs have to give up authority because they're not—yet—Christians. The "guardianship" exercised over Indian governments is necessary because they are not Christian rather than because Indians are innately, as the U.S. Supreme Court had it, in a permanent state of "pupilage." What they need are their "rights," and like the U.S. Native writers, Jones is not optimistic about the possibility of the Canadian government's recognizing them. "I know of no legal impediment to their possessing [civil] rights; the difficulty lies in the tenure by which they hold their lands," he observes. "It is my firm conviction that many of the Indians are sufficiently instructed in the knowledge of civil affairs to be able to use the rights of British subjects as judiciously as many of their white neighbours. The names and numbers might be inserted were it of any avail" (217–18). While Jones argues that Ojibwes should be recognized as British subjects, he also believes they should be able to govern themselves.

Jones's description of the progress of his always-prone-to-backsliding people would seem to leave no room—no place—for traditional beliefs, and yet they're still present in his book, albeit marginally. For example, at the beginning of his book, he takes the time to relate several "absurd" narratives about thunder when he describes the traditions of his deluded people. The Ojibwes, he writes, "consider the thunder to be a god in the shape of a large eagle that feeds on serpents, which it takes from under the earth and the trunks of hollow trees" (85–86). He adds in a footnote, however, the following personal note:

> I have in my possession two family gods. One is called *Pabookowaih*—the God that crushes or breaks down diseases. The other is a goddess named *Nahneetis*, the guardian of health. This goddess was delivered up to me by Eunice Hank, a Muncey Indian woman, who with her friends used to worship it in their sacred dances, making a feast to it every year, when a fat doe was sacrificed as an offering, and many presents were given by the friends assembled. She told me that she was now restored to worship the Christians' God, and therefore had no further use for it. (87n)

Like David Cusick, Jones collects the artifacts of his own history—which, given his other statements, seems odd for someone who repudiates the past with such vehemence. Jones was never very healthy throughout his life either; one has to wonder, then, why this devout Christian held on to these particular idols, although he is of course silent on this matter.[45] By the mid-1840s, however, Jones, like other Native intellectuals appearing before white audiences, was compelled to dress in appropriate Indian attire, which, as has been noted, he found "odious," a broadside for a lecture in that period promises the exhibition of "several specimens of Heathen Gods and Indian Curiosities."[46] Perhaps the artifacts he mentions in his book are the ones he displayed in order to supply the white audience with the requisite curiosities so that they would contribute to his effort to build schools for Native children in Canada. As much as Jones condemns traditional practices and beliefs, his exact relationship to them remains elusive.

Like all of the other Ojibwe writers, Jones writes about the importance of dreams in Ojibwe religious experience and thought generally. In a passage where he doesn't stop to condemn the beliefs of his own people, Jones relates how "the Indian youth from the age of ten to manhood are encouraged by their parents and the old people to fast": in order to "[gain] favour with some god" (87). The children "rise before the sun, take a piece of charcoal, which they pound to powder, and with it blacken their faces, the girls only blackening the upper part" (87). This is what Jones himself did as a child, as he notes further on. They fast for several days, and "all this time they notice every remarkable event, dream, or supernatural sound; and whichever of these makes the most impression on their minds during their fast, suggests the particular spirit which becomes their personal *munedoo* as long as they live, and in all emergencies and dangers they will call upon him for assistance" (87–88). Jones then repudiates the Ojibwe belief in the "*little gods*," even as he keeps relating the stories about them. He mentions a "pious Indian" named Thomas Magee who spoke at a religious meeting about the many "*munedoos*" he used to worship, "[thanking] the Great Spirit that he had been brought to know the vanity of idol-worship, and that he now worshipped the one true God" (88).

Dreams count as a kind of deluded knowledge.

To dream of seeing an old grey-headed man is taken as a token of long life; or of a pretty woman, that they will be blest with more wives than one. If they happen to dream of sharp-pointed instruments, or anything that is proof against the arrow, tomahawk, or bullet, they fancy themselves protected against the shot of their enemy. When they dream of animals or fowls they imagine they are invested with the power of self-defence as possessed by these creatures. A poor Indian at Lake Huron used to boast that he had obtained the spirit of a bat. (88–89)

Jones relates several stories of the importance of a dreams about personal "little gods" to Ojibwe warriors. And he adds an interesting personal note. As a child, he tried to fast and dream of his "little gods," but it never quite worked out, which it turns out was all for the better. One day, he writes, when he was fasting, he became thirsty and "took a sip of water." "The moment I had done so," he writes, "the thoughtless act filled me with sorrow, and I wept the greater part of the night, fearing that now no munedoo would ever communicate himself to me" (91). He never did, Jones reports. "In all my fastings I never had any vision or dream, and, consequently, obtained no familiar god, nor a spirit of the rank of a pow-wow. What a mercy it is to know that neither our happiness nor success depends upon the supposed possession of these imaginary gods, but that there is *one* only true and living God, whose assistance none ever did, or ever can, seek in vain!" (91). One might indulge in speculation on Jones's interior life here, but there isn't much to go on; for whatever reasons, he—or his editor—doesn't go into detail. It can be said, though, that Jones's writing represents some of the complex effects of historical change on Ojibwe people. Donald Smith points out in his biography of Jones that at about the time Jones would have gone on a vision quest as a boy, the War of 1812 was raging around him and his people. Jones reports visiting a battlefield full of corpses with his brother, and his grandmother, who was lame and unable to be moved, was left behind when the band fled the U.S. attack on Fort York in May 1813 (34–35). "The trauma the Mississaugas experienced around 1800 cannot be overemphasized," Smith writes; this trauma included "the entry of thousands of foreigners, the introduction of frightening new diseases like smallpox, measles, and tuberculosis, the decline of the game population" (36). In that chaos, some Ojibwe people began to repudiate traditional practices and beliefs and turned to Christianity, as Jones himself did. Jones's relation to his own history is more complicated than his habit of denying its validity suggests. Maybe he couldn't reconcile a Native future with the Native past—but maybe he didn't have the opportunity to write it down. Like most of the writers included in this book, his political responsibilities to his nation occupied most of his time.

Peter Jones and William Warren each had a well-defined social position in relation to the subject matter of their books: Jones was a faithful missionary, Warren a knowledgeable interpreter. Copway, on the other hand, is somewhat

Peter Jones in Indian dress, while on tour in 1845 to raise funds for a Native boarding school. Jones detested appearing in costume, which his audiences by the 1840s apparently expected; he wrote to his wife in 1845 complaining of his "odious Indian Costume." Nevertheless, his fundraising speeches were billed as lectures on "the manners, customs, and religion" of the Ojibwes and included exhibitions of "specimens of heathen goods and Indian curiosities" (Smith, Sacred Feathers, 203–4). Calotype portrait by David Octavius Hill and Robert Adamson of Edinburgh; courtesy of Yale Collection of Western Americana, Beinecke Rare Book and Manuscript Library, Yale University.

more complex. As A. LaVonne Brown Ruoff points out, Copway's first book combines ethnology, autobiography, conversion narrative, travel narrative, and history.[47] Indeed, his title suggests the reflections of a well-traveled gentleman of leisure, not the life of a pious Indian missionary. However, he makes the same arguments as Jones and Warren about the autonomy and historicity of the Ojibwes, and, like them and the other writers included in this book, he argues that the current state of Native peoples in the United States was the result not of the inherent difference and inferiority of Native peoples but the result of willful, deceitful actions of whites.

Where he departs from Jones and Warren, and perhaps picks up from William Apess, is in his portrait of the radical change suffered by the Ojibwes, the violent transition that they must make when faced with modernity and its effects. In fact, Copway's description of the conflict between tradition and Christianity may shed some light on Jones's comments on tradition in his book. Many critics seem to enjoy ganging up on Copway, mocking his sentiment, questioning his psychological state, and his sentimental and wrenching accounts of his own participation in converting other Ojibwes to Christianity make him an easy target.[48] In his *Life, Letters, and Speeches*, he includes repeated scenes of his participation in the destruction of his fellow Ojibwes' beliefs and spirituality in order to convert them to Christianity. One critic argues that Copway suffered from a "lack of psychological and cultural coherence," that his writing "conveys little real sense of Copway as 'one of Nature's children,' the description he proffers in his opening self-presentation" in *Life*, an assessment that other critics share.[49] Copway is not a model Indian: he's separated from his nation through his own improprieties, and he is not particularly on the forefront of political battles, despite his plan for an Indian territory—which he named after himself. He seems to have been a man with a knack for self-promotion. Rather than assailing him for not knowing who he is, we should pay attention to what Copway had to say about his experiences. He leaves a record of living and thinking at a point of radical change for Native peoples, a change that was difficult enough for people to live through, more difficult still to represent in English.

Copway's *Life* is the history of himself—his own and his family's conversion to Christianity, his efforts as a missionary, his travels in the eastern United States, and himself as the exemplary Indian converting to Christianity and EuroAmerican society. He leaves out of his story the fact that before it was published, in 1846, Copway had been ousted from his position as a Methodist missionary in Canada on being accused of financial improprieties at two different missions. Born in 1818, Copway was from the Rice Lake band of Ojibwes or

Portrait of George Copway made at Philadelphia's leading daguerreotype studio and published in the second edition of his book Life, Letters, and Speeches of Kah-ge-ga-gah-bowh *(1847). The book went through seven reprintings during its first year. From* George Copway, Life, Letters, and Speeches, *frontispiece. Photograph courtesy of the Edward E. Ayer Collection, Newberry Library, Chicago.*

Mississaugas, who lived on Lake Ontario—a band that, Donald Smith points out, William Warren considered not truly Ojibwe. By 1825, whites had begun settling in the area, and Peter Jones had arrived at Rice Lake accompanied by other Native missionaries, who converted Copway's father, then his mother. The missionaries started a school at Rice Lake that Copway attended as a child before his own conversion after his mother's death in 1830. He was a good student and a pious child. By 1834, along with several other Ojibwe converts, he went to Minnesota to be a missionary among the Ojibwes. After being assigned to various stations, including a period spent at La Pointe, where he translated two portions of the Gospel that were later published in Boston with Rev. Sherman Hall, an ABCFM missionary, Copway was sent to a missionary school in Illinois, which the church financed, in 1837. On graduating in late 1839, he decided to go back to Rice Lake. On his return to Canada, he met and married Elizabeth Howell, the daughter of a farmer. Peter Jones performed the ceremony at his Credit River mission. From 1839 to 1842, Copway and Elizabeth were missionaries in Minnesota, again in territory between the warring Ojibwes and Dakotas. After returning to Canada in 1842, Copway, by then Peter Jones's protégé, was sent to missionary stations in Canada, where he got into financial trouble, first at Walpole Island on Lake St. Clair, and then at Saugeen mission on Lake Huron, where in 1845, he failed to account for 125 pounds of the mission's money and was charged with embezzlement. Eventually, because he was unable to pay his debts—the money he "misappropriated"—Copway went to prison in Toronto. He was released when the Indian Department decided it would cost too much to prosecute him. The Canadian Methodist church then expelled him. The next record of Copway is in December 1846, when he registered the publication of his book under the title *The Life, History, and Travels, of Kah-ge-ga-gah-bowh (George Copway), a Young Indian Chief of the Ojebwa Nation, A Convert to the Christian Faith, and a Missionary to His People for Twelve Years.*[50]

Copway is an intriguingly self-invented character, but rather than speculate on his psychological state, it is more useful, I think, to consider what it was he had to say about the confrontation between tradition and modernity as it was experienced by Ojibwe people in the early nineteenth century. In Copway's account, Christianity and education are the means of restoring order to a society under attack. Christianity's emphasis on temperance provided a structure for rejecting alcohol, and education provided a means—literacy—of resisting the colonial bureaucracy. In his *Life*, Copway recounts how his father became friendly with the white settlers and "learned the manners, customs, and worship of the [settler] nation" (16). (Copway uses both the terms "white" and "settler.") "And I know the day when he used to shake the hand of the white man, and *very friendly*, the white man would say, '*take some whiskey*' " (16). Copway's father does not abandon alcohol until he becomes a Christian. "If Christianity had not come," Copway writes, "and the grace of God had not take possession of his heart, his head would soon have been laid low beneath the fallen leaves of the forest, and I, left, in my youthful days, an orphan" (17). At gatherings for the purpose of distributing annuity payments, alcohol had not only personal but also political effects when settlers and traders swindled Indians of their money (127–28). Copway's description of the social effects of alcohol and Christianity's effects on alcohol use cannot be dismissed as religious sentimentality. At a Methodist "centenary tea party," an Ojibwe chief tells how he was converted and how it affected his life: "Now, I drink *tea* instead of *whiskey*, and have religion with it; now my house is comfortable; and my children are pious and happy. I expect to pursue a Christian course till I arrive in heaven" (100). This type of scene might be read as a capitulation to colonialism, and the influence of Christianity inevitably causes serious conflicts that Copway's writing inadvertently makes evident, but Copway's objectives must first be recognized. He argues throughout his writing that were Ojibwe people able to achieve social stability, they would not abandon each other or the Ojibwe Nation but would instead fight to remain together on territory.

Copway's religious conversion has as much to do with education as with Christianity. While his parents had been converted earlier than he had, and he had apparently begun attending a mission school, Copway describes being converted himself at a camp meeting in the summer of 1830, in which "several hundred" other Indians were also converted. Before his conversion, Copway writes, "I had only begun to spell and read. I now resumed my studies with a new and different relish. Often, when alone, I prayed that God would help me to qualify myself to teach others how to read the word of God; this circumstance I had not told to anyone. On Sabbath mornings I read a chapter in the New Testament, which had been translated for my father, before we went to meeting" (63). At the beginning of his narrative, Copway writes, "I loved the woods, and the chase. I had the nature for it, and gloried in nothing else. The mind for letters was in me *but was asleep*, till the dawn of Christianity arose, and awoke the slumbers of the soul into energy and action" (11). The combination of Christianity and education might make for a kind of utilitarian approach to the advancement of the Ojibwe Nation, and indeed, passages of Copway's works certainly read that way. Christianity and education are inseparable in the Ojibwe struggle against colonialism: "When we have a press of our own, we shall, perhaps, be able to plead our own cause. Give us but the *Bible*, and the influence of a *Press*, and we ask no more" (141).

At the same time, in dramatizing the meeting of Christianity and Ojibwe traditions, Copway inadvertently describes the will of many Native peoples to hold onto their beliefs as well as the severity of the social disruption that would cause them to give up those beliefs. Ojibwe tradition and Christianity battle one another, as when, at a mission near Aunce Bay, Ojibwes who had gathered in the spring to visit a leader named Spear Maker "for the purpose of uniting with him in dancing, and in their medicine worship," on finding out that Spear Maker had converted to Christianity "sent word to all, that they could excel us in worshiping in the Great Spirit and that they intended to hold their regular spring Grand Medicine Worship. Every night we held meetings. They commenced with their *paw-wahs* (singing), and beating of drums on the other side of the bay, and continued it for a whole week. We kept up our usual meetings; and at the end of the week, their drumming, singing, and dancing ceased. We continued our meetings for two months. The Chief of this place, was yet unconverted" (73). Copway's descriptions of his own assault on Ojibwe traditions in *Life* are disturbing, although, as I argue below, Copway himself cannot ultimately deny the importance of those traditions. In relation to his missionary activities, however, Copway pays a great deal of attention to scenes of Ojibwe conversion in which a recalcitrant Indian gives up his or her traditions by emptying out a medicine bag. He repeats a story told by John Sunday, another Ojibwe convert and preacher: "He mentioned . . . an instance of an Indian who brought his medicine sack with him to the meeting, but on being converted, he scattered its contents to the four winds of heaven. These sacks were held very sacred among the Indians" (64). Unlike his settler contemporaries, the ethnologists and historians to whom a medicine bag was not unknown, Copway knows just how important this medicine is in the lives of Ojibwe people, describing the Grand Medicine Lodge rituals and noting their importance in both his *Life* and *Traditional History and Characteristic Sketches of the Ojibway Nation*.

Spear Maker himself had been a particularly difficult conversion project for the missionaries. According to Copway, Spear Maker, like "many of the unconverted," is "very revengeful." The difference between Copway's use of the stereotype and settlers' use of it is that in Copway's tale, Indians change, whereas in settlers' representations of Indians the stereotypically vengeful Indian is proof that Indians cannot change and should be dispossessed. "*Kah-be-wag-be-ko-kay*, i.e., Spear Maker, threatened to tomahawk us," Copway writes, "if we should come to his wigwam 'with the white man's religion'; 'for,' said he, 'already some of my family are very sick and crazy' " (70). Although Copway does not tell why Spear Maker's family is "sick and crazy," the possible reasons are evident. Copway and the other missionaries succeed in converting Spear Maker's children, although Spear Maker himself resists for some time, until one day when Spear Maker is sick he wants Copway to come and pray with him. "He could not speak; but sat sobbing and sighing over the fire. We conversed with him, and then left him; but before breakfast he entered our house with his large medicine sack containing little gods of almost every description. He stood before us, and said '*Ah bay, ah was ah yah mook*,'—here, take this. He cast the bag, or sack, down upon the floor, and wept and sobbed bitterly, saying, 'I have done all that I could against you, but you have been my friends. I want you to pray for me, and to burn these gods, or throw them where I can never see them' " (70–72). In another melodramatic scene of Ojibwe destruction and conversion, Copway describes an Ojibwe woman's dedication to Christianity: "an old Indian woman of about eighty years" named Anna, unable to walk, crawls to a camp meeting (73). "Before her conversion," Copway notes, "she was a celebrated conjurer, and a dread to the nation; every one was afraid to incur her displeasure. The last time I saw her, was in 1842, and she was still confiding in the Lord" (74).

What Copway attempts to destroy in Ojibwe people, their "traditions," is also the basis of his own efforts toward poetry, and it is his desire for the literary that particularly forces the contradictions of his thinking to the surface. The contradictions manifest themselves not only in terms of the narrative—as above, in his attempts to explain Ojibwe life and beliefs as valid while he also destroys the mainstays of those beliefs in the conversion scenes—but also in terms of the language available to convey his experience. Copway believes in his own worth—and by extension, that of Indian people generally—as a thinking, experiencing being, no different, essentially, from anyone else, but his narrative consistently returns to the difficulty of finding a means of writing his experience that does not ultimately deny that experience. In describing Ojibwe society and beliefs, he remains an unrepentant Ojibwe nationalist: "As far as I am able to learn, our nation has never been conquered; and have maintained their ground wherever they have conquered" (44). He describes their defeat of the Sacs, the Hurons, and the Iroquois, indicating that the power of the Ojibwes caused even the formation of the League of the Iroquois (45).[51] He describes Ojibwe government, including treaty-making between the Ojibwes and other Indian nations (45–46). These observations lead to a description of the "*future state* of the Ojebwas" in which Copway follows his more evocative commentary on Indian experience with remarks on Indians' pre-Christian "delusion":

> The favored warrior entered the fields of paradise, amidst the shouts and welcome of his fellow warriors, who had preceded him to this land of plenty. The deer, the moose, the elk, and all kinds of animals, fruits, flowers, and the singing of birds fill and charm the land. While the ever rolling valleys are visited with delightful and refreshing winds. To kill, eat, and shoot, are their only employments. No sickness, no fatigue, no death, will ever visit them. The valleys and the mounts are to be clothed with evergreens. No winter to chill the earth. A carnal heaven indeed! A sensual paradise! Oh! the credulous and misguided Indian. (47–48)

Copway employs inflated sentimental rhetoric to describe the lost world of the Indians but by the end of the passage must make sure to condemn Indians for being so misguided, which would seem to be a violation of sentimental conventions. The sentimental Indian exists in a fantasy world without connection to historic events or the lives of actual Indians; the point is for the white reader to *enjoy* the idealized description of Indian life. No one condemns Indians in sentimental stories for being deluded. Copway is a contradictory figure because of who he is and what he is trying to do with writing. In his life, Copway's Christianity causes him to destroy his own society, at least in his autobiography, but, ironically, his literary ambitions are centered on representing that very society. The only literary imagery available for him to describe his experience essentially denies that an Indian could produce literature in the first place or that his experience even exists. Copway's best and most effective writing is when he breaks through this impasse, as in his description of Spear Maker's despair.

The sentimental depiction of the "credulous and misguided Indian" leads Copway to a well-known passage from Alexander Pope's *Essay on Man* (1733):

> Lo! the poor Indian whose untutored mind,
> Sees God in clouds, or hears him in the wind;
> Whose soul proud science never taught to stray
> Beyond the solar walk or milky way.
> Yet simple nature to his hopes has given,
> Beyond the cloud top'd hill, a humble heaven,
> Some safer world in depths of woods embrace,

Some distant Island in the watery waste.
Where slaves once more their native land behold,
Nor fiends torment, nor Christian thirsts for gold. (48)

Copway leaves out the concluding lines of this stanza: "He asks no angel's wing, no seraph's fire; / But thinks, admitted to that equal sky, / His faithful dog shall bear him company" (3.110–12). He would have had to edit. Pope writes about the order of the English Enlightenment universe, where Indians are man in a state of nature, and despite the common notion that "human nature is the same everywhere," that order cannot be violated by one who steps out of his place, as Copway does. The fact that he considers his dog his equal in the afterlife marks the Indian as inhabiting the lowest state of humanity. For Copway, however, the Indian's supposed "untutored mind" has a meaning entirely different from that in Pope's poem, since Indians' "untutored" state was to Copway temporary, one which could be remedied, while for Pope the notion established Indians' permanent inferiority. "The thought of *perishing!* how *insufferable!* O how *intolerable!*," Copway writes. When he invokes the sentimentality of nineteenth-century Protestant Christianity and the imagery of Indian doom, he necessarily, if not consciously, changes the meaning of the words, since for him the point really was that Indians should *not* perish (49).

In the summer of 1839, at the end of his two years of missionary training at Jacksonville, Illinois, Copway traveled through several U.S. cities before returning home to Rice Lake. He visited Chicago, Detroit, Buffalo, Rochester, Albany, New York, Newark, Providence, and Boston, among other cities, seeing the sights and relying on the kindness of Christian clergy, who invited him to preach and gave him books (92). Although he found Boston "much overrated" (it is "far behind New York, Philadelphia, and perhaps Baltimore, and New Orleans"), he stayed two weeks (94–95). Copway preaches and visits the Bunker Hill Monument and State House, from which he looks out over the "works of the white man"—wharves, steamboats, towns, railroads, factories—and thinks "of the noble race of red men who once lived and roamed in all the land, and upon the waters as far as my eye could reach" (95). "The following thoughts arose in my mind," he adds, "which I have since penned":

Once more I see my fathers' land
  Upon the beach, where oceans roar;
Where whiten'd bones bestrew the sand,
  Of some brave warrior of yore.

The *groves* where once my fathers roam'd—
    The *rivers*, where the beaver dwelt—
The *lakes*, where angry waters foam'd—
    Their *charms*, with my fathers, have fled.

O! tell me, ye "pale faces," tell,
    Where have my proud ancestors gone?
Whose smoke curled up from every dale,
    To what land have their free spirits flown?
Whose wigwam stood where cities rise;

On whose war-paths the steam-horse flies;
    And ships, like mon-e-doos in disguise,
Approach the shore in endless files. (95–96)

When an Indian writer asks the question "Where have my proud ancestors gone?" the question is not merely sentimental rhetoric, the point of which is to establish what EuroAmericans ought to feel without their having to actually do anything. If Copway were to answer that question himself, he would be forced to confront the contradictions in his own thinking. "Ships like mon-e-doos in disguise" begins to approach these contradictions (the common modern spelling is "manitou"). That the ships descend like spirits pushes Copway's use of the doomed Indian theme into an invocation of Ojibwe knowledge assaulted by settlement. Settlers might be "happy in the Lord," but in their concerted action they attempt to destroy Indian people, who do not inevitably recede but who are rather quite able to name and criticize settlers' actions.

WILLIAM WARREN'S TRIBAL KNOWLEDGE

Like Jane Schoolcraft, William Warren was from a fur-trading family. He was born in 1825 at La Pointe on Lake Superior, where John Johnston moved after his marriage to establish himself in the fur trade. Warren's family was Ojibwe and French on his mother's side and English on his father's. His mother is described as "three-fourths Indian," and like the Johnston children, he spoke Ojibwe fluently. The oldest of eight children, Warren attended mission schools in La Pointe and then boarding schools in New York, where his father was from, including the Oneida Institute, which was run by an antislavery minister. In 1841, when he was sixteen, he returned home to become a government interpreter in Michigan—like Jane Schoolcraft's brothers. He married the daughter of another fur trader in 1842 at age eighteen; his health began to fail soon thereafter. By 1845, he had moved to Minnesota and had begun supplementing his government duties with farming; he was elected to the Minnesota territorial legislature in the fall of 1850.[52] In a biographical essay included in the 1885 edition of his *History of the Ojibway People*, J. Fletcher Williams reported that people who knew Warren described him as a story-teller. Williams writes that Warren "was fond . . . of telling the Indians stories which he had learned in his reading, and would for hours translate to them narratives from the Bible, and Arabian Nights, fairy stories, and other tales calculated to interest them. In return for this, they would narrate the legends of their race."[53] After Warren joined the legislature, he met the publisher of the *Minnesota Democrat*, Colonel D. A. Robertson of St. Paul, who asked him how he had discovered the "Ojibwa myths" that Warren had often told him. Robertson explained in a letter to Williams that Warren had told him the stories were "from the old men of the tribe, and that he would go considerable distances sometimes to see them—that they always liked to talk with him about those matters, and that he would make notes of the principal points. He said this was a favorite pastime and pursuit of his. He had not at this time, it seems, attempted to write out anything connected, and the matter which he had written down was not much more than notes, or memoranda" (15). Robertson asked Warren to write down some of these stories, which he published in the *Democrat* in several articles beginning in February 1851. The articles were popular, and Robertson encouraged Warren to write a book: "I finally suggested to him that if he would gather them [the stories] up, and with the other material which he had, work them into a book, it would sell readily, and possibly secure him some profits. The idea seemed to please him, and I am certain it never occurred to him before. He at once set about it, and from time to time when I saw him during the next two years, he assured me he was making good progress. At this period he was in poor health and much discouraged at times, suffering from occasional hemorrhages, as well as from financial straitness" (16). When he finished his book in 1852, he traveled to New York to find a publisher as well as a doctor for himself.

In 1885, Warren's biographer describes the book as if it were a collection of quaint or thrilling frontier Indian stories, but the book is not at all like that. It is instead a serious work of history in which Warren violated every convention for writing about Indians. Unlike the other writers included in this book, he had no credentials as a Christian missionary to offset this violation. In *History of the Ojibway Nation, Based upon Traditions and Oral Statements*, Warren says explicitly about Ojibwe tradition what Jones only implies and Copway generally just touches on. Like Jones and Copway, he invokes the difference and doom rhetoric while rejecting the notion of inherent difference. He disputes the misrepresentation of Indians and insists on the authority of tradition and the historicity of the Ojibwes. The last is the element I want to address here, as Warren's entire book is an argument for both. Unlike Copway and Jones, he is not writing an autobiographical conversion narrative, and so does not have the imperative to demonstrate the superiority of Christianity relative to the progress of the Ojibwe people. This in a sense frees him to address directly how the Ojibwes perceive their own history.

Warren offers himself, and specifically the connection of his family, his blood relations, as the means through which he claims valid knowledge of the Ojibwes, although his use of the biological connection is at best ambiguous and is for the most part defined historically and socially. He takes on "eminent authors" who have already written about the "red race" (which includes Schoolcraft, whose work he disputes in several instances), directly and indirectly. He maintains that their information comes only from "transient sojourners" who, "not having a full knowledge of their character and language, have obtained information through mere temporary observation—through the medium of careless and imperfect interpreters, or have taken the accounts of unreliable persons" (24). Warren's blood connection gives him a social connection to the Ojibwes, which allows for more accurate—but not complete—knowledge. On his mother's side, he writes, his ancestors "have been in close connection with this tribe for the past one hundred and fifty years" (25). He speaks the language "perfectly" and is "connected with them through the strong ties of blood" (25). Moreover, "he has ever felt a deep interest in their welfare and fate, and has deemed it a duty to save their traditions from oblivion, and to collect every fact concerning them, which the advantages he possesses have enabled him to procure" (25). His work, he writes, "does claim to be one of truth, and the first work written from purely Indian sources, which has probably ever been presented to the public" (26). On this count, it's not surprising that he couldn't find a publisher.

The book begins with the present location of the Ojibwes, their division into totems, their origins, the "me-da-we" religion, their account of their migration to their settlement at La Pointe on Lake Superior, where they first came into contact with Europeans, their dispersal from La Pointe in the aftermath, and then their history of wars with the Dakotas through the U.S. Treaty of Fond du Lac in 1826. Throughout, Warren continually returns to the theme of whites not having access to Native knowledge. He maintains that Indians don't tell whites everything and that whites cannot assume the superiority of their

William Whipple Warren died in 1853 at the age of twenty-eight, shortly after returning from an unsuccessful trip to New York City to find a publisher for his History of the Ojibway Nation. *He was at the time a representative to the Minnesota territorial legislature. Photograph courtesy of the Minnesota Historical Society.*

knowledge. "I have taken much pains to inquire and made use of every advantage, possessed by speaking their language perfectly, being related to them, possessing their friendship and intimate confidence," but even with his intimate knowledge, Warren admits, "I frankly acknowledge that I stand as yet, as it were, on the threshold of the Me-da-we lodge" (65–66). Still, he insists that he "has full as much and more general and true information on this matter than any other person who has written on this matter, not excepting a great and standard author [this would be Schoolcraft] who, to the surprise of many who know the Ojibways well, has boldly asserted in one of his works that he has been regularly initiated into the mysteries of this rite, and is a member of the Me-da-we Society" (66). "This is certainly an assertion hard to believe in the Indian country," Warren continues, "and when the old initiators or Indian priests are told of it, they shake their heads in incredulity that a white man should ever have been allowed *in truth* to become a member of the Me-da-we lodge" (66).

Warren's account of Ojibwe knowledge is notable for what he says that he doesn't know and information to which he says he does not have access, as well as for his insistence on the validity of Ojibwe knowledge, even though he distinguishes between the "vague and figurative traditions" of the Ojibwes and the "accurate history" of the European written tradition (76). Given the way in which Warren describes Ojibwe knowledge, the distinction becomes one of kind, not of validity. Warren's account of Ojibwe origins, for example, begins with the history that he is able to surmise from what he understands of the "Me-da-we-gaun" ceremonies or Grand Medicine Lodge (77). He writes of standing outside of the lodge while the people inside perform ceremonies, which he describes as well as he can. Warren is both honest about his own lack of knowledge and critical of those scholars, like Schoolcraft, who claim total knowledge for themselves while denying the validity of Ojibwe knowledge.

> As I partially understood, and could therefore appreciate, the meaning and objects of their strange ceremonies, and could partially understand their peculiar religious idiom, I stood, watched, and listened with a far deeper interest than could be felt in the mind of a mere casual observer, who is both unacquainted with the objects of the rites or the language of these simple children of nature, and who, in his greater wisdom, deems it but the unmeaning mummery and superstitious rites of an ignorant race, buried in heathenish darkness. (77–78)

Warren then seeks out a priest, who gives him a more explicit story about the travels of the Ojibwes from the Atlantic Coast to the Great Lakes. The priest tells him that on the East Coast, "while congregated in a great town, and while they were suffering the ravages of sickness and death, the Great Spirit, at the intercession of Man-ab-o-sho, the great common uncle of the An-ish-in-aub-ag, granted them this rite wherewith life is restored and prolonged" (79). After that, the Ojibwes began their move west. Warren writes that "it is only from such religious and genuine traditions that the fact is to be ascertained" (80). He notes that "the common class of the tribe . . . when asked where they originally came from, make answer that they originated from Mo-ning-wuna-kaun-ing (La Pointe), and the phrase is often used in their speeches to the whites, that 'Mo-ning-wuna-kaun-ing' is the spot on which the Ojibway tribe first grew, and like a tree it has spread its branches in every direction" (80). "A superficial inquirer would be easily misled by these assertions," Warren writes, "and it is only through such vague and figurative traditions as the one we have related, that any degree of certainty can be arrived at" (81). As Daniel Butrick observed to John Howard Payne, not every Indian can account for his or her history accurately.

Warren's account of the Ojibwes' telling of their own history is remarkable for the lack of white people in it, even though it concerns Ojibwe history after contact with whites. For the most part, the bulk of Warren's history addresses ongoing conflicts between the Ojibwes and the Dakotas over land in central and western Minnesota. The presence of white people is apparently not the most important element to the Ojibwes themselves. Warren collects "the annals of this tribe" from "the old men from home," some of whom attribute the dispersion of the Ojibwes from La Pointe to having obtained guns from whites to the east, which enabled them to attack their enemies to the west, the Dakotas and Fox, and to settle farther inland (108). This allows them, Warren writes, to "better . . . get over this fearful portion of their history," in which their society suffered almost total breakdown and chaos (109). Others of the old men, however, attribute the westward movement, which was "sudden and entire," to the fact that "the Evil Spirit had found a strong foothold amongst them, during the latter years of their residence" at La Pointe (109). The truth is then even more unsettling: "Evil practices became in vogue.—Horrid feasts on human flesh became a custom. It is said by my informants, that the medicine men of this period had come to a knowledge of the most subtle poisons, and they revenged the least affront with certain death" (109). Warren does not describe a prepolitical state of nature that naturally degenerates on account of contact with whites but rather a more complicated scenario of social break-down—and there had to be order before the disorder—in which whites themselves may or may not have been the motivating cause. He maintains that he is writing his history from the perspective of the Ojibwes themselves; the story he writes is one of a society that becomes disordered and needs to be put back into order, but that disorder is not explained entirely in terms of whites.

The Ojibwes' history of their own experience after European settlement, Warren maintains, can be favorably compared with the written tradition of whites. "So far as their own tribe is concerned, the Ojibways have preserved accurate and detailed accounts" of their contact with whites; "the information which their old men orally give on this subject, is worthy of much consideration, although they may slightly differ from the accounts which standard historians and writers have presented to the world" (113). Even though "standard historians and writers," who rely on the firsthand accounts of Jesuit missionaries and various adventurers and traders are "more reliable and authentic than the oral traditions of the Indians," the Ojibwes' own accounts of themselves are still valid, since "we have undertaken to write their history as they themselves tell it" (113). Further, "the writer is disposed to consider as true and perfectly reliable, the information which he has obtained and thoroughly investigated, on this subject" (114). Warren takes time to dispute conclusions about the first contact between Ojibwes and whites written by both George Catlin and George Bancroft, pointing out that Bancroft's account, in his ever-expanding *History of the United States*, "is not altogether corroborated by the Ojibways" (115).

Despite the minimal presence of white people in the Ojibwes' conception of their own history, Warren himself describes the "contact" between Europeans and Ojibwes, in which he tells a story not of inevitable degeneration but of coexistence on the part of the French and failed coexistence on the part of the British and Americans. His account of "contact" is one of explicitly political relations, and his criticism of the Americans is on the count of their undermining of Ojibwe government. Moreover, the success or failure of EuroAmerican coexistence with Native peoples depends on EuroAmericans' ability to adapt themselves and recognize the authority of Native governments.

The Ojibways learned to love the French people, for the Frenchmen, possessing a character of great plasticity, easily assimilated themselves to the customs and mode of life of their red brethren. They respected their religious rites and ceremonies, and they "never laughed" at their superstitious beliefs and ignorance. They fully appreciated, and honored accordingly, the many noble traits and qualities possessed by these bold and wild hunters of the forest. . . . It is probable that their character in many respects was more similar, and adapted to the character of the Indian, than any other European nation. (132)

While the French incorporate themselves into Ojibwe political organization, the British and the Americans who come after them seek to undermine it. The French, Warren writes, were careful to "conform . . . to their system of governmental polity, of which the totemic division formed the principal ingredient. They were circumspect and careful in bestowing medals, flags, and other marks of honor, and appointing chiefs, and these acts were never done unless being first certain of the approbation of the tribe, and it being in accordance with their civil polity" (135). The British and Americans, however, both government officials and the traders themselves, "have appointed chiefs indiscriminately or only in conformity with selfish motives and ends, and there is nothing which had conduced so much to disorganize, confuse, and break up the former simple but well-defined civil polity of these people" (135). Echoing William Apess, Warren observes that the entire disorganization of Native societies is the result of EuroAmericans meddling in various ways in Native governments. "Utter disorganization" is "one of the chief stumbling-blocks which has ever been in the way of doing good to the Indian race," he writes (135).

The book ends with this account of the Treaty of Fond du Lac in 1826:

At the treaty . . . the United States commissioners recognized the chiefs of the Ojibways, by distributing medals amongst them, the size of which were in accordance with their degree of rank. Sufficient care was not taken in this rather delicate operation, to carry out the pure civil polity of the tribe. Too much attention was paid to the recommendation of interested traders who wished their best hunters to be rewarded by being made chiefs. One young man named White Fisher, was endowed with a medal, solely for the strikingly mild and pleasant expression of his face. He is now a petty sub-chief on the Upper Mississippi. From this time may be dated the commencement of the innovations which have entirely broken up the civil polity of the Ojibways. (393–94)

The practice of the United States of recognizing the members of a foreign nation most amenable to its own policies only serves to systematically destroy Native government. When "the tribe is without a head or government," Warren notes, it "has become infinitely difficult to treat with them as a people" (135). As the governments are undermined, so are the treaties that are supposed to recognize those governments undermined, a situation that, he points out, resulted in "the Creek, Seminole, and Black Hawk wars" (135).

SENTIMENT AND PERFORMANCE

The painter George Catlin's exhibitions and publications in the late 1830s and 1840s mark the explosion of the display of Indians in U.S. popular culture. Catlin spent, as his promotional material always pointed out, eight years among the Indians in the West, in Indian Territory, St. Louis, and elsewhere, painting mainly portraits, and in 1839 he organized his first exhibitions of what he called his Indian Gallery. He hung the pictures, most of them the same size, row upon row, like a giant catalog on four walls. He also gave lectures on the manners and customs of the Indians, the famous warriors he had met, and his adventures. The gallery was enormously popular; it toured eastern cities, and then Catlin moved it to Europe, where he remained through most of the 1840s. The portraits in some respects provided the audience a representation of the "Indian mind" that Schoolcraft described in *Algic Researches*. One newspaper reported that "we have visited [the Indian Gallery] repeatedly, and have studied its contents, with close attention, as the best exposition of savage character and life that has ever been given to the world. . . . The hardships of Indian existence are brought before us with a bold effect; the few refinements by which it is comforted, are impressively presented: the labors by which it is sustained are shown; and the romance which makes it charming, is brilliantly and copiously exhibited."[54] Presumably, this is what white people went to these displays or performances of Indians to experience and it is what caused them to buy books afterward.

Like Catlin, George Copway and Maungwudaus were entrepreneurs: both made livings, briefly, as Indian performers, although they had different approaches. There seems to be little information on Maungwudaus; he took his troupe to Europe in 1845, joined up with Catlin's Indian Gallery, and visited the great cities. He published accounts of his experiences to be sold at the shows, one in England and another in Boston, after the troupe returned from Europe in 1848. These were his only published works, and after his troupe appeared in Toronto and Cleveland in 1851, there is little record of him—other than, Smith notes, the 1889 obituary for one of his sons, which describes his son, Saigitoo, as a "medicine man" and the "son of the well known Indian doctor Maungwudaus."[55] The obituary also notes that "Saigitoo had just visited Urquhart's Medical Hall in Oakville with 'a full supply of medicines from his father's recipes.' "[56]

While Maungwudaus, as an Indian performer among whites, took perhaps the most established route toward making a living, Copway followed a different path. The publication history of his books and the many notices of him in newspapers and journals between 1847 and 1851 suggest that his capacity to promote himself was quite remarkable. His autobiography was published first in Albany in early 1847 (it was registered in December 1846), and the second edition, published in Philadelphia also in 1847 (probably in the fall), included a daguerreotype frontispiece by the city's best studio; letters from reputable citizens to the publisher, James Harmstead, attesting to the significance of the book; and reviews and several pages of hymns in English and Ojibwe. As has been noted, Copway altered the title from *Life, History, and Travels of Kah-ge-ga-gah-bowh* to *Life, Letters and Speeches of Kah-ge-ga-gah-bowh*, both of which bespeak a genteel literary milieu, not savages on the frontier or pious Indians converting to Christianity. Between 1847 and 1848, the book went through seven printings and Copway became well known. In 1847, he introduced himself to Longfellow, who wrote in his journal about taking Copway to see a statue of a dying Indian and a lecture by Louis Agassiz on the inherent inferiority of all people other than whites; he knew historian Francis Parkman (who soon soured on him); and the ethnologist and self-styled archaeologist Ephraim George Squier refers to Copway as an authority on Ojibwe tradition in several articles published in the *American Whig Review* in 1848. Copway himself published an essay on his plan for an Indian Territory in that same journal in 1849, as well as a story called "The Two Cousins" in *Graham's Monthly Magazine of Literature, Art and Fashion*. In addition to giving lectures on temperance, by 1849, he was lecturing on Indian traditions and his plan for an Indian Territory. Longfellow recorded his attendance at Copway's lectures in his journal; he reports that Copway gave "a rambling talk, gracefully delivered, with a fine various voice, and a chief's costume, with little bells jangling upon it, like the bells and pomegranates of the Jewish priests." In 1850, Copway published under his own name *The Ojibway Conquest*, a long narrative poem written by someone else. Also in that year, through his new well-connected friends, he finagled an invitation to the International Peace Conference in Frankfurt, and he spent time in the summer and fall traveling in Europe. After he returned to the United States, he published *Traditional History and Characteristic Sketches of the Ojibway Nation*, with illustrations by F. O. C. Darley, the most popular illustrator in mid-nineteenth-century U.S publishing, who had illustrated the books of Poe, Dickens, Cooper, Irving, Longfellow, and Hawthorne. He includes some of Warren's articles from the *Minnesota Democrat* in his book. In the summer of 1851, he began publishing his short-lived newspaper, *Copway's American Indian*. His eponymous news-paper joined another being published at the same time: after a break with the Garrisonian antislavery movement sometime in the spring of 1851, Frederick Douglass had changed the title of the newspaper he published in Rochester, New York, from *The North Star* to *Frederick Douglass's Own*. Much of the content of Copway's newspaper was given over to unattributed essays on such topics as "The Coliseum at Rome," "China As It Is," and "Feeling and Poverty," as well as columns on "Art News" ("Jesse Talbot has finished a large landscape, of the headwaters of the Nile") and "New Music" ("We have this week the following pieces of Music from the publishers, William Hall & Son, Broad-way"). Copway also printed material on Indians, some of it written by himself but much of it reprinted from elsewhere, but for the most part, the inspiration for putting his name in the title of his newspaper may owe more to *Ned Buntline's Own* than to Frederick Douglass. Buntline was one of the founders of what came to be called the Know-Nothing Party, which surfaced in New York City in 1849 and with which Copway became associated. The newspaper folded in October 1851. That same year, he published *Running Sketches of Men and Place, and of Notable Men and Events*, which he described in the news-paper as having been "got up for the parlor for our numerous friends through-out the country by Mr. Riker [publisher J. C. Riker], whose taste for book-making is much superior to the common book makers of our city." "We cannot praise our own," Copway adds; "we leave it to the hands of a scrutiniz-ing public to say what it deserves at their hands."[57]

Copway resembles no one so much as Nathaniel Parker Willis, the star literary man of the era and a diligent entrepreneur of genteel middle-class culture, who was at least an acquaintance of Copway's, if not a supporter.[58] If the Cherokee spokesmen were intent on having the Cherokees counted as civilized in the legal and philosophical senses, Copway sought to bring himself within the realm of the emerging middle-class society, at least in terms of being recognized as a literary man, if not an intellectual, on the model of Willis. That he circulated in this particular world brings up the issue of his wife's influence on his work. There is a lingering question as to how involved his wife was in his work; he acknowledges in his *Life* that he had editorial help in putting it together, although he insists that all of the writing is his. Smith points out that Copway's wife, Elizabeth, the daughter of a Canadian farmer whose family abandoned her when she married Copway, "once considered becoming a con-tributor to the *Christian Advocate*, a newspaper in Buffalo, New York," and that "she had an easy and agreeable writing style."[59] He argues that Eliza-beth's influence can be seen in the epigraphs from literary figures such as

Broadside advertising a public speech by George Copway in Boston, 1849. Like Peter Jones, his former mentor, Copway was obliged to present his plans for the well-being of contemporary Native peoples couched in a display of authentic Indian traditions. Unlike Jones, however, Copway never expressed misgivings about the display, which was fundamental to his literary career. Photograph courtesy of the American Antiquarian Society.

Shakespeare and Pope that appear in every chapter of *Traditional History*, as well as much of the material incorporated into *Running Sketches*. Copway probably did receive help from his wife with his writing, and possibly a lot of help, but it's impossible to say for sure how much. He certainly seems to have had the initiative to invent a career for himself, however, and the kinds of things he writes about in his books, even when they are couched in the elaborate sentimental language that suggests at least his wife's influence, if not her actual writing, exceed the conventions for the sentimental representation of Indians.

Both Copway and Maungwudaus violated the terms of convention and audience expectation for representing Indians—although as William Apess pointed out, often whites came just to *see* Indians, so what Indians actually *said* didn't really matter that much. Nevertheless, their writing has to be examined for its violation of those terms because it demonstrates an engagement with and critique of representation that will continue to be employed by other writers.

Maungwudaus's pamphlet, *An Account of the Chippewa Indians, Who Have Been Traveling Among the Whites, in the United States, England, Scotland, France and Belgium; With Very Interesting Incidents in Relation to the General Characteristics of the English, Irish, Scotch, French, and Americans, with Regard to their Hospitality, Peculiarities, Etc.*, is an ironic reversal, in the manner of William Apess, of the narratives of white travelers among Indians, which is all the more interesting given Maungwudaus's association with George Catlin in Europe, as Catlin was one of those white travelers. Maungwudaus observes that the English are lewd, the French not so bad but somewhat frivolous, the Scots dirty, and the Irish oppressed. He appends hymns "translated and composed by me" in both English and Ojibwe.[60] The pamphlet begins as a straightforward travelogue of the places the troupe visited, from its formation in 1843 through its travels in Europe. It includes the descriptions of quaint and naïve Indian savages experiencing civilization for the first time that Maungwudaus's audience would probably have expected in this kind of writing. The members of the troupe go to the "Queen's house" in England and find that "she is a small woman but handsome," although "there are many handsomer women than she is. . . . We got tired before we went through all the rooms in it" (4). The naïveté is somewhat stylized. "We saw three men out of the Zoological Gardens going up to the country of stars," Maungwudaus writes; "they had something very large in the shape of a bladder over their heads; they called it a balloon" (5). One can imagine the audience's pleasure in reading this account of the quaintness of the savage Indians experiencing the marvels of modern life.

Maungwudaus, or George Henry, second from left, with his troupe of Ojibwe performers in 1851. In a pamphlet sold at performances, Maungwudaus claimed to be "The Self-Taught Indian of the Chippewa Nation," which was not exactly true, as he had been converted to Christianity at fourteen and was even regarded as a good prospect for minister before he abandoned Christianity and formed his troupe. Photograph courtesy of the Chicago Historical Society.

Maungwudaus's account is not without a certain amount of bawdiness, which may demonstrate that he knew his audience very well. He tells the story of English officers inviting the troupe to dinner, at which there were many ladies:

When we got ready to leave, one of the officers said to us, our ladies would be glad to shake hands with you, and we shook hands with them. Then they were talking amongst themselves; then another officer said to us, "Friends, our ladies think that you do not pay enough respects to them, they desire you to kiss them"; then we kissed them according to our custom on both cheeks. "Why! they have kissed us on our cheeks; what a curious way of kissing this is." Then another officer said to us, "Gentlemen, our pretty squaws are not yet satisfied; they want to be kissed on their mouths." Then we kissed them on their mouths; then there was a great shout amongst the English war-chiefs. Say-say-gon, our war-chief, then said in our language to the ladies; "That is all you are good for; for wives, you are good for nothing." The ladies wanted me to tell them what the war-chief said to them. I then told them that he said he was wishing the officers would invite him very often, that he might again kiss the handsome ladies. Then they said, "Did he? then we will tell our men to invite you again, for we like to be kissed very often; tell him so." They put gold rings on our fingers and gold pins on our breasts, and when we thanked them for their kindness, we got in our carriage and went to our apartments. (5–6)

Purposefully mistranslating for whites is a time-honored strategy for dealing with them; it might be described as a convention of Native discourse. One might also see it in terms of Daniel Butrick's letter: there's much that Native peoples do not want white people to know, and there are many ways of deflecting whites' seemingly relentless inquisitiveness. Here Maungwudaus is playing two sides as both performer and critic by entertaining his audience with a bawdy story and criticizing the behavior of supposedly morally superior whites, although these whites are British.

Maungwudaus's narrative doesn't have a consistent tone of light entertainment, however; people die in it. Mrs. Catlin dies in Paris, two of his troupe die there, and then another dies in London. In Edinburgh, two of Maungwudaus's children die, and then his wife dies in Newark, England. As the brief narrative advances, it becomes more pointedly critical. He witnesses an execution in Norwich in which the condemned man "was hanging in the air with the cord that was around his neck, his hands tied together behind his back. Then he began to kick and twist for his life, and one of the murderers ran down and caught hold of his legs and pulled him down, and very soon killed him. They said that he was not fit to live on earth, but we believed that he is gone to the happy country in the other world, where he will be out of mischief forever" (8). They visit Edinburgh, which stinks of "the dirt thrown in the streets" (8), and Edinburgh's famous medical school, where they witness "about seventy young men, who are to be medicine men" performing autopsies on "thirty dead bodies": "They were skinning and cutting them same as we do with venison" (8).

Then Maungwudaus tells this story:

Riding through a town in our native costume, we saw a monkey performing in a street upon a music box, about fifty young men looking at him. He was dressed like a man. When the young men saw us, they began to make fun of us, and made use of very insulting language, making a very great noise;—at the same time when the monkey saw us he forgot his performances, and while we were looking at him, he took off his red cap and made a bow to us. A gentleman standing by, said to the audience, "Look at the monkey take off his cap and make a bow in saluting those strangers; which of the two the strangers will think are most civilized, you or the monkey? You ought to be ashamed of yourselves. You may consider yourselves better and wiser than those strangers, but you are very much mistaken. Your treatment to them tells them that you are not, and you are so foolish and ignorant, you know nothing about it. I have been traveling five years amongst these people in their own country, and I never, not once, was insulted, but I was always kindly treated and respected by every one of them. Their little children have far better manners than you. Young men, the monkey pays you well for all the pennies you have given him; he is worthy to become your teacher." We then threw some money to the monkey, and he jumped down from his platform and put the money into his master's mouth, and he made another bow to us as we were going away; at the same time we heard one of the young men saying to his friends, "See the teacher making another bow to the Indians." "Yes," said another, "this is to teach you, for you are the very monkey that was making fun and blackguarding the Indians." (9)

This account is very much in keeping with Apess's use of ironic reversals, but Maungwudaus's story also evokes the scientific racism of the mid-nineteenth century. Indians were supposed to be little better than monkeys. At the same time, he displaces the criticism of white behavior from Indians onto whites themselves, in the white man passing by who has traveled among the Indians and scolds the young men for their behavior, perhaps in deference to his audience. That aspect is referenced when the monkey puts money thrown at him into his master's mouth: like the Indians dressed for the part, no matter how civilized a being he is, he's still beholden to the man who pays him. Maungwudaus's attitude toward the idea of playing Indian is at the very least nuanced, and it's unfortunate he didn't write anything else.

Copway never seems to have been critical of the idea of performing his Indi-anness in the way that Maungwudaus was. After Copway's first book launched his career as a platform speaker, he seems to have pulled together some of his lecture material, with quite a lot of padding, to make a second book published in 1851 to take advantage of his popularity. Originally titled *Traditional History and Characteristic Sketches of the Ojibway Nation* and later *Indian Life and Indian History, by an Indian Author*, it includes substantial sections copied from other sources, material on contemporary Christian Ojibwe government taken from *Life*, as well as material that appeared previously in newspapers. Frequently there is little or no transition or even connection between topics within chapters. But there are several chapters that could well be material Copway presented in his lectures, "descriptive of the worship or religious belief of the Indian—his poetry, songs and his eloquence," as the broadside for one lecture had it.[61] In this second book, less constrained by the need or desire to present his Christian credentials, Copway begins to reconcile Ojibwe tradition with his desire for the literary. Dressed as his audience's concept of an Indian, Copway's remarks likely presented to them a contradiction of that same concept. Copway told his audience that what they called Indian "myths and legends" were both a history of and resistance to colonization; that the Ojibwe language has an aesthetic quality of which speakers were intensely aware; and that dreams were valid knowledge, knowledge that only Indians could explain.

In the chapter entitled "Their Legendary Stories and Historical Tales," Copway writes that Ojibwe stories are specifically for "winter evening instruction and amusement" and that they are individual performances: "I have known some Indians who would commence to narrate legends and stories in the month of October and not end up until quite late in the spring, and on every evening of this long term tell a new story" (97, 98). Most significantly, he wrote, "these legends have an important bearing on the character of the children of our Nation. . . . The fire-blaze is endeared to them in after years by a thousand happy recollections. By mingling thus, social habits are formed and strengthened" (98–99). Noting that Schoolcraft had collected "many of these fanciful stories," which may indicate the type of story Schoolcraft translated, Copway writes, "It is not my purpose to unnecessarily extend this work with a large number of these. I will, however, in this connection narrate a few, in order to give you some idea of the manner in which my people amuse themselves in their wigwams, and promise to send you, at some future day, a good handful from the forest" (98).

Of the three "classes" of stories (the Amusing, the Historical, and the Moral), Copway narrates the historical (99). They are historical in the sense that, unlike Schoolcraft's pristine narratives of the era of stone tools, for Copway colonization is the condition of the narrative, even when the narrative takes place before that. "The Star and the Lily" begins:

There was once a time when this world was filled with happy people, when all nations were as one, and the crimson tide of war had not begun to roll. Plenty of game was in the forest and on the plains. None were in want, for a full supply was at hand. Sickness was unknown. The beasts of the field were tame, they came and went at the bidding of man. One unending spring gave no place for winter—for its cold blasts or unhealthy chills. Every tree and bush yielded fruit. (99–100)

This is at once a generic Eden and one that is specifically precolonial from the perspective of Indians. Copway writes, "It was at such a time, when earth was paradise and man worthily its possessor, that the Indians were the lone inhabitants of the American wilderness" (100). The story about the morning and evening stars and the white lily takes place during the wars between the Iroquois and Ojibwes, which form a significant part of the more formally historical part of *Traditional History*.

It may be some indication of Copway's manipulation of the traditional material in "The Long Chase" that he begins this story by writing, "The long continued wars which once existed between the Ojibways and the Iroquois, gave rise to the following legend, which was originally related to me by an Ojibway Chief, whose name was Na-nah-boo-shoo," which seems to be one of the variations on the name of the Ojibwe trickster figure (104). This story about an Ojibwe girl, whose warning that Iroquois spies were in the camp was first ignored and then believed, also has literary touches. When they discover the Iroquois spies, Ojibwe warriors "became quite frantic, and giving their accustomed yell, the whole multitude started after them as swift as the flight of birds": "The waters of the mighty lake were without a ripple, other than that made by the swiftly gliding canoe, and the beautiful fish moved among their rocky haunts in perfect peace, unconscious of the chase above" (106). When the people capture the spies, they intend to torture them until "an aged warrior" says that they ought to let the spies go so that "they may go and tell their people of our power" (108). They let one of the spies go and burn the other at the stake. The story also bears the marks of the influence of Christian moralizing on Copway's thinking. "The spot where the sacrifice took place has been riven by many a thunderbolt since that eventful hour," Copway writes, "for the god of war was displeased with the faint-heartedness of the Ojibways for valuing a man more highly than the privilege of revenge" (108–9). Indians who refuse to be converted are always vengeful in Copway's writing, although vengefulness is not a permanent characteristic but lasts only as long as the Indian in question remains unconverted.[62]

In his last story, titled "An Historical Tale. The Effects of Liquor," Copway shows how traditional practices incorporate new experiences and the resistance to colonization. The history and the location are very specific. The culprits in this narrative are the French, who "brought into the Indians' possession implements of steel, and that bane of the civilized world, 'fire-water' " (118). The location is "the peninsula which is formed by the three lakes, Huron, Erie and Ontario," where "the people had already commenced to inhabit the islands along the river St. Marie, when a quantity of liquor was landed at a point near Grand De Tour, between St. Marie and Mackanaw" (118). The Indians who come to trade furs with the French "began to use this liquor quite freely, in order to see its curious effects upon them," which resulted in a variety of reactions in the people who drank it (118). "During this experimenting," Copway writes, "two intimate friends had a quarrel, which resulted in the death of one of them" (119). When the murderer flees into the woods, the murderer's brother readies himself to be executed in the murderer's place (119). The brother paints himself and begins to sing a death song, and says to the crowd, thinking his brother might be near, that he "will not dishonor the clan I belong to. . . . If you can endure the idea that hereafter the Nation will look upon us as a race of cowards, live! but I would choose to die in your stead" (120–21). The brother then runs from the woods and tells them " 'I am not a coward. I ran to the woods to get sober, that I might not be killed like a dog' " (121). The murderer then paints himself in the same way and sings his death song, and then he's killed by warriors, "the second Indian victim of intemperance" (121).

Copway appends a note to the story: "This traditional story was related to me by *Ne-gah-be-an*, in the year 1834, while we camped near Drumwoood's Island on our way up the Sault Ste. Marie. It was my purpose some time since to have published a volume of Indian stories, and trust that I shall be able to do so in a short time" (121). Given this example, one has to wonder what Copway's book of traditional stories would have included. If Ne-gah-be-an's story taught Ojibwe people to resist the influence of alcohol, Copway's presentation of that story to a white audience shows that Indians adapt to the conditions and effects of colonization but remain Indians, which is of course their main threat. Copway called this narrative "A Historical Tale" and also a "traditional story." As contemporary Native writers often point out, the experience of colonization and the struggle against it become incorporated into existing practices, and thus this story about the effects of alcohol on Ojibwe society becomes "traditional," illustrating how alcohol disrupts Ojibwe society and how people might resist that disruption by recognizing alcohol's effects and staying away from it. The story then has the same kind of purpose (on one level) as the Christian temperance movements: the restoration of order in a society that the introduction of alcohol throws into chaos. One need go only so far as the epigraph to the chapter, however, for an idea of the inability of Copway's audience to recognize what he was saying: "'Tis a story, / Handed from ages down; a nurse's tale, / Which children open-eyed and mouthed devour, / And thus as garrulous ignorance relates, / We learn it and believe—" (97). Who inserted the epigraphs (which appear in all of the editions of the book) and why remains mysterious. Copway's wife, who had a penchant for poetry, is often named as a possible source. Indian stories, following from the epigraph's logic, can only be stories of "garrulous ignorance," for the amusement of children. Copway says nothing of the kind. His written traditional narratives both resist the effects of colonization and aspire to the literary; it is likely that his audience could fathom neither of these acts, born of Indians' desire to remain Indians on territory in a changed world.

Copway continues his impossible insistence on Ojibwe autonomy and heterogeneity in a chapter on Ojibwe "Language and Writings." Citing School-craft's observations on the Ojibwe language, Copway agrees and elaborates:

> I cannot express fully the beauty of the language, I can only refer to those who have studied it as well as other languages, and quote their own writing in saying, "every word has its appropriate meaning, and with additional syllables give additional force to the meaning of most words." After reading the English language, I have found words in the Indian combining more expressiveness. There are many Indian words which when translated into English lose their force, and do not convey so much meaning in one sentence as the original does in one word. (123)

The chapter's epigraph again provides the clue to understanding just how radically Copway's comments differ from the received notions about Indian languages. The quotation is brief and from Shakespeare: "Here are a few of the most unpleasant words / That ever blotted paper" (122). Indians, of course, can only be inarticulate brutes. When they occasionally have the capacity for language, a tradition of representation that emerges along with the written treaties in the eighteenth century, Indians only have the capacity for metaphorical language, which is treated as a spontaneously occurring habit, not something that Indians might choose for logical or aesthetic reasons. Copway assumes that Indians can be both poetic and reasonable, a impossible combination, which the epigraph demonstrates.

Copway was called upon to translate when he was a missionary, and while in school at Jacksonville, Illinois, he collaborated with Sherman Hall on translations into Ojibwe of the Gospel of Luke and the Acts of the Apostles, which were published in Boston in 1837 and 1838 for the American Board of Commissioners for Foreign Missions.[63] Although lists of Indian words and their English equivalents were common in books on Indians and had been for some time, those lists were generally made up of words useful for trade. Copway addresses the aesthetics of Ojibwe in comparison with English. "Observe the smoothness of its words," he writes, inserting a list of twenty Ojibwe words and their English equivalents:

Ah-nung-o-kah	The starry heavens.
Bah-bah-me-tum	Obedience.
Che-baum	Soul.
De goo wah skah	The rippling wave.
E-nah-kay-yah	The way. (124)

Copway expects his settler audience to be able to believe that Ojibwe is a beautiful and expressive language. In addition to its aesthetics, Copway points out that Ojibwe is a written language and that those written records help to preserve tradition: "The records of the Ojibways have a two-fold meaning; the hieroglyphic symbols of material objects represent the transmission of a tradition from one generation to another. This refers more particularly to their religion, which is itself founded on tradition" (126). Copway then interprets a series of war-song "hieroglyphics" and translates them into English verse (127–28). "When I was young I was taught this," he comments, "and while singing I could, in imagination, see the enemy, though none were within a hundred miles" (128). Thus, "with these [figures] . . . Ojibways can write their war and hunting songs" and can also "send a communication to another Indian, and by them make himself as well understood as a pale face can by letter" (132). Settlers therefore do not have exclusive claim to the technology of writing.

Despite his own Christianity, Copway continues to describe Ojibwe religious belief, insisting that it is profound, mysterious, and must be approached with respect, particularly by Christians. In Chapter 12 of *Traditional History*, "Their Religious Belief," he describes not just what he calls the Medicine Worship—to which he refers many times and which he explains on more than one occasion—but dreaming as the method of gaining knowledge of medicine. The narrative concerns the dreams of exactly the type of "conjurer," this time a woman, whose knowledge and tribal authority he was at pains to destroy in

Life, Letters and Speeches. Dreams (and medicine) are forms of traditional knowledge, an "other" epistemology that denies the authority of misrepresentation and cannot be contained by it.

In *Life*, Copway describes two dreams, one he had when he was twelve and the other he had after his conversion. As a child, Copway has a dream that his father must interpret, a form of knowledge that Indians have and to which only Indians have access. After his conversion, he describes a highly romanticized, sentimental dream about the death of a cousin of his, in which he sees the cousin going off to the gates of heaven and discovers later that he had had the dream at the exact moment that the cousin died.[64] Copway thus attempts to conform the importance of dreams in Ojibwe society to the conventions of writing in English, in particular to the sentimentality favored by Christians and literary types alike. But Copway cannot deny the importance of dreaming, and when he puts that form of knowledge into mid-nineteenth-century American English, he dramatizes the inevitable epistemological confrontation between tradition and the practice of writing. Copway's dream as a boy must be explained by his father—it is a form of Ojibwe traditional knowledge. His Christian dream can be understood by his white readers because it is fully conventional.

Copway's narrative of the woman conjurer's dreams in *Traditional History* is something else again: he must be in the position of his father, interpreting that knowledge into English, which itself must be transformed. The chapter begins with Copway's representation of the " 'gods innumerable' " of the Ojibwes as romanticized "spirits." "The Ojibway, as he reclines beneath the shade of his forest trees, imagines these gods to be about him. He detects their tiny voices in the insect's hum. With half closed eyes he beholds them sporting by thousands on a sunray" (149). This leads him to reflect on "the god of Medicine" and on the importance of dreams in Ojibwe society. Copway writes that "men or women are deemed capable of learning the virtues of roots from [the god of Medicine], and often fast in order to gain his favor"; the object of fasting is to bring on the dreams through which the knowledge of medicine may be gained (149). In a note to his narrative "Manabozho; Or, the Great Incarnation of the North" in *Algic Researches*, Henry Rowe Schoolcraft observes of the ritual fast and dreams that

> it is at this period that the young men and the young women "see visions and dream dreams," and fortune or misfortune is predicted from the guardian spirit chosen during this, to them, religious ordeal. The hallucinations of the mind are taken for divine inspiration. The effect is deeply felt and

strongly impressed on the mind; too deeply, indeed, to be ever obliterated in after life. (149)

The importance of dreams in Ojibwe society, according to Schoolcraft, unfits them for Christianity, as they are more devoted to "the Manitoes or spirits whose influence and protection they wish to engage or preserve" rather than "the Great Spirit or Creator" (149–50).

To explain "the influence of dreams upon the Indian's mind," Copway tells "the story of an Indian damsel, who according to the custom of fasting, determined to do so in a remarkable romantic spot, near Grand Island" (150). The story about "woman conjurer" thus begins in sentimental convention. The "damsel" had been "coasting along the southern shore" in the summer accompanied by her friends and her family. "Suddenly," Copway writes, "she became pensive":

> Evening after evening passed, and on each she took her accustomed stroll along the beach, picking up Cornelian stones, which are found there in great numbers. One evening she was seen standing on the peak of the pictured rocks; and as the sun was passing the horizon, and the waves dashed furiously, she was heard to sing for the first time. Her long black hair floated upon the wind, and her voice was heard above the rustling of the leaves and the noise of the waters. When night came, she could not be seen. She had fled to the rocky cave, from whence were to go up her petitions to the gods. (150–51)

At first, the people, along with her parents, go looking for her. "They looked in every place—in woodland, in glades, upon the shore and in the caves of the rocks, yet could not find her. Day passed. Night came. They called her by name, 'Shah-won-o-equa' (Lady of the South), but she answered not, and they were left in great distress, conjecturing about her situation" (151). The people hear Shah-won-o-equa's voice but still cannot locate her, and they conclude, since they hear her voice but find no footprints, that "it was not her voice but that of a spirit they had heard, and that she had been taken away by the Great Spirit whose track was seen on the rocks" (152). Finally, the people see "the lost maiden" on "a lofty peak . . . gazing at the departing sun, and chanting her evening prayer to the gods of her fathers" (152). The next day her parents find her in a cave, where she says she has decided to fast (152–53).

The break in the sentimental narrative occurs when Copway begins to discuss the substance of the dreams. Although her mother comes every day to try to persuade the girl to come out of the cave, she refuses, and waits for the dreams to begin: "In the cave, on the ledge of rocks, she waited to receive the god of war, the god of the vegetable kingdom, and the god of the waters, whom she expected would visit her in her dreams, or in a visible form, and converse with her" (153). The dreams begin to move Copway's narrative out of convention. Shah-won-o-equa first dreams of a "young warrior . . . who standing over her, gazed at her as her raven hair was tossed about by the wind" (153). The warrior asks her "What will you have? The furs from the woods—the plumes of rare birds—the animals of the forest—or a knowledge of the properties of the wild flowers?" (153). But the girl tells him she is not interested in these things: "I want a knowledge of the roots that I may relieve the Nation's sufferings, and prolong the lives of the aged who live among us" (154). The "damsel" wants the knowledge of medicine: "The woods had their charms for me when I was small, but now the long wail of my people over their accumulating woes sounds in my ears. . . . I loved to gather the lilies and the flowers, till I learned there was life in them and a power to impart it. Then I hasted to this secluded spot, and, that I might learn the secret of the herbs and flowers, I have fasted here in seclusion, waiting the approach of thy fathers to teach them to me" (154). The romanticized narrative about a raven-haired damsel who coasts up the shore of the lake with her friends in the manner of European travelers of the leisure classes becomes a narrative about a woman who wants the knowledge that will "relieve the Nation's sufferings," which, given Copway's perspective, cannot result from anything other than the ravages of European settlement. The woman conjurer seeks traditional knowledge as a means of preserving the "Nation," the political entity, from disintegration.

Shah-won-o-equa then has "a number of remarkable dreams," Copway writes (156). In the first, "she was placed on the edge of a high rock which was suspended over the great prairies of the West, and . . . before her many Nations assembled to join in a great ball play" (154). Shah-won-o-equa "observed that the women were the fleetest, and that one of them actually won the prize" (154). The warrior, now a "stranger," appears again and tells her that she will be as "that maiden among the crowd. . . . So will your Nation look to you, when an assembled multitude gather to join in the Nation's ball play" (155). Interestingly, however, the warrior/stranger tells her that "if this will satisfy you, go now, return to your mother": but Shah-won-o-equa does not return home, when her mother comes to the cave the next day (155).

While storms rage outside the cave—"The earth trembled as the thunder growled above it"—Shah-won-o-equa continues to dream. "Numerous individuals surrounded her.—One was clad in scarlet—another in blue—another in black, and another in white cloth. They sang a song, then left, with the exception of one, who it appeared remained to reveal to her the purport of what she saw. He was old and quite bald-headed" (155). This knowledge has to be interpreted and explained. The "bald-headed" one tells the woman that "they are the birds you see in the forests—they will always sing for you." " 'And I am their parent,' said a great Bald Eagle, adjusting his wings, and suddenly starting off. The next morning these same birds came and sang near her head, while she was musing over her pleasant dream. The Red-breast Robin, the Scarlet birds, the Blue Jays, and the tiny Humming-birds, were about her.—She thought the gods had been propitious to her, and her heart filled with emotions of gratitude" (156).

Copway describes these dreams in succession with just that amount of explanation, which leaves the reader open to a sentimental interpretation: birds talk to a beautiful Indian maiden in the woods. In another dream, "two beings" take Shah-won-o-equa to the top of a hill, and then mountains, from which she could see the course of life. There, "One of the maiden's companions touched her head, when one-half of her hair was changed to snowy whiteness. Then she awoke, much exhausted" (157). In her last dream, Shah-won-o-equa "saw a canoe sailing upon Lake Superior," and when she gets into the canoe, "one of her visiters [*sic*] began to chant a song:—'Ba bah mah she yon nee beeng gay, / Ba bah moo say a keeng gay.' / 'I walk on the waves of the sea, / I travel o'er hill and dale' " (158). The canoe then goes "far from the sight of land," where "the waters around them were unmoved" (158). The beings tell her to sing this song "when becalmed . . . and you will hear us whisper to you" (158). Sha-won-o-equa then wakes up, when "the storm was yet raging, and the voices of the gods were heard in the winds among the trees" (158).

Given Copway's romanticized depiction of her dreams—and how else could he depict them—it is necessary to remember why Shah-won-o-equa was dreaming in the first place, which is to say, for the benefit of her nation, which Copway notes is under attack. After she returns to her people, Shah-won-e-qua tells them, "[By fasting,] I have received the favor of the gods. . . . I have traveled the journey of life, and have learned that I shall not die until half my hair has turned white" (158). As in the traditional story on the effects of liquor, it is at the end that Copway offers a glimpse of his connection to this narrative:

Since that time, I have seen that girl but once. In the year 1842, while sailing along Lake Superior, on its southern shore, I came rather unexpectedly to a cluster of wigwams, where I saw Shaw-won-a-qua [*sic*], and listened with deep interest to her relation of the dreams of her childhood. I gave her a few wild ducks from my boatload of game, and a yard of scarlet cloth—a fabric which is esteemed very highly by the Indian women. This I did in payment for those early impressions she had made upon my mind, leading me to believe that the noble deeds of man are those, and those only, which are performed for the good of others; and that virtue will be alike rewarded in the future, whether it be found and cherished in pagan lands or in Christian temples. (158–59)

Copway himself was evidently one of the people traveling with Shah-won-o-equa when she decided to go in search of the knowledge of medicine. That Copway records the year of his visit calls to mind the other powerful woman he met in 1842, the "celebrated conjurer" Anna, who accepted Christianity and in her old age crawled to a missionary meeting. The coincidence of the years and their status as powerful women begs the question whether Anna and Shah-won-o-equa might be the same person, although it is impossible to say. To Copway's audience, accustomed as it was to religious sentiment, Anna's story may have been the more plausible of the two; Shaw-won-o-equa's story, however, is more consistent with the works of the Native writers who follow Copway. Copway narrates the existence of an "other," Ojibwe, knowledge, which is knowledge that is the means of resistance to colonization and that must also, when he puts it into writing, break the bounds of the epistemology within which he writes. In this last scene, Copway demonstrates his respect for a powerful Indian woman (a depiction in itself highly unusual, even unthinkable, for readers in mid-century America), because of the traditional knowledge that she had given him. He also describes that knowledge—which contradicts the endless production of the identity of all Indians, that contradicts the denial of Native political organization and intelligence—as a version of the Golden Rule.

This does not mean, however, that Copway is a failure or is an inferior writer whose works may be set aside and justifiably ignored. In invoking a recognizable tenet of Christianity, Copway did what many Native intellectuals did and still do when they must insist, in the face of knowledge about racial difference, that Indians are no different, in one sense, from whites or anyone else, but are reasonable beings who ought to be able to live their lives without harassment. Copway's writing may be uneven and contradictory at times, but that is its importance. His writing dramatizes the inevitable epistemological struggle in Native writing in the wake of settlement and colonization. Remarkably, given the time in which he wrote and the writing of those who were his ostensible supporters, Copway disregards received knowledge and instead describes dreams as valid knowledge, knowledge that is about "medicine," medicine that helps to preserve the political life of the nation. That he had a certain naïveté about the capacity of his audience to accept the validity of what he wrote about should not detract from the fundamental importance of what he wrote. The contradictions of Copway's writing do not make him the stereotypical Indian of literary critics, one who has taken up English and therefore abandoned oral tradition. The power of Copway's writing is that he did *not* abandon the authority of tradition.

After the collapse of his newspaper in 1851, Copway seems to have begun a protracted slide into obscurity. The literati grew tired of him, and, at least according to Donald Smith, his behavior became somewhat erratic. He begged support from potential wealthy patrons, was thrown into jail in Boston for debt, and helped steal Red Jacket's bones while on a lecture tour in Buffalo in 1852. N. P. Willis entertained Copway at his country house in upstate New York when Copway was on a lecture tour in 1855.[65] Like Henry Rowe Schoolcraft and many other self-respecting men of the time, he petitioned the U.S. government for a bureaucratic position. He left his wife, then reconciled with her for a few years. She later took their surviving youngest child and went to live with her father in Ontario. In the early 1860s, Copway turns up in Geneva, New York, along with his brother David, recruiting Canadian Indians for service in the Civil War. He's listed in a business directory in Geneva at about this time as "Indian doctor. 58 Pultney."[66] In the late 1860s, he was in Detroit, advertising his services as a root doctor in the *Detroit Free Press*. Finally, in 1868, he appears in the account of a French Catholic missionary at the Grand Island reserve in Ontario, having been at first accepted as a healer by the Iroquois and Ojibwe converts there but then losing favor with many of them, as he chose to be baptized in the Catholic church. He died in January 1869, only a few days after having been baptized with a new name, Joseph-Antoine.[67]

CHAPTER FOUR

Reclaiming Red Jacket and the Confederacy in Iroquois Writing

LEARNED PAGANS

In 1838, Henry A. S. Dearborn—adjutant-general of Massachusetts, son of a Revolutionary War hero and early secretary of war, and former student of the Cherokees' lawyer William Wirt—kept a detailed journal of his experiences at the negotiation of the Buffalo Creek Treaty, which he attended because Massachusetts had historic claims to the land in question through colonial charters and the convolutions of New York state Indian policy. While there, he befriended a Mr. Cone, whom he described as "a very intelligent young Indian of the Tonnawanda Band."[1] This Mr. Cone was likely Nicholson and Ely Parker's brother Spencer.[2] The Buffalo Creek Treaty was, as historian Laurence Hauptman writes, "one of the major frauds in American Indian history."[3] The bribery, duplicity, and coercion involved in making the treaty are well known; in fact, a furor was raised almost immediately after the requisite signatures were secured in January 1838. The purpose of the treaty was to acquire title to most of the remaining Seneca land in western New York and to provide for the removal of the Senecas to Indian Territory. A primary motivation for the treaty was the Ogden Land Company's interest in acquiring the last Native-held land in the vicinity of Buffalo, so that it could sell the land to investors eager to expand and improve the port there. Buffalo itself was the endpoint of the transportation network built in New York west of Albany from the late eighteenth to the early nineteenth centuries, built largely on Six Nations or Iroquois land. None of the members of the Iroquois Confederacy—the Mohawks, Oneidas, Onondagas, Cayugas, Senecas, and Tuscaroras—was exempt from the web of largely illegal real estate deals.

According to Dearborn's journal, Mr. Cone serves as Dearborn's guide and informant at the council, which includes not just formal meetings but a range of other events that take place in association with it. He takes Dearborn to "a Corn Feast of the Pagan portion of the tribe" and lacrosse games; they go to dances, which, Dearborn relates, "are formal religious rites, over which some of the principal chiefs always preside" (69). He tells Dearborn about the properties of plants and recounts Seneca traditions, which Dearborn sets out in his journal, including "The Creation of the World" and "The Origins of the Seven Stars," through which, Dearborn writes, the Great Spirit admonished the people to continue performing their ancient ceremonies (67, 69). Mr. Cone tells Dearborn about his grandfather Black Face's experiences in wars with the western tribes and his own cure by a medicine man at Cattaraugus, one of the six remaining Seneca reservations. He describes a prophesy made by an old Seneca man at Buffalo Creek, which Dearborn records as follows:

> [The prophet] dreams like the patriarchs of old & sees visions. . . . Very recently this learned pagan, reports that he went to hell, in one of his spiritual nocturnal excursions. He passed over an immense prarie [sic] & at the distant end beheld an enormous stone edifice, without doors or windows, but the guide, who accompanied him,—being a special messenger from the Great Sp[irit] knocked against the wall & instantly an opening was made, from which issued a blaze that ascended hundreds of feet above the roof, & he beheld within huge potash kettles, filled with boiling oil & moulten lead, & there were the wicked rising & falling & tumbling over in the bubling [sic] fluids, & ever & anon as the heads of some were thrown above the top of kettles they gave a horrid yell & down they plunged again. There he was told would be punished all the chiefs who advocated emigration. (91)

Dearborn doesn't comment on the clear message in this particular story. He's instead more interested in the origin of the Iroquois name for the president of the United States, which was first held by George Washington and is translated as "Town Destroyer" (96). The name, Dearborn notes, refers to the Iroquois experience at the hands of General John Sullivan during the Revolutionary War. Sullivan commanded a notoriously destructive 1779 Revolutionary War campaign through western New York to retaliate against the Iroquois for their raids on the frontier.[4] The circumstances and devastation of the expedition were well known in the early nineteenth century through such books as David Ramsay's *History of the American Revolution* (1789) (which was reprinted many times and became the standard history of the Revolution), Samuel Gardner Drake's *Biography and History of the Indians of North America*, James Seaver's *Narrative of the Life of Mrs. Mary Jemison* (1824), and William L. Stone's *Life of*

Joseph Brant (1838). In his official report, quoted by Stone in *Life of Brant*, Sullivan writes that "the Town of Genesee contained one hundred and twenty-eight houses, mostly large and very elegant. It was beautifully situated, almost encircled with a clear flatt [*sic*], extending a number of miles; over which extensive fields of corn were waving, together with every kind of vegetable that could be conceived."[5] Sullivan destroyed everything. Since George Washington was Sullivan's commander, he became associated with the devastation as well, Dearborn adds, "in the true Grecian & Roman style," as befitted the leader of a republic (96).

In the 1850s, Mr. Cone's brother, Nicholson Parker, lectured on Indian topics in western New York, telling his white audiences the same kinds of things his brother had told Henry Dearborn. Parker devoted an entire lecture ("Indian Dances and Their Influence") to the importance and meaning of dancing in Iroquois tradition, making the point that dancing cannot be separated from the history of the nation or its political claims. Dancing, he explained, "is regarded as a thanksgiving ceremonial acceptable in itself to the Great Spirit" and "as a divine art"; most importantly, it is "the instrumentality for arousing patriotic excitement and keeping alive the spirit of the nation" (279). War dances also included speeches—some witty, others serious. At a council in 1846, Parker writes, "Da-geh-sa-deh, a distinguished chief" lamented the present state of the Iroquois:

> We have been reduced and broken by the cunning and rapacity of the white race. We are now compelled to crave as a blessing that we may be allowed to live upon our own lands, to cultivate our own fields, to drink from our own spring and to mingle our bones with those of our fathers. Many winters ago our wise ancestors predicted that a great monster with white eyes would come from the east and as he advanced would consume the land. This monster is the white race and the prediction is near its fulfillment. They (our ancestors) advised their children when they became weak to plant a tree with four roots, branching to the North, the South, the East and the West; and then collecting under its shade to dwell together in unity and harmony. This tree I propose shall be at this very spot. Here we will gather, here we will live, and here we will die. (282–83)

Henry Dearborn appears not to have been able to connect his education in the practices and beliefs of the Iroquois with an appreciation for the merits of their political struggle, which seems to have been Mr. Cone's purpose, as well as his brother's. Frustrated with the treaty negotiations at one point, he bursts out in his journal:

It is a rediculous [*sic*] mockery of sovereignty,—a contemtable [*sic*] show of respect & gravity, to be treatying with men, who are incapable of comprehending the simplest state; & who should be made to do, what the intelligence and kindness of the government, have deemed indispensable, for their comfort and moral elevation. How preposterous is it for such characters to be talking about their ancient rights their independence and customs. . . . The . . . power of the nation [must be] substituted for this sham exercise of diplomatic authority & respectful treatment towards a people, who are incapable of managing their own affairs & providing for this own means of subsistence. (99–100)

Dearborn soon recovers himself, however, observing that the Indians "are to be treated as children, by a kind & merciful & generous parent," and, more ominously, "be compelled to so conduct as to merit consideration esteem, respect & honor" (100). Further on, like Edward Everett, he waxes poetic on the transportation revolution and the glories of the American landscape, reflecting on the advancement of civilization in western New York: "The American Hercules has gone forth, to achieve more wonderful exploits than those of the son of Alcmena. He went forth to *destroy*, but this republican adventurer to *create*" (109).

In her *License for Empire*, Dorothy Jones writes that an "Iroquois mystique" was a factor in British-Iroquois relations in the eighteenth century. While the idea of Iroquois supremacy stretches back to the seventeenth century, Jones points out that the British, and after them the Americans, used this conception as a means of acquiring influence for themselves through the Iroquois by various means, including manipulating conflicts among other members of the Confederacy or by representing themselves as allies of an Indian empire (34). Cadwallader Colden, a New York colonial official whose *History of the Five Indian Nations of Canada* first appeared in 1727, followed by an expanded version in 1747, was an important contributor to this mystique. Using extensive excerpts from the seventeenth- and eighteenth-century treaty documents, he described the (then) Five Nations as a primitive republic, its leaders as Roman statesmen, and argued for Britain's alliance with the Iroquois Confederacy in order to advance its own economic and political interests. In the nineteenth century, after it had been thrown into confusion by the American Revolution and suffered the depredations of New York land speculators, the Iroquois began to be represented as a once-great but now eclipsed empire rather than a quasi-Roman republic. By 1851, when Lewis Henry Morgan published *League of the Iroquois*, it was quite common to figure the Iroquois

Confederacy as the fallen empire that, as Morgan wrote, was "our [predecessor] in . . . sovereignty," that occupied "the highest position among the Indian races of the continent living in the hunter state" (143, 55).

The idea of Iroquois supremacy was also held by the Iroquois themselves, Jones writes. Iroquois were brought up in an atmosphere that continually proclaimed their destiny and the supremacy of the Confederacy. I want to elaborate on Jones's observation, because I think it provides a means of thinking about the Iroquois writers under consideration here—David Cusick, a Tuscarora; and Maris Bryant Pierce, Nathaniel T. Strong, and Ely and Nicholson Parker, all Senecas. Like the Cherokees, all of these writers wrote relatively little besides official correspondence and the like, and published less. Like the Cherokees, they were all called upon to support and defend their nations in times of crisis. For the Iroquois, the struggle to retain ancestral land and to resist an always imminent removal elsewhere lasted from the American Revolution to at least the middle of the nineteenth century; the fight over the Buffalo Creek Treaty of 1838 was not resolved until the 1890s. As a result of the dislocations suffered in the American Revolution, the Iroquois leadership shifted from the Onondagas—the historic leaders of the Iroquois Confederacy, who lived in central New York and suffered the loss of much of the territory in the immediate post-revolutionary years—to the Senecas in the western part of the state. From the end of the eighteenth century, the Tuscaroras lived close by the Senecas, in a settlement northeast of Niagara Falls.[6] The works of these writers are dominated by the history and legacy of the Confederacy and in particular by Red Jacket, a Seneca leader who famously rejected any white influence and sought to maintain sovereignty at a time when EuroAmerican writing reduced the Iroquois Confederacy, a political entity with which Euro-Americans historically had had to make agreements, to a mythical Iroquois "empire" that is eclipsed by the rising "Empire State" of New York, positioning Red Jacket as the last heroic, eloquent vanishing savage. These writers—Cusick, Pierce, the Parkers, and Strong—historicize the Confederacy and ultimately historicize Red Jacket himself, so that the Confederacy is an organization under assault but neither vanquished nor forgotten, and Red Jacket is not a vanishing savage but a contemporary leader in the struggle against the destruction of governments and the loss of territory.

Behind that shift in EuroAmerican representation of the Iroquois from quasi-republican state to eclipsed empire lies an especially complicated legal history involving the Iroquois, the U.S. government, Massachusetts, New York, and land speculators. Immediately after the Revolution, in 1784, the United States attempted to position itself as having effected a "conquest" of the Iroquois by virtue of having won the Revolution in the Treaty of Fort Stanwix. Ten years later, however, the United States negotiated the Treaty of Canandaigua, which, like the other renegotiated treaties of the time, formally recognized the political autonomy of the Iroquois, following Henry Knox's plan for U.S. Indian policy. The United States had recently concluded a war with Indian nations in the Ohio Valley, and the British in Canada were a continuing threat; it returned 1,600 square miles of land it had summarily taken from the Senecas at the Treaty of Fort Stanwix, acquired Iroquois claim to land in the Ohio Valley, and recognized Iroquois reservations in New York.[7] The Senecas agreed to give up their claims in the Ohio Valley and to other land in New York in order to secure the U.S. government's recognition of the bulk of the lands they occupied and to protect themselves from the actions of the state of New York and land speculators eager to divest them of their territory.

Even before the close of the Revolution, forward-thinking speculators and businessmen in New York City and Albany began to imagine a transportation network of roads, canals, and riverways that would link the riches of the western United States with the eastern seaboard through Lake Erie, supported by towns and cities established through the central and western portions of the state. The Iroquois held much of that land. New York's actions in regard to the Iroquois feature a peculiarity to which Iroquois writers often return and which make relations between EuroAmericans and Native peoples there especially complicated. At the Hartford Convention in 1786, in order to end a historic disagreement with Massachusetts over the status of land in western New York that went back to royal charters that had granted the same land to both colonies, New York ceded the right of preemption of Native land within the disputed territory to Massachusetts in exchange for Massachusetts's recognition of New York's jurisdiction over the land. New York sold not the land itself to Massachusetts, but rather the right to buy the land from the Native peoples on it. The valuable thing that Massachusetts had then was the right to sell the right to buy; it did not have claim to the land itself, as New York retained— eventually, after Indians had consented to sell—political jurisdiction of the land. Once the right to buy the land is itself a commodity, rather than the inalienable right of the national or state government, Dorothy Jones points out, land speculators could enter into the mix "at the highest level," which they promptly did (182). In April 1788, Massachusetts sold the right of preemption to Native land in the state of New York to two land speculators, Oliver Phelps and Nathaniel Gorham. When Phelps and Gorham could not succeed in getting title to the land through agreements with Indians, they relinquished their claim to Massachusetts, which then sold it in 1791 to the land speculator Robert

Morris, "the legendary financier of the Patriot cause in the American Revolution" in 1791.[8] By the mid-1790s, however, Morris was facing financial difficulties and still had not secured Native consent to sell the land within the territory. He then sold his right to preemption to a group of European investors operating as the Holland Land Company on the condition that Morris would be able to secure mainly Seneca consent to sell their land. In 1810, the Holland Land Company sold its preemption rights to Seneca and Tuscarora land to the Ogden Land Company, founded by the Holland Land Company's former counsel David Ogden, which then aggressively pursued the purchase of Seneca land and the removal of Seneca people from western New York until the middle of the nineteenth century.[9] Throughout the nineteenth century, the federal government did little if anything to stop the actions of New York and the speculators. It wasn't until 1985 that the Supreme Court, in a test case brought by the Oneida Nation, held that New York's actions were in violation of federal law at the time, which, beginning with the first of the Indian Trade and Intercourse Acts in 1790, establishes that only the federal government has the capacity to treat with Indian nations. The Court also held that New York must compensate the tribes for the fraud, but officials have so far put off settlement, as hundreds of thousands of acres taken from the Mohawk, Onondaga, Cayuga, and Seneca Nations, in addition to the Oneidas, from Albany west, may be in contention. As of this writing, all five tribes are in litigation with the state of New York to force settlement of their claims.[10]

The right of preemption is disputed by Iroquois orators and writers, including Red Jacket, from the beginning of the conflict. The doctrine of preemptive right is a legal manifestation of Indian difference; the concept is founded on the familiar assertion that, because Indians are inherently unable to use land as it should be used, productively and for profit, white people have a superior claim to that land. The preemptive right is essentially a declaration of white superiority, a fact that all of the Iroquois writers recognized. In New York, the separation of the preemptive right from the state stripped away the political basis for treaty relations with Indian nations. While Henry Knox could endorse diplomatic alliances with Indian nations and offer the U.S. government as their protector—all while attempting, one way or another, to secure their consent to sell as much of the land as he could get—in New York, those political and diplomatic relations between Indian nations and EuroAmerican states were no longer important. It simply became a matter of a range of interested parties wearing down Native peoples in order to secure their still necessary consent to surrender land.

Reciting the history and formation of the Confederacy has been a central part of the ceremonies binding the Iroquois together since the formation of the Confederacy before EuroAmerican settlement. Iroquois writing can be understood in relation to that political tradition, and it in large part can be seen as an extension of that tradition in different forms. Writing itself complicates this process. The writers discussed in this chapter provide almost an overview of Native strategies for dealing with misrepresentation and its political effects in the nineteenth century. To begin, both Red Jacket and David Cusick dispute misrepresentation, but they don't address themselves to analyzing its political or psychological effects. They also write and speak from the traditions of the Confederacy and its constituent nations. They both describe to white audiences a different and equally legitimate political system that the United States violates and attempts to destroy. Such narratives—about the history of the Confederacy, apparently careful explanations of why the Iroquois live or think in the way that they do—are a staple of the seventeenth- and eighteenth-century treaty documents. One might also consider Mr. Cone, Ely and Nicholson's brother, with Henry Dearborn at Buffalo Creek: tradition— beliefs, practices, knowledge—can't be separated from the political structure with which EuroAmericans must engage. Red Jacket and David Cusick are working from that same model.

Despite ample sarcasm directed at whites on Red Jacket's part and a pointed challenge to white knowledge about Indians on Cusick's, neither of these early writers directly addresses the psychological or political effects of misrepresentation. These points are taken up by Maris Bryant Pierce in his address on the Senecas in 1839. Like other Native intellectuals in the 1830s—Boudinot and Apess in particular—Pierce rejects racial difference by arguing that Native peoples have all the requisite traits of civilized human beings. However, like Boudinot at least, he sets aside the past in order to do so. In the 1840s and 1850s, Ely and Nicholson Parker become, like their brother Spencer before them, responsible for explaining Iroquois knowledge and history to a white public, and their works evidence the difficulty of reconciling Native tradition, which they see as authoritative knowledge, with the political claim that Native peoples are rapidly becoming civilized. Red Jacket himself becomes a means of reconciling tradition and modernity. In speeches given by Nicholson Parker, Nathaniel Thayer Strong, and, in 1884, Ely Parker, Red Jacket becomes a means of telling the history of the Confederacy not as the story of inevitable decline and disappearance, but as resistance to subordination to EuroAmerican authority. Finally, in his lectures on Indian topics in the 1850s, Nicholson Parker insists on the authority of tradition but also represents something new: Native intellectual production in English that draws on traditional knowledge to represent contemporary experience. Like George Copway, Nicholson Parker begins to reconcile tradition and modernity, so that Native experience is not split between the past and the present, between the past before colonization and progress.

CONTRARY ELOQUENCE IN RED JACKET AND DAVID CUSICK

By the late eighteenth century, the eloquence of Indians was a widely accepted fact in the United States; it was promulgated in schools from the primary level to Harvard and Yale.[11] Cadwallader Colden had quite a lot to do with the popularization of the notion of Indian eloquence in the eighteenth century, as did the printing for general readers of about fifty colonial treaties between various British colonies and Native tribes; Benjamin Franklin, who as a commissioner for Pennsylvania attended many treaty conferences with the Iroquois and other tribes, printed a series of them from the 1740s to the 1760s. Iroquois treaty practice was especially well known because of their importance to Britain and because of the ceremony with which treaties were conducted; the Iroquois adapted the ceremonies they previously used for the Confederacy to the new circumstance of having to establish relations with Europeans. The written versions of the treaties usually consist of exchanged speeches with a narrative of the treaty conference's events, which could last for several weeks. The treaty documents are a remarkable record of EuroAmerican colonials writing down a version of what Native peoples say that often preserves Native insistence on their autonomy and the validity of their knowledge, very much in keeping with the Native writers under consideration in this book. However, when EuroAmericans, first and foremost Colden, wrote about the Iroquois and the treaties, what the Indians said generally recedes and is replaced by the concept of their eloquence, which becomes an inherent Indian trait. Indians' oratory can be picturesque, metaphorical, and bold, but they do not have reason, and therefore they do not have the capacity for forming civil societies.[12] The notion of Indian eloquence reduces the ceremonial practice in treaty negotiations into a signifier of Native difference and inferiority. Native speeches are removed from a historical setting in which at least the effort must be made to understand Indians as accurately as possible for whites to achieve what they want to achieve—underhandedly or not—to the figure of the Indian that denies the very idea of political relations with Native peoples in the first place.

Red Jacket first came to the attention of the U.S. government in treaty negotiations in 1790, at the age of about thirty-two. He was neither a hereditary chief nor a warrior—in fact, he endured rumors of his cowardice in battle throughout his life—but was rather an orator called upon to convey the wishes of the Senecas. He sometimes spoke on behalf of Iroquois and Seneca women, who held positions of political authority in the nations and the Confederacy. After about 1817, when the Senecas split into Christian and pagan factions, however, Red Jacket's recorded positions were probably his own rather than sanctioned by the Senecas as a whole. Several translated and widely circulated speeches made Red Jacket the predominant figure of Indian eloquence in the first part of the nineteenth century, and he became known as signally resistant to white influences and white efforts to buy Native land and remove the inhabitants elsewhere. Several of his speeches, sometimes published with those of two fellow Senecas, Farmer's Brother and Cornplanter, but also separately, first appeared in print in 1809 and 1811. They were often reprinted, under various titles, and he soon became quite famous. Between 1822 and 1823, Henry Inman, George Catlin, Charles Bird King, and Robert Weir had either painted or drawn his portrait, Catlin and King more than once. His speeches continued to be reprinted after his death in January 1830, in a variety of popular forms; both Samuel Gardner Drake and Benjamin Thatcher included Red Jacket in their Indian biographies of 1832. During the height of the Mashpee conflict, William Joseph Snelling reprinted one of Red Jacket's speeches against missionaries in the *New England Galaxy* in July 1833.[13]

"Red Jacket's Reply to Reverend Cram" (1803), reprinted in Christopher Densmore's *Red Jacket: Iroquois Diplomat and Orator*, begins with the narrative voice of an Indian agent introducing Cram, who is from the Boston Missionary Society, insisting that the missionary has "not come to get your lands or your money, but to enlighten your minds" and bring Christianity, the "one true religion" (136). "If you do not embrace the right way," Cram says, "you cannot be happy hereafter" (136). Red Jacket's reply exemplifies what might be called the difference argument: essentially, he says, Indians have a different society and a different religion, and Christianity isn't necessary to them. Critics often read this insistence on difference in early writing as insistence on cultural difference exclusively. However, Christianity did not just change Native peoples' minds about spirituality. One could think of the example of Rev. John F. Schermerhorn here, the Dutch Reformed minister who not only served as Jackson's agent in forcing the New Echota Treaty on the Cherokees but also had a hand in the 1838 Buffalo Creek Treaty.[14] In the context of the times, rejecting Christianity was a defense of political autonomy as much as a defense of culture. As William Apess pointed out, missionary activity often gave rise to increased factionalism among Native peoples in times

Portrait of Red Jacket, which appeared in the first volume of McKenney and Hall's Indian Tribes of North America. *Red Jacket is wearing the medal that George Washington presented to him in 1792, when he requested that Red Jacket and other Iroquois leaders represent the United States' interests in peace on a diplomatic mission to Indian nations on the western border. Photograph courtesy of the Edward E. Ayer Collection, Newberry Library, Chicago.*

of great stress, as it did among the Senecas. It often led to the destruction of Native governments, thereby impeding Native peoples' ability to resist further white interference.

Red Jacket's reference to the history of colonization and settlement in the beginning of the speech marks that political context. After an introduction that employs conventional treaty speech—the "Great Spirit . . . has taken his garment from before the sun, and caused it to shine with brightness upon us. Our eyes are opened, that we see clearly; our ears are unstopped, that we have been able to hear distinctly the words you have spoken"—Red Jacket launches into a history of contact between whites and Native peoples (137). He insists that the world as the Iroquois knew it was created for and "owned" by their ancestors and that "all this [the Great Spirit] had done for his red children, because He loved them" (138). When whites came, however, it was "an evil day." He then recites the story of the English pilgrims fleeing persecution and notes that the Indians "took pity on them" and gave them land (138). "We gave them corn and meat," he says, "and they gave us poison in return" (138). As the white population increased, he says, "they wanted more land; they wanted our country. Our eyes were opened, and our minds became uneasy" (138). Here Red Jacket employs a version perhaps of the discourse of Indian doom, but it is one that frequently appears in eighteenth-century treaties: "Brother: Our seats were once large and yours were small. You have soon become a great people, and we have scarcely a place left to spread our blankets. You have got our country, but are not satisfied; you want to force your religion on us" (138). This is perhaps more accurately described as an accounting of whites' failure to live up to their obligations to Native peoples, whose aid they had previously sought; it is a call to remember a longstanding relationship, and an assertion that the relationship ought not change when the relative power of those involved changes. The politics of religion are inescapable here: it is not just about culture but about power as well.

Red Jacket deploys the "Indians who are more Christian than Christians themselves" theme, perhaps sarcastically. He points out that the white religion "is written in a book," but the Great Spirit didn't see fit to give that book to Indians. "We only know what you tell us about it," he says; "how shall we know when to believe, being so often deceived by white people?" (138–39). Further, if there is only one true religion, Red Jacket asks, "why do you white people differ so much about it?" (139). The politics are certainly present in Red Jacket's critique of white Christianity. He notes in closing that missionaries have been preaching to whites in the vicinity of Buffalo and observes, "We will wait a little while, and see what effect your preaching has upon them. If we find it does them good, makes them honest, and less disposed to cheat Indians; we will then consider again of what you have said" (139). Like William Apess, Red Jacket's criticism of Christian missionaries is that the political effects of Christians were often devastating to Native peoples.

Another of Red Jacket's speeches, given to a Rev. John Alexander at a council in 1811, first appeared in the pamphlet *Native Eloquence*, which was published at Canandaigua in 1811 and reprinted many times afterward. Red Jacket actually gave two speeches at this council at Buffalo Creek in May 1811, in which the newly formed Ogden Land Company was attempting, as ever, to buy Seneca land, the other to an agent of the Ogden Land Company named Mr. Richardson. This speech was not reprinted in *Native Eloquence* and was not as well known, Densmore writes, although as the removal controversy became national in the 1820s, it began to be printed in reform and abolitionist periodicals (74). The Alexander speech essentially reprises the Cram speech, rejecting Christian missionaries and insisting on Seneca autonomy, although it is much more direct.

The Richardson speech is unmistakably about political conflict and provides the circumstances for rejecting missionaries. In the opening, Red Jacket seems to be mocking the businessman's need to get to the point, in contrast to his use of treaty language in the Cram speech. "In doing important business," Red Jacket says, "it is best not to tell long stories, but to come to it in a few words" (143). So he gets to the point: "Your application for the purchase of our lands is to our minds very extraordinary. It has been made in a crooked manner—you have not walked in the straight path pointed out by the great Council of your nation" (143). Red Jacket points out the problem of jurisdiction in this speech. The Ogden Land Company claimed the preemptive right to purchase the land, which Red Jacket points out is a federal right, maintaining, "You have no writings from the President" (143). He then accounts for the history of land sales, insisting that the Senecas "have remembered how the Yorkers purchased our lands in former times. They bought them piece by piece for a little money paid to a few men in our nation, and not to all our brethren; our planting and hunting grounds have become very small, and if we sell these we know no where to spread our blankets" (144). He maintains that the Senecas do not accept the notion of the preemptive right. "You tell us your employers have purchased of the Council of Yorkers a right to buy our lands—we do not understand how this can be—the lands do not belong to the Yorkers; they are ours, and were given to us by the Great Spirit" (144). "We think it strange," he continues, in an indication that he is well aware of the Ogden Land

Company's plans, "that you should jump over the lands of our brethren in the East, to come to our Council fire so far off, to get our lands. When we sold our lands in the East to the white people, we determined never to sell those we kept, which are as small as we can live comfortably on" (144).

This is the same point the Cherokees made in the 1820s: they had sold as much land as they could while retaining enough to reasonably maintain their population. And like the Cherokees, Red Jacket explicitly rejects removal, on the ground that whites would still want their land wherever they went: "We should soon be surrounded by the white men, who will there also kill our game, come upon our lands, and try to get them from us" (144). This is clearly a problem of political relations, not of cultural difference. "We are determined not to sell our lands, but to continue on them," Red Jacket reiterates, "We like them—they are fruitful and produce us corn in abundance, for the support of our women and children, and grass and herbs for our cattle" (144).

At treaties, Red Jacket says, "the white man with sweet voices and smiling faces told us they loved us, and that they would not cheat us, but that the king's children on the other side of the lake would cheat us. When we go on the other side of the lake the king's children tell us your people will cheat us, but the sweet voices and smiling faces assure us of their love and they will not cheat us" (144). "These things puzzle our heads," Red Jacket says disingenuously, "and we believe that the Indians must take care of themselves, and not trust in your people or the king's children" (144). The politics of the preemptive right are plain here. "The white people buy and sell false rights to our land," Red Jacket says; "our lands are of great value to us, and we wish you to go back with your talk to your employers, and to tell them and the Yorkers that they have no right to buy and sell false rights to our lands" (145).

Red Jacket's celebrity led to notices of his public activities, although, again, his insistence on Seneca autonomy could be variously interpreted or ignored altogether. In 1802, he had become involved in the trial of Stiff-armed George, a Seneca man who was accused of killing a white man in Buffalo, tried in state courts, and pardoned by the governor after white petitions on his behalf. In 1822, Densmore reports, Red Jacket went to court to argue Seneca jurisdiction in another trial, this one much more sensational (61–63). In May 1821, Kau-qua-tau, a Seneca woman, was killed at Buffalo Creek, her throat cut, and a Seneca chief named Soonongize or Tommy-Jemmy was accused. The Seneca woman had been denounced in council as a witch, and Tommy-Jemmy had carried out the death sentence against her. In July, a local Albany newspaper described the scene in court:

At the trial both Red Jacket and Captain Pollard testified about Seneca usages, and Red Jacket in particular took offense at the idea that the belief in witchcraft was absurd. He reminded the court that white men in Salem had executed witches: "What have your brothers [the Senecas] done more than the rulers of your people have done? And what crime has this man committed by executing in a summary way, the laws of his country and the injunctions of his God?"

Red Jacket was then asked whether he believed in a Supreme Being and in future rewards and punishments, to which he replied: 'Yes! much more than the white men, if we are to judge by their actions'" (96). John C. Spender, the Senecas' attorney, argued that the Senecas were a sovereign nation and that the laws of New York did not apply. The jury in Buffalo agreed, but the court sent the case to the New York Supreme Court, which, Densmore writes, was "unable to render a judgment" and sent the matter to Governor DeWitt Clinton, who went to the legislature (96–97). In April 1822, the legislature passed a law declaring that only New York state had authority to punish crimes, but it also pardoned Tommy-Jemmy, acknowledging that he had acted on the authority of the Seneca Nation. This is an interesting contradiction between theory and actual conditions, similar to the U.S. government's problems in asserting its authority over Indian nations after the Revolution. In theory, New York unilaterally declared its authority over Indians, but because of extant conditions, which probably included the necessity of gaining future Seneca consent to sell land, it also had to recognize Seneca political autonomy.

A different contradiction is at work in the record of Red Jacket's public appearances. From January to April 1829, Red Jacket took a well-publicized "leave-taking" tour through the eastern United States to Albany, Boston, New York, and Washington, where he met with Andrew Jackson. He appeared at Masonic Hall in New York City, accompanied by "other warriors [who] danced and sang and revealed the customs of their people."[15]

Red Jacket's biographer William Stone, writing in 1841, presents a different view of his leave-taking as he performed it in Albany, where Stone himself witnessed Red Jacket's undercutting his audience's expectations. In contrast to the tawdriness that Stone thought characterized Red Jacket's other public appearances, at Albany "great pains were taken to collect a political audience" for Red Jacket.[16] These largely New York legislators and Jackson Democrats, Stone writes, eagerly anticipated a speech from the great Indian orator celebrating the virtues of their leader. As in the case of William Apess's *Eulogy on King Philip*, however, this audience did not get what it expected. "Instead of eulogizing the man who was at that time the popular idol of the nation," Stone writes, Red Jacket "spoke of his former visit to George Washington, drew an outline of *his* character, and then instituted a comparison between it and that of General Jackson, greatly to the disadvantage of the latter" (389–90). This produced predictable results: "The applause with which the orator was greeted on his first appearance, was changed into rude manifestations of displeasure, and the audience rapidly grew thin by the departure of those who had been most eager to come" (389–90). Stone concludes by insisting that "the speech was feeble and puerile . . . and delivered without energy or grace," further evidence that Red Jacket was past his prime and at death's door (390).

Red Jacket knows what his audience wants but refuses to supply it. He does not, however, directly confront the representation of himself as eloquent savage, which supersedes anything he actually says. Still his constant return to autonomy, his dismissal of EuroAmericans' views on Indian inferiority, and his manipulation (although this is all through translation) of both treaty discourse and the discourse of Indian doom are all tactics used by those who write in English. Above all, his emphasis on the sovereignty of Native governments was common knowledge in the era. He was even called into service in the Cherokee resistance, when a pamphlet attributed to him was published in 1830, the year of his death. Titled *First Impressions on Reading the Message of the Governor of Georgia, 1830, Relative to the Indian*, the essay repeatedly exposes the illogic at work in the Georgians' arguments in support of Indian removal, revealing that force itself and political oppression lay beneath.[17]

In 1826, the Ogden Land Company convinced the U.S. government to help it pursue a land sale at the Buffalo Creek reservation. A treaty was signed in August 1826, despite Red Jacket's resistance. He appealed to the Quakers, who sent the Senecas' objection to Washington, where they were rejected. Red Jacket himself then went to Washington to lobby the Senate, which did not ratify the treaty but instead "adopted a resolution . . . 'to disclaim the necessity of an interference by the Senate' on the matter."[18] Despite the lack of Senate ratification, however, the Ogden Land Company got what it wanted: the remaining Seneca lands along the Genesee River in the central part of the state, "large tracts from the Buffalo and Tonawanda Reservations, and . . . a small tract from Cattaraugus." Only the Oil Spring and Allegheny reservations in the south-central part of the state were spared. By October 1827, the company began selling the land it had acquired, placing an advertisement in the *Geneva Palladium* on 17 October 1827 insisting that its title to the lands was "indisputable."[19]

This was about the time that David Cusick, a Tuscarora, published his *Sketches of Ancient History of the Six Nations*. It was noticed in Philadelphia and New York newspapers in July and August 1827 in a reprinted paragraph that listed its contents and noted that Cusick "has . . . placed himself at once among the literati of our country" and "has embodied in his work the traditions of his nation, and given a most interesting narrative to the public, told, as we gather it, in the phraseology peculiar to the people of his complexion."[20] The notice appeared in at least the *New-York Gazette & General Advertiser*, the *New York Daily Advertiser*, the *Philadelphia Gazette*, the *Pennsylvania Enquirer*, and the African American newspaper *Freedom's Journal*. The Erie Canal was probably the reason why Cusick's book made it from the outpost of Lewiston, a village north of Buffalo near the Tuscarora reservation where it was first printed, to the Atlantic coast. The book must have been popular: when it was reprinted in 1828, the new edition carried with it on the title page the notice that it was the "Second edition of 7,000 copies—Embelished [*sic*] with four engravings." The engravings were Cusick's own and in the 1828 edition appear as the frontispiece, which unfolds from a large sheet of paper. At least one source suggests that the book was printed for the tourist trade at Niagara Falls—which is entirely plausible, if not probable.[21] From the 1820s to at least mid-century, tourists visiting the falls included a trip to Tuscarora Village, which was about ten miles distant, some of them going so far as to attend Sunday church services in order to get a closer look at the Indians.[22] Like Red Jacket, the only forum open to Cusick to get his message out is one that also insists on him performing his difference, in his case, the tourist trade.

Cusick's book must be seen in relation to works written in the 1820s by Elias Boudinot and William Apess, no matter how apparently different in perspective, as well as against the background of the Iroquois struggle against removal and especially in relation to Red Jacket's speeches and activities at the time. Written at the height of a particularly intense struggle with the Ogden Land Company over a fraudulent treaty, *Sketches of Ancient History of the Six Nations* establishes the history of Iroquois tenure on the land in terms of the traditions of the people and the political structure of the Iroquois Confederacy. Cusick's book cannot be reduced to sentimental Indian trope by EuroAmerican readers—it's much too strange a document—and he is certainly not eloquent, by conventional standards, in English, which in itself marks both the historical necessity of learning English to accommodate radical change and the difficulties for Native peoples, at that moment, of getting an English education, as it was commonly called.

David's father Nicholas was an important leader at the Tuscarora reservation and a devout Christian who is usually noted as having been the bodyguard of Lafayette. Though there was for a time, between 1815 and 1820, open conflict

DAVID CUSICK'S

SKETCHES OF ANCIENT HISTORY OF THE

SIX NATIONS;

—COMPRISING—

First—A TALE OF THE FOUNDATION OF THE

GREAT ISLAND,

(NOW NORTH AMERICA,)

THE TWO INFANTS BORN,

AND THE

CREATION OF THE UNIVERSE.

Second—A REAL ACCOUNT OF THE EARLY SETTLERS
OF NORTH AMERICA, AND THEIR DISSENTIONS.

Third—ORIGIN OF THE KINGDOM OF THE FIVE NATIONS.
WHICH WAS CALLED

A LONG HOUSE:

THE WARS, FIERCE ANIMALS, &c.

Second edition of 7,000 copies.—Embelished with 4 engravings.

Tuscarora Village.
(Lewiston, Niagara co.)
1828.

Title page of the second edition of David Cusick's Sketches of Ancient History of the Six
Nations *(1828), which may have been sold to the nascent tourist trade at Niagara Falls.
Photograph courtesy of the American Antiquarian Society.*

between "pagan" and Christian parties on the reservation, historian Douglas Boyce describes the state of Christianity as "non-committal" on the part
of many people, who attended churches but did not whole-heartedly reject
"pagan" practices. Nevertheless, after 1820, he reports, "overt conflict for religious reasons was a thing of the past . . . and the New York Tuscarora were
known thereafter as Christians."[23] Like his father, David Cusick is often mentioned in travelers' and missionaries' accounts.[24]

In 1803, a missionary report described the teacher of the school at the nearby Buffalo Creek reservation as a "young Indian." Boyce surmises this may have been David Cusick, who had been educated at the Oneida reservation by the missionary Samuel Kirkland—who was himself known for his advocacy of Oneida land sales.[25] On being introduced to David Cusick in 1822 by a Tuscarora "who had lately received his education in New-York," Philip Stansbury, in an account of his "pedestrian tour" of the Great Lakes, Canada, and New England, wrote that David was "celebrated for his ingenuity in the art of painting," adding, "[He] had in his possession, a variety of relics of their former implements and arms, such as stone axes, flint arrows, war-clubs, belts of wampum, and some curious ornaments; and his drawings, though the materials were coarse, exhibited a striking and clear manner, the council meetings, the rites of worship, and the modes of dancing practised by their forefathers."[26] Secretary of War Thomas McKenney met Cusick in 1826, on his way back from the Treaty of Fond du Lac with the Ojibwes in Wisconsin. In his memoir, *Sketches of a Tour to the Lakes*, McKenney describes Cusick as "a cripple with the rheumatism [who] has been bedridden for eight years. He is now quite white. We found him in bed in a sitting posture, with his legs doubled under him."[27] McKenney "purchased some moccasins of him, a painting by one of the tribe, which illustrates a tradition, and several other drawings, hunting, traveling scenes, &c" (433). One drawing, McKenney writes, represents the story of "an enormous bear [that] entered their country to dispossess them of it," although the Iroquois repelled it (433). The picture "represents the bear, and showers of arrows flying in the direction of his head; and a giant, before whom the natives are flying in great terror" (433). "All this is executed with spirit," McKenney adds (433). Cusick was also "thought a good doctor by both whites and Indians," although the source for this information, a late-nineteenth-century Episcopal priest turned expert on the Iroquois, does not say what kind of doctor Cusick was.[28]

In his preface to the book, Cusick very specifically describes himself as writing history.[29] Though he had "been long waiting in hopes that some of my people, who have received an English education, would have undertaken the work as to give a sketch of the Ancient History of the Six Nations," Cusick writes, "no one seemed to concur in the matter," and he concludes that he must write the book himself. But the history is "involved with fables," he continues, and he worries about his own lack of education: "It was impossible for me to compose the work without much difficulty." So he starts the book, abandons it, but returns to it. "I have taken much pains procuring the materials, and translating it into English language," he writes; "I have endeavored to throw some light on the history of the original population of the country, which I believe never have been recorded. I hope this little work will be acceptable to the public." There is a certain urgency in Cusick's account of his coming to write the book; he insists that people must know this history, which in light of other works of Iroquois historiographers, one can certainly relate to the political conflicts at hand. It is possible to read Cusick's urgency, then, in relation to Dearborn's record of Mr. Cone, Red Jacket's speeches on sovereignty, the prophet at Buffalo Creek, Handsome Lake, and the colonial treaties. There is a record of Cusick commenting on current political conflicts over treaty rights. In 1838, McKenney began the first volume of his elephant folio edition of *Indian Tribes of North America* with an entry on Red Jacket in which he mentioned another picture of Cusick's he had seen. "There is, or was, an Indian artist, self taught, who, in a rude and most graphic drawing, exhibited upon canvass [*sic*] the events of a treaty between the white men and an Indian tribe," he writes:

> The scene was laid at the moment of settling the terms of a compact, after the proposals of our government had been weighed, and well nigh rejected by the Indians. The two prominent figures in the front ground, were an Indian chief, attired in his peculiar costume, standing in a hesitating posture, with a hand half extended towards the scroll hanging partly unrolled from the hand of the other figure. The latter was an American officer in full dress, offering with one hand the unsigned treaty to the reluctant savage, while with the other he presents a musket and bayonet to his breast.

"This picture was exhibited some years ago near Lewistown, New York, as the production of a man of the Tuscarora tribe, named *Cusick*," McKenney notes, and then he gives a convoluted reading of the picture. Although "it was an affecting appeal from the Indian to the white man," he observes, "in point of fact, the Indians have never been compelled, by direct force, to part with their lands." Instead, McKenney writes, "we have triumphed over them by our superior power and intelligence, and there is a moral truth in the picture, which represents the savage as yielding from fear, that which his judgments and his attachments should have withheld."[30]

Cusick's claim to write history in contradistinction to "fables" or myths and legends directly counters settlers' depictions of Indians' traditions. After addressing the "creation of the universe," the story of the Good Mind and the Bad Mind, and the creation of the real people in Part I, Cusick offers in Part II "a *real account* of the early settlers of North America" (emphasis added), settlers who are the ancestors of the Iroquois. In Part III, he provides a narrative of the "origin of the Kingdom of the Five Nations," which largely concerns the Five Nations' political alliances and military exploits. Cusick seems to pattern the structure of his narrative after that of settler histories: first there is a narrative of the settlers' origins in the distant past, then a narrative of the first settlers, and then a narrative of the state's foundation. *Sketches of Ancient History of the Six Nations* indeed concerns the formation of political entities and the struggle of those political entities to protect their integrity over time. In this respect, he argues the same point as did Apess, the Cherokees, and the Iroquois negotiators at Lancaster, and, like his predecessors but in a more obvious manner owing to the form in which he makes this argument, he insists that unwritten oral tradition is as valid a measure of accuracy as are written records.

Insisting on the validity of Native traditions or knowledge, and on that knowledge as historical, ultimately concerns Indians' political authority. Many of the narratives in Parts II and III present the "real people" and then the Iroquois defending themselves against attack from outsiders, whether monsters or other Indian tribes. The narratives establish that the Iroquois form political entities of ancient lineage that claim territory, form governments and alliances, and that, by implication, must endure. The history that begins with the Holder of the Heavens breathing life into the real people ends with the founding of the Long House:

> The Long House were free and independent nations, and have been acknowledged in such treatise made them by the neighboring nations—Every independent nation have a government of their own: they have a national committee meet occasionally: they have a Chief Ruler, named *Aukoyaner*, a peace-maker who is invested with authority to administer the government. Each nation have a right to punish individuals of their own nation for offences, committed within their jurisdiction; each nation are bound to oppose any hostile invasions of the enemy. (33–34)

This particular passage was part of a section of material added to the end of Part III in the second 1828 edition. Cusick's history is a history of the Iroquois both before and after Columbus. When he writes that he is presenting a "real account" of that history, the fundamental point, the truth claim he makes to readers who are outside of Iroquois tradition, is that the political entity that existed in the far past will continue to exist in the future.

Well aware of the disbelief that his non-Native readers might feel for stories about Stonish Giants and Flying Heads, he persists in presenting what he knows as accurate historical knowledge. When describing how the Tuscarora people, after their separation from the "five families" and their journey to the south and then east, "discovered a grape vine lying across the [Mississippi] river by which a part of the people went over," Cusick adds a footnote: "By some this may seem an incredible story. Why more so than that the Israelites should cross the Red Sea on dry land" (21). After describing the Stonish Giants' attacks on the people, Cusick appends this footnote:

> It appears by the traditions of the Shawnees, that the Stonish Giants descend from a certain family that journeyed on the east side of Mississippi River, went towards the northwest after they were separated, on account of the vine broke. The family was left to seek its habitation, and the rules of humanity were forgotten, and afterwards eat raw flesh of the animals. At length they practiced rolling themselves on the sand by means their bodies were covered with hard skin these people became giants and were dreadful invaders of the country. It is said that Sir William Johnson, the Superintendent of the Six Nations, had a picture of the giant. Probably the English have recorded in the Historian respecting North America. (22)

In this instance, Cusick reverses the relation between the oral and written records so that the written will confirm the oral, which takes precedence, and not vice versa. He was also aware of the histories of America that would deny that any such confirmation could be made. The Holder of the Heavens comes to the aid of the people and destroys all the Stonish Giants except for one, who "seeks an assylum in the regions of the north." "The families were now preserved from extinction," Cusick adds. Cusick's vocabulary—his use of such charged words as "conquest," "extinction," "extermination"—and his references to the Bible, Columbus, historians, and Sir William Johnson indicate that, like William Apess, he was aware of what settlers wrote about Indians and rejects the claims of such written accounts to accuracy and superiority.

After the creation of the universe, a group of the real people camped "on the bank of a majestic stream . . . named Kanawage, now St. Lawrence" but they "could not enjoy tranquility, as they were invaded by the giants called Ronnongwetowanca" (16). Two aspects of Cusick's history persist throughout the narrative: first, that the real people and then the Iroquois spend much of their time defending themselves against attacks that would destroy them entirely; and second, that a contemporary English placename almost always accompanies the Iroquois name. In this, Cusick implicates the ongoing political struggles of the Iroquois and attaches Iroquois political history to places claimed and renamed by settlers. Another giant attacks another Kanawage town when "there was no person in the town except an old chief and an attendant named Yatatonwatea," who escaped "out the back door and deserted the aged chief to

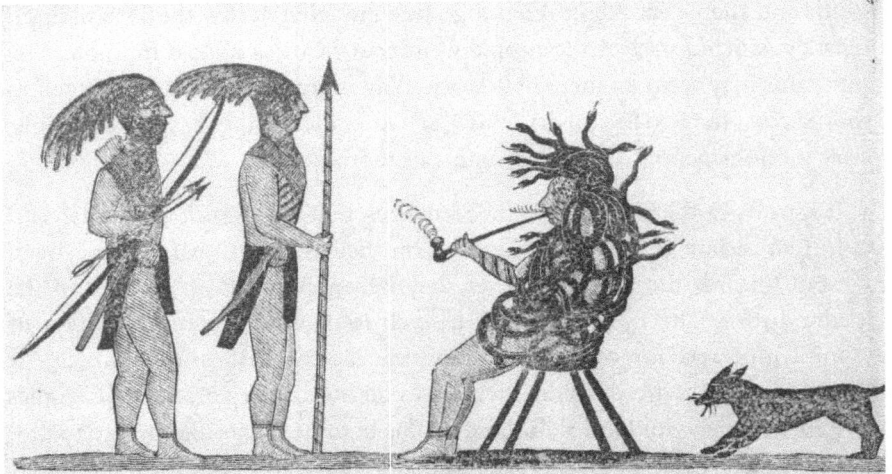

ATOTARHO, A FAMOUS WAR CHIEF, RESIDED AT ONONDAGA.

A WAR DANCE.

Frontispiece woodcuts by David Cusick from the second edition of his Sketches of Ancient History of the Six Nations *(1828). Cusick's paintings, watercolors, and woodcuts*

THE **FLYING HEAD** PUT TO FLIGHT BY A WOMAN PARCHING ACORNS.

THE STONISH GIANTS.

illustrated aspects of Iroquois tradition and history. Photograph courtesy of American Antiquarian Society.

the fate" (17–18). Yatatonwatea flees but is pursued; he attempts to hide himself and to distract the giant, but the giant persists. Yatatonwatea then meets two warriors and together they fight the giant until it "was exterminated" (18). He returns to the village and tells the other members of the tribe about the dangers: "As soon as the people received the intelligence immediately returned to their settlements, and a convention were held by the chieftains in order to take some measures to defend their country" (18).

The real people must form a larger political organization to protect themselves. After a period of safety for "many winters," the people were again attacked, this time by "a mischievous person named Shotyerronsgwea." Then they are attacked by "Big Quisquiss (perhaps the Mammoth)" and "Big Elk," but they always beat back the monsters (19). It was "about this time," Cusick writes, that "the northern nations formed a confederacy and seated a great council fire on river St. Lawrence" (19). When an "Emperor" in the south began to make incursions on the northern people, by building "many forts throughout his dominions," the real people "determined to defend their country against any infringement of foreign people" (19). The wars continue for one hundred years, but "the people of the north were too skillful in the use of bows and arrows and could endure hardships which proved fatal to a foreign people," and "at last the northern nations gathered the conquest and all the towns and forts were totally destroyed and left them in the heap of ruins" (19). Despite their successes, the northern people eventually destroy themselves. First a serpent on Lake Ontario "produced diseases," killing many people before being itself killed; then "a blazing star fell into a fort situated on the St. Lawrence," destroying the people there (19). This was "a warning of [the] destruction" of the northern nations: eventually they fall into war with each other "which continued until they had utterly destroyed each other." After that, "the island again become in possession of fierce animals" (19). Cusick's narrative of the real people defending themselves against attack but being felled by disease and intertribal warfare can certainly be seen in light of Indian nations' more recent experiences with the effects of colonization and settlement, with which Cusick himself would have been familiar.

In Part III, the Holder of the Heavens leads out the survivors of the northern people, who were "concealed in the mountain at the falls named Kuskehsaw-kich, (now Oswego)" to become the "five families" or Five Nations, in addition to the Tuscaroras (20). The people then have another chance at forming a political organization for their mutual protection. The Holder of the Heavens (Tarenyawagon) leads them eastward to "a river . . . named Yenonanatche, i.e. going around a mountain, (now Mohawk)" and beyond the Hudson, where they camped for a few days. Then the different tribes of the Five Nations split up, moving westward from the Shaw-na-taw-ty or Hudson River, first the Mohawks, then the Oneidas, then the Onondagas, then the Cayugas, and finally the Senecas. Cusick then continues the story with the "sixth family," which goes south and then east, "[making] their residence near Cau-ta-noh, i.e. Pine in water, situated near the mouth of Nuse river, now in North Carolina, and the family was named Kau-ta-noh, now Tuscarora" (21). Each tribe's placenames give territory a history that precedes European settlement and a connection to political organization, as does each tribe's language, which, Cusick writes, was "altered" at each settling of a tribe, although the "six families did not go so far as to lose the understanding of each other's language" (20, 21). The Holder of the Heavens sends the five families an "agent" who gives them seeds for their crops and tells them how to hunt. He "instructs them in various things respecting the infinity, matrimony, moral rules, worship &c . . . [and] warns them that a evil spirit was in the world and would induce the people to commit tresspasses against the rules he had given them" (21).

Cusick describes both intertribal conflict and attacks from the outside—again, not unlike the more recent history of the Iroquois post-European contact. About a hundred years after leaving the mountain and at time when "the Holder of the Heavens was absent from the country," the people were "invaded by the monsters called Ko-nea-rau-heh-neh, i.e. Flying Heads" (21). The people defend themselves against attack from "the monster of the deep," Stonish Giants, a human-headed serpent. Cusick describes how forts are constructed, so that the people could protect themselves from "monsters," as they "could not enjoy but a short space of time without being molested" (22). When the Confederacy forms, "perhaps 1000 years before Columbus discovered the America," its purpose is to prevent conflict among the Five Nations so that they may better defend themselves against outside attacks:

> About this time the Five Families become independent nations, and they formed a Council fire in each nation, &c. Unfortunately a war broke out among the Five Nations: during the unhappy differences the Atotarho was the most hostile chief, resided at the fort Onondaga; his head and body was ornamented with black snakes;—his dishes and spoons were made of skulls of the enemy; after a while he requested the people to change his dress, the people immediately drove away the snakes—a mass of wampam were collected and the chief was soon dressed in a large belt of wampam; he became a law giver, and renewed the chain of alliance of the Five Nations and framed their internal government. (23)

The five families form *nations* that have *governments*. A "tree of peace" was planted at Onondaga that "reached the clouds of Heaven"; the "Senators" met and deliberated and "smoke the pipe of peace as ratification of their proceedings" (23). The Atotarho is the "King of the Five Nations," which is "governed by the senate, chosen by the people annually; the successor of the kings to follow the woman's line" (23).

The balance of Cusick's history is a recital of the events occurring during each Atotarho's reign with the relation to Columbus carefully noted. The conjunction of Columbus and the Iroquois Atotarho demonstrates the continuity of Iroquois political organization, just as the Cherokees invoke "time immemorial" as the basis of their argument for continued autonomy. During the reign of Atotarho III, Cusick writes, "perhaps about 800 years before the Columbus discovered the America . . . the Twakanhahors, (now Mississaugers,) ceded the colonies lying between the Kea-nau-hau-sent (Oak-Orchard,) and the river Onyakara, (Niagara) to the five Nations" (25). During the reign of Atotarho VI, "perhaps 650 years before the Columbus discovered the America," warriors are sent "out to make an incursion upon the enemy that may be found within the boundaries of the kingdom" (26). The threat to the Five Nations may be Stonish Giants, Oyalquarkeror or the Big Bear, or other Indian tribes (the Ottawas, Mississaugas, Eries), or a combination of these. Cusick moves easily from military history to descriptions of a monster's frightening powers. At the same time, he describes laws and practices, including punishments for murder, adultery, and recovery of debt. He tells why the Iroquois changed their burial practices in a narrative about a man coming upon a ghost eating a dead person (30). As Susan Kalter points out, he describes the Iroquois as not in need of civilizing, but rather as already civilized.[31] The Iroquois were also expecting whites and their disruptions. Hundreds of years before Europeans arrive, the Five Nations are warned about their arrival: the threat Europeans pose is the same type of threat posed by monsters or other Indian tribes. Cusick's history presents the future in the past; as it leads up to the arrival of Columbus, his history demonstrates the resistance to the settlement that Columbus symbolically opens by his continual insistence on the "sovereignity" of the Indian nations (34).

SENECA HISTORIANS IN THE WAKE OF RACIAL DIFFERENTIATION

While David Cusick's history was apparently largely forgotten, Henry Rowe Schoolcraft's use of the history in his *Notes on the Iroquois* (1847) brought it to the attention of EuroAmerican intellectuals with an interest in Indians, who—

predictably—dismissed it.[32] Schoolcraft remarks of the "Tuscarora legendary" and his writing of tradition: "No people in the world have ever, probably, so completely mingled up and lost their early history, in fictions and allegories, types and symbols as the red men of this continent. Making no sort of distinction themselves, between the symbolic and the historical, they have left no distinctions to make the true from the false."[33] Henry David Thoreau remarked in one of his notebooks on Indians written in the 1850s that Cusick's book was "almost entirely fabulous & puerile—only valuable as showing how an Ind. writes history," although he added that it might be useful though for "some . . . interesting and suggestive traditions."[34] Francis Parkman related Cusick's "preposterous legend" of Iroquois origins in his *The Conspiracy of Pontiac and the Indian War after the Conquest of Canada* (1851).[35] Albert Gallatin gave Cusick no credence whatsoever. "Very little reliance can be placed on their [Indian] legends, tales, or pretended historical traditions," he writes in *Transactions of the American Ethnological Society*, "many of which are indeed fabrications ascribed to them," despite the fact that "the evidently fabulous annals of the Iroquois were . . . invented by a pure Indian (Kussick?)."[36]

In the disparate records of David Cusick, Mr. Cone, and Nicholson Parker's lecture on dancing, there's a pattern of presenting and explaining Iroquois history, practices, and beliefs to EuroAmericans in such a way that the differences in practices and beliefs cannot be separated from political relations, in particular, political negotiations. They are explaining what they believe and how they think to whites with whom they need to establish a political relationship. For the Iroquois, this can perhaps be understood as a practice going back to the necessity of incorporating Europeans into their ceremonies for alliances in the seventeenth and eighteenth centuries—which Europeans had to do, although plenty of them, like Henry Dearborn, complained about it.[37] At Lancaster in 1744, for example, Witham Marshe, the secretary for the commissioners for Maryland, left a journal of the negotiations in which he notes that the colonial officials were invited to dances held at night after the negotiations, the significance of which was explained to them by interpreters.[38] Whereas Europeans, at least the ones who wrote down accounts of their experiences, tended to understand these events as exotic or curious displays, the Iroquois accounts seem to portray them as a matter of explaining the political entity as a whole, where their histories, knowledge, practices, and beliefs are brought to the negotiation.

One might think that Native peoples dealing with Europeans, no matter how desperately those Europeans needed Indians on their side, would be quite familiar with the fact that Europeans thought them inferior savages and their practices and beliefs utter nonsense—if curious and even intriguing nonsense. As Daniel Butrick explains to John Howard Payne, Native peoples were quite used to their knowledge being mocked to their faces. In political negotiations, both sides come together as autonomous entities, as equal autonomous governments, and the recognition of that autonomy and equality extends to a kind of respect conferred on the other party or parties to the negotiations. The mutual recognition of political autonomy in a treaty negotiation extends to mutual recognition that differences do not mean inferiority or make agreements impossible.

The Iroquois writers in the early nineteenth century can be understood as picking up from past practices in their explaining Iroquois difference to a white public in terms of their political claims. Their explanation of their difference is not for the sake of describing difference, but rather part of a long-standing tradition in their dealings with EuroAmericans that cannot be separated from their struggle over their political autonomy. But the setting in which they do that explaining of their difference changed radically in the nineteenth century, and EuroAmerican society at large became even less receptive to hearing what they had to say about themselves, as the learned commentary on Cusick's book indicates. Their difference was by then completely reified, separated from its political context, and turned into the means of their political disfranchisement.

I want here to look at writing by two Iroquois leaders who were chosen to be negotiators with whites: Maris Bryant Pierce and Ely Parker. Both of them were called upon to help negotiate with New York State and the U.S. government, as well as represent the Senecas and Iroquois to the white public, as very young men. Pierce's 1839 speech, *Address on the Present Condition and Prospects of the Aboriginal Inhabitants of North America, with Particular Reference to the Seneca Nation*, his only published work, is very much within the parameters set out by John Ridge and Elias Boudinot. Pierce argues that the Iroquois are rapidly progressing, catching up with whites, and that past traditional practices and beliefs are really past, the moment from which the Iroquois started on their rapid path to progress. Still, like John Ross, he cannot separate the nation from the land, and like William Apess, he invokes a noble lineage of Native leaders, Iroquois and others, who fought for autonomy and sovereignty. More than Pierce, Ely Parker was marked out as a young man to be a leader and a negotiator with whites and their governments. He was extremely well connected: he was the great-great-grandson of Handsome Lake and a grand-nephew of Red Jacket; he served as interpreter for his maternal grandfather, James Johnson (also Jimmy or Jemmy Johnson; his Seneca name was Sose-ha-wa), who was the spiritual leader of the Handsome Lake religion at the time.[39] By the time he was in his twenties, he was an experienced hand at dealing with politicians in Albany and in Washington. In his mainly fragmentary public writing at this time, Ely Parker argues for both Iroquois progress and political claims as well as their traditional difference, on which, in part because of his family connections, he is looked to as an expert. As a very young man, Ely Parker had important political responsibilities both to a modernizing Seneca Nation and to Seneca and Iroquois tradition, and in his public speaking to white audiences, he hasn't quite reconciled the two. This is revealed in Parker's invocation of Indian difference on these public occasions; the only thing available to him rhetorically, in a nonpolitical context, is the reification of Indian difference and the reiteration of their impending doom. In the early 1850s, that rhetoric is like a too-tight suit of clothes Parker tries on, in which he just can't move. The language available to him cannot convey the complexity of his position.

The controversy over the Buffalo Creek Treaty produced two Seneca writers who took opposite sides of the controversy: Maris Bryant Pierce, at the time a sophomore at Dartmouth called by his tribe to a leadership position because of his education; and Nathaniel Thayer Strong, who was employed by the Ogden Land Company as an interpreter during the treaty negotiations and produced an extended defense of the Company's actions, *Appeal to the Christian Community on the Conditions and Prospects of the New York Indians* (New York, 1841). Daniel F. Littlefield Jr. argues that the Seneca resistance to the treaty provided the impetus for the beginnings of Seneca literature and points out that both Pierce and Strong reject subordination and assertions of Indians' ontological difference, insisting on the history of colonization and oppression.[40] Both of them reject the notion of whites' preemptive right to the land. But although he rejects whites' assertion that they have a superior claim to the land because they are white, Strong also concedes that Indians could at that point do nothing about it—whites could claim the preemptive right and Indians were powerless to challenge it, wrong as it was.[41]

Pierce explicitly returns to history in his critique of the Buffalo Creek Treaty, but reserves for it a place apart. The past really is past and, at least in this essay, he sees no element of Seneca tradition in the present, only an increasing movement toward the practices and beliefs characteristic of EuroAmerican society. Pierce's *Address on the Present Condition and Prospects of the Aboriginal Inhabitants of North America, with Particular Reference to the Seneca Nation* was presented at a Baptist church in Buffalo in August 1838 and published in January 1839 in Philadelphia as part of the continuing effort against the Buffalo

Creek Treaty.[42] Like William Apess, Pierce turns to the history of Native leaders, and that of the Iroquois, to demonstrate that there are no essential differences between whites and Indians, but rather only the differences of "*circumstances* and *education*" (3). Like Apess, he mocks the doomed Indian trope, observing that "it has been said and reiterated so frequently as to have obtained the familiarity of household words that it is the *doom* of the Indian to disappear—to vanish like the morning dew, before the advance of civilization: and melancholy it is to us—those doomed ones—that the history of this country, in respect to *us* and its civilization, has furnished so much ground for the saying, and for giving credence to it" (4). That is to say, if Indians are doomed, it's not because of their supposed difference, but rather because of the history of relations between Indians and whites. "It has been so long and so often said as to have gained general credence, that our *natural constitution* is such as to render us incapable of apprehending, and incompetent to practice, upon those principles from which result the *characteristic* qualities of christian civilization," he writes, reiterating the arguments about false knowledge made by African American and other Native writers in the era (4). "Under the sanction of acknowledged principles of moral law," he continues, "we must yield ourselves sacrifices, doomed by the constitution which the Almighty has made for us, to that *other race* of human beings, whom the same Almighty has endowed with a more noble and more worthy constitution" (4). "These are the premises; these the arguments; these the conclusions," he concludes, "but they are not *true*, and *just*, and *legitimate*" (5).

Pierce points out that the anger and resentment that Indians may feel for whites is fully justified by their historical experiences, as is the apparent suspicion that many Indians—Red Jacket would certainly have been in the minds of his Buffalo audience—feel for the "civilizing" efforts of whites (5–6). Indians do not differ from whites biologically, emotionally, morally, or intellectually. Pierce writes:

It is not denied that [the Indian] is susceptible of hatred, and equally of friendship,—that he even can love and pity, and feel gratitude,—that he is prone to the adoration of the Great Spirit,—that he possesses an imagination, by which he pictures fields of the blessed in a purer and more glorious world than this,—that he possesses the faculty of memory and judgment, and such a combination of faculties as enable him to invent and imitate,—that he is susceptible of ambition, emulation, pride, vanity,—that he is sensitive to honor and disgrace, and necessarily has the *elements* of a *moral sense* or conscience. All these are granted as entering into his *native spiritual constitution*. (7)

Undated daguerreotype of Maris Bryant Pierce. Pierce was made a chief while still a student at Dartmouth and remained a leader among the Senecas throughout his long life, serving as interpreter and secretary of the Seneca Nation. He died in 1874. Photograph courtesy of the Buffalo and Erie County Historical Society.

To support his point of there being no essential difference between Indians and whites, Pierce, like William Apess, turns to the history of Indian leaders—Osceola, Red Jacket, Tecumseh, and King Philip—who possessed those "*natural endowments*, which, by *cultivation*, give to the children of civilization their great names and far-reaching fame" (7). And these are all leaders who insisted on Native political autonomy and struggled, as did Osceola, against "the white man's treachery and cruelty" (8).

Despite his insistence on Native equality, or rather because of his insistence on Native sameness to EuroAmericans, Pierce describes the Iroquois past before the advent of whites as disconnected from the civilized present. The Senecas, he writes, do not "wish to return to . . . the habits of life which

prevailed when the country was first taken possession of by the Europeans"—
the moment in which European thought freezes Indians in time (16). Indeed,
Pierce writes, the Senecas "desire to renounce those habits of mind and body,
and adopt in their stead those habits and feelings—those modes of living, and
acting and thinking, which result from the cultivation and enlightening of the
moral and intellectual faculties of man" (16).

What the Senecas and other Indians do have, however, that establishes
continuity between past and present is land. Pierce maintains that civilizing
Indians can occur only "by remaining where we are now located" (13). "The
right and possession of our lands is undisputed—so with us it is a question of
appealing directly *to our interest*; and how stands the matter in relation *to
that?*" (13). That their lands belong to them is accepted by all; when the
removal question comes up, it's a matter of explaining to these rational Native
peoples the benefits of removing—of which there are none. Their land is
fertile; their ancestors and history are there; there are opportunities for "improvement" in their proximity to "enlightened" whites; all of the goods they
might need are available. "We here are more in the way of instruction from
teachers, having greater facilities for getting up and sustaining schools; and as
we, in the progress of our improvement, may come to feel the want and
usefulness of books and prints, so we shall be able readily and cheaply to get
whatever we may choose" (13–14). Thus, "there is no inducement for removing" (14). There is no inducement to sell either: "The fact that whites want our
land imposes no obligation on us to sell it," he writes (14). "We neither know
nor feel any debt of gratitude which we owe to them . . . that should cause us
to make a sacrifice of our property or our interest, to their wonted avarice,
and which, like the mother of the horse leach, cries Give, give, and is never
sated" (14).

Like the Cherokee spokesmen, Pierce would deny traditional knowledge but
retain land. He remained an important leader among the Senecas for the rest
of his life, although after the initial struggle over the Buffalo Creek Treaty, he
produced no further orations or lectures; his time was taken up with political
and tribal business. In the 1840s, Ely Parker began to perform a similar func-
tion to Maris Pierce, even before he was twenty years old. Parker's father
William had fought with the Americans in the War of 1812 and farmed wheat
and raised horses on the Tonawanda Seneca reservation, northeast of Buffalo
Creek. Nicholson Parker's grandson Arthur C. Parker relates that although Ely
was not the eldest son, his mother Elizabeth had had a dream while she was
pregnant foretelling Ely's destiny as one who would "be distinguished among
his nation as a peace-maker" and who would "become a white man as well as

an Indian."[43] While still a schoolboy, Ely Parker was chosen by the tribe to become involved, first as an interpreter and later as a tribal leader, in their endless disputes with the Ogden Land Company, the state of New York, and the federal government. He left school at eighteen because of his political responsibilities. By the time he was in his late teens, he had had dinner at the White House with President Polk and had met Daniel Webster, Henry Clay, and John Calhoun, all of whom considered Ely "a great favorite . . . though his costume was of buckskin and his hat of doeskin and feathers."[44]

Ely was especially close to his older brother Nicholson, who seems not to have had the pressures put on him as a boy that Ely had, which may have been owing to their parents' sense of Ely's destiny. Arthur Parker, who trained as an anthropologist at Harvard and became state archaeologist of New York at the turn of the century, writes that Ely and Nicholson each received a classical education in their different boarding schools but also discovered for themselves the written accounts of "the fine qualities possessed by the old leaders of the race before the time when contact had caused too great corruption." Such accounts were written by the likes of Samuel Gardner Drake and B. B. Thatcher, who both published Indian biographies in 1832. Arthur Parker writes that Ely and Nicholson "read with the joy of discoverers of Tecumseh and Pontiac, of Philip of Pokanoket and of Garangula" (76). "Spurred on [by] ambition," as schoolboys Ely and Nicholson "[delivered] in oration and essay, heroic defenses of the Indian," although the seeming contradiction between defending "savage" Indians while partaking of a "civilized" education "led to many interesting arguments, and both Nicholson and Ely felt compelled to deliver orations explaining why they were seeking a white man's education if the Indian way was so superior" (76). However, Ely and Nicholson put their common interests to more prosaic uses too; Arthur Parker writes that they would often submit the same paper or a variation of it in their schoolwork, since they went to different schools. He observes that "this was at least brotherly reciprocity even if it had some suspicion of a lack of ethics" (76–77). One of their shared papers, titled "Original Thoughts Impossible to Man," won a prize, although for which brother Arthur Parker doesn't say (77).

They were also reading William Apess. In what survives of his school papers at the Buffalo and Erie County Historical Society, Nicholson copied out the beginning of Apess's *Eulogy on King Philip*: "I do not arise to spread before you the fame of a noted warrior whose natural abilities shone like that of the great and mighty Philip of Greece or of Alexander the Great or like those of Washington whose virtues & patriotism are engraven upon the hearts of my audience. Neither do I approve of *war* as being the best method of bowing the haughty tyrant *Man* & civilizing the world."[45] Although Nicholson studied Apess, it is Ely's account of "King Philip's Last Speech to his Countrymen" that survives. Ely writes that King Philip "could . . . see many a son of the forest, in refusing to give place to his white neighbor, killed and dragged through the streets in order to exterminate them in the most disgraceful manner, while others were taken and carried to a land beyond the salt waters and exhibited in shows like wild beasts, thus clearly proving that by a great number they are looked upon as not unequal to the brute." Ely's version of King Philip's speech concludes: "We have suffered greatly from [whites'] injustice. . . . We are now on the verge of ruin, a few suns more shall seal the fate of us all; but the Great Spirit will revenge the wrongs of his red children for he delights not to have them oppressed."[46] Nicholson and Ely were schoolboys, learning how to write, and their discursive models for themselves, for Indian people, could only convey their own doom and destruction. Yet, Apess's model comes through in their writing, in their refusal of racial difference and their need to write history. In Nicholson's writing in particular, too, it's possible to see the delight in language that Apess's work makes evident, the traces of his work as a widely praised orator.

In the late 1840s, Ely and Nicholson, along with their sister Caroline and brother Levi, worked closely with Lewis Henry Morgan, the main architect of the nineteenth-century enshrinement of the Iroquois empire, providing much of the information through which Morgan produced that narrative. In *League of the Iroquois* (1851), which was dedicated to Ely and featured illustrations of Caroline and Nicholson in traditional Seneca dress, Morgan observes that the Iroquois held "the highest position among the Indian races of the continent living in the hunter state."[47] Their achievements were so remarkable because Indians had little or no inclination to form governments since they were inveterate hunters who only wanted more and more land to hunt on. "The effect of this powerful principle," Morgan writes, "has been to enchain the tribes of North America to their primitive state" (57). Even the Iroquois, however, were unable to stop the advance of the "Saxon . . . race" (58). Nevertheless, Morgan writes, "their institutions have a real, a present value, for what they were, irrespective of what they might have become. . . . Our country they once called their country, our rivers and lakes were their rivers and lakes, our hills and intervals were also theirs" (143). The Iroquois, with their long recorded history of diplomatic, military, and economic relations with European settlers, provided a suitably heroic past for the United States, an empire that was admirable in many respects but that was doomed to fade before the emerging republic with its population of freedom-loving Anglo-Saxons.

In *Playing Indian*, Philip Deloria describes how Morgan first formed his fraternity with the idea of its members helping to produce an authentically American literature. By the 1840s, however, Morgan began to envision his Indian fraternity in relation to ethnology. In an absurd, even obscene, embodiment of EuroAmerica's obsession with incorporating Indians epistemologically, psychologically, and politically, members of Morgan's fraternity would participate in an "Inindianation" ceremony, through which they would acquire an Indian persona, after which they would then set out to acquire as much "accurate" information on the Iroquois as they possibly could. They then would write up this information and discuss it at their meetings. The political, the actual, became a problem, however, because in the interest of greater authenticity, Morgan began to cultivate the Parker children as informants. He met Ely—in a bookstore—when Ely accompanied a Seneca delegation to Albany as an interpreter for negotiations with the state government.[48] Ely, in turn, used his connection with Morgan to further the cause of the Senecas' contestation of the Buffalo Creek Treaty, enlisting Morgan and the members of the New Confederacy in a letter-writing campaign. Morgan even went to Washington on the tribe's behalf. This contradiction between necessarily disappeared Indians who were figured as the prehistory of the United States and actual Indians who were fighting for treaty rights led, Deloria writes, to "a new, more complicated set of rationalizations that would eventually explain away the contradictions of Indianized American identities in the modern terms of ethnography" (83). That rationalization consisted of making a distinction between Indian people who "were not necessarily physically vanishing" and their culture, which *was* vanishing (91).

I would argue that a more complicated set of rationalizations than had existed previously was not even required. As the response to all of the writers who preceded the Parker children's involvement with Morgan shows, it was quite easy for nineteenth-century EuroAmericans to distinguish between "real" Indians who produced their racial difference and the—many—anomalous "civilized" Indians who were only postponing the inevitable. Deloria notes that Morgan lost interest in his fraternity by early 1847; after he published *League of the Iroquois* in 1851, he did not return to writing about Indians until his *Ancient Society* in 1877 (92). One does wonder whether the contradiction between the Indians of ethnology and the Senecas who wanted his help on treaty rights was too much to sustain intellectually. If anything, Morgan was relying on Native peoples who, though younger and not quite as well educated as he was, were nevertheless quite well educated by middle-class American standards and who were at the same time vastly knowledgeable about Seneca tradition and history.

Scott Michaelsen has considered Ely Parker's contributions to *League of the Iroquois* in some detail—specifically his translations of the speeches of Abraham LaFort and Jimmy Johnson (the latter of whom relates the Handsome Lake revelations)—and concludes that Ely is "racialist" in his descriptions of Iroquois difference.[49] Leaving aside the problem of reading Ely Parker's translation of ceremonial speech as if it were simply his own thoughts on the topic, Michaelsen neglects entirely to examine the speeches in the context of Iroquois writing of the era, although they are completely congruent with the recorded positions of Red Jacket, David Cusick, and even Timothy Alden's account of Cornplanter's presumably lost history. For example, at a council in October 1847 Abraham LaFort says that "the human race was created and divided into different classes, which are placed separate from each other, having different customs, manners, laws and religions."[50] This is an insistence on different political jurisdictions characteristic of Iroquois and other Native groups' discourse. Ely Parker's translation of Jimmy Johnson's recitation at a mourning council in October 1848 at Tonawanda makes essentially the same point. Johnson recounts Handsome Lake's experiences, revelations, and commands. He admonishes the Iroquois by warning them, "We are surrounded by the pale faces, and in a short time the woods will all be removed. . . . The pale-faces are pressing you upon every side. You must therefore live as they do. How far you can do so without sin, I will now tell you. You may grow cattle, and build yourselves warm and comfortable dwelling-houses. This is not sin; and it is all that you can safely adopt of the customs of the pale-faces. You cannot live as they do" (250–51). Johnson goes on to relate that Handsome Lake prohibits intermarrying with whites, saying that the Great Spirit "has made us, as a race, separate and distinct from the pale-face. It is a great sin to intermarry, and intermingle the blood of the two races. Let none be guilty of this transgression" (252). As with Red Jacket's speeches, this appeal to racial difference must be seen in the political context. The object here is for the Iroquois to retain their autonomy and land in a period of great upheaval; intermarriage with whites often historically had adverse effects on the cohesiveness of Native governments and therefore on their ability to resist white encroachment. If Jimmy Johnson describes what might be read as an endorsement of racial difference, he's using the concept in a sense diametrically opposed to that of his white contemporaries—for political reasons.[51] One has to take into account the conditions at hand: Johnson is talking to other Native peoples, trying to keep them together as a community in the face of enormous pressure driving them apart.

Ely Parker and the other writers included here are talking to whites, however, and with the treaty relationship foremost in the struggle, they recognize that to appeal to racial difference would be politically counterproductive. That awareness is evident in their arguments against racial differentiation as it is manifested in false knowledge about Indians. Michaelsen notes that Parker's version of the "Inindianation" ceremony he wrote for Morgan's fraternity, apparently in 1847, for example, can be read as in some respects satirical. He points out that Parker uses such charged rhetoric of Indian difference as "wigwam" when he "knew full well" that the Iroquois traditionally lived in longhouses and describes the ceremony as "one great laugh at the naivete of Morgan's Grand Order" (91). Parker has the "Sachem" speak as follows: "The birds of the air have places to build their nests, the beasts of the earth are bountifully supplied with all the comforts necessary for their subsistence. Alas! Alas, there is no place left, where the red man can lay his head, or repose his weary limbs in peace and comfort. The blackness of despair surrounds him, as he sits in his lonely wigwam. It accompanies him during the chase, it returns with him at night, to rack his mind as he lies upon his bearskin, seeking that rest that he so much needs."[52] The Inindianation ceremony can be read as an exercise in the doom and disappearance discourse of Indians and is indeed a joke at the expense of white men who want to be Indians.

At the same time, entering into this discourse on Indians, as a writer like George Copway shows, can be contradictory and confusing, for both writer and reader. Ely Parker surely knows, as the Inindianation ceremony and his other writings demonstrate, that the idea of Indians' ontological difference is misrepresentation. The problem is that virtually the only rhetorical device for representing Native peoples in EuroAmerican discourse is that inescapable figure of Indian doom, especially after 1840. William Apess, for example, could manipulate his audience's expectations about pious Indian preachers, but after 1840, that kind of representation virtually disappears, as the possibilities for EuroAmerican thinking about Native peoples are reduced even further.

One might also consider, or imagine, Ely Parker's place, and that of his brother Nicholson as well, in society, particularly after becoming Morgan's informant. In the early 1850s, when, with Morgan's help, he had taken a job as an engineer at Rochester, New York, on—ironically—the canal system, Ely was helping Morgan to complete *League of the Iroquois*, active in the local Masonic Lodge and the Fifty-fourth Regiment of the New York Militia, and a member of the Rochester Athenaeum and Mechanics Association. In 1851, he was installed, at the age of twenty-three, as one of the fifty sachems of the Iroquois Confederacy. As William Armstrong notes in *Warrior in Two Camps*,[53] although the fifty sachems were traditionally equal, Ely's high profile in Euro-American society led whites at first to construe him as first among the fifty,

Although Ely Parker did not appear publicly in Indian dress, he often appeared wearing the Red Jacket medal, as in this 1855 daguerreotype. On Red Jacket's death, the medal had passed to Ely Parker's grandfather Sose-ha-wa or James Johnson, a nephew of Red Jacket's who was also the grandson of Handsome Lake. Johnson succeeded Handsome Lake in relating the prophet's teachings; Ely Parker, who served as his grandfather's interpreter, inherited the medal from him. Photograph courtesy of the Western Reserve Historical Society, Cleveland, Ohio.

referring to him as " 'the Chief of the Six Nations' " or the " 'Head Sachem' of his people," a designation that was accepted by Native peoples, given Ely's important duties despite his relative youth (51). He was regularly called upon to go to Washington to bring the Seneca case to the commissioner of Indian affairs or to the president himself—which he did, with more than one president and commissioner. He was also, apparently, giving lectures, perhaps to the Masons or the Athenaeum, although only his notes survive.

In his writing at least, Parker never wavered on the fact that he was Seneca, on the importance of the history of the Senecas, or on the political rights of the Senecas. As with all of the writers included in this book, I don't think the problem is that Parker doesn't know who he is, as one critic once put it in reference to George Copway (which begs the question how we are supposed to delve into his innermost thoughts if even he doesn't know what they are). Rather the issue is that he had to find a means of representing Senecas and of being Seneca in radically changed circumstances—in particular, in the face of a dominant society that egregiously misrepresented him and all Native peoples.

Perhaps psychological speculation is inevitable in these circumstances, but in Ely Parker's writing as a young man at least, it's his contradictions and impasses that become intriguing. For example, in "Indian dances, games, and social and domestic habits," a partial text and collection of his lecture notes from about 1850 on, one can see Ely trying to sort out conflicting discourses. The bulk of the lecture notes are a straightforward catalog of ethnological information: Seneca marriage practices, ceremonies, games, hospitality. This is the knowledge about Indians' quaint and strange practices (sometimes titillating in the case of courtship and marriage practices) in which a polite Rochester audience at the Masonic hall or the Athenaeum would be interested, and which Lewis Henry Morgan himself supplied with the help of the Parker family—all of whom, one can imagine, had other things in mind than the disappearance of the Iroquois. The most extensive written material from the lecture is the introduction, which begins with the unattributed and slightly edited first few lines of Apess's *Eulogy on King Philip*:

> Ladies & Gentlemen,
>
> I do not present myself here for the purpose of spreading before you the fame of a noted warrior, whose natural abilities shone like that of the great and mighty Philip of Greece, or of Alexander the Great, or like those of Washington, whose virtues and patriotism are engraven upon the hearts of my audience.

But it is to bring before you beings made by the God of nature, and in whose hearts has planted sympathies that will [live?] forever in the memory of the world, so that the most cultivated, whose powers shown with equal luster were not able to prepare mantles to cover the burning elements of an uncivilized world.

Those noble traits that marked the wild man's course lie buried in the shades of night, and who shall stand? I appeal to the lovers of liberty, justice, humanity and permit me to present before you the North American Indians, and especially those who once peopled the length and breadth of your Empire State.

But Ladies & Gentlemen I have appeared before you, as an isolated fragment of that once powerful and magnanimous, but now feeble, scattered and nearly extinct race.

How often have I listened with delighted wonder to the history of our race, detailed by my people, as it has been handed down by them from generation to generation, having been thus preserved in tradition as historic record. When I have harkened to their heroic deeds, their patriotism, their multitudinous feasts, the extent and support of their "*Long House*," I have enquired with an anxious and swelling heart "Where are they all now"? Whither have they fled? Shall I not come to some of these great council fires yet, and see their greatness and glory? And then to hear in answer, "My son, you will never see such mighty feasts, such council gatherings, such a great people of the race of the *Red Man*, as our ancestors were wont to see and enjoy."[54]

A comparison with Apess is helpful here. The context for Apess's references to the "God of nature" in the *Eulogy on King Philip* in 1836 is natural law, the underpinning of the controversy over the meaning of treaties in the 1830s. By 1850, when "nature" in relation to Native peoples can be understood only in the romantic sense, the setting for discussion of Native peoples has changed radically, and Parker, still a young man of twenty-two or twenty-three, can't quite find a means to talk about the history that leads up to himself and the Senecas' struggle against the Ogden Land Company. With the Cherokees in the public eye and their "removal" a political and moral crisis in the 1830s, Apess was able to incorporate himself and other New England Native peoples into an ongoing history of political struggle. Ely Parker's personal life is the embodiment of that struggle; conceptually, however, the words aren't yet there to convey it to an audience of whites for whom Native political demands have become incomprehensible.

Ely Parker's surviving writing is fragmentary. He spoke publicly, either with or without notes, and no written lecture survives, although he apparently gave many throughout his life. What survives, however, cannot be written off as "racialism." Ely's account of the history of the Iroquois Confederacy that he wrote down at about the age of twenty, for example, is a history of government. "The plan of alliance was at first simple," Parker writes. "It provided for the establishment of a confederacy, enjoying a democratic form of government. The civil and legislative power was to be vested in a certain number of wise men who would be styled civil sachems, and the military and executive power in another third of men who would be styled military sachems."[55] He hesitates on whether or not the Iroquois account of the Confederacy's origins are exactly accurate, observing, "I cannot tell how much reliance can be placed upon this tradition, which is more allegory than real. The main facts of its origin may be embodied in allegory, while it has been painted at by the imagination of the Indians." Then he copies out an account of the Confederacy origins that the Moravian missionary John Heckewelder heard from the Delawares earlier in the nineteenth century and concludes that while he is "not able now to say which of the two traditions can most be relied on" as "they both are plausible," "historical disclosures and present existing traditions go far to show that the Iroquois are right in regard to the place where their Confederacy was formed." The "imagination" of Indians is an accurate account of the past—as Native writers who didn't abandon the past always maintained.

REPOLITICIZING RED JACKET

In speeches given in 1853 and 1863, Nicholson Parker and Nathaniel Strong tell the recent history of the Iroquois through Red Jacket in such a way that their relative disunity in the wake of the American Revolution and their near-constant struggles against land speculators in the first half of the nineteenth century can be represented as a moment in time, a historical experience, and not as the providential end of the Confederacy.

The circumstances of the disinterment of Red Jacket's bones are not entirely known. In 1852, George Copway was in Buffalo on a speaking tour, and either in advance of or as a result of his lecture, he heard about Red Jacket's neglected gravesite on the Buffalo Creek reservation, which was in the process of being abandoned as it had ultimately not been saved from the Ogden Land Company. Copway, along with a businessman named Wheeler Hotchkiss and an undertaker named Farrell, apparently decided to dig up the bones for a proper burial. In his biography of Red Jacket, Densmore reports that Hotchkiss had the bones at first, but when the people on the Buffalo Creek reservation found out and demanded them, they were eventually handed over to Ruth Stevenson, Red Jacket's stepdaughter, who lived at the Cattaraugus reservation. One story circulated that Moses Stevenson and Daniel Twoguns of Buffalo Creek went to a local lawyer named Hugh Cameron for advice, telling the lawyer that Copway "intended to illustrate his lecture with the skull of Red Jacket" (122). Cameron, the story goes, told them not to take legal action but rather to secrete the bones somewhere safe as soon as possible. They were then hidden at Cattaraugus but were not forgotten by those who wished to rightfully memorialize the celebrated orator of the vanished Iroquois empire. While Nicholson Parker's speech "The American Red Man" was given while he was a student at Albany Normal School a year after the bones' disappearance, Strong's speech was motivated by the idea of reinterring the bones at Buffalo's Forest Lawn cemetery, an up-to-date park cemetery on the model of Mount Auburn in Cambridge, Massachusetts. However, the bones were not reinterred until 1884. In 1876, William Clement Bryant, the head of the Buffalo Historical Society, got permission from the Senecas to rebury Red Jacket at Forest Lawn, along with other Senecas from the Buffalo Creek mission cemetery (122). The reinterment finally took place in October 1884, and at the celebration the night afterwards, Ely Parker was the featured Indian speaker (122).

In "The American Red Man," Nicholson Parker explains why Red Jacket appeared to have rejected whites entirely; the reasons are not racial, but rather political. When the tribe was in dire straits, Nicholson writes, surrounded by whites who "advanced upon them with gigantic strides," and when war had failed as a strategy, "it was then that Red Jacket stood forward as a patriot, defending his nation with fearless eloquence and denouncing its enemies with fierce invective, or bitter sarcasm" (266). Nicholson alludes to Red Jacket's supposed cowardice in war, pointing out that his "moral courage" in the crisis faced by the nation "showed a mind of too high an order to be influenced by the base sentiment of fear" (266). He then addresses the circumstances of Red Jacket's apparent rejection of white practices, pointing out that the combination of social change and political oppression made for particular and difficult circumstances that Red Jacket dealt with by arguing against whites entirely.

The Indians were asked not only to sell their country, but to embrace a new religion, to change their occupation and domestic habits, and to adopt a novel system of thought and action. Strange as these propositions must have seemed in themselves, they were rendered the more unpalatable when dictated by the stronger party, and accompanied by occasional acts of oppression. It was at this crisis that Red Jacket stood forward, the intrepid defender of his country, its customs, and its religion, and the unwavering opponent of all innovations. He yielded nothing to persuasion or bribery, or to menace, and never, to his last hour, remitted his exertions in what he considered the noblest purpose of his life. (266)

Nicholson thus provides the context for Red Jacket's apparent rejection of all things white. He quotes "an intelligent gentleman" who describes Red Jacket as "a *perfect Indian* in every respect—in costume, in his contempt of the dress of the white men, in his hatred and opposition to the missionaries, and in his attachment to and veneration for the ancient customs and traditions of his tribe" (266–67). Nicholson Parker, though a young man when he wrote this, was versed in both the EuroAmerican classics and his own tradition, had been brought up Christian, and would eventually marry a white woman. He recognized that Red Jacket's choices were political ones made at a particular moment in time.

As Nicholson describes it, in a council held between the Iroquois and the governor of New York, a dispute arises about a point in a previous treaty. Red Jacket says to the American agent, " 'You Yankees are born with a feather between your fingers; but your paper does not speak the truth. The Indian keeps his knowledge here; this is the book the Great Spirit gives us; it does not lie!' " (267). Nicholson adds that "a reference was immediately made to the treaty in question, when to the astonishment of all present, and to the triumph of the red statesman, the document confirmed every word he had uttered" (267). When Red Jacket knew he was dying, Nicholson writes, he visited the Senecas and talked to them about "the conditions of the nation, in the most impressive and affecting manner. He told them that he was passing away. . . . He would run over the history of his people from the most remote period to which his knowledge extended, and pointed out, which only few could do, the wrongs, the privations and the loss of character, which almost of themselves constituted that history" (267). Wrongs, privations, and loss of character: the sequence is important. Like Apess, Nicholson explains how loss of character becomes a fact of existence, but first you have to be wronged. Red Jacket then says that while he's going to "join the spirits of my fathers," the Senecas themselves are in trouble; they "are soon to be scattered and forgotten" (267). Nicholson writes that "with him fell the spirit of his people. They gazed upon his fallen form and mused upon his prophetic warnings, until their hearts grew weary with grief" (267–68). Even here, the doom discourse is counterbalanced by Nicholson's representation of Red Jacket's own historicizing of experience.

Ten years after Nicholson Parker's comments on Red Jacket, Nathaniel Strong begins his own speech on Red Jacket with the doom and extinction discourse, while also noting the close connections between the founders of the "great Republic" and Iroquois leaders. "But with this difference between us the race to which I belong, the doomed children of nature, are passing, a mournful procession, toward the Spirit Land and are leaving no monuments behind them," he writes. "Yea, it may be said that the race *has* passed away. This is meet—for the Great Spirit wills it. A new race has taken their seats." But after this appeal to sympathy, Strong tells a story by Aesop that becomes a mocking refrain throughout the speech. A forester and a lion meet in the woods and begin to argue about the superiority of their "respective races." The forester, in order to prove his superiority, "pointed to a monument on which was sculptured in marble the statue of a man striding over the body of a vanquished lion. 'If this,' said the Lion, 'is all you have to say, let *us* be sculptors and you will see the lion striding over the vanquished man.' " Strong continues: "Yes Ladies and Gentlemen, 'Indians are no sculptors.' He, who would now address you, found great difficulty, groping amid the highlights of Seneca tradition, in gleaning a few kernels of grain, a few meagre facts in the history of the life and times of one of the most extraordinary men that has appeared on the theatre of public action among the people of his nation and among your fathers in the century which is just closed."[56] It may seem remarkable, given the arguments in Strong's only published work, that he can so forcefully point out in this anecdote that those with power write the history that's taken as truth—and to an audience of well-off white people at the Buffalo Historical Society. In the pamphlet from 1839, however, Strong does not concede Native inferiority but rather argues that, given whites' behavior up to that point, the Senecas would be better off out of their proximity. The anecdote may appear to be a rhetorical flourish, but it is instead a recognition of the politics of representation.

In his speech at the Buffalo Historical Society, Strong emphasizes from the beginning that Red Jacket was deeply involved in the politics of the Senecas and the Iroquois from the time he was a boy, first as a messenger for the chiefs. These messages were evidence of "grave and patient deliberation on the part of those Indian Senators and in which were involved the welfare and peace of whole communities and nations" (5). Red Jacket, Strong explains, "grew up to manhood in the councils of his people. The sachems and chiefs appreciated his thoughtful and sedulous attentions to them. No wonder that he was a favorite with them all. Indeed it is said that he was petted by them" (5). Red Jack-et's grandmother put him forward as a suitable chief, Strong points out, taking the occasion to dispute the stereotypical portrayal of Indian women as drudges. "The popular notion that woman was degraded and shorn of all indulgence among the Six Nations of Indians is erroneous," he writes. "The Indian woman, it is true, performed much laborious toil, but she has a potential voice in naming the rulers of her people, and withal was invested with an influence and a dignity such as the boasted chivalry of our pale-face brothers has never clothed her" (6).

Strong describes Red Jacket's eloquence in terms of its political and intellectual power, and also its social grace. "His oratory moved all men," Strong writes. "His words often times swayed and changed the destinies of kindred tribes. His powerful understanding comprehended all subjects which came before the Councils and he elucidated them before his associates by tracing cause and effect into their . . . simple forms" (7). Red Jacket is "courteous" and "considerate," never sarcastic or "vituperative"; his "voice was clear and melodious—charming and attractive in the highest sense, his gesticulations too were graceful and impressive" (7). Strong would seem to be attempting to capture Red Jacket's eloquence in his own writing: "His thoughts were clothed in a garb that glittered with the gems and was gorgeous with the blossoms which nature scattered with so prodigal a hand about the homes and forests of the Red children of the forest," he writes (8). Red Jacket is exemplary in the way that William Apess's King Philip is exemplary—equal to whites, but more naturally talented than most.

Strong then begins a history of the Iroquois' relations with the United States, from the time of the American Revolution, observing that "the acknowledgement of the independence of the United States by Great Britain was the darkest hour to the Six Nations of Indians in their whole national existence" (13). The Revolution that EuroAmericans celebrate is the destruction of the Iroquois. After the Iroquois realized that they had been abandoned by Great Britain, "the thought for the first time struck them—that perhaps the result would be the loss of all their lands—their favorite hunting grounds . . . forfeited, their wives and children homeless. The result was unlooked for by them. They were for a time paralyzed. They did not know what to do" (13). They consented to a provisional treaty in 1783, then the Treaty of Fort Stanwix in 1784 recognized Iroquois territory but also ceded a large amount of land to the United States. This caused a lifelong rift between Red Jacket and Cornplanter, Strong writes, and only after the treaty was concluded did Cornplanter have second thoughts, petitioning George Washington for redress. Cornplanter's appeals to Washington went unheard: "History has not recorded an instance where the white man, when he placed his foot upon Indians land by some pretended color of right has ever retraced his steps" (17). The dominance of sympathetic discourse about Indians allows for reference to whites' transgressions within the conventional lament for disappeared Indians. Strong necessarily exceeds what would have been expected of him as an Indian speaker at the Buffalo Historical Society in this somewhat veiled reference to the preemptive right, given that the land on which he spoke, as well as the livelihoods of a good part of his audience, were probably directly related to the advantages gained by whites as a result of that particular "pretended color of right."

Strong also addresses the shift that took place in U.S. policy from the close of the Revolution to the mid-1790s. As Dorothy Jones describes, this was when the United States changed its policy from one of declaring conquest when no conquest had been effected to that of recognizing in treaties the sovereignty of Indian nations on its frontiers, including the Iroquois. Strong observes that "the real cause of uneasiness and difficulty on the part of the Indians of the Six Nations after the treaty of peace at Fort Stanwix was that the Congress of the U.S. had acted upon the principle that the treaty with Great Britain invested them with the fee of all Indian lands within the boundaries of the U.S." (20–21). That is, the United States acted as if, having made peace with Great Britain, all of the Indian territory within the territory claimed by Britain was now part of the United States, as if previously recognized Indian treaties and territories meant nothing. The Iroquois held their ground that they "were the only rightful proprietors of the soil," a "principle" which, Strong notes, the U.S. Congress "acceded to . . . in its instructions to General St. Clare in 1787 and 1788," and which "is the basis . . . of all subsequent treaties with the Indians of the U.S." (21). Without mentioning George Washington directly, Strong is also telling of the occasion of Washington's partial redemption from his identity as "Town Destroyer"—though the name was permanent—to friend of the Indian when under his administration the United States reversed its initial policies and established a policy of recognizing Native sovereignty.

The manuscript of Strong's speech itself records the conflict between what Native writers would say and how their white audiences would interpret it. William Clement Bryant, the president of the Buffalo Historical Society, apparently at one point either printed or prepared for printing Strong's manuscript, which he edited. It's unclear whether or not Strong's manuscript was ever published, however.[57] Bryant's small neat hand obtrudes in the manuscript when Strong begins to tell the history of the Iroquois' struggle to maintain autonomy after the Revolution and Red Jacket's pivotal role in that struggle, inserting passages that push Strong's manuscript back into line with convention. The Revolution "not only shook the foundation of the League [Confederacy] but it cut in two," Strong writes. In this situation, the "great sachems . . . reconstruct the League and . . . settle the relations that should hereafter exist between it and the new government, which then for the first time had made its appearance among the Nations of the Earth! The great Spirit seemed to have ordered that such men as Red Jacket and Cornplanter should be the actors on the public theater at this period of the history of mankind" (30). Bryant then inserts a passage that shifts the emphasis from a crisis of governing in light of the appearance of a new EuroAmerican government to the inevitable fate of the Indian. "Every wind from the east bore a low but swelling murmur from the advancing tide of pale-face immigration that was to inundate the land and overburden the ancient League in destruction," Bryant writes. "The white man's axe awoke strange echoes in the primeval forest" (31).

Strong nevertheless remains focused on the problem of government. Red Jacket's actions, he writes, have caused some "sorrow and surprise" among Indians, and adds, "I can only account for Red Jacket's neglect to warn his people of their danger in part that he, and his people were ignorant of the nature or system of the new government into which the whirlwind of the Revolution had thrown them" (31). Strong speculates on the difficulty that Red Jacket and the Senecas had in distinguishing the exact nature of the U.S. government's structure from the British system to which they had been accustomed.

> They had an idea that the Government was similar to that under which they had relations with the King. He was the Government. So after the independence of the United States the Red man had an idea that George Washington was the Government; it was George Washington with whom they had formed relations of peace and friendship and not with any one of the 13 council fires[;] that even Congress was a mere advisory body to George Washington. Red Jacket had no idea of "states rights." He had faith in George Washington. He thought the treaties were paramount to any law, so that there was no danger of state encroachment. He therefore rested easy in the enjoyment of what he supposed his sacred rights and that of his people. (31)

George Washington here becomes not the hero of the Revolution and savior of Indians (and that because of the renegotiated Treaty of Canandaigua, which recognized Iroquois autonomy) but rather a figure misunderstood by the Iroquois, a man whose personal appeals stood for something else and so, by implication, could not really be trusted. "States rights" was indeed the cry of those—in Georgia, New York, and elsewhere, and still today—who would unilaterally abrogate treaties and assert authority over land. The reference to states' rights (as well as his reference to the Iroquois "Confederacy") is inevitably doubled-edged in 1863, as it is the Confederate States of America's justification for its existence as well. Strong's implication is that if the United States goes to war in 1863 to defend federal supremacy, so also ought it to abide by that same federal supremacy in regard to treaty relations with Indians, and the Senecas specifically.

Bryant again intrudes in the manuscript when Strong begins to talk about Red Jacket's celebrated defenses of sovereignty at the trials of Stiff-armed George in 1803 and of Tommy Jemmy in 1821. Strong writes that Red Jacket fought for sovereignty, noting, "I am sustained in this view by the position that Red Jacket took on the two important occasions when he appeared in the courts of law of this state as a Counsel" (31). He is not allowed to tell the story of Red Jacket's defenses of sovereignty, however, as at that point Bryant's small neat hand reappears. The story of sovereignty becomes the story of romanticized Indians and their impending doom. Bryant writes, "Red Jacket appeared in court with all the pride and dignity of an Indian Prince"—not a republican orator; his speeches "[drew] a vivid and touching picture of the wrongs and sufferings of his people" (32). While Red Jacket "proceeded to argue from their treaties and relations with Great Britain and the U.S., that his nation was independent of the laws of the State of New York," and that "George Washington's treaty" (the 1794 Treaty of Canandaigua) never claimed jurisdiction over the Iroquois, Bryant's narrative then poses some rhetorical questions, the answers to which are provided as the speech continues (32). "When had the Iroquois renounced their sovereignty over their territory? When had they adopted the written laws of the whites? Had those laws ever been read or proclaimed to them?" Bryant asks (32). "No, the Iroquois were not vassals or slaves. They would mete out justice and punish the guilty among their own people after the manner of their Fathers. Born free,—an independent nation, they would not bow to the authority of laws which they had no part in enacting and whose purport even never had been disclosed to them!" (32). The long conclusion of the speech is still in Bryant's neat hand, and he provides the answer to these rhetorical questions: the claim of sovereignty matters only for its futile nobility. Red Jacket's popularity faded later in his life, as "intemperance caused the great orator to bow beneath the slowly increasing degradation and sorrow" (37). He "drooped silently, uncomplainingly for a little time and then sank into his grave." When he dies, the manuscript reads, "Thus perished the pride and glory of my nation. His efforts to resist the advances of civilization among his people sprang from a mistaken patriotism. He knew not the irresistible power that influenced the progress of that civilization. The stalwart oak with its hundred arms could not hope to beat back the tornado" (37).

Red Jacket is the figure for the Iroquois, and for the speaker himself, as Bryant has it. Red Jacket "lived to see his nation decline, its power, its influence, its numbers fading away like the mists of the morning." Strong (writes Bryant) "[stands] before you now in the late hours of a death-stricken people" (38). At this point the manuscript lapses into an elaborate outburst of the kind of sentiment Edward Everett favored: "To-night I address you as an alien in the land of my fathers," writes Bryant for Strong; "I have no nation, no country and I might say I have no kindred. All that we loved, and prized and cherished is yours. The land of the rushing river, the thundering cataract and the jeweled lakes is yours. All those broad, flowery fields, those wooded hills, and laughing vallies are yours, only yours. I would that I had the eloquence of Red Jacket that I might fitly speak of the wrongs and sorrows of my people" (38). Thus far, as a complete manuscript with a conclusion in Strong's hand either doesn't exist or hasn't yet been found, how Strong concluded the speech before the historical society remains mysterious.

What's not quite so mysterious is the text crossed out in the manuscript and replaced with Bryant's ode to the vanishing savage. Where Bryant intrudes on Strong's discussion of Red Jacket's defense of Seneca autonomy in the trials of Stiff-armed George and Tommy-Jemmy in the manuscript, Strong writes that Red Jacket "appeared in the courts of law in this state in the character of an advocate," adding, in parentheses and underlined, *"there is no question that nature had designed him for the Bar!!"* (33). Red Jacket "in each case . . . strongly insisted that the Seneca Nation was Independent from the State of New York" (33). One couldn't find a more graphic illustration of just how racial difference works to deny Native political status. Nathaniel Strong, like Maris Bryant Pierce, worked for the Seneca Nation—his only other appearance in the archives is in his membership on a committee of the Seneca Nation that reported on financial abuses by its treasurer in 1853. He wrote several brief notes that appeared in the Buffalo Historical Society Collections—two on the origin of the name of the city of Buffalo, and another, in an anonymous note appended to this manuscript, "in relation to the marking out of the road from Clarence to the Tonawanda [reservation] (now Batavia) in 1801, by 'White Chief' for Joseph Ellicott, by whom the route was adopted." From the manuscript, it appears that Bryant substituted his page for Strong's, and so his account of Red Jacket's appearance at court is incomplete. Nevertheless, one can tell something from where the excising stops. At the end of the excised portion, Strong notes that "it must be admitted, that the state itself had doubts on the question" of Seneca autonomy; Bryant permits the text to pick up at the point when Strong writes, "Red Jacket persevered in his opposition to the encroachments of civilization among his people to the last" (33). This too is telling. In Strong's canceled out version, Red Jacket's resistance to EuroAmerican practice and belief is an extension of his struggle for Seneca autonomy; tradition and government are one and the same. Bryant's intrusions are again a graphic illustration of the fact that EuroAmerican thought has to deny the validity of the government and reify tradition in order to elide the political struggle.

EMPIRE OF THE REAL

That defending the truth of Iroquois traditional knowledge is incongruent with both acceptance of the notion of inherent racial difference and its associated Indian doom rhetoric can be seen in the works of Ely's brother Nicholson in the 1840s and early 1850s, when he occasionally gave lectures on the Iroquois or Indians in general. While Ely was put forward as a liaison to the white world, Nicholson was free, in some respects, to live his own life. By 1847, Nicholson was graduating from Alexander Academy, and in the early 1850s, he graduated from Albany State Normal School. According to his grandson Arthur C. Parker in his *Life of General Ely S. Parker*, it was at this time that Nicholson made a foray into "platform-speaking" on "many subjects, but his longest discourses were always on Indian topics" (92). After graduation, he managed Ely's farm at Tonawanda while Ely was pursuing his career in engineering and then moved on to working as "interpreter, printer and clerk" to the missionary Asher Wright at the Cattaraugus reservation. By 1855, he had married Asher Wright's wife's niece and started farming (191). Arthur C. Parker remembers his grandfather reading him *Paradise Lost*, *King Lear*, and *A Midsummer Night's Dream*; he "even tried to teach me algebra" (195). But in the house were also "the heirlooms of the family, that is, such as could be exhibited . . . quaint old Indian trophies, beaded sashes, tomahawks, scalping-knives that had seen service, old flint-locks and pictures of famous members of the family all in Seneca regalia"—along with portraits of his white grand-mother's ancestors, and "a wonderful engraving of 'Christian, the Pilgrim'" (193). Nicholson, unlike Ely, insisted on appearing at important occasions in Native dress: "He was ever proud of his blood and ancestry, and . . . often appeared at celebrations and historical exercises dressed in the full regalia of a

Seneca chief. . . . When taken to task for emulating his ancestors he said, 'I can be as much a gentleman in the costume of my fathers as is a Scotch lord in costume celebrating his native events. Even Englishmen affect their old-time dress on old-time occasions' " (199). Nicholson was an officer of the Iroquois Agricultural Society for many years, and " 'clerk of the nation,' or as the greater republic would say, 'Secretary of State.' " His grandson writes, "besides being clerk of the nation, United States interpreter, census agent, marshall of the nation, orator, agriculturalist and civil engineer, my grandfather was the drum major of the Seneca Indian Silver Cornet Band. He was a versatile and useful citizen of the Seneca Republic" (195, 197).

Three complete lectures by Nicholson are extant—one in manuscript, "Intellectual Character of the Indian," which may have been given on Nicholson's graduation from Alexander Academy in 1847, and two from 1853 that Arthur Parker includes in his *Life of General Ely S. Parker*, "Traits of Indian Character," which was presented over two nights at Canandaigua, New York, and "The American Red Man," given when Nicholson was a junior at Albany State Normal School. (Arthur Parker also includes a partial copy of "Indian Dances and Their Influence" in his *Life of General Ely S. Parker*.) At least in part, his model seems to have been George Copway, who had appeared in Buffalo in the 1850s. "Traits of Indian Character" appears to owe quite a lot of its material to Washington Irving's essay of the same title (the same one that William Apess reprints in the appendix to *A Son of the Forest*). The lectures were advertised as "Indian Historical Lectures, by Ga-i-wah-go-wa." The poster promises: "This talented young Indian, a descendant of the Iroquois, will give two select Lectures, on the history of his race, their manners, customs, national festivities, costumes, literature, and religion, to the citizens of Canandaigua, in the Seminary Hall, on Monday and Tuesday evenings, the 7th and 8th of March, 1853." In smaller print below the poster continues: "Ga-i-wah-go-wa is a brother of Do-nih-ho-ga-wah, or Ely S. Parker, of Rochester, N.Y., who is Head Chief of the Six Nations, and recently acknowledged as such by Gov. Seymour, and is a distinguished Civil Engineer in the Government service. Ga-i-wah-go-wah, (Nicholas [*sic*] H. Parker) is a fine specimen of the noble Aborigines of this country. He possesses testimonials of a thorough education, and native powers of eloquence, and will not fail to interest any intelligent audience, that may listen to his delineation of Indian History, Character and Traditions." And, finally: "The Lectures will be delivered in Indian costume."[58]

Unlike the material he supplied to Lewis Henry Morgan on Seneca beliefs and practices, Nicholson's speeches were mainly about Native peoples and history. The three complete speeches all address the problem of Indian "char-

INDIAN

HISTORICAL

LECTURES,

BY

GA-I-WAH-GO-WA.

This talented young Indian, a descendent of the Iroquois, will give two select Lectures, on the

HISTORY OF HIS RACE,

Their Manners, Customs, National Festivities, Costumes, Literature, and Religion, to the citizens of **CANANDAIGUA**, in the

SEMINARY HALL,

ON

MONDAY AND TUESDAY EVENINGS,

The 7th and 8th of March, 1853.

GA-I-WAH-GO-WA, is a brother of DO-NIH-HO-GA-WAH, or Ely S. Parker, of Rochester, N. Y., who is Head Chief of the Six Nations, and recently acknowledged as such by Gov. Seymour, and is a distinguished Civil Engineer in the Government service. Ga-i-wah-go-wo, (Nicholas H. Parker) is a fine specimen of the noble Aborigines of this country. He possesses testimonials of a thorough education, and native powers of eloquence, and will not fail to interest any intelligent audience, that may listen to his delineation of Indian History, Character and Traditions.

The Lectures will be delivered in full Indian costume.

Lectures to commence at 7 1-2 o'clock.

Admission 12 1-2 Cents.

Printed at the Ontario Messenger Office, Canandaigua.

acter" in much the same terms as William Apess does with King Philip, that is, by arguing that any differences between Indians and whites are the product of history, not providence. The two that interest me here, "Intellectual Character of the Indian" from 1847 and "The American Red Man" from 1853, directly confront the racial differentiation of Native peoples in the figure of the Indian. Although he was a very young man, probably in his late teens for the first speech and his early twenties for the second, Nicholson Parker describes Native intellectual life as different and historically specific but also as recognizably intellectual and therefore the "same" as that of whites, with whom Native thinkers must communicate.

In "Intellectual Character of the Indian," Nicholson begins by observing that "expansion and progress is the great law in intellectual life and there is no society however degraded that does not in some degree exemplify this principle."[59] Therefore, he continues, "where nature rules and education is shut out, there we need not expect much intellectual worth; for there they have nothing upon which to exert their dormant energies." It appears (for the moment) that he has accepted the position of Indians as excluded from universal progress, but this is not the case. He continues, noting that "where men are governors and nature exhibits her sternest features, there people are industrious; and they use every means to improve their physical and intellectual nature," which is exemplified in the ancient Greeks, the Scottish highlanders, and the "enterprising people" of New England, "with all her mountains and vallies" (1–2). Here Nicholson is doing something of a turn on the standard environmentalism of the eighteenth and nineteenth centuries; he argues that intellect itself can be correlated to the geography in which people find themselves, so that those who must struggle with the environment and exhibit "hardihood and perseverance" become the most developed intellectually (2). Thus, Indians can be perceived as intellectuals:

Poster advertising an 1853 public lecture by Nicholson Henry Parker. Like George Copway, Peter Jones, and his own younger brother, Ely Parker, Nicholson Parker gave speeches on the traditions of his people. According to his grandson, Arthur C. Parker, Nicholson, unlike Ely, was happy to appear in Native dress on public occasions. In 1855, Nicholson married the missionary Asher Wright's niece and started farming at the Cattaraugus reservation, after which his platform speaking apparently ceased. From A. C. Parker, Life of General Ely S. Parker, *91. Photograph courtesy of the Edward E. Ayer Collection, Newberry Library, Chicago.*

But, if you would see the human mind in its native energy, turn to the aborigines of your country, yes, to the simple native, who walks as the natural Lord of the American forest. We behold him in the bosom of the lonely forest, where an enlightened person may fancy there is not knowl- edge, but we see him gathering lessons from the unwritten column of Na- ture. It is indeed a mystery to him what causes the seasons of the years—but in watching the motions of the heavenly bodies, there he sees the Great Spirit moving among the stars, and as [he sees?] the firey [bounty?] passing away, many a son of the forest has attempted to prove, and read, in its transient glare, the future destiny of the Indians. (2–3)

Indians have the same intellectual capacity as whites, although their historical experiences are different. Invoking the same figures of exemplary Native talent and character as Maris Bryant Pierce and William Apess, Nicholson observes that "Red Jacket and Cornplanter are ranked superior to Cicero and Demos- thenes. Osceola and Tecumseh were but little inferior to Napoleon and Wash- ington in commanding military prowess. We view Philip of Mt. Hope, who not only ruled the surrounding tribes with prowess but he even swayed their minds to a degree, that none but a Philip could do" (3). Nicholson appears to be invoking Apess's arguments in the *Eulogy on King Philip*. "Such is the mind produced by nature," he continues, "as to be allied to the genius of a Wash- ington for courage, policy, and address [in wars]" (3).

There is a problem, however, in that "those natural minds" have not had the opportunity to become "enlightened" and so to "[rival] a Newton or Franklin in Philosophy" (3). As in Apess's *Eulogy*, "nature" is not a permanent state but a historical and material state. At this point—and Nicholson is graduating from secondary school here, so he's not quite a polished writer—he shifts from the intellectual abilities of Indians to the historical oppression they have suffered.

But not willing to pass, without saying something on the subject, which so much concerns the Indians at the present day. I would say that I regret to think on the past scenes, which the red sons of America have passed through. In the circumstances under which they are now placed, they have cause to fear that soon the key of oppression will be turned against them and they will be dragged from their hearths and the grudgeing whiteman [*sic*] will take their places. Now to contemplate a forced removal of the Indians and the heartrending scenes that must accompany such removal is shocking to every sentiment of justice and humanity. To see a great and powerful nation lending its aid to oppress the weak and helpless must tend to loosen the attachment of the people to their government, and would do more to weaken the bond of our national union than all the enemies of a just people could ever effect. The United States by the peculiar nature of their institutions stands conspicuously before the world. (4)

He does not reconcile this shift from an assertion of historical difference but essential equality to the invocation of a history of oppression, but the main elements of the critique put forward by Pierce and Apess are present. Although he evokes the standard "sympathy for Indians" discourse, Nicholson characterizes it more dramatically—Indians "will be dragged from their hearths"—and also demands that his white audience consider the effects on their own government of such oppression. "On the purity of your national administration," he writes, "depends not only the prosperity of your citizens, but, perhaps, the success of one of the most momentous and interesting experiments which has ever been exhibited to the view of mankind" (4–5). He implies the existence of treaties when he invokes the high ideals and exemplary philosophical foundations of the United States.

By the time he gives his Albany Normal School address, "The American Red Man," Nicholson has refined his analysis to the point where he universalizes the figure of Indian doom and uses it as a rebuke to white authority at the same time that he elaborates on the theme of Native intellect begun in the earlier speech. Indeed, he simultaneously uses that figure to challenge his audience—presumably fellow students and graduates of the state teachers' school—to take him seriously as a thinker. He begins, "I am no orator. . . . I stand here a simple Indian, a son of the forest, a relic of the wreck of the Iroquois, a band of nations who once peopled the length and breadth of your Empire state" (263). Like Maris Pierce, Nicholson lingers over the popular moniker for the state of New York, implying, in context, its history of oppression of the Iroquois "empire" invented by Morgan and Schoolcraft. He thus historicizes the doomed Indian trope. Then, like William Apess, he challenges his audience to see him as a human being, not as a stereotypical Indian speaking, reduced to the racial characteristic of eloquence—an eloquence that he knows elides the substance of what the Indian speaker is saying. "If there be any present to whom the form and address of an Indian is displeasing, I speak not to them," he says. "I speak to those, to whom real knowledge has taught that all men are made of one blood, created free and equal, entitled to the same rights and privileges, and accountable to the same God" (263). Nicholson insists that Indians be included in the universal category of human intellectual endeavor: "I speak to those who can appreciate the merits of talent and intellectual worth, who are lovers of true knowledge, and who are lovers of eloquence" (263).

An 1853 daguerreotype of Nicholson Parker, one of several Native students, men and women, admitted to Albany State Normal School in the 1850s. From A. C. Parker, Life of General Ely S. Parker. *Photograph courtesy of the Edward E. Ayer Collection, Newberry Library, Chicago.*

His topic, he says, is "The People Gone" (263). "Why weep over their fate, those brave hearted hermits of the wilderness?" he asks, invoking, again, the doomed Indian trope (263). He puts that figure, however, in a large, even grand, context:

> Their destiny was accomplished, they uttered their voice, they filled up their portion of the great universe plan, their hour upon the clock of time was struck,—and they were not! Such is the law of fate, beneath whose stern mandate other nations have wrapt around themselves the solemn drapery of the sepulchre and bowed their glorious foreheads in the dust. Birthplaces of the monarch minstrel, the blind old man of Scio, and he who plucked the last laurel from the olden tree of song, what are ye? Mouldering monuments, erected by the Destroyer to show the foot-prints of the eternal world march, the *stern, unbending, necessary law!* . . . Without and within, is force, resistless force, moving spirit and matter; moves and starts onward. Under the power, man and world must be alike pushed off the stage of existence to make room for others. System rushes on system, generation on generation, nation on nation, in everlasting battle; a fearful war, in which the defensive must ever surrender; some expiring with a long melancholy wail, and others breathing their last in a loud, warrior shout. So died the "People Gone." The forest fire shot up fiercely in the end, and brave souls glanced defiance in the death struggle. (263)

Here Nicholson puts Native peoples on the world stage, which removes them from the closed discourse of Indians' particular doom and forces his audience to consider the oppression of Native peoples philosophically. "Were this people wronged?" he asks. "You do not feel disposed to investigate the subject. If wronged, then wrong is the very divinity of the inevitable laws which produced their ruin. Man's feeble eye cannot pierce the cloud; man's circumscribed mind can not roll away the mists which envelop the Empire of the Real" (264). Certainly, Native peoples *were* wronged, according to Nicholson Parker, and the "divinity of the inevitable laws which produced their ruin" is wrong as well. Positing the inevitability of Native disappearance is wrong, and, according to Nicholson Parker, certainly not divine, but rather, as every Native writer included in this book points out, manmade. And certainly white people do not "feel disposed to investigate the subject" of the false divinity that they ascribe to the effects of their own willful behavior.

That Parker continues to position whites' treatment of Native peoples in the United States in the larger context of world history calls to mind Apess's maps of the United States and the world in his house at Mashpee. "When you dismiss the subject" of Indians and their fate, Parker writes, "another arises which you may think of much more importance, *the doing of justice* to the characters of those, whom the 'law' forced you to destroy; the rescuing of their names from oblivion and the placing of them within their proper sphere in history" (264). That is, whites were players on the world stage in the destruction of Native peoples, and justice demands that they not forget the history of the people whom they have destroyed. He himself must now address the history of Native peoples in North America—first by, once again, maintaining that the characteristics, such as cruelty, that have been ascribed to them as inherent are in fact borne of historical circumstances. He then returns to the theme of Indians' "intellectual character" (264).

The Indian's mind, Parker writes, "has always been underrated." "The only faculty which you have allowed him to a high extent is that of *oratory*. But we fearlessly challenge the whole white race to afford more striking instances of judgment, caution, calculation and consideration, than can be found in Powhattan, Pontiac, Tecumseh, Philip and, last though not least, Osceola" (264). Again, like Apess, Nicholson does not argue the essential difference of Indians, but rather their possession of universal human characteristics. His first example is Powhattan; his second is Philip. He continues to make the same points as William Apess: "There is not a character either in the staid lore of history, or the splendid pages of romance, more martial, dignified and brilliant, than the renowned Philip. Brave, merciful and talented, he is the very *beau-ideal* of the wise, the chivalrous and the good" (265).

Nicholson closes with what he calls "mind." He insists on an intellectual life for Indians, and if his rhetoric sounds inflated today, it is in keeping with the EuroAmerican rhetoric with which he had to engage. Certainly intellect was not a particularly advanced feature of the Indian's character as described by the likes of Lewis Henry Morgan or, for that matter, virtually any other white writer of the time. Intellectual life, Nicholson points out, requires freedom from harassment and oppression. "Has not the Indian his Cadmus," Nicholson asks, footnoting Sequoyah. "If his invention had been given a fair trial among redmen in time of peace and prosperity, who can say the epic and the lyric, the essay and the oration, the biography and the history which would have sent the name of the red man down to a future, whose heart should thrill beneath his memory, and whose tongue might hymn his praises?" (268). Nevertheless, "these unsophisticated denizens of the unshorn forest possessed in a high degree, that noble faculty which runs like lightning fire through the world, *mind*, arming vivifying and creating until the beautiful, august and godlike, start forth in entrancing loveliness and undying grandeur; the glory of man, and the cynosure of time" (269).

The "love of the beautiful and the grand," or "ideality," produces literature—and this appears to be what Nicholson himself is in pursuit of here (269). Again, the differences between Indians and whites are not inherent but rather the differences of time and circumstances.

> Why with all their sparkling, forcible, unique imagination, did the Indian progress no farther? This may perhaps be accounted for by continuous exertion and the absolute necessity of sharpening the physical faculties which his lot demanded. But after all, had he not literature, unwritten to be sure, but effective? There are many things of service besides books. Yes, he had a literature, the literature of the sun in unison with the breeze as it struck its harp of the wilderness, uttering in the grave council and thrown from the burning lips of eloquence. There is another literature also; that written in marble, the poems of architecture. This literature is always the result of religion, whatever other phases it may assume. Temples we know were the first fabrics. A literature such as this the Indian did not feel in need of. He was compelled to live mostly in the open air; his nature called but little for shelter; so he made the boundless forest his worshiping place, the steadfast sky was its dome, the winds its choir, and the eternal lights of the blue infinitude its lamps. A right brave temple that, a temple which God built, and where angels might adore; a temple too with free seats. (269)

Finally, in their religion, the intellect of Indians is revealed. "Is there not intellect in the conception of . . . Indian heaven? Is there not beauty in the wide stretching hunting grounds with their graceful animals, emerald trees and crystal rivers, and over all the spirit of love throwing its soft splendor, like a beautiful banner woven of sunbeams? Peace! Peace everlasting!" (269).

The closing returns to the idea of the inevitability of Indians' demise as well as to the white people who are responsible for that apparent inevitability, thus demonstrating that his invocation of Indian doom is a critique of white knowledge. Indeed, here the Indian doom rhetoric itself becomes a critique and a rebuke:

> A few more years, a few more massacres, a few more sighs, and not a descendant of that people will stand upon the soil of his fathers. The very grave of the warrior will be nameless, his dust mingled almost without a memorial with the universe atoms. The tides of life will rush over the silent

realms of death, and the deep sea-like voice of other generations rise where a lost people have not even left an echo. And you the arrogant, what of you? Look to the *"inevitable, necessary law, of destiny."* In three thousand years may not two nations slumber, where but only one now lies in the icy pall of unconsciousness. (269–70)

Nicholson takes the doom narrative, specific and localized to Indians, puts it on the world stage, and then uses it as a rebuke and a critique, even a threat, to white society, not entirely in terms of what they have done but of what will happen to them. He turns the Indian doom figure into a philosophical meditation and, in the terms of literary writing that he himself has set out, a product of a Native literature itself.

In 1884, Red Jacket's bones were finally reinterred at Forest Lawn Cemetery in Buffalo, along with those of several other Seneca leaders who had been buried at the Buffalo Creek settlement. As president of the Buffalo Historical Society, William Clement Bryant presided over a ceremony the next day, making the usual remarks about disappeared Indians, the nobility of the Iroquois, their reputations as the "Ciceros of the wilds." Several other people spoke besides Bryant, including "the venerable ex-Judge George W. Clinton," Indian chiefs in "picturesque costume," and Ely Parker.[60] The venerable ex-judge provided the ritual account of Iroquois difference, inferiority, savagery, and disappearance. After musical selections and a speech in Seneca by Chief John Jacket, one of Red Jacket's descendants, Ely Parker addressed the audience in English. Parker's remarks, later published in the journal of the Buffalo Historical Society,[61] center on treaties and the violation of agreements between nations. Speaking "without notes" (40), he begins by saying, "I wish to direct attention to one phase of their character, which, in my judgment, has never been brought out with sufficient force and clearness, and that is, their fidelity to their obligations and the tenacity with which they held to their allegiance when once it was placed." He then discusses the succession of Iroquois alliances with the French, the Dutch, and the English, who, despite the Iroquois' aid to them during the Revolution, "in the treaty of peace which followed the English entirely ignored and forgot their Indian allies, leaving them to shift for themselves" (41).

As in Nathaniel Strong's remarks on Red Jacket, Parker cites Sullivan's campaign as an attack that effectively undermined Iroquois political power:

The Indians left to themselves and bereft of British aid made Sullivan's success an easy one. He drove them from their homes, destroyed and burnt

> their villages, cut down their corn-fields and orchards, leaving the poor
> Indians homeless, houseless and destitute. We have been told this evening
> that the "Long House" of the Iroquois had been broken. It was indeed truly
> broken by Sullivan's invasion. It was so completely broken that never again
> will the "Long House" be reconstructed. (42)

This is the George Washington to whom Strong could not allude, and it is also
the answer to the venerable ex-judge's account of Iroquois disappearance. It's
not heredity that causes the "decline" of the Iroquois, but the violence and
rapacity of whites. The Iroquois are not a doomed empire, but an embattled
people.

When the Indians sought peace, however, George Washington and the Americans granted it, along with "small homes in the vast domains they once claimed
as absolutely and wholly theirs by the highest title known among men, viz., by
the gift of God." "The mercy of the American people," Parker adds, "granted
them the right to occupy and cultivate certain lands until some one stronger
wanted them." George Washington is not the saint some would portray him to
be. Like Strong, Parker doesn't mince words on the subject of land rights.
Parker's audience of middle-class whites, patrons of historical societies and
civic organizations, wanted, indeed expected, to hear the story of Indian doom
and American superiority, couched in an elaborate display of sympathy. As in
Red Jacket's orations, and even Strong's, Parker employs a certain amount of
sarcasm and dissembling:

> The Indian mind has never to this day been able to comprehend how it is
> that he has been compelled to buy and pay for that which has descended to
> him from time immemorial, and which his ancestors had taught him was
> the gift of the Great Spirit to him and his posterity forever. It was an
> anomaly in civilized law far beyond his reasoning powers. (42)

Parker perhaps refers to Red Jacket's similar disingenuous questions in his
1811 speech to Richardson, the Ogden Land Company agent. Red Jacket, said
Parker, who "labored hard for the recognition and restoration to his people of
their ancient rights . . . did not embrace that peculiar doctrine now so strongly
believed in, that 'to the victors belong the spoils'" (43). Red Jacket "did not
know that the Sullivan campaign had taken from his people all the vested
rights which God had given them, and when, subsequently, he was made to
understand that a preemptive title hung over the homes of his people he was
amazed at the audacity of the white man's law which permitted and sanctioned
the sale and transfer by one person to another of rights never owned and

properties never seen" (43). This reference to the preemptive right also appears in the last of Red Jacket's speeches, likewise addressed to an agent for Ogden Land Company.

To Parker, Red Jacket's burial illustrates the ironies of Native-white relations. Despite Red Jacket's insistence "that white men should not dig his grave and that white men should not bury him," he ends up being buried by those same people. "How forcibly now comes to us the verity and strength of the saying that 'man proposes, but God disposes,'" Parker says, reminding his audience that Red Jacket's people were "removed" from their reservation and that his grave "remained unprotected, and ere long was desecrated" (43). What he does not say directly is that the desecration and abandonment of Red Jacket's grave was the result of the succession of treaties, beginning with the Buffalo Creek Treaty of 1838, through which the Senecas eventually lost the Buffalo Creek reservation, where Red Jacket lived and was first buried. Red Jacket's grave is desecrated as the Seneca lands are stolen and desecrated. In the end, the "good men of the Buffalo Historical Society . . . take charge of his [Red Jacket's] remains" as they take charge of the land.

Parker urges that the monument that the Buffalo Historical Society provides for Red Jacket "should tell his story to all future generations"—but it is unlikely that the story Ely Parker tells would be on that stone, and Parker knew it. He concludes by addressing the sympathy of whites, so flagrantly on display at the ceremonies, offering one final rebuke:

> While a silent spectator of the ceremonies to-day, the words of the blessed Saviour forcibly presented themselves to my mind, "the foxes have holes and the birds of the air have nests, but the Son of Man hath not [sic] where to lay His head." I applied this saying to the Indian race. They have been buffeted from pillar to post. They once owned much, but now have hardly anything they can call their own. While living they are not let alone—when dead they are not left unmolested. (44)

This is the same language Parker provided to Lewis Henry Morgan for his "Inindianation" of white men forty years before. Then, as a young man, Parker mocked the white men who would be Indian, but in 1884, the reference has a more pointed significance. Parker is talking to people who are already convinced that they're right: the terms are not up for debate, and he has to work within a hostile structure. Parker is a "silent spectator"—to whites. One can wonder how the Native members of Parker's audience—also silent—received his comments. Parker compares Indians to Jesus with no excuses and returns, once again, to the facts of history. He rejects the reburial of Red Jacket as a grand tribute; it is rather more harassment. "I thank you for your kind atten-tion," Parker concludes, "and I now bid you all, and each of you, a fair good-night; and may you retire to sweet slumbers and pleasant dreams"—of the violence, destruction, and desecration of his ancestors.

That in closing Parker returns to the doomed Indian discourse—"Mournful memories are brought to their minds in the sad ceremonies in which they have been both participants and witnesses, but their griefs are all assuaged and their tears dried up by your kindness. They will carry back to their people nothing but good words of you and yours" (44)—should remind us that that discourse is as available to Parker to be manipulated as it is to white writers. He is not, as literary critics often maintain, merely slavishly producing the representation that whites would find palatable because he has "assimilated" to white society. Rather he presents a complex figure, a thinker who knows that his white audi-ence will refuse to recognize or understand the validity of his experience, who uses the conventions with which his audience would be familiar to refute—*almost* silently—the logic of racial difference and its erasure of Native peoples from history and from political relations.

CONCLUSION

Were this people wronged? You do not feel disposed to investigate the subject. If wronged,
then wrong is the very divinity of the inevitable laws which produced their ruin. Man's
feeble eye cannot pierce the cloud; man's circumscribed mind cannot roll away the mists
which envelop the Empire of the Real.
—Nicholson Parker, "The American Red Man," 1853

If there's one thing that almost every student who walks into my classroom for the first time knows, it's that Indians were torn between two cultures—in fact those are often the words they use. It seems to mean, at least for the students, that Indians will never be able to choose, never be able to have both old ways, the life before Columbus, and white ways, the modern world. Every Indian is an abstraction removed from history. People considered to be members of ethnic groups, in contrast, often aren't understood to be "torn"; rather they are understood—in popular as well as scholarly discourses—to go through gradual changes through the generations. In most people's lives, there might be conflicts between one way of thinking and doing things and another, but that is a condition of their existence, something they negotiate on a daily basis. It doesn't stop them from being who they are; it doesn't stop them from being people in time. In fact, the conflict itself marks them historically. It usually isn't understood to destroy them psychologically. For Native peoples in the United States, the difference is the degree to which what was lost was lost violently and systematically and the degree to which they must live misrecognized by the world around them. These are political and historical conditions, to which all of the writers included in this book attest. The idea of "tornness," however, implies an inescapable, inevitable impasse, where Indians will be crushed— "caught between two cultures" as it is often construed—when the two cultures (white and Indian) slam into each other in the Indians' individual psyches.

What's truly inescapable, however, is the "clash of cultures" (to cite yet another variation on the theme) as an explanation, even today, for U.S. history. To take one example, one might consider the visitors center at the Little

Bighorn Battlefield National Monument in Montana—which was until recently Custer Battlefield National Monument but was renamed, much to the consternation of Custer buffs worldwide. At the entrance, just before the display case featuring Custer's toothbrush and various changes of costume and around the corner from the eerie full-color busts of two soldiers that were reconstructed from skulls recently discovered in the field, the title above opposed pictures of Sitting Bull and Ulysses S. Grant reads: "Political leaders in a clash of cultures." This is how the *Official Map and Guide* explains it: "The Battle of the Little Bighorn was but the latest encounter in a centuries-long conflict that began with the arrival of the first Europeans in North America. That contact between Indian and white cultures had continued relentlessly. . . . It reached its peak in the decade following the Civil War, when settlers resumed their vigorous westward movement. These western emigrants, possessing little or no understanding of the Indian way of life, showed slight regard for the sanctity of hunting grounds or the terms of former treaties. The Indians' resistance to those encroachments on their domain only served to intensify hostilities."[1] To summarize: "Resistance . . . only . . . [intensified] hostilities." If only Indians had just cooperated and gone to the reservations, none of this violence would have happened. The government's guide summarizes the whole tragic history, observing that "although the Indians won the battle, they subsequently lost the war against the white man's efforts to end their independent, nomadic way of life." Perhaps in keeping with an institutional imperative to be all things to all people, the guide both praises the essential "vigor" of the pioneers and condemns their ethnocentric bias. Still, one can substitute "race" here for "culture" and get the narrative current at the time of the battle: The Indian culture/race is, unfortunately, inherently incompatible with the white culture/race and therefore inevitably will disappear. Despite the contemporary preoccupations of the displays—of the flotsam of celebrity and of the wonders of scientific detection, as if the soldiers were long-ago crime victims rather than battlefield casualties—it's the same old story all over again. According to the U.S. government, discrete massed cultures confronted one another at the Little Bighorn, not political entities disputing the meaning of written documents and verbal agreements, agreed-upon and violated boundaries, a complicated history of economic and political conflicts. The visitors center accounts for the unfolding of the battle almost minute by minute, divines not only the combatants' precise movements but even their physical attributes (those of the U.S. soldiers anyway) through archaeological research, while the larger conflict lacks detail. The narrative implies that treaties were merely sites of inevitable cultural misunderstanding; given that whites think one way and

Indians think another, nothing could be done. At the Little Bighorn National Monument, culture displaces history and gives the visitor something to appreciate about Indians, even though culture got them into trouble in the first place, and now, sadly, it's gone. Because once they lose their "nomadic way of life," how can Indians be Indians any more, if that is what defines them?

The Crow Nation, hereditary enemies of the Lakotas, who supplied scouts for the U.S. Army at the Little Bighorn, runs the battlefield gift shop, which is a source of necessary employment, as the Crow Nation surrounds the battlefield today. Visitors to the battlefield might wonder how "torn" the clerks feel as they punch up purchases. In *Custer Died for Your Sins*, first published in 1969, Vine Deloria Jr. had this to say about the psychologized "two cultures" narrative as an explanation for any pathologies manifested in any Native person or group:

> Lumping together the variety of tribal problems and seeking a demonic principle at work which is destroying Indian people may be intellectually satisfying. But it does not change the real situation. . . . Regardless of theory, the Pyramid Lake Paiutes and the Gila River Maricopas are poor because they have been systematically cheated out of their water rights, and on desert reservations water is the most important single factor in life. No matter how many worlds Indians straddle, the Plains Indians have an inadequate land base that continues to shrink because of land sales. Straddling worlds is irrelevant to straddling small pieces of land and trying to earn a living. (86)

It *is* "intellectually satisfying" to pronounce that Indians are torn between two cultures. As an explanation, it makes sense because it has never gone out of style. The cliché locks Native peoples in time, always in the state of not being able to reconcile one "way of life" with another, just as in earlier formulations of this same thinking, they were always in the state of being just about ready to disappear. The reliance on cultural difference as an explanation merely reprises the nineteenth-century platitude that when "civilizations" clash and inferior meets superior, Indians must disappear. Although today even homogenized cultures are ostensibly not conceived hierarchically, using this logic does invoke the victim-victimizer relationship, and everybody knows how that turned out. This maintains in scholarly disciplines as it does in popular discourses, as I have argued. In literary studies, the observation that one writer or another is "torn between two cultures" is regularly offered up as critical insight. In historiography, the popularization of the "middle ground" concept as a paradigm for studies of Native-EuroAmerican relations has allowed for narratives that describe how "cultures" met and mixed in U.S. history but ultimately failed to produce a just society in the end because people could not get along, as they were too different.[2] As both of these paradigms are focused on explaining the coherence of the United States, neither can allow for or recognize the validity of the persistence of Native struggles for political autonomy.

Nicholson Parker's question, "Were this people wronged?," is important here. Conceding that Native peoples were "wronged" means that somebody chose to wrong them, that is, that what happened wasn't inevitable but rather very much willed, calculated, and politically motivated in the face of vocal Native resistance, a point that all the writers in this book make repeatedly. If one concedes that Native peoples were "wronged" despite sustained resistance, then one must concede that the "inevitable laws"—of European superiority, Native difference and inferiority—that justified such actions against Native peoples are themselves wrong. Because Nicholson Parker, like all the writers included in this book, knows how the politics of knowledge works for Native peoples, he points out that it was those inevitable laws that produced Native peoples' "ruin," that is, knowledge about Indian difference justifies willful political oppression. It's not that white people can't help it because the doom of Indians was inevitable; they chose to not listen. To carry Parker's point a little further, while the social construction of knowledge is an axiom of contemporary academic thought, still, the predominance of cultural difference as an explanation of Native-European relations in the United States retains the notion of determining difference, the sense of inevitability, and the erasure of Native political claims that Nicholson Parker and the other writers included in this book well understood and dismantled. Parker notes that "you do not feel disposed to investigate the subject." In both the nineteenth century and today, that involves not continuing to rely on unexamined notions of difference but rather addressing the difficult details of political conflict that are all the more difficult to articulate because they have been so necessarily occluded. To the extent that scholars refuse to recognize Native political autonomy as a category for analysis, they continue to participate in a colonial epistemology.

Parker's last, cryptic sentence speaks to the continuing problem of knowledge about Indians and to Native peoples' resistance to and critique of it. Native difference is still the thing that has to be accounted for, pinned down, and fully explicated. I want to think about this in relation to the writers included in this book and to Native discourse generally today. All of the writers included here made this point: Native peoples cannot be known by whites in the way that whites represent themselves as knowing them; whites often do not know what they're talking about. The "Empire of the Real" is a comment on the American empire of Henry Dearborn and Edward Everett, which was rapidly eating up Iroquois land in the nineteenth century, and on the Iroquois empire that Lewis Henry Morgan invented to serve as its predecessor. And, as William Apess insisted on countering the misrepresentation of Native peoples with their "experience" as he and they told it, Parker insists that the knowledge that Native peoples have about their reality can be truly communicated only by them, and in the last instance, they guard that knowledge from misappropriation—from circulation in an economy of misrecognition. This is no small matter. Daniel F. Littlefield Jr. has pointed out, for example, that in recent years tribal governments have been increasingly ready to limit outsiders' access to their knowledge, and among Native scholars, discussion of what sovereignty might mean—politically, historically, and aesthetically—continues.[3]

As noted above, developments such as these often irk the affected non-Native parties who want that knowledge for their own and who seem to consider their desire for that knowledge free and clear of political ramifications. In the afterword to a book that consists of anthropologists' reconsiderations of his critique in *Custer Died for Your Sins* thirty years after, which is titled "Anthros, Indians, and Planetary Reality," Vine Deloria Jr. observes, "The conflict between Indians and anthropologists in the last two decades has been, at its core, a dead struggle over the control of definitions. Who is to define what an Indian *really* is? The generations of anthros [sic] now retiring and passing way have not been at all willing to surrender its entrenched position on this matter."[4] When the knowledge about Native peoples has construed them as different and sought to account for their difference ad infinitum, and when Native intellectuals have recognized that that knowledge about their difference is the means to justify political oppression, it should come as no surprise when efforts are made to counter and stop the flow of misrepresentation. Native writers have been doing this since they have been writing in English.

There isn't much difference, then, between how Native peoples were perceived in the nineteenth century and how they are perceived today. In fact, knowledge of Indian difference may be more entrenched today, given the insidious nature of the culture concept as it is commonly used. People may mean well, but the concept itself is deceptive and has a peculiar history with regard to Native peoples. What has changed is the proliferation of Native writing and of Native readers. Although the writing discussed in this book was generally aimed at a non-Native audience, the example of William Apess reading the *Experiences of Five Christian Indians* to the people at Mashpee, helping them to articulate their knowledge about their reality, cannot be an isolated incident. Nicholson and Ely Parker in turn read Apess's *Eulogy on King Philip* as schoolboys and took it as a rhetorical model; they probably knew George Copway and read his books, given Copway's activities in Buffalo with regard to the theft of Red Jacket's bones. Apess knew Boudinot and read the *Cherokee Phoenix*; Peter Jones followed the struggle against removal and thought the idea of removal "wicked." The Senecas sent a delegation to support the Cherokees in 1834.[5] It's too bad that Nicholson Parker didn't write more, but he had his responsibilities, as his grandson put it, "as a versatile and useful citizen of the Seneca Republic," which took precedence over writing at the time. He was needed in other ways. The terms that these early writers set out, however—the dispute over the meaning of difference, the fight for political claims, the struggle with misrepresentation, and the ongoing thought about the relation of the past to the present and of tradition to modernity—continue to animate Native writing in its myriad forms today. They are not the only things that Native writers write about by any means, but they recur enough to be fundamental. The contemporary situation, with the continued struggle over knowledge and continued agitation over the political status of Native peoples, is in some respects the nineteenth-century situation writ large or perhaps circumstances the nineteenth-century writers would have liked to have had, with so many more Native peoples able to write and produce knowledge in a wider range of settings. That contemporary writers often make the same kinds of arguments as the nineteenth-century writers is evidence not of intellectual stagnation on their part but rather of the difficulty of their struggle and, I would argue, the profoundly political importance in the United States of knowledge of Indians' difference. Now, however, Native writers may have reached a kind of critical mass, so that the goals of the nineteenth-century writers are achievable but on a much larger scale.

NOTES

INTRODUCTION

1. This ad was produced by Keep America Beautiful and is universally known as the "crying Indian" PSA; it is also possibly the most famous PSA ever produced. The organization resurrected the central image in a 1998 antilittering PSA titled "Back by Popular Neglect." The actor in the PSA was Iron Eyes Cody, who had made a career in Hollywood films as an Indian, claiming that his mother was Cree from Canada and his father was Cherokee from Oklahoma, but was actually a "full-blooded Italian" born in Louisiana. Unlike many other "wannabe" Indians, however, Cody supported Native peoples and causes; he was recognized for his work late in his life (he died in 1997) by First Americans in the Arts, an organization of Native film professionals. In 1936, Cody married Bertha Parker, the daughter of Arthur C. Parker and great-granddaughter of Nicholson H. Parker. Bertha was an archaeologist's assistant at the Southwest Museum in Los Angeles, and together she and Iron Eyes operated an Indian museum in their home. See Aleiss, "Iron Eyes Cody." The original PSA is available on Keep America Beautiful's website, ⟨http://www.kab.org/psa1.cfm⟩ (9 April 2003).

2. See the Advertising Council's website for a video of the PSA: ⟨http://www.ad council.org/campaigns/I_am_an_American⟩ (9 April 2003).

3. "Treaty with the Indians of the Six Nations," 103–4.

4. Hoxie, "Why Treaties?," 87.

5. As a British colony, Canada relied on the Proclamation of 1763, which recognized Native autonomy in all of Britain's North American colonies. It did not start making formal treaties with Indian nations until the late nineteenth century, after the U.S. government announced that it would no longer make treaties with Indian nations. See Harring, White Man's Law, and Macklem, Indigenous Difference.

6. See, for example, Saler, "Empire for Liberty," and Onuf, Jefferson's Empire.

7. In Crow Dog's Case, Harring writes that throughout the period of colonization, "Indian people understood themselves to be sovereign, acted as if they were sovereign in the most responsible way they could under the circumstances, made judgments concerning ways to defend their sovereignty, and both retained Indian law and used that law to structure their actions. Therefore, the record of Indian peoples' attempts to protect their sovereignty defines the legal concept of sovereignty more accurately than does a long line of ambiguous federal cases, and the history of this struggle is a vital part of the U.S. legal tradition" (14–15).

8. On the history of the term "Indian nation," see ibid., 57–58, n. 4.

9. Dirlik, *Postmodernity's Histories*, 183–84.

10. See, for example, Krupat, "Scholarship and Native American Studies," and Prucha, *American Indian Treaties*.

11. On representations of Indians, see Berkhofer, *White Man's Indian*; Dippie, *Vanishing American*; and Pearce, *Savagism and Civilization*.

12. See, for example, Said, *Culture and Imperialism*, and Ashcroft, Griffiths, and Tiffin, *Empire Writes Back*. On the exclusion of Native peoples from considerations of race in the United States, see the fall 2002 issue of *American Literary History* on "Race and Antebellum Literature," which includes only articles on whites and African Americans.

13. Deloria and Wilkins, *Tribes, Treaties, and Constitutional Tribulations*, 158.

14. Wilkins, *American Indian Sovereignty*, 366–67.

15. O'Brien, *American Indian Tribal Governments*, 51–52, 77–78.

16. Wilkins, *American Indian Politics*, 55.

17. Deloria and Wilkins, *Tribes, Treaties, and Constitutional Tribulations*, 162.

18. Wilkinson, *American Indians, Time, and the Law*, 5.

19. In *American Indian Sovereignty*, Wilkins observes that the Court has historically and in the present day practiced "retrohistory"—a "rhetorical ability to *retroactively* generate an interpretation of historical events that contradicts the actual occurrence" (303; emphasis in original).

20. Hoxie, "Why Treaties?," 92–93.

21. Ibid., 90, 92, 97.

22. In *White Man's Indian*, Berkhofer notes that the book was quite influential, "particularly . . . in shaping [U.S.] leaders' comprehension of the Indian" (48). In 1777, it was printed in London, Dublin, Florence, Leipzig, Maastricht, and Paris; in 1778, it was reprinted in London, Paris, and Venice; in 1780, London, Paris, and Pisa; in 1783, London and Venice; in 1786, Leipzig; in 1787, Vienna; in 1788, London; in 1790, Basel; in 1793, Vienna and London. In Europe from the end of the eighteenth century to 1845, the book was published in Stockholm, Dublin, London (many times), Basel, Edinburgh, Strasburgh, Venice, Alston, Paris, Palermo, and Barcelona; the second book on Columbus's voyages was reprinted in Istanbul in 1879–80, and the entire book was reprinted in Paris in 1891. The North American printings followed the European pattern. The first appeared in New York in 1798. In Philadelphia in 1799, two extra sections on the settlement of New England and Virginia that Robertson's son completed after his death were printed, then the whole book with the two extra sections was reprinted in Walpole, New Hampshire; Halifax, Nova Scotia; Philadelphia (several times); Cincinnati; Albany; and New York. The second American edition, printed in Philadelphia in 1822, included the Declaration of Independence plus a "correct facsimile of the signatures," and by 1831, the New York editions included "questions for the examination of students" by the editor, John Frost. A different edition, edited by Dugald Stewart, was

included in Harper's Family Library series, beginning in 1844 in New York. The last American edition appeared in New York in 1859.

23. Robertson, *History of the Discovery and Settlement of America*, 123.

24. Scott, "Universalism and the History of Feminism," 3–4.

25. Mills, *Racial Contract*, 15, 16–17 (emphasis in original).

26. D. V. Jones, *License for Empire*, 147.

27. Knox, "Report from H. Knox," 13. Literary critic Helen Carr disputes historian Reginald Horsman's claim that Knox "created the basis of a humane official policy toward the Indian"; she argues that Knox's policy was "oscillating and confused. . . . There emerges . . . a clash between his patriotic enlightenment rhetoric and the far from humane compromises and prevarications of his practice; in addition that very rhetoric opens up the possibility of its own subversion" (*Inventing the American Primitive*, 46, 41).

28. Jefferson, *Notes on the State of Virginia*, 221.

29. Bancroft was one of a group of influential antebellum American intellectuals, including Edward Everett, George Ticknor, Henry Wadsworth Longfellow, and John L. Motley, who brought romanticism to the United States as a result of studying in Germany in the early part of the century. Horsman writes that the histories of both Bancroft and Motley exalted "the basic Germanic and Anglo-Saxon character of the American people" (*Race and Manifest Destiny*, 161–62, 182–83). See also Levin, *History as Romantic Art*.

30. Stewart, "Emergence of Racial Modernity," 182, n. 2.

31. *Johnson v. M'Intosh*, 573, 574. On the history of *Johnson*, see G. E. White, *Marshall Court and Cultural Change*, 708–10.

32. Harring, *Crow Dog's Case*, 27.

33. G. E. White, *Marshall Court and Cultural Change*, 675–76.

34. *Cherokee Nation v. Georgia*, 4–5.

35. See G. E. White, *Marshall Court and Cultural Change*, 730. The book published by the Court's reporter is R. Peters, *Case of the Cherokee Against the State of Georgia*.

36. Harring, *Crow Dog's Case*, 25.

37. *Worcester v. Georgia*, 544–45.

38. Story, "History and Influence of the Pilgrims."

39. V. Deloria, "Intellectual Self-Determination." See O'Brien, *American Indian Tribal Governments*, 77–91, for U.S.-Native relations, and Allen, *Blood Narrative*, for a comparative account of American Indian and Maori political and literary resurgence in the post–World War II era.

40. For an overview of the criticism, see Littlefield, "American Indians, American Scholars."

41. See, for example, the discussion of C. Walker, *Indian Nation*, below.

42. Dirlik, "Culturalism as Hegemonic Ideology," 398.

43. In literary criticism, the difference between how scholars and Native writers use

the term "oral tradition" is striking. While critics separate that which is "Western" from that which is "Native American" in literary works using the presence or absence of identifiable aspects of "oral tradition" or Native American "culture", Native scholars and writers tend to describe the concept in historical terms, so that it encompasses change over time and relations among Native peoples. See, for example, V. Deloria, *Red Earth, White Lies*, 51–52; Ortiz, "Towards a National Indian Literature" and the introduction to his collection *Woven Stone*; Revard, "History, Myth, and Identity"; Tapahonso, *Blue Horses Rush In*, ix–xv; and Walters, *Talking Indian*.

44. Krupat, *Voice in the Margin*, esp. 202–32.

45. See, for example, Bellin, *Demon of the Continent*; Bergland, *National Uncanny*; Powell, *Ruthless Democracy*; and Rowe, *Literary Culture and U.S. Imperialism*.

46. Guillory, *Cultural Capital*; Kuper, *Culture*, 240.

47. Peyer, *Tutor'd Mind*, 19, 3.

48. Quoting Daniel, "Beyond Black and White," and McFee, "The 150% Man."

49. C. Walker, *Indian Nation*, 10–11.

50. Quoting Heat-Moon, *PrairyErth (a Deep Map)*, 16.

51. S. Baker, "William Least Heat-Moon," 55. Philip Deloria's *Playing Indian* addresses the phenomenon of white impersonations of Indians from the Boston Tea Party to the Grateful Dead and includes a chapter on the founding of the Boy Scouts. See also Rose, "Great Pretenders."

52. See C. Walker, "Guest Expert Transcript." The company for which Walker served as expert, BeyondBooks.com, sells interactive online textbooks to middle and high schools.

53. Despite occasional criticism of this taxonomy, college textbook editors habitually put translated Native narratives at the beginning of American literature anthologies as a means of representing, one suspects, the essentially American or the first American. The anthology then tracks the movement from traditional to modern, from tribal to democratic, from precolonization to postcolonization, from culture to art. The fact that there is seldom information on how or why or when or under what circumstances these narratives were written down is secondary to the more fundamental requirement of incorporating Indians—somehow—into the United States. The anthologies then incorporate later Native writers in English (including the writers whose work this book addresses) either as representing their "cultures" or as rightfully criticizing EuroAmericans and desiring inclusion as citizens of the United States.

54. In a discussion of Iroquois treaties in the eighteenth century in her book *Eloquence Is Power*, Gustafson maintains that eloquence is a "shared" cultural value that links Europeans and Native peoples (117).

55. Berkhofer, *White Man's Indian*, 195–96.

56. Sayre, *Les Sauvages Americains*, 321.

57. Maddox, *Removals*, 5.

58. See Cook-Lynn, *Anti-Indianism in Modern America*, "The American Indian Fiction Writer," "Literary and Political Questions," and "Who Stole Native American

Studies?"; Warrior, *Tribal Secrets*; Womack, *Red on Red*; Weaver, *That the People Might Live*; Allen, *Blood Narrative*; J. Armstrong, *Looking at the Words of Our People*; Forbes, "Colonialism and Native American Literature"; Justice, "We're Not There Yet, Kemo Sabe"; and Mihesuah, *Natives and Academics*.

59. Warrior, *Tribal Secrets*, xix, 111–15.

60. Womack, *Red on Red*, 4.

61. Krupat, *Turn to the Native*, 20. Krupat returns to the controversy in his most recent book, *Red Matters*.

62. Lincoln, *Sing with the Heart of a Bear*, xii, 10.

63. Fraser, "Rethinking Recognition," 108.

64. Dirlik, "History without a Center?," 252.

65. Dirlik, "Is There History After Eurocentrism?," 18.

66. Apess, *Eulogy on King Philip*, 287.

67. Copway, *Life, Letters, and Speeches*, 145.

68. Cusick, *Ancient History of the Six Nations*, 34.

69. Dirlik, *Postmodernity's Histories*, 216.

70. Smith, *Sacred Feathers*, 204 (emphasis in original).

CHAPTER ONE

1. DiPietro, "A Jeep Cherokee History." Alcatraz was occupied by Native activists in 1969; the Trail of Broken Treaties march in 1972 ended with the occupation of the Bureau of Indian Affairs; the conflict between the American Indian Movement and the FBI at Wounded Knee occurred in 1973. For a general history and overview of U.S.-Native political relations, see D. Wilkins, *American Indian Politics*. Arthur Penn's film *Little Big Man*, based on a 1962 novel by Thomas Berger, appeared in 1970; Cher's hit song "Half-breed" was a single from an album of the same name that was certified a gold record in October 1973. See //www.rockonthenet.com/artists-c/cher—main.htm (19 August 2002).

2. See, for example, Deloria, *Custer Died for Your Sins*, 3–4.

3. The issue of Clinton's heritage seems to have come up first in a televised forum on his "race initiative," which was broadcast on the Public Broadcasting System in July 1998. In discussion with a panel of journalists, scholars, and writers, Clinton observed that "he didn't know much about the American Indians while growing up in Arkansas" but that his grandmother was one-quarter Cherokee. Sherman Alexie, a Spokane/Coeur d'Alene writer, when asked by panel moderator Jim Lehrer, "How do you get people to talk about race?" responded, "Just walk into a room. . . . What they will do is come up to me and tell me they're Cherokee. But that's usually what it amounts to." See Scales, "Few Have Spoken Easily in Nation's Discussion on Race." In a November 1998 magazine article that appears to refer to the exchange described above, a genealogist from the Cherokee Heritage Center is quoted as saying, "If you lived in Arkansas . . . give it up," because, the brief article continues, "the roots of the tribe are Oklahoma-,

Texas-, and North Carolina–based. Worse, the White House didn't find his kin's name to compare against the official Cherokee rolls" ("Meet Chief Panderbear").

4. In *The Racial Contract*, Mills describes the "norming" of space in the racial contract, where whites mark the division between "civil" space and "wild space" (41). "These strange landscapes (so unlike those at home), this alien flesh (so different from our own), must be mapped and subordinated," Mills writes; "creating the civil and the political here thus requires an active *spatial* struggle (this space is resistant) against the savage and barbaric, an advancing of the frontier against opposition, a Europeanization of the world" (43). "Indian country" then cannot contain true civil governments, and white "encroachment" on Native territory can be understood as the advancing tide of civil polity on territory where it does not yet exist, being inhabited by Indians.

5. The term "Cherokee spokesmen" is from Sweet, *American Georgics*.

6. Perdue, "Clan and Court"; Dowd, "Spinning Wheel Revolution"; Sweet, *American Georgics*.

7. McLoughlin, *Cherokee Renascence in the New Republic*, xvii.

8. On Ross and slavery, see Moulton, *John Ross*, 13. Peyer reports that while Boudinot didn't own slaves himself, his feelings about slavery are elusive; he points out that while the Cherokee Council endorsed African slavery, the missionaries on whom the *Phoenix* depended for support didn't, and so what appears in the *Phoenix* on African Americans "remains ambiguous at best" (*Tutor'd Mind*, 189). McLoughlin discusses slavery in the Cherokee Nation in *Cherokee Renascence in the New Republic*, 337–48.

9. The motivations for the Treaty Party's actions appear to have been mixed. Some scholars argue that Ridge and his family stood to gain financially from the treaty; others argue that Boudinot was motivated by a sincere belief that the Cherokee Nation could not survive the kind of assault it was weathering and that the only way to preserve it was to move. On the events surrounding the Treaty of New Echota and subsequent removal, see, for example, Dale and Litton, *Cherokee Cavaliers*; Foreman, *Indian Removal* and *The Five Civilized Tribes*; McLoughlin, *Cherokee Renascence in the New Republic*; and T. Wilkins, *Cherokee Tragedy*.

10. Foreman, *Indian Removal*, 264–69.

11. Perdue, "Introduction," 28–29.

12. Perdue, "Clan and Court," 566. Moulton writes in *John Ross* that Quatie, also known by her English name Elizabeth Brown Henley Ross, was born about 1791 and died during the removal to Indian Territory, on 1 February 1839; she was buried at Little Rock. He writes that her "background remains a mystery. Some sources say she was a full-blood Cherokee of the bird clan, while others contend that she was the daughter of Thomas Brown, a mixed-blood who owned the ferry at Moccasin Bend on the Tennessee River. The best evidence suggests that she was the daughter of a Scottish trader and the sister of Judge James Brown of the Cherokees, thus a mixed-blood but with a stronger Cherokee line than Ross" (12).

13. On John Howard Payne and the Cherokees, see Baillou, "Introduction," esp. 4–5;

Moulton, *John Ross*, 66, 70, 124; and Foreman, "Introduction" and *Indian Removal*, 268, n. 5.

14. Debo, *History of the Indians of the United States*, 97–98.

15. Perdue, "Introduction," 5–6, 12–13, 10.

16. Ibid., 9–13.

17. Peyer, *Tutor'd Mind*, 355, n. 53.

18. Ridge, "John Ridge on Cherokee Civilization in 1826," 79.

19. Review of *An Address to the Whites*, 474.

20. *Vindication of the Cherokee Claims*, 3–4.

21. In *Cherokee Renascence in the New Republic*, McLoughlin writes: "Carefully read, their speeches do not display strong faith in the progress or equality of the Indians, but they contained strong arguments against Jackson's policy toward them" (434).

22. Andrew, *From Revivals to Removal*, 8, 21, 27, 62, 184–85.

23. The most famous representation of William Penn is Benjamin West's *William Penn's Treaty with the Indians*, painted for one of Penn's descendants in 1771. The painting was soon reproduced in Britain and the United States on all manner of consumer goods, including linens, curtains, dishes, and banknotes. The Quaker painter Edward Hicks reproduced the central group of Penn and the Indians in his painting *Peaceable Kingdom*, of which he produced over sixty versions between the 1820s and the 1840s. The "Treaty Elm" under which Penn supposedly made the treaty was a familiar landmark in Philadelphia until a storm blew it down in 1810. See Brinton, "Benjamin West's Painting of Penn's Treaty with the Indians"; and Mather and Miller, *Edward Hicks*.

24. Andrew, *From Revivals to Removal*, 189.

25. Interestingly, one of the leading historians of Indian relations in this era, Francis Paul Prucha, has made the very same argument in a book entitled *American Indian Treaties*. Prucha notes that Indian treaties throughout the nineteenth century both recognize Native autonomy and provide for Native subordination in various ways, which he explains by referring to John Marshall's assessment of Indian relations in *Cherokee Nation v. Georgia*, that is, "the relation of the Indians to the United States is marked by peculiar and cardinal distinctions which exist nowhere else" (1). Prucha reads Marshall's statement as an accurate assessment of relations that need be analyzed no further.

26. Foreman, *Indian Removal*, 229.

27. A. Jackson, "President Jackson on Indian Removal," 48.

28. Sweet, *American Georgics*, 125.

29. Walker and Sarbaugh, "Early History of the Cherokee Syllabary," 72.

30. John Ross to George Gist [*sic*], 12 January 1832, in Ross, *Papers*, 1:234.

31. Boudinot, "Inventing a New Alphabet," in *Cherokee Editor*, 48–63.

32. John Ridge, "Speech of John Ridge," *Liberator*, 10 March 1832, 39.

33. D. S. Butrick to John Howard Payne, 29 December 1840, Payne Typescript, vol. 4, pt. 1, p. 12, John Howard Payne Papers, Edward E. Ayer Collection, Newberry Library, Chicago.

34. John Ross to Cherokee Antiquarians, 15 September 1835, in Ross, *Papers*, 1:353.

35. Foreman, *Indian Removal*, 268, n. 5. Payne describes his experiences in a long missive that was published under the title "John Howard Payne to His Countrymen" in the *Knoxville (Tenn.) Register* in November 1835 and later in the *August (Ga.) Constitutionalist*. See Payne, *John Howard Payne to His Countrymen*. Moulton writes that "in this polemic Payne embraced so entirely the sentiments of the Ross faction that [John] Ridge thought it had been prepared at Ross's suggestion. Ridge found the trace 'diametrically opposite' his views and asked that his name be withdrawn as a member of the delegation. Ross countered that his views were not set on any fixed course and that Payne had written the account based on his own impressions. Ridge must have accepted these explanations, for he remained a part of the delegation and journeyed on to Washington" (*John Ross*, 70). Moulton also reports that Ross asked Payne to help with his manuscripts, apparently, although how much can't be determined; he also asked Payne to help write petitions (124).

36. Payne, "Cherokee Cause," 17.

37. Despite the fact that scholars over the years have consulted Payne's manuscript at the Newberry Library in Chicago, it is only now that part of it is being prepared for publication by the University of Nebraska Press.

38. Overmyer, *America's First Hamlet*, 321–22.

39. Ibid., 335.

40. Boudinot, "Letters and Other Papers," 176.

41. Ibid., 177.

42. Ross, *Letter from John Ross*, 5.

43. Boudinot, "Letters and Other Papers," 160.

44. Peyer, *Tutor'd Mind*, 214.

CHAPTER TWO

1. John Ridge to Stand Watie, 6 April 1832, in Dale and Litton, *Cherokee Cavaliers*, 8.

2. T. Wilkins, *Cherokee Tragedy*, 235.

3. The Congregational-Unitarian controversy was still raging in Boston in 1832, although Beecher himself was doing most of the actual raging. Channing preferred to avoid rancorous public conflict. See Cayton, "Who Were the Evangelicals?"

4. Gabriel, *Elias Boudinot*, 77.

5. Louisa Jane Park to Agnes Major Park, 29 April 1832, Park Family Papers (1800–1890), American Antiquarian Society, Worcester, Mass. Louisa Park (1802–92) was from a prominent family in Worcester, Massachusetts. Her books include *Alfred* (Boston, 1836); *Joanna of Naples* (Boston, 1838); *Miriam: A Dramatic Poem* (Boston, 1838); *The Sheaves of Love* (Boston, 1861); and *Verses* (Cambridge, 1892).

6. See Corn, "Sam Houston." In 1832 Sam Houston was a notorious ex-governor of Tennessee who was living among and serving as an agent of a group of Cherokees who

had emigrated from Tennessee and Alabama to western Arkansas in 1810. In October 1829, the Cherokees in the western part of the state granted Houston citizenship, and he either married or lived with a woman who seems to have been the mixed-blood daughter of a local white trader whose mother's family was influential among the Cherokees. In addition to writing newspaper articles defending Indian rights, when Congressman Stanberry of Ohio made offensive remarks about the Cherokees on the floor of the House of Representatives, Houston "met him on a dark street and soundly caned him" (Corn, "Sam Houston," 43). Houston was arrested, tried, found guilty by the House, and fined. By 1833 he had moved on to Texas, leaving his Cherokee wife behind. See also Hoig, "Diana, Tiana, or Talihina?"; and Gregory and Strickland, *Sam Houston with the Cherokees.*

7. "Rev. Wm. Apess [*sic*] of the Pequot Tribe of Indians," *Boston Evening Transcript*, 24, 25 April 1832; Bowen, *Bowen's Picture of Boston*, 70–71.

8. "William Apess, a Missionary of the Pequod Tribe of Indians," *Liberator* 2, no. 20 (19 May 1832); "Rev. William Apes, a Missionary of the Pequod Tribe of Indians," *Liberator* 2, no. 21 (26 May 1832); "Rev. William Apes Will Preach the Ensuing Sabbath," *Liberator* 2, no. 23 (9 June 1832); "Rev. William Apes Will Preach the Ensuing Sabbath," *Liberator* 2, no. 27 (7 July 1832); "Rev. Wm. Apes Will Preach To-morrow," *Liberator* 2, no. 28 (14 July 1832).

9. Hershberger, "Mobilizing Women, Anticipating Abolition," 37 (Hershberger indicates that the masthead change happened after the passage of the Indian Removal Bill, but the bill was passed in May 1830); "William Apes, a Missionary of the Pequod Tribe of Indians," *Liberator* 2, no. 20 (19 May 1832).

10. Drake, *Indian Biography*, 268.

11. Drake, *Biography and History of the Indians* (1851), preface. Drake writes in the preface to the 1851 edition that by 1835 this book had a circulation of about 5,000, having gone through five editions since the first in 1832, increasing in size from a "small duodecimo of 348 pages" to an octavo of at least 600 densely printed pages. The title of the book was changed to *The Book of the Indians of North America* in the 1833 edition, then became *Biography and History of the Indians of North America* in the third, 1834 edition, although both titles were used, even apparently when the book was printed twice within one year. Drake published several other books in the 1820s and 1830s relating to King Philip's War. His annotated edition of Benjamin Church's history of King Philip's War (1716), which included illustrations, footnotes, and an appendix on the colonial history of Indians, was first published in Boston in 1825; subsequent editions appeared frequently in Boston and in Exeter, New Hampshire, in the 1820s and 1830s (Simpson and Simpson, "Introduction," 53, 183). In 1833, Drake published *The Old Indian Chronicle*, a collection of accounts of King Philip's War published in London in 1675 and 1676, which was reprinted in 1836. He also edited Daniel Gookin's *An Historical Account of the Doings and Sufferings of the Christian Indians of New England, in the Years 1675, 1676, 1677* for inclusion in volume 2 of the *Proceedings of the American Antiquarian Society* in 1836.

12. Review of *A Son of the Forest*, 149, 150.

13. Advertisement for Drake's Antiquarian Bookstore in Drake, *Biography and History of the Indians* (1837), [iv].

14. Stern, *Antiquarian Bookselling*, 11. Sparks solicited Lewis Cass's views on Indians and removal, which incensed the missionary community in Boston. Soon after the appearance of that review, the editorship of the *North American Review* passed to Alexander Hill Everett, Edward's brother, who published Jeremiah Evarts's summary of the antiremoval position in October 1831.

15. "Savage," *Boston Investigator* 2, no. 5 (27 April 1832).

16. Campisi, *Mashpee Indians*, 77–79.

17. Sylvannus Phinney, "The Mashpee Plantation," *Barnstable Patriot*, 24 July 1833.

18. Freeman, *History of Cape Cod*, 701–2.

19. At the peak of its political power in Boston in 1833–34, the Antimasonic Party formed from a larger antimasonic movement, which arose from suspicion among the middle classes about the influence of freemasons in government and business. Generally moralistic, antimasonry often appealed to orthodox Congregationalists, who were disgruntled by the increasing prominence of Unitarianism. The political party collapsed in the mid- to late 1830s. See Formisano, *Transformation of Political Culture*, 197–221. After deciding against Associate Supreme Court Justice John McLean as its presidential candidate in 1832, the party chose instead William Wirt, the Cherokees' lawyer. For a brief history of antimasonry in Boston, see Goodman, *Towards a Christian Republic*, 148–52. Goodman notes that William Lloyd Garrison was an Antimasonic Party supporter, attending the state conventions in 1832 and 1834 as a member of the Boston delegation and endorsing the party in the pages of the *Liberator* (239–40). Those who were attracted to antimasonry, historian Donald Ratcliffe writes, included "dissatisfied and energetic men, usually newspapermen or young lawyers, [who] saw in an appeal to a popular cause a means of recouping their declining fortunes or establishing a career" ("Antimasonry and Partisanship in Greater New England," 218). Like Apess himself, Hallett was a somewhat notorious political gadfly. At the time of the Mashpee conflict, he was attempting, through the pages of the *Advocate*, to force Edward Everett to declare himself an antimason. While Hallett was arguing the Mashpee case in the legislature, he was also testifying to it on the dangers of masonry. See Sylvannus Phinney, "The Hon. Edward Everett," *Barnstable Patriot*, 24 July 1833. On Everett and the antimasons, see also Cumings, *Journal*, entry for Saturday, 8 February 1834.

20. See Hinks, *To Awaken My Afflicted Brethren*; Peterson, *"Doers of the Word,"* 56–73; M. Stewart, *Maria W. Stewart*; and Easton, *"To Heal the Scourge of Prejudice."* For a detailed history of the antislavery movement of the 1830s that attends to the role of free African Americans in guiding its ideals, see Goodman, *Of One Blood*. See also Ernest, "Liberation Historiography."

21. Ruoff introduced William Apess and many other early Native writers to literary criticism in her article "Three Nineteenth-Century American Indian Autobiographers"

and her book-length study *American Indian Literatures*. O'Connell's edited collection of Apess's works, *On Our Own Ground*, can be said to have initiated the minor explosion of interest in Apess, and O'Connell's interpretation of Apess's writing in the collection's introduction remains the one from which almost all subsequent readings derive, at least in part. O'Connell argues that Apess's republican rhetoric demonstrates his desire to become a citizen of the United States (lxxiii–lxxvi), an argument followed by Ashwill in "Savagism and Its Discontents"; L. J. Murray in "Aesthetic of Dispossession"; Sundquist in "The Frontier and American Indians"; and C. Walker in *Indian Nation*. Gaul, in "Dialogue and Public Discourse in William Apess's *Indian Nullification*," follows this orientation but adds that the structure of *Indian Nullification* demonstrates that Apess endorses Native-white "dialogue." O'Connell argues that Apess's Methodism helped him to achieve a Pequot psychological and cultural identity (lv), which is the topic of essays by Haynes, "'A Mark for Them All to . . . Hiss At'"; Tiro, "Denominated 'SAVAGE'"; and Wyss, "Captivity and Conversion." Finally, O'Connell argues that Apess is properly seen as an "antiracist" writer, whose works can be connected to those of African Americans and abolitionists (xv, lxviii), an argument followed especially by Gustafson, "Nations of Israelites"; Dannenberg, "'Where, Then, Shall We Place the Hero of the Wilderness?'"; Sayre, "Defying Assimilation, Confounding Authenticity"; and Peyer, *Tutor'd Mind*. In *Forked Tongues*, David Murray argues that Apess rejects a discourse of "Indianness" and instead exhibits several psychological "identities" in his writing (61, 64). O'Connell's assessment that Apess essentially writes like a white person is followed by Moon in "William Apess and Writing White" but was first argued by Krupat in *Voice in the Margin*, 143–49, 171–77. Krupat returns to Apess in *Ethnocriticism*, 221–29.

In recent years, Apess has been incorporated into multicultural histories of antebellum American literature, on the grounds of his supposedly desiring to be a citizen of the United States; these include Bergland, *National Uncanny*; Bellin, *Demon of the Continent*; and Powell, *Ruthless Democracy*. Michaelsen considers Apess as an "autoethnographer" in *Limits of Multiculturalism*.

Observations regarding Apess's use of "reversals" abound in the criticism, appearing first in Murray's discussion of Apess in *Forked Tongues*. In his introduction to *On Our Own Ground*, O'Connell describes Apess's practice of "mirroring and reversals" as similar to the "wiliness" suggested in the African American critics' discussion of "signifying" in African American literature (xxiii, xxii). Other scholars discussing the theme of reversals in Apess's writing include Ashwill, Bergland, Haynes, Peyer, and Sayre. Apess makes his appearance as the closer in three recent works of early American history: Waldstreicher's *In the Midst of Perpetual Fetes*, Lepore's *Name of War*, and Richter's *Facing East from Indian Country*. All present Apess as a critic of white hypocrisy who demonstrates the historical failure of the United States to incorporate all people as citizens, and whose criticism prefigures a true multicultural present, or at least one to which we all ought to aspire. Richter ends his book by observing, "Somehow the very violence with which [whites] revolted against an empire that suggested that White and Indian people might live beside each other, the very violence with which they rejected their own history, exposes the reality of the threat they faced: the racialized world the revolutionaries created was not the only one that might have been. As William Apess understood far too well, that was the real American tragedy" (252–53).

22. Mather, *Early History of New England*, 151. Mather incorporated the account written at the end of the war by the settlers' leader, John Mason, at the request of the Connecticut Assembly.

23. Salisbury, *Manitou and Providence*, 222.

24. Campisi, "Emergence of the Mashantucket Pequot Tribe." See also DeForest, *History of the Indians of Connecticut*, 246–47, 423–37.

25. O'Connell, " 'Once More Let Us Consider,' " 172–73.

26. Without evidence of Pequot beliefs or values in *A Son of the Forest*—indeed, in " 'Once More Let Us Consider,' " O'Connell remarks that it is "almost completely mysterious both why and how Apess comes to identify himself as a Pequot" (171)— O'Connell argues in his introduction to Apess's works that the sequence of events in *A Son of the Forest*, in which Apess becomes a Christian, then a Methodist, and then returns to a Pequot community, demonstrates that Methodism's emphasis on community, but especially orality (prayers are extemporaneous, not rehearsed), allows Apess to develop an "affirmative identity" as a Pequot (lv–lix). Even though O'Connell himself recognizes that appeals to an anthropologically pristine Pequot culture make no sense, his conceptual model still requires a kind of essential Pequotness, hidden from Apess himself, half-forgotten. For similar views, see also Haynes, Tiro, and Wyss.

27. Warrior, "William Apess," 191. Ruoff also points out, in an early article, that Apess does not write about his "culture." See Ruoff, "Three Nineteenth-Century American Indian Autobiographers," 254.

28. Stevens, "William Apess's Historical Self," 73–74.

29. O'Connell, editorial comment in Apess, *On Our Own Ground*, 10, n. 4.

30. See Hatch, *Democratization of American Christianity*; and Treat, *Native and Christian*.

31. Stevens, "William Apess's Historical Self," 76. Laura Murray shares Stevens's tentativeness in attempting to assess Apess's intentions in the appendix; she suggests that Apess may have included much of the material, even Washington Irving's "Traits of Indian Character," only to demonstrate that whites could be sympathetic to Indians, despite the fact that much of what writers like Irving had to say about Indians we recognize today as racist (L. J. Murray, "Aesthetic of Dispossession," 222–23).

32. These patrons have never been identified. O'Connell speculates that the New York abolitionist Lewis Tappan might have helped Apess. Considering Apess's appearance with Elias Boudinot in Boston, Boudinot himself, Jeremiah Evarts, and even Edward Everett might also be candidates, as well as any other of the prominent Bostonians who were involved in the resistance to removal. It is worth nothing that Alexander Hill Everett, Edward's brother and a state legislator in Massachusetts, was

the editor of *North American Review* when it published Jeremiah Evarts's dismantling of the proremoval position and that he was a visible supporter of the Mashpees when they brought their case to the legislature in 1834.

33. Boudinot, *Star in the West*, 152.

34. Quoted in L. J. Murray, "Aesthetic of Dispossession," 222.

35. On Apess's mistake, see Velikoa, " 'Philip, King of the Pequots.' "

36. Stevens, "William Apess's Historical Self," 74.

37. On antiabolitionists' hysteria over the possibility of "amalgamation" between the races, see J. B. Stewart, "Emergence of Racial Modernity," 198–99.

38. Mayer, *All on Fire*, 115. See also Hinks, *To Awaken My Afflicted Brethren*, for an account of the *Appeal*, its distribution, responses to it, and effects.

39. O'Connell insists that Apess may be partly African American (see " 'Once More Let Us Consider,' " 162), and other scholars have repeated his speculation. Critics generally associate Apess with African Americans in very broad terms; see, for example, Dannenberg, " 'Where, Then, Shall We Place the Hero of the Wilderness?' " 75–76; Haynes, " 'A Mark for Them All to . . . Hiss At,' " 39–40; Tiro, "Denominated 'SAVAGE,' " 653; Sayre, "Defying Assimilation, Confounding Authenticity," 1; Peyer, *Tutor'd Mind*, 165; and Krupat, *Ethnocriticism*, 225–29.

40. Garrison, *Thoughts on African Colonization*, pt. 2, p. 5.

41. See Hershberger, ""Mobilizing Women, Anticipating Abolition"; and Kerber, "Abolitionists' Perception of the Indian."

42. In *Africans and Native Americans* (260–63), Forbes writes that, while "color" was a category included in the first U.S. census in 1790, the usage of the term "people of color" was not entirely consistent, especially in Massachusetts in the early nineteenth century. It could sometimes refer to all Native peoples of mixed descent—which, as far as whites were concerned, would probably include most Native peoples. Nevertheless, Native peoples who lived either in independent nations or in recognized Indian towns were generally excluded from the term.

43. D. Walker, *Appeal*, 1. In *To Awaken My Afflicted Brethren*, Hinks argues that part of Walker's plan for distribution of the *Appeal* in the South included sending it to the Cherokees and other Indian nations. Samuel Worcester and Elizur Butler had been imprisoned in Georgia for having Walker's *Appeal* and for admitting African Americans into their school for Native children (127). Hinks speculates that Walker may have sent the *Appeal* to Worcester and Butler, as well as other missionaries to the Indians, because he "believed the Native Americans would probably be likely allies in the struggle against slavery and racial oppression" (130–31).

44. The looking-glass metaphor was also used by writers on religious controversies, including Benjamin Shaw, *The Fatal Looking-glass, or Universalism Looked in the Face* (Woodstock, Vt., 1828); and Edward Sharman, *The Christian World Unmasked, or, an Enquiry into the Foundation of Methodist Camp Meetings with a Plan for their Correction and Improvement, as Recommended by Mr. John Wesley, and, a Looking-glass for Talkative Professors of Religion* (Watertown, N.Y., 1819).

45. Sylvannus Phinney, "Black Hawk," *Barnstable Patriot*, 26 June 1833. In his introduction to *Black Hawk: An Autobiography*, Jackson writes that on his tour Black Hawk became more of a celebrity than a prisoner and, strangely, that Andrew Jackson himself was touring the same cities at the same time. Bank notes that in Baltimore, Black Hawk upstaged Jackson when they appeared at the same theater performance; afterward, Jackson took care to arrive in town before Black Hawk (Bank, "Staging the 'Native,'" 476). Black Hawk includes an account of his tour in his autobiography (4–15). Phinney founded the *Barnstable Patriot* in 1830 and sold it in the 1850s. In *Barnstable*, Trayser writes that Phinney's "virtues as an editor included frankness, fearlessness, a liberality which opened his columns to religious controversies when strong prejudices existed, and a buoyant good humor" (471–72).

46. Apess, *Indian Nullification*, 172.

47. Sylvannus Phinney, "Trouble in the Wigwarm," *Barnstable Patriot*, 10 July 1833. This is the language as it was widely reported in Boston and Cape Cod newspapers, but Apess toned it down in *Indian Nullification*, changing the original to read: "And now we would say to our white friends, we are wanting nothing but our rights betwixt man and man. And now, rest assured that said resolutions will be enforced after the first day of July, 1833" (180).

48. Jonathan Howe was active first in Charlestown and then in Boston between 1807 and 1855. His publications include quite a few for Baptist organizations, books on antislavery and (in the 1830s) antimasonic themes, and books on botanic medicine.

49. Massachusetts, *Documents Printed by Order of the Senate*, 11–12.

50. Levi Lincoln to Josiah Fiske, 20 June 1833, Folder 1-1, Marshpee Disturbance, 1833–34, Guardians of Indian Plantations, Massachusetts Archives, Boston (this is a manuscript copy of the letter and might be misdated; according to Campisi, *Mashpee Indians*, 102, Fiske left for Mashpee on 30 June); Phineas Fish to Levi Lincoln, 28 June 1833, Folder 1-1, Marshpee Disturbance, 1833–34, Guardians of Indian Plantations, Massachusetts Archives, Boston.

51. Massachusetts, *Documents Printed by Order of the Senate*, 19.

52. Josiah Fiske to Levi Lincoln, 3–4 July 1833, Folder 1-2, Marshpee Disturbance, 1833–34, Guardians of Indian Plantations, Massachusetts Archives, Boston.

53. Massachusetts, *Documents Printed by Order of the Senate*, 22, 23.

54. Levi Lincoln to Josiah Fiske, 5 July 1833, Folder 1-2, Marshpee Disturbance, 1833–34, Guardians of Indians Plantations, Massachusetts Archives, Boston; Massachusetts, *Documents Printed by Order of the Senate*, 16.

55. Josiah Fiske to Levi Lincoln, 3–4 July 1833, Folder 1-2, Marshpee Disturbance, 1833–34, Guardians of Indian Plantations, Massachusetts Archives, Boston.

56. "Notice," *Liberator*, 20 July 1833, 115; also 27 July, 3 August 1833. The overseer was Lemuel Ewer of South Sandwich; the bond was $100 and the fine $100, which O'Connell points out was an exorbitant amount at the time ("Introduction," xxxviii).

57. After the initial confrontation, Apess conducted a revival with Joseph Amos in August. The meeting, they said in an announcement that appeared several times in the

Liberator, "will be held upon their plantation, in the woods, for want of a meeting-house.... We shall erect tents and make seats to accommodate as well as we can.... The friends of religion, without regard to color, are invited to attend; and Ministers of all orders, who are willing to look to heaven for their reward, are invited to come and labor, and do us good" ("Notice," *Liberator*, 20 July 1833, 115; see also 27 July, 3 August 1833).

58. Sylvannus Phinney, "Court of Common Pleas," *Barnstable Patriot*, 11 September 1833.

59. Massachusetts, *Documents Printed by Order of the Senate*, 25.

60. Sylvannus Phinney, "Trouble in the Wigwarm [*sic*]," *Barnstable Patriot*, 10 July 1833. The title of the editorial can be found in *A Son of the Forest*, where Apess uses the phrase to describe one of the white households where he was briefly employed, in which the mistress drank too much (35).

61. "Just Published," *Liberator*, 17 March 1834.

62. Hallett, *Rights of the Marshpee Indians*, 5–28.

63. The Mashpees were made citizens of Massachusetts in 1869. Mashpee Joseph Amos, by then an old man, opposed the proposal to make the Mashpees citizens and divide their land into individual allotments because he felt many Mashpee people were still vulnerable, saying, "We are not capable of taking care of the [land], and the white man, the foreigner from anywhere, would be likely to get away from us our properties, because they had more understanding; they were more shrewd, and knew better how to use themselves" (Commonwealth of Massachusetts, *Hearing Before the Committee on Indians at Marshpee*, 18). He argued that the Mashpees had not yet received a sufficient degree of education to protect themselves from predatory whites: "If this generation, now in their school-rooms, can be allowed to complete their education before this change [allotment] takes place, I think when that is done we shall be ready for it" (19). Amos's description of the disadvantages of Native peoples does not figure them as essentially inferior but rather recognizes the actual, historical difficulties they faced and the necessity of being able to protect themselves from the age-old depredations of whites.

64. "The Marshpee Indians," *Boston Daily Advocate*, 26 March 1834; "A Triumph of Civil Rights," *Boston Daily Advocate*, 29 March 1834.

65. "An Act to Establish the District of Marshpee," reprinted in *Boston Daily Advocate*, 26 March 1833.

66. On Harvard's status as a bastion of Unitarianism, see R. Story, *Forging of an Aristocracy*, esp. 7–8, 79. On the Congregational-Unitarian controversy in Boston in the period, see Cayton, "Who Were the Evangelicals?" The problem of Fish's religious conservatism was noted in a letter to Josiah Quincy from William Whitman, one of Fish's local supporters. In a reference to Quincy's predecessor Samuel Kirkland, who was a Unitarian minister himself, Whitman insists that Fish has fulfilled his ministerial duties "though his Creed is not so liberal as President Kirkland suffered, when he attended [Fish's] ordination—yet I believe him sincere, pious and decent, and I inquire

no further." William Whitman to Josiah Quincy, 1 February 1834, UAI.20.811, Marshpee Indians, 1811–41, Harvard University Archives, Cambridge, Mass.

67. Trayser, *Barnstable*, quoting (without citation) Rev. Enoch Pratt's manuscript history of West Parish Church, Cotuit, Mass., 91.

68. Phineas Fish to Josiah Quincy, 6 December 1833, Marshpee Indians, 1811–41, UAI.20.811, Harvard University Archives, Cambridge, Mass.

69. Fish's cause could not have been helped, however, by the fact that, of the two Mashpee men sent to demonstrate their support for Fish during the legislative session, one spent his days drunk in the boardinghouse room arranged for him by the overseers. Harvard's records include an affidavit of sorts from a Mrs. Dimmas Wallace, the landlady, who wrote that "Mr. [Nathan] Pocknet was incapable of attending to his meals some part of the time being intoxicated and when he was not able to leave his Bed he would Call for Rum and this he Repeated a Number of times—And other things in the way of Conversation that was very much against any Gentlemans Characture [*sic*]." Dimmas Wallace, "Certificate Respecting Nathan Pocknet and William Amos," 3 February 1834, UAI.20.811, Marshpee Indians, 1811–41, Harvard University Archives, Cambridge, Mass.

70. Fish, *Memorial*, 4.

71. "The Rev. Wm. Apes," *Boston Morning Post*, 19 June 1835. The *Post* observed, "Mr. A proves, very clearly, that the Marshpees have been most shamefully abused and neglected, and that while our far-reaching philanthropists were weeping over the fate of '*the poor Cherokees*,' they were guilty of grosser injustice toward the Indians in their own State than ever was inflicted upon the red men by the Georgians." The *Post* had a few words for Governor Lincoln as well, noting that his "threat to attend the *military operations* against the handful of Marshpees, in case they refused to yield to his commands, is the most ludicrous affair which has occurred since his excellency's recommendation to tunnel the Hoosack."

72. Sylvannus B. Phinney, "William Apes' Book," *Barnstable Patriot*, 1 July 1835.

73. "Indian Nullification," *New England Magazine* 9, no. 1 (July 1835): 79. The *New England Magazine*, published in Cambridge, Massachusetts, from July 1831 to December 1835, had among its contributors Henry Wadsworth Longfellow, Edward Everett, Noah Webster, Lydia Sigourney, and John Greenleaf Whittier. Hawthorne published fifteen stories in the magazine, which always included a selection of reviews of books, lectures, and addresses. According to Edward Chielens, "very little contemporary oratory or writing went unremarked" by the magazine. Washington Irving, James Fenimore Cooper, William Ellery Channing, Elizabeth Peabody, Emma Willard, and Jared Sparks, along with William Apess, all received notice. See Chielens, *American Literary Magazines*, 270.

74. R. Story, *Forging of an Aristocracy*, 89.

75. James Walker, "Dr. Walker's Queries as to the State of the Indians (Fall 1835)," UAI.20.811, Marshpee Indians, 1811–41, Harvard University Archives, Cambridge, Mass.

76. James Walker, "Facts in Regard to the Difficulties at Marshpee," [17 October 1835], UAI.20.811, Marshpee Indians, 1811–41, Harvard University Archives, Cambridge, Mass.

77. Benjamin Hallett reported this fact in the memorial he presented to the Massachusetts legislature in 1834, which was printed in the Massachusetts records and which Apess reprints in *Indian Nullification* (233–34). In "Cherokees and Methodists, 1824–1834," McLoughlin notes that because the Methodist hierarchy in particular did little to support the Cherokees in their fight against removal, the Cherokees repudiated the Methodists and their missionaries. Elias Boudinot was vocal on this point in the pages of the *Cherokee Phoenix* as early as January 1831 (57).

78. Phineas Fish to James Walker, 3 October 1835, UAI.20.811, Marshpee Indians, 1811–41, Harvard University Archives, Cambridge, Mass.

79. Remini, *Revolutionary Age of Andrew Jackson*, 24. See also Tregle, "Andrew Jackson and the Continuing Battle of New Orleans." While the Mashpee conflict was brewing in late June 1833, Jackson was visiting Boston. In an article entitled "Reception of the President in Boston," the *New Bedford Mercury* of 28 June 1833 describes the ceremony greeting Jackson when he arrived in Boston, which included decorated Fire Department engines: "The bucket-carriage of Fire Company No. 10, had a banner inscribed 'January 8, 1813,' [*sic*] supported by a hickory branch." On this same trip, Jackson received an honorary L.L.D. from Harvard ("Doctor Jackson," *New Bedford Mercury*, 5 July 1833). On 8 January 1836, Alexander Hill Everett addressed a celebration of Andrew Jackson convened by the Democrats of Salem, Massachusetts, where his oration, Sylvannus Phinney wrote in the *Barnstable Patriot* of 13 January 1836, focused "with much force and effect upon the great civil and military services of the President, and his peculiar moral and intellectual strength of character."

80. Apess himself remarks on the competing factions at Mashpee. Perhaps Apess was too flamboyant, too public, too confrontational for the Mashpees, who had been battling their white oppressors for 200 years before he appeared on the scene. Apess was also, still, an outsider: in an 1834 list of people living at Mashpee, Apess, his wife Mary, and a twelve-year-old daughter are each listed as "a Stranger [who] came here in May 1833" ("A Record of Names and Ages of the People Who are Not Proprietors in Marshpee District for the Year 1834," Mashpee Indian District, Historical Commission, Mashpee, Mass.). According to Mrs. Reuben Attaquin Sturgis, a Mashpee, William Apess had two daughters who married brothers named Chummuck at Mashpee (Speck, *Territorial Subdivisions*, 89–90).

81. "Petition of Sundry Indians of Marshpee for the Preservation of the Parsonage," January 1836, UAI.20.811, Marshpee Indians, 1811–41, Harvard University Archives, Cambridge, Mass.

82. See Cumings, *Journal*, entries for 4, 7, 8, and 13 January (199), 13 and 15 January (200); and 17 January (201).

83. Notices appeared in several Boston newspapers: in the *Liberator* (a weekly) on 2 January 1836 and in the *Morning Post*, the *Evening Transcript*, and the *Daily Advocate*

on 6 and 7 January. Tickets were sold at the bookstores of Ticknor, Loring, Stimson, Muzzey or Mooney, and Drake.

84. Huntzicker, *Popular Press*, 13.

85. Bowen, *Bowen's Picture of Boston*, 71–73; Cumings, *Journal*, entry for 8 January 1836. Bowen estimates the Odeon had a capacity of 3,000, including those who stood. "Every part of the extensive establishment," he writes, "orchestra, auditory, and smaller rooms, has been furnished with gas apparatus, so that in the evening, all parts of it can be beautifully lighted. The public have only to examine the alterations and improvements made in this building by the Academy [of Music], to perceive its admirable adaptation to the purposes for which it is designed, as well as to all great public occasions" (73).

86. "The Indian King Philip," *Boston Morning Post*, 25 January 1836. The same announcement appeared in the *Advocate*, and both appeared on 26 January as well.

87. Everett, "Address Delivered at Bloody-Brook," 610.

88. See Coward, *Newspaper Indian*, 75. Coward notes that *Niles' Weekly Register* frequently reprinted material from the *Cherokee Phoenix*. The *Register* noted the theft of the *Phoenix*'s press and type by the Georgia Guard in an article reprinted from the *New York Star* on 31 October 1835. On 5 December 1835, the *Register* printed a long account of the Cherokee Council's resistance to signing what would be the New Echota treaty, reprinting a petition from the Cherokee Council and a letter from Lewis Ross describing John Ross's arrest by the Georgia Guard (Coward, *Newspaper Indian*, 138–39).

89. The Mashpees submitted a petition to Harvard in May 1836 to remove Fish and use Harvard's money to support Native schoolteachers at Mashpee instead ("Petition of the Marshpee Indians to Trustees of Williams Fund," 10 May 1836, UAI.20.811, Marshpee Indians, 1811–41, Harvard University Archives, Cambridge, Mass.).

90. Webster, *Discourse*, 17.

91. Most critics see the *Eulogy* as Apess's claim of American identity for Native peoples, reading Apess's demand for Native political rights as a demonstration of membership in American "culture," which is always conflated with U.S. citizenship. The standard interpretation of Apess's *Eulogy* remains the one set out by Barry O'Connell, who argues that Apess rewrites history in order to include Native peoples in the category of the "American." In that vein, Cheryl Walker's *Indian Nation* offers the following assessment of Apess's rhetorical strategies: "For William Apess the task was . . . to elevate his (Indian) people so that they could take their appropriate place among Americans of all description, protected by the laws and exercising the rights of full citizens" (180). Also following O'Connell, Laura J. Murray reads the *Eulogy* as Apess's fusing of Native history and "the political discourse of republicanism" in order to "demand legal rights and protections for Native Americans," that is, Apess desires to become a U.S. citizen ("Aesthetic of Dispossession," 307). In " 'Where, Then, Shall We Place the Hero of the Wilderness?,' " Dannenberg situates the *Eulogy* in relation to the rise of scientific racism and American nationalism, arguing that Apess makes an "im-

plicit" case for "cultural relativism" (72). In *Tutor'd Mind*, Peyer also relates Apess's writing to the rise of abolitionism and reform movements such as the temperance movement; he characterizes Apess's representation of King Philip as "primitivist," while noting that Apess "[pulls] on a variety of ideological strings—democratic republicanism, abolitionism, revivalism, romantic primitivism—in what can be considered one of the strongest pro-Indian statements in the history of American Indian literature" (160, 159).

92. O'Connell cites a brief list of early-nineteenth-century literary versions of Puritan historiography and King Philip's War as precursors to Apess's version, beginning with Webster's 1820 oration and including Washington Irving's sketch "Philip of Pokanoket," which appeared in *The Sketch-book* (1819/1820) and which Apess excerpts in the appendix to *A Son of the Forest*; J. W. Eastburn and R. C. Sands's *Yamoyden*, a long narrative poem about King Philip's War (1820); and John Augustus Stone's popular play *Metamora; or, The Last of the Wampanoags* (1829) ("Introduction," xix, n. 9). Besides literary critics, historians also make use of this list, often writing as if it has already been established, for example, that Apess read and was directly responding to Daniel Webster's 1820 speech. See Richter, *Facing East from Indian Country*; and Lepore, *Name of War*. Lepore writes that Edwin Forrest appeared in *Metamora* at the Tremont Theatre in Boston in November 1833 and describes the newspaper coverage of a group of Penobscot Indians' attendance at the play, noting that that was a "not uncommon" event (212). Although there is no evidence for this, she asserts that Benjamin Hallett's expostulations on behalf of the Mashpees in the *Daily Advocate* "[seem] to have been inspired by *Metamora* itself" (216). Apparently unaware of Apess's claim in the first paragraph of *A Son of the Forest* that "my grandfather . . . married a female attached to the royal family of Philip, King of the Pequot tribe of Indians" (3), she writes that *after* the events at Mashpee, Apess became "fascinated" with King Philip, implying that *Metamora* had something to do with that fascination (216).

93. "Historical Society's Lectures," *Boston Evening Transcript*, Monday, 25 January 1836. Gray had been on the Board of Fellows at Harvard during the Mashpee revolt but resigned in 1836. He was a friend of Sparks, Webster, and Lemuel Shaw, among others. The son of William Gray of Salem, a wealthy merchant, Gray was somewhat known as an orator and intellectual; in 1832, on the centennial of George Washington's death, he delivered to the Massachusetts legislature an oration that was later published. See Bolton, "Memoir of Francis Calley Gray."

94. Buell, *New England Literary Culture*, 201.

95. See Gould, *Covenant and Republic*; and Lepore, *Name of War*.

96. See, for example, N. Morton, *New England's Memorial*, 196n; Winthrop, *History of New England*, 134; and Choate, "Importance of Illustrating New-England History by a Series of Romances Like the Waverley Novels." In fact, Choate actually argues that New Englanders ought to ignore the ugly details of history and instead concentrate on—to the point of inventing—its "romance," in order to "reassemble . . . the people of America into one vast congregation" (343–44).

97. Drake, *Book of the Indians*, 3, 37–38 (emphasis in original).

98. J. Story, "History and Influence of the Pilgrims," 465.

99. Bartlett, "Edward Everett Reconsidered," 437. Bradley Newcomb Cumings (1811–76), a young man in Boston in the 1830s, left a journal in which he records his efforts at self-improvement. Cumings seems to have attended a historical lecture by one of Boston's leading political or intellectual lights every few weeks in the 1830s, including ones by Everett, Joseph Story, and Jared Sparks. Cumings, *Journal*, entries for 8 September 1834 (126); 14 October 1834 (132); 22 October 1834 (132); 29 October 1834 (134); 5 November 1834 (135).

100. Review of "An Address Delivered at Bloody-Brook," 465, 466.

101. Apess uses Book 3, chaps. 1 and 2, of Drake's 1833 edition of the *Book of the Indians* for the account of King Philip's War that is at the center of the *Eulogy*, esp. chap. 2, rearranging, compressing, expanding, editing, and copying Drake's account of the war's events, Philip's character, and settler violence. George H. Callcott writes that such use of another source without citation was a common practice in the era (Callcott, *History in the United States*, 136). In his edition of "The Eulogy on King Philip," Dexter notes that Drake's third edition of the book, *Biography and History of the Indians of North America* (Boston: O. L. Perkins, 1834), was "no doubt used as a source by Apes" (65). An 1834 edition was not available to me, but I assume that Drake did not make extensive revisions to the King Philip narrative.

102. Drake, *Book of the Indians*, Book 3, 13.

103. See Harring, *Crow Dog's Case*, 27–36.

104. Bright, "The State in the United States in the Nineteenth Century," 126.

105. Harvard Corporation Records, vol. 7, 21 July 1836, 432–33, UAI.5.30.2, Harvard University Archives, Cambridge, Mass.; Campisi, *Mashpee Indians*, 107–8. In his *History of Cape Cod* (1860), Freeman does not discuss the details of Fish's struggle, perhaps out of a sense of decorum. "It falls not within our province to go farther into the affairs to which we have alluded, leading to the new organization of the Mashpee tribe," he writes; "the whole is of too recent occurrence. Less we would not record in faithfulness; more need not be written" (712).

106. O'Connell, "'Once More Let Us Consider,'" 168. In his headnote to Apess's *Experiences of Five Christian Indians of the Pequot Tribe*, Krupat writes: "Only recently have obituaries in the New York *Sun* and New York *Observer* been found recording [Apess's] death, as a result of alcoholism, in New York, in the spring of 1839" (121). In *Notable Native Americans*, Wellburn understands the conclusion of death from apoplexy and the autopsy details to indicate "a head injury possibly related to alcohol" (16). In his chapter on Apess in *Tutor'd Mind*, Peyer concludes that Apess died "from the effects of alcoholism" (147–48). This is just a sampling of the many versions of Apess's death by alcoholism.

107. Goodman, *Towards a Christian Republic*, 190–91; Hallett, *Oration at Palmer*. Hallett remained active in the Democratic Party for the rest of his life.

108. The first edition, in 1839, was called *Indian Captivities, Being a Collection of the*

Most Remarkable Narratives of Persons Taken Captive by the North American Indians, or, Relations of Those Who, by Stratagem or Desperate Valor, Have Effected the Most Surprising Escapes from their Cruel Hand: To which are Added Notes, Historical, Biographical, &c. In 1841, the second edition's title became even more sensational: *Tragedies of the Wilderness; or, True and Authentic Narratives of Captives, Who Have Been Carried Away by the Indians from the Various Frontier Settlements of the United States, from the Earliest to the Present Time. Illustrating the Manners and Customs, Barbarous Rites and Ceremonies, of the North American Indians, and their Various Methods of Torture Practised Upon Such as Have from Time to Time, Fallen into their Hands.*

109. Drake, *Biography and History of the Indians* (1836), [iii].

110. O'Connell, "Introduction," xliii–xliv. Drake wrote on his copy of *Indian Nullification*: "This work was written by William J. Snelling, who often consulted me during the progress of it. It was done at the request of Wm. Apes, whose name appears in the Title."

111. Drake, Autograph Collection, 2:3, Wisconsin Historical Society, Madison, Wis.

112. Ibid., 116.

113. Ibid., 18.

114. Flanagan, "Introduction," ix–x, xv–xvi. Henry Mayer notes in *All on Fire* that Snelling wrote the preamble for the statement declaring the formation of the New England Anti-Slavery Society (129–30).

115. Snelling, review of *Life of . . . Black Hawk*, 68–69.

116. An almost perfect example of Robertson's discussion of the inability to Native peoples to form governments because of their inability to form real attachments to one other can be found in Snelling's observation that "the refinements of modern chivalry, the tenderness due to the weaker sex, are things of which Black Hawk never heard. Such principals are the natural consequence of the state of aboriginal society" (ibid., 72).

117. Drake, "Indian Miscellany."

118. I. Mather, *Early History of New England*, 151. On Pequot history after 1638, see the section titled "Experiences" above.

119. O'Connell notes in "Introduction" that in the *Bibliography of American Literature*, Smyers and Winship observe that "the source of the Snelling attribution is probably the *Catalogue of the Private Library of Samuel G. Drake . . .*, Boston, 1845, No. 544, where Drake . . . assigns authorship to Snelling. It was possibly edited or put into final shape by Snelling. The copyright is in Apes's name" (xliv). According to the records of the Wisconsin Historical Society, Drake's autographical biography was sold in 1876, in a sale of Drake's books that took place after his death.

120. Pease and Pease, *Web of Progress*, 200.

121. In July 1835, the reviewer of *Indian Nullification* in the *New England Magazine* wrote that Apess "is a full-blooded Indian, one of the last of the Pequots, and makes his descent from one of the daughters of the heroic Metacom, a matter of boast. He had, consequently, a natural claim on the sympathies of the people he addressed [at Mashpee], and they invited him to settle among and preach to them, which he has done

since, with great effect—receiving nothing for his clerical services, but supporting himself by the labor of his hands, and by vending books" (79).

122. *Ezra Tobey v. Wm. Apess*, Barnstable Court of Common Pleas, April 1837 Term, case no. 1069.

123. *Phebe Ann Weden (by Pro Ami) v. William Apess*, Barnstable Court of Common Pleas, September 1836 Term, case no. 1168.

124. *Enos Ames v. William Apess and Trustee*, Barnstable Court of Common Pleas, September 1837 Term, case no. 1199. One other case was lodged against Apess, *William Pope v. William Apess*, Barnstable Court of Common Pleas, April 1836 Term, case no. 1035, but in this instance neither party appeared in court.

125. Mortgage, William Apess to Richard Johnson, 11 September 1836, First Book of Personal Property Mortgaged, Marshpee Indian District, Mashpee Historical Commission, Mashpee, Mass. My thanks to Rosemary H. Burns of the Mashpee Historical Commission for providing me with this information.

126. Ibid. R. Story characterizes elite Boston's "love for books" in the era: "The library was an important token of cultural attainment and family stability for professionals, scholars, politicians, and businessmen alike (*Forging of an Aristocracy*, 114).

127. Tebbel, *History of Book Publishing in the United States*, 1:223; Tryon and Charvat, *Cost Books of Ticknor and Fields*, xv–xvi.

128. The *Boston Daily Evening Transcript* reported that Apess's wife was a "white woman" (12 April 1839); the *Boston Morning Post* insisted that Apess "has left a widow, an Indian woman" (13 April 1839).

129. Coroner's Inquest for William Apes, 10 April 1839, New York County Coroner Inquests, Roll no. 16, July 1838–August 1840, Department of Records and Information, Municipal Archives of the City of New York, New York.

130. Ibid. On the importance of lobelia in Thomson's system, see Thomson, *New Guide to Health*, esp. 46–47. Jonathan Howe was the printer of *Indian Nullification* in 1835. For an account of the history of botanic medicine by an advocate of a later development of the practice (called "eclectic medicine" at the turn of the nineteenth century), see Wilder, *History of Medicine*. For a contemporary consideration of botanic medicine, see Estes, "Samuel Thomson Rewrites Hippocrates." Estes cites other research to the effect that Native knowledge of the medicinal properties of plants had little influence on European settlers.

131. Coroner's Inquest for William Apes, 10 April 1839, New York County Coroner Inquests, Roll no. 16, July 1838–August 1840, Department of Records and Information, Municipal Archives of the City of New York, New York. In *Elements of Medical Jurisprudence*, the standard text on U.S. medical jurisprudence for the first half of the nineteenth century, Theodoric Romeyn Beck and John B. Beck observe that coroner's juries, made up of laypersons and led by a coroner who generally wasn't a medical doctor, had authority over the doctors enlisted to perform autopsies, even to the point of stopping the dissection in progress; they also note that doctors generally were not

compensated for inquest duty (1:2–3). In the autopsy protocol that Beck and Beck describe, the first procedure is to open the skull and examine the brain (1:8).

132. On the symptoms of apoplexy in nineteenth-century medicine, see, for example, Copland, *Of the Class, Nature and Treatment of Palsy and Apoplexy*, esp. 90–96, 132–42, 213–14.

133. Mohr, *Doctors and the Law*, 89–90.

134. The fact that a detailed account of the death of an Indian writer was published in at least three New York newspapers—the *Observer*, *Sun*, and *Star*—may be owing to the manner of his death, as well as to changes in the newspaper business. Founded in 1833, the *New York Sun*, for example, is credited with being the first of the penny newspapers, which emphasized the lives and struggles of white working-class people rather than the political and economic concerns of elites. It featured humorous accounts of the foibles of the poor in New York City's Police Court, as well as interesting or remarkable accounts of deaths gathered at the coroner's office. At the same time, the medical establishment in New York constantly attacked the practitioners of botanic medicine, particularly in New York. In 1809, Samuel Thomson was jailed for murder after a patient of his died after being administered lobelia, as Apess had. See Huntzicker, *Popular Press*, 1–3; Mott, *American Journalism*, 220–27; and Wilder, *History of Medicine*, 462–91. Mayer writes in *All on Fire* that Thomson found a devotee in William Lloyd Garrison, who took regular vapor baths at Thomson's establishment on Pleasant Street (272). There is even a connection between Thomsonian medicine and the Mashpees. In *American Vegetable Practice*, Morris Mattson writes that the Mashpees—"of Martha's Vineyard"—regularly used "vapor baths" as well as lobelia as an emetic, "closely analogous to [the practice] of Dr. Thomson," adding that "according to tradition, they were in the habit, even a century and a half ago, of taking a vapor bath, on the first attack of disease, followed by an emetic of lobelia, if they could obtain it, and if not, they employed some other emetic herb" (x).

135. "An Inquest Was Held at New York," *Boston Daily Evening Transcript*, 2 April 1839; "William Apes," *Boston Morning Post*, 13 April 1839.

136. "Under the Head of 'Suicide No. 3,'" *Yarmouth Register*, 18 April 1839.

137. "An Inquest Was Held at New York," *New Bedford Mercury*, 19 April 1839.

138. "Death of Apes," *Greenfield (Mass.) Gazette and Mercury*, 7 May 1839.

139. Sylvannus Phinney, "Death of the Indian Preacher," *Barnstable Patriot*, 17 April 1839.

140. In the field of literary studies, there is one major exception: Allen, *Blood Narrative*.

141. Putney, "Richard Johnson," 46.

142. Grover, *Fugitive's Gibralter*, 122.

143. Ibid. Shortly after Johnson's death in 1853, William C. Nell wrote in *Colored Patriots of the American Revolution* that "Mr. Johnson was always ready to extend the hand of relief to his enslaved countrymen, and no one was more ready to assist,

according to his ability, in the elevation of his people. . . . He was one of the earliest friends of Mr. Garrison; a subscriber to his paper, from the time the first number was issued in Baltimore, and for several years an efficient agent for the *Liberator*; and very active in circulating Mr. Garrison's 'Thoughts on Colonization,' in 1832. In all the vicissitudes through which the anti-slavery cause has been called to pass, Mr. Johnson always maintained a straight-forward, consistent course, frankly adhering to the pioneer who first sounded the alarm" (91). Nell also mentions the Mashpees in this book, noting that the Mashpee District sent twenty-seven soldiers to die for the Americans in the Revolution. Interestingly, Nell attributes the changes the legislature made to Mashpee government to Benjamin Hallett, who was still active in politics at the time, which possibly makes the attribution politically motivated (95–96).

144. Grover, *Fugitive's Gibralter*, 121; "Richard Johnson Appointed Agent for *The Weekly Advocate*," *Weekly Advocate*, 7 January 1837. Johnson is listed as agent for the *Colored American* in its 4 March 1837 issue.

145. Grover, *Fugitive's Gibralter*, 88; Harris, *Paul Cuffe*, 15, 30.

146. Grover, *Fugitive's Gibralter*, 121, 133.

147. "The Whale Fishery," 108.

148. O'Connell, " 'Once More Let Us Consider,' " 175. He notes that he's quoting correspondence, otherwise unidentified, from Erwin Apes.

149. Apess is also recorded to have had two daughters who came with him and his wife Mary to Mashpee in 1833 and were made members of the tribe; the daughters are remembered to have married men from Mashpee (Speck, *Territorial Subdivisions*, 89–90).

150. O'Connell, "Textual Afterword," 320.

CHAPTER THREE

1. Bieder, *Science Encounters the Indian*, 151–52.

2. Horan, *McKenney-Hall Portrait Gallery*, 105–9. McKenney also had portraits painted of Native leaders who visited Washington for diplomatic reasons, then exhibited the pictures in his offices as an "Indian Gallery," which became a popular tourist attraction in the 1820s. After Andrew Jackson dismissed him in 1830, McKenney sought to have the portraits published in a lavish three-volume elephant portfolio, with biographical entries on each of the subjects and a concluding historical essay by his collaborator, James Hall, a lawyer, magazine editor, and historian in Cincinnati. Subscribers to the set were relatively few but included Maris Bryant Pierce, then a student at Dartmouth and the only Native subscriber; Andrew Jackson; and the king, queen, and Princess Victoria of Britain, as well as the king of France.

3. Alden, *Account of Sundry Missions*, 140. I have been unable to determine whether or not York's manuscript survived. In 1902, William Walker Canfield published a book called *Legends of the Iroquois*, in which he says that he is editing stories that Cornplanter himself told from a manuscript in his possession that an unnamed man allowed him to see. Canfield writes that "a few years after the close of the war of the Revolution

one of the pioneers of Western New York, who was in the service of the Holland Land Company, made the acquaintance and won the friendship of the Seneca Chief, Cornplanter. . . . The friendship continued as long as the two men lived and was marked by its cordiality. In their intercourse they were thrown together many winters, and the Cornplanter was led to talk freely of his people, their past, their present condition, and their future, and it was during these confidences that the Indian told his white friend many of the Iroquois legends. To the recollections of the Cornplanter was added the knowledge possessed upon the subject by the Nephew (Governor Blacksnake), who resided upon the same reservation in the immediate vicinity. . . . The legends were preserved in outline notes upon the blank pages of some diaries and civil engineer field-books which the white man was accustomed to keep; and these outlines, with full oral explanations came finally into the possession of the present writer" (15–16). Canfield further notes that "some of the most intelligent Indians in New York" verified the material as true, including the Tuscarora chief John Mountpleasant (husband of Caroline Parker, the sister of Ely and Nicholson Parker), Harrison Halftown, Elias Johnson (who wrote his own history of the Iroquois in the late nineteenth century), and John Kinjocity (16).

4. Seaver, *Narrative of the Life of Mary Jemison*, ix. Although the book was reprinted in London in 1826 and in New York City in 1829, for the most part it was reprinted in western New York during the time in which the Iroquois struggle against removal, which was led by the Senecas, was at its height. It appeared in Buffalo in 1834, Rochester in 1840 and 1841, Utica in 1842, and Batavia in 1844. The 1856 edition, published in Rochester, featured notes by Lewis Henry Morgan and an authenticating letter by Ely S. Parker. Parker wrote: "Many years ago, I perused Seaver's book with great interest, and have since had good opportunities of testing its reliability, by comparing it with the traditional history preserved of her among the Indians with whom she lived and died, all of which more than corroborates every incident related in the narrative. I have, therefore, every reason to believe it to be entirely true" (29).

5. On Mary Jemison, see Burnham, " 'How Extravagant the Pretension' "; and Walsh, " 'With Them Was My Home.' " On Black Hawk, see Bellin, " 'How Smooth Their Language' "; Wallace, "Black Hawk's Autobiography"; Sweet, "Masculinity and Self-Performance in *The Life of Black Hawk*"; Schmitz, "Captive Utterance"; and Boelhower, "Saving Saukenuk."

6. Smith, *Sacred Feathers*, writes that in the mid-seventeenth century, Jesuits began calling a band of Ojibwe people who settled on the north shore of Lake Ontario Mississaugas after the Mississagi River, which was near their settlement. The French and English afterward called any Native group living on the north shore of Lake Ontario Mississaugas, regardless of whether or not they were Ojibwes. Smith notes that whatever EuroAmericans called them, the people designated "Mississaugas" considered themselves Ojibwes or, in their own language, Anishinabegs (17–20).

7. Schmalz, *Ojibwa of Southern Ontario*, 151.

8. Harring, *White Man's Law*, 11.

9. J. F. Williams, "Memoir of William W. Warren," 14. Bellin, in *Demon of the Continent*, implies that Copway lobbied Congress on behalf of the 1853 Treaty of La Pointe. It appears instead that though Copway endorsed the treaty by publicly praising Millard Fillmore's relationship with Indians, he lobbied Congress on his own plan for a western territory. The Ojibwes sent representatives to Congress, but Copway was not one of them. See Kugel, *To Be the Main Leaders of Our People*, for a comprehensive history of Ojibwe-U.S. political relations in the era.

10. Knobel, "Know-Nothings and Indians," 180–81; Sweet, "Pastoral Landscape with Indians," 12–14.

11. Copway, "American Indians," 637.

12. P. Jones, *History of the Ojebway Indians*, 172.

13. Bremer, *Indian Agent and Wilderness Scholar*, 93.

14. On Native women in the fur trade, see Van Kirk, *"Many Tender Ties"*; Sleeper-Smith, "Women, Kin, and Catholicism"; and J. S. H. Brown, *Strangers in Blood*. On Native women as "cultural mediators," see Kidwell, "Indian Women as Cultural Mediators."

15. Mason, "Introduction," xxiii.

16. B. Peters, "John Johnston's 1822 Description of the Lake Superior Chippewa," 32, quoting John Johnston to Lewis Cass, 19 May 1822, National Archives, Microfilms of Bureau of Indian Affairs Correspondence, Records to the Michigan Superintendency of Indian Affairs, Letters Received, January–June 1822.

17. Bieder, *Science Encounters the Indian*, 146–49. On Schoolcraft's convoluted publications, see Hallowell, "Concordance of Ojibwa Narratives."

18. Bieder, *Science Encounters the Indian*, 152–54.

19. H. R. Schoolcraft, *Personal Memoirs*, 89, 181, 184.

20. Bieder, *Science Encounters the Indian*, 154.

21. Bushman, *Refinement of America*, 282.

22. McKenney, *Sketches of a Tour to the Lakes*, 181.

23. Mason, "Introduction," xxvi.

24. H. R. Schoolcraft, "Unchangeable Character of the Indian Mind," 108.

25. [Johnston?], "Character of Aboriginal Historical Tradition," 5.

26. J. J. Schoolcraft, "To a Friend Asleep," 59.

27. J. J. Schoolcraft, "Otagamiad," 62, 63.

28. Zipes, "Introduction," xviii–xix.

29. J. J. Schoolcraft, "Origin of the Robin," 66.

30. J. J. Schoolcraft, "Forsaken Brother," 69.

31. J. J. Schoolcraft, "Mishosha," 64.

32. H. R. Schoolcraft, *Literary Voyager*, 176–77, n. 79.

33. J. J. Schoolcraft, "Moowis," 67.

34. H. R. Schoolcraft, "Moowis," 90.

35. Bremer, *Indian Agent and Wilderness Scholar*, 110.

36. Ibid., 111, quoting Henry Rowe Schoolcraft to Jane Schoolcraft, 24 November 1830, Henry Rowe Schoolcraft Papers, Library of Congress, Washington, D.C.

37. H. R. Schoolcraft, *Personal Reminiscences*, 107–8.

38. Booth, "Lessons of the Medusa," 267, 265, 270.

39. Hallowell, "Concordance of Ojibwa Narratives," 138–39.

40. Jameson, *Winter Studies and Summer Rambles*, 69–70.

41. H. R. Schoolcraft, *Algic Researches*, 9.

42. Hallowell, "Concordance of Ojibwa Narratives," 140.

43. Smith, *Sacred Feathers*, 1–6, 40–45, 317, n. 78, 54–55, 187–88.

44. Michaelsen, *Limits of Multiculturalism*, 107.

45. The editor of Jones's journals published after his death "under the direction of the missionary committee, Canada conference" of the Methodist church notes Jones's frequent ill health after 1838, when his journals conclude. However, at least in the published material, Jones does not complain about being ill. See Peter Jones, *Life and Journals of Kah-ke-way-quo-na-by*, 409–13. Jones's biographer, Donald B. Smith, writes that Jones told his sons "Indian stories and legends," as did his mother, who taught his sons Ojibwe and when she visited her son's home "kept to her own customs and . . . slept on her blanket on the floor, never a bed" (*Sacred Feathers*, 227–28).

46. Smith, *Sacred Feathers*, 204.

47. Ruoff, "Literary and Methodist Contexts of George Copway's *Life, Letters, and Speeches*," 7.

48. See esp. Smith, "Life of George Copway"; Bellin, *Demon of the Continent*, esp. 187–90; Peyer, *Tutor'd Mind*; and C. Walker, *Indian Nation*.

49. C. Walker, *Indian Nation*, 85. Walker relies on Smith and on Knobel, "Know-Nothings and Indians: Strange Bedfellows?," for her view of the state of George Copway's Indianness. In *Limits of Multiculturalism*, Michaelsen comments on Smith's (and by extension Walker's and Knobel's) assessment of Copway's Indianness at 112–13.

50. Smith, "Kahgegagahbowh," 23–33.

51. Copway may be referring to the contemporary interest in the Iroquois. Schoolcraft's *Notes on the Iroquois* appeared in Albany in 1847, as did Copway's first edition of *Life, History, and Travels of Kah-ge-ga-gah-bowh*.

52. J. F. Williams, "Memoir of William W. Warren," 12–14.

53. Ibid., 13.

54. *Atkinson's Saturday Evening Post* 18 (13 April 1839): 2.

55. Smith, *Sacred Feathers*, 218.

56. Ibid.

57. Ruoff, "Literary and Methodist Contexts," 5; S. Longfellow, *Life of Henry Wadsworth Longfellow*, 2:135, 137, 188; Francis Parkman to Charles Eliot Norton, 3 March 1849, in Parkman, *Letters of Francis Parkman*, 59–60; Francis Parkman to Ephraim George Squier, 18 November 1849, in ibid., 65–66; Squier, "Ne-she-kay-be-nais," 255; Squier, "Manabozho and the Great Serpent," 397; Squier, "Historical and Mythological

Traditions," 177; Copway, "American Indians" and "Two Cousins"; McFeely, *Frederick Douglass*, 168–69; *Copway's American Indian*, 23 August 1851.

58. T. N. Baker, *Sentiment and Celebrity*; Tomc, "Idle Industry." Willis is listed as a contributor to *Copway's American Indian*, along with Lewis Henry Morgan, William Gilmore Simms, Henry Rowe Schoolcraft, Francis Parkman, Washington Irving, and William Cullen Bryant.

59. Smith, "Kahgegagahbowh," 30.

60. Maungwudaus, *Account of the Chippewa Indians*, 14.

61. *Kah-ge-ga-gah-bowh, a Chief of the Ojibwe Nation of North American Indians.*

62. The unconverted Spear Maker in *Life, Letters, and Speeches* is one example of Copway's notion of Indian "vengefulness."

63. Copway and Hall, *Minuajimouin Gainajimot au St. Luke*; and Copway and Hall, *Odizhijigeuinius Igiu Gaanonijig = Acts of the Apostles in the Ojibwe Language.*

64. In *Life, Letters, and Speeches*, Copway describes his childhood dream at 39–41; he describes his dream after the death of his cousin Thomas Kezhig, from consumption, at 104–6.

65. Black, *Cornwall*, 8.

66. *Boyd's Business Directory*, 327.

67. Smith, "Kahgegagahbowh," 43–48.

CHAPTER FOUR

1. Dearborn, "Journals," 176, 187.

2. W. H. Armstrong, *Warrior in Two Camps*, 8. My thanks to Alyssa Mountpleasant for pointing out Cone's likely identity.

3. Hauptman, *Conspiracy of Interests*, 67.

4. On Sullivan's campaign, see Graymont, *Iroquois in the American Revolution*, chap. 8.

5. Stone, *Life of Joseph Brant*, 2:33.

6. Hauptman, *Conspiracy of Interests*, 107–8.

7. Ibid., 74. The treaty remains centrally important to the Iroquois, then and in the present day, as it unequivocally recognizes their sovereignty. See Jemison and Schein, *Treaty of Canandaigua*, 2000.

8. Hauptman, *Conspiracy of Interests*, 88.

9. Ibid., 91–114.

10. Woods, "Long-Running Indian Claims," 1; Chen, "Battle over Iroquois Land Claims Escalates."

11. Carr, *Inventing the American Primitive*, 63. Carr points out that in *Lectures on Rhetoric and Belles Lettres* (London, 1783), a book that became "the single most popular work of literary criticism in the States from the time of their publication until the mid-nineteenth century. (They were a set text at Yale by 1785, and at Harvard by 1788)," Hugh Blair maintains that Indians "are governed by imagination and passion more

than reason. . . . Their speech must be deeply tinctured by their genius. . . . This is the character of the American and Indian languages: bold, picturesque, and metaphorical; full of strong allusions to the sensible qualities, and to such objects as struck them most in their wild and solitary life" (Carr, *Inventing the American Primitive*, 64–65, 63).

12. On colonial treaties and especially Iroquois treaties, see Jennings et al., *History and Culture of Iroquois Diplomacy*; DePuy, *Bibliography of the English Colonial Treaties with the American Indians*; and Van Doren, "Introduction" to *Indian Treaties Printed by Benjamin Franklin*.

13. Densmore, *Red Jacket*, xv–xvii, 63–69, 74.

14. See Hauptman, *Conspiracy of Interests*, esp. 178–86. Hauptman notes that both John Ross and Maris Bryant Pierce denounced Schermerhorn publicly.

15. Bank, "Staging the 'Native,' " 473.

16. Stone, *Life and Times of Sa-go-ge-wat-ha or Red Jacket*, 389.

17. [Red Jacket], *First Impressions on Reading the Message of the Governor of Georgia*, 2.

18. Densmore, *Red Jacket*, 113.

19. Ibid., 107, 111.

20. "Indian Literature," *Freedom's Journal* (New York, N.Y.), 3 August 1827, 82. The same notice appeared in the *New-York Gazette & General Advertiser* and the *New York Daily Advertiser* on 4 July 1827. There might be some evidence that Cusick was known to the literati in New York at the time in that Fitz-Greene Halleck's poem "Red Jacket" is subtitled "A Chief of the Indian Tribes, the Tuscaroras." The poem, with a headnote, "On looking at his portrait by Weir," describes Red Jacket as a fit king to precede the democratic republic. Halleck also describes, mysteriously, Red Jacket's "hatred—of missionaries and cold water." See Halleck, *Poetical Writings*, 46–50.

21. Rita Reif, "A Man Who Traded Everything for an Indian Trove," *New York Times*, 16 May 1999: sec. AR. The article describes the Frank T. Siebert collection of Indian and western books and manuscripts to be sold at Sotheby's that month. An 1828 edition of Cusick's book is noted as "one of the 'gems' of the collection," and Reif writes that it was "produced to be sold as a souvenir at Niagara Falls," although she isn't specific about her source for that information.

22. Jasen, *Wild Things*, 50. Jasen describes travelers' comments on the Tuscaroras (41–45) and Native peoples selling souvenirs to tourists (50–51). General Peter B. Porter, developer of roads and canals, speculator in Iroquois land, congressman, and former commander of Iroquois troops in the War of 1812, allowed Native women to sell beadwork on land he owned on the U.S. side of the falls as a reward to Native peoples for service during the war. David Cusick himself was a veteran of that war, having served at the garrison at Lewiston on the Niagara River, along with other Tuscarora volunteers to the U.S. cause. On Porter, see Hauptman, *Conspiracy of Interests*, 121–27; and Dubinsky, *Second Greatest Disappointment*, 66. On Cusick's service during the War of 1812, see Johnson, *Legends, Traditions, and Laws of the Iroquois*, 167.

23. Boyce, "Tuscarora Political Organization," 125–26, 142–43.

24. See Duncan, *A Sabbath among the Tuscarora Indians*, 57; and Johnson, *Legends, Traditions, and Laws of the Iroquois*, 134. Johnson writes that Nicholas's son James was ordained a Baptist preacher in 1838. An advocate of removal, James led a party of emigrants to Indian Territory, most of whom were members of his church, in 1846. About a third of the people died within a year, and the rest came home. Cusick then went to Canada as a missionary at the Grand River Iroquois reserve. He returned to Tuscarora Village in 1860 and died there in 1861 (137–39). Johnson reports that a temperance society was formed at Tuscarora Village in 1830, with Nicholas as its president and James as its secretary and treasurer (154). He also reports that David Cusick, along with many other Tuscarora men, was stationed at Lewiston during the War of 1812 to guard the river (165–66).

25. Boyce, "Tuscarora Political Organization," 131. On Samuel Kirkland's machinations, see Hauptman, *Conspiracy of Interests*, 70.

26. Stansbury, *A Pedestrian Tour*, 98, quoted in Brydon, "Ingenuity in Art: The Early Nineteenth Century Works of David and Dennis Cusick," 67. In his encounter with Cusick, Stansbury also "was informed" about Tuscarora history, from the migration from North Carolina to the extent of their present reservation. He reported: "My Tuscarora conductor, favoured me with a song in his own house, in which he was joined by a number of Indians formed in a ring. The song commenced with these lines, which he inscribed for me upon a piece of paper. 'Ka ro ri ni kough ri go stayh / Ne sa qua riyat ni yo— / Oni a qua a ta qua yah / Sa we a na to teak to.' Seldom was I better pleased with singing: the young squaws with their 'silver voices,' added considerably to the harmony" (99).

27. McKenney, *Sketches of a Tour to the Lakes*, 432–33. McKenney describes Cusick's famous father at 431–32. In *An Account of Sundry Missions Performed among the Senecas and Munsees*, Timothy Alden visits the mission house at Buffalo Creek where David Cusick's brother Dennis had been a teacher. Although Dennis died soon after Alden saw him in 1826—"of a pulmonary disorder, which is frequent among the Senecas"—he notes that Dennis "had left numerous pieces of writing" at the mission house, "of different hands, showing a skill in penmanship seldom surpassed by any one. He has a natural taste for drawing, and some of the specimens of his ingenuity in this art, which we had opportunity to examine, indicate a genius worthy of encouragement" (119).

28. Beauchamp, *Iroquois Trail*, 41. Beauchamp's source of information on David Cusick was one of Cusick's descendants. Nicholas Cusick had at least three sons: Dennis, David, and James. James, the Baptist minister, who "published a collection of Indian hymns, and died in Canada," provided information to Schoolcraft for his *Notes on the Iroquois*; Schoolcraft prints a version of his notes and correspondence from James Cusick at 473–75 (42). James's son, unnamed, married an Onondaga woman and had a son named Albert, who was Beauchamp's informant on his notes to David Cusick's history. In 1864, Albert Cusick became hereditary chief of the Iroquois but left that position after ten years to become an Episcopalian. Beauchamp writes, "[Albert Cusick] has aided me and others much, and for many years was lay reader and inter-

preter for the Onondaga Episcopal Mission, besides being active in temperance work. In the Church of the Good Shepherd, Onondaga Castle, he was made a deacon by Bishop Huntington, October 1, 1891. Much interesting and valuable matter in this volume is credited to him" (42). Beauchamp wrote many books on the Iroquois during his long lifetime (he died in 1925 at age 95) ("Beauchamp, William Martin," 103–4). In *The Iroquois in the Civil War*, Hauptman provides some background information on the Cusick family in his remarks on David Cusick's nephew Cornelius C. Cusick (son of James Cusick and uncle of Albert Cusick), who became a lieutenant in the U.S. Army during the Civil War and served in the campaigns against the western Indians thereafter (39–45).

29. Most critics who write about Cusick's book indicate that its representation of history and sovereignty is not as interesting as its representation of Iroquois culture, or what is described as its conflation of history and myth. See Schmitz, *White Robe's Dilemma*, 11; and Bellin, *Demon of the Continent*, 201–3. Bellin reads Cusick's insistence that he tells history and not myth as "intercultural" and thus representative of the "accommodation of diverse stories" one finds in a multicultural United States. While admitting that Cusick's book is indeed an "antiremoval" text, Michaelsen contends in *The Limits of Multiculturalism* that Cusick's most important contribution is that he "constructs an Amerindian identity entirely circumscribed by colonial relations and in which the Iroquois are colonizers every bit the equal of the Europeans. Amerindian identity is . . . both relational and decentered, and at the same time it is curiously identical to Anglo identity" (50, 54). That is, Cusick's book shows that he "constructs" a representation of his own culture that cannot escape the constructions of the colonizers whom he critiques. In "David Cusick's *Ancient History of the Six Nations*," Judkins argues that Cusick's book "constitutes an early and significant attempt to coordinate Iroquois and Euro-American knowledge systems, to have them share and exchange world views, and to experience one another as intellectual equals" (26). Though he notes that Cusick uses "a linear-time-sequence format to trace Iroquois life from Creation to the early historical period," he argues, like Bellin and Michaelsen, that the most important aspect of the book is what he understands as its conscious synthesis of Indian and white worldviews or cultures. He argues, for example, that in the Columbus chronology Cusick "correlates the two historical experiences and the two world views, by correlating their chronologies, thus affirming the validity of each, and the universe it represents, by the fact of the existence of the other" (35).

30. McKenney and Hall, *Indian Tribes of North America*, 1:2.

31. Kalter, "Finding a Place for David Cusick," 32.

32. Pechuman, "Introduction," 4. A notice seeking a copy of the book appeared in the 20 November 1839 *Lockport Democrat and Balance*. Pechuman also reports that Cusick was likely born in Madison County, New York, on or near Oneida land, and "apparently retained his connections in Madison County and is believed to have died there in 1840 or 1841" (3).

33. Schoolcraft, *Notes on the Iroquois*, 263.

34. Quoted in R. F. Sayre, *Thoreau and the American Indians*, 128 [Notebook 10, 109].

35. Parkman, *Conspiracy of Pontiac*, 10, n. 1. Parkman also recounts: "Cusick was an old Tuscarora Indian, who, being disabled by an accident from active occupations, essayed to become the historian of his people, and produced a small pamphlet, written in a language almost unintelligible, and filled with a medley of traditions in which a few grains of truth are inextricably mingled with a tangled mass of absurdities. He relates the monstrous legends of his people with an air of implicit faith, and traces the presiding sachems of the confederacy in regular descent from the first Atotarho downwards. His work . . . is illustrated by several rude engravings representing the Stone Giants, the Flying Heads, and other traditional monsters" (12, n. 1).

36. Gallatin, "Hale's Indians of North-West America," quoted in Judkins, "David Cusick's *Ancient History of the Six Nations*, 30.

37. See, for example, Weiser, "Weiser's Report on the Treaty at Albany."

38. Marshe, "Journal of a Treaty Held with the Six Nations."

39. W. H. Armstrong, *Warrior in Two Camps*, 3, 9.

40. Littlefield, " 'They Ought to Enjoy the Home of Their Fathers,' " 93–97.

41. Strong, *Appeal to the Christian Community*, 27. Like Elias Boudinot, Strong argues that there would be no stopping whites and their ill effects until Indians could escape them entirely, and so they must remove in order to preserve themselves as a political entity. Also, as Littlefield points out, Strong insisted that the civilizing of Indians would not make any inroads until Indians could possess land as individual property owners, which, he argued, is the foundation of civilization (31). Like Boudinot, Strong has as his objective the continuity of Seneca political existence, but he is, at this point early in his adult life anyway, a pragmatist in despair: he sees no way out but to get away from whites and start over. Iroquois history is nowhere referenced in his essay.

42. Vernon, "Maris Bryant Pierce," 19–41.

43. A. C. Parker, *Life of General Ely S. Parker*, 48.

44. Ibid., 77.

45. Nicholson Parker, partial copy of William Apess's "Eulogy on King Philip" (manuscript), mislabeled "by N. H. Parker" (by Arthur C. Parker), in Folder 4, Writings of Nicholson H. Parker, 1845–46 and undated, Papers of Arthur C. Parker, A64-94, Buffalo and Erie County Historical Society, Buffalo, N.Y.

46. Ely S. Parker, "King Philip's Last Speech to His Countrymen," no date, Ely S. Parker Papers, A00-450, Buffalo and Erie County Historical Society, Buffalo, N.Y.

47. Morgan, *League of the Iroquois*, 55.

48. Bieder, *Science Encounters the Indian*, 202.

49. Michaelsen, *Limits of Multiculturalism*, 95.

50. Morgan, *League of the Iroquois*, 232.

51. The political context of the Handsome Lake religion can also be seen in the account Johnson gives of George Washington in his own special purgatory. Handsome Lake, led by messengers, "saw an inclosure upon a plain, just without the entrance of heaven. Within it was a fort. Here he saw the 'Destroyer of Villages,' walking to and fro

within the inclosure" (Morgan, *League of the Iroquois*, 257). Washington's "counte-nance indicated a great and good man," because at the end of the Revolution, when the Iroquois were abandoned by their supposed ally Britain and suggested that the "Great American . . . might kill [the Iroquois] if he liked," Washington "judged that this would be cruel and unjust. He believed that they were made by the Great Spirit, and were entitled to the enjoyment of life" (257). The messengers explain Washington's fate to Handsome Lake in this way: "[He] was kind to you, and extended over you his protec-tion. For this reason, he has been allowed to leave the earth. But he is never permitted to go into the presence of the Great Spirit. Although alone, he is perfectly happy. All faithful Indians pass by him as they go to heaven. They see him, and recognize him, but pass on in silence. No word ever passes his lips" (257).

52. E. S. Parker, "New Initiation of the Wolf Tribe of the Cayuga Nation, one of the Confederate Nations of the Grand Confederacy of the Iroquois," [June 1847?], Ely S. Parker Collection, American Philosophical Society Library, Philadelphia, Pa.

53. W. H. Armstrong, *Warrior in Two Camps*, 44–60.

54. E. S. Parker, "Draft of lectures on Indian dances, games, and social and domestic habits," [ca. 1850?], MS 674, Folder 1, page 2, Edward E. Ayer Collection, Newberry Library, Chicago, Ill.

55. E. S. Parker, "Iroquois or Confederacy of the Five Nations," [May 1848?], A00-450, Ely S. Parker Papers, Buffalo and Erie County Historical Society, Buffalo, N.Y.

56. Nathaniel T. Strong, "Speech on Red Jacket," B00-2, page 1, 2–3, Indian Collec-tion, 1788–1955, Buffalo and Erie County Historical Society, Buffalo, N.Y.

57. Personal communication from Daniel F. Littlefield Jr., 17 November 2001.

58. A. C. Parker, *Life of Ely S. Parker*, 277.

59. N. H. Parker, "Intellectual Character of the Indian," ms., Writings of Nicholson H. Parker, 1845–46 and undated, Folder 1, A64-94, Papers of Arthur C. Parker, Buffalo and Erie County Historical Society, Buffalo, N.Y.

60. Bryant, "Obsequies at Forest Lawn Cemetery," 17, 24.

61. E. S. Parker, "Remarks on Red Jacket," 41.

CONCLUSION

1. U.S. Department of Interior, National Park Service, *Little Bighorn Battlefield Offi-cial Map and Guide*.

2. R. White, *The Middle Ground*, is the origin of the concept. For recent examples of work influenced by White's thesis, see Merrell, *Into the American Woods*; and Richter, *Facing East from Indian Country*. For a critique of how the concept has developed in historiography, see Herman, "Romance on the Middle Ground."

3. Littlefield, "American Indians, American Scholars."

4. V. Deloria, "Anthros, Indians, and Planetary Reality," 215.

5. Smith, *Sacred Feathers*, 124; John Ross, "To the Seneca Delegation," in Ross, *Papers*, 1:284–87.

BIBLIOGRAPHY

ARCHIVES

Boston, Mass.
   Massachusetts Archives
   Massachusetts Historical Society
Buffalo, N.Y.
   Buffalo and Erie County Historical Society
      Indian Collection, 1788–1955
      Papers of Arthur C. Parker
      Ely S. Parker Papers
Cambridge, Mass.
   Harvard University Archives
      Harvard Corporation Records, vols. 7 and 8
      Marshpee Indians, 1811–41
Chicago, Ill.
   Newberry Library
      Edward E. Ayer Collection
         John Howard Payne Papers
Madison, Wis.
   Wisconsin Historical Society
      Samuel Gardner Drake, Autograph Collection, 3 vols., Ms. ZGT D7
Mashpee, Mass.
   Mashpee Historical Commission
New York, N.Y.
   Municipal Archives of the City of New York
Philadelphia, Pa.
   American Philosophical Society Library
      Ely S. Parker Collection
Washington, D.C.
   National Archives
      Records of the Bureau of Indian Affairs
Worcester, Mass.
   American Antiquarian Society
      Park Family Papers

NEWSPAPERS

Barnstable Patriot. Barnstable, Mass. 1833–39.

Boston Daily Advocate. Boston, Mass. June 1833–April 1834.

Boston Evening Transcript. Boston, Mass. April 1832–April 1839.

Boston Investigator. Boston, Mass. April 1832.

Boston Morning Post. Boston, Mass. June 1835–April 1839.

Colored American. New York, N.Y. 1837.

Copway's American Indian. New York, N.Y. August–September 1851.

Freedom's Journal. New York, N.Y. August 1827.

Greenfield Gazette and Mercury. Greenfield, Mass. May 1839.

The Liberator. Boston, Mass. 1832–36.

New Bedford Mercury. New Bedford, Mass. 1833–39.

New England Galaxy. Boston, Mass. July 1833.

New York Daily Advertiser. New York, N.Y. July 1827.

New-York Gazette & General Advertiser. New York, N.Y. July 1827.

Niles' Weekly Register. Baltimore, Md. November 1834.

Weekly Advocate. New York, N.Y. 1837.

Yarmouth Register. Yarmouth, Mass. April 1839.

PUBLISHED SOURCES

Abu-Lughod, Lila. "Writing against Culture." In *Recapturing Anthropology: Working in the Present*, edited by Richard G. Fox. Santa Fe, N.Mex.: School of American Research Press, 1991.

Advertising Council. "American" public service announcement. ⟨http://www.adcouncil.org/temp/American—feedback.html⟩. 20 February 2002.

Agassiz, Louis. "The Diversity of Origin of the Human Races." *Christian Examiner and Religious Miscellany* 49, 4th ser., 14 (July 1850): 110–45.

Alden, Timothy. *An Account of Sundry Missions Performed among the Senecas and Munsees; in a Series of Letters*. New York: Printed by J. Seymour, 1827.

Aleiss, Angela. "Irony Eyes Cody: Wannabe Indian." *Cineaste* 25, no. 1 (Winter 1999): 30.

Allen, Chadwick. *Blood Narrative: Indigenous Identity in American Indian and Maori Literary and Activist Texts*. Durham: Duke University Press, 2002.

Andrew, John A., III. *From Revivals to Removal: Jeremiah Evarts, the Cherokee Nation, and the Search for the Soul of America*. Athens: University of Georgia Press, 1992.

Apess, William. *Eulogy on King Philip* (1837). In *On Our Own Ground: The Writings of William Apess, a Pequot*, edited by Barry O'Connell, 277–310. Amherst: University of Massachusetts Press, 1992.

———. *Experiences of Five Christian Indians of the Pequod Tribe* (1833). In *On Our Own Ground: The Writings of William Apess, a Pequot*, edited by Barry O'Connell, 119–61. Amherst: University of Massachusetts Press, 1992.

——. *Indian Nullification of the Unconstitutional Laws of Massachusetts; or, the Pretended Riot Explained* (1835). In *On Our Own Ground: The Writings of William Apess, a Pequot*, edited by Barry O'Connell, 166–274. Amherst: University of Massachusetts Press, 1992.

——. *On Our Own Ground: The Writings of William Apess, a Pequot*. Edited by Barry O'Connell. Amherst: University of Massachusetts Press, 1992.

——. *A Son of the Forest: The Experience of William Apess, a Native of the Forest* (1831). In *On Our Own Ground: The Writings of William Apess, a Pequot*, edited by Barry O'Connell, 3–112. Amherst: University of Massachusetts Press, 1992.

Armstrong, Jeannette, ed. *Looking at the Words of Our People: First Nations Analysis of Literature*. Penticton, British Columbia: Theytus, 1993.

Armstrong, Nancy. "Who's Afraid of the Cultural Turn?" *differences* 12, no. 1 (2001): 17–49.

Armstrong, William H. "Red Jacket's Medal: An American Badge of Nobility." *Niagara Frontier* 21, no. 1 (Spring 1974): 26–36.

——. *Warrior in Two Camps: Ely S. Parker, Union General and Seneca Chief*. Syracuse: Syracuse University Press, 1978.

Ashcroft, Bill, Gareth Griffiths, and Helen Tiffin. *The Empire Writes Back: Theory and Practice in Post-Colonial Literatures*. London: Routledge, 1989.

Ashwill, Gary. "Savagism and Its Discontents: James Fenimore Cooper and His Native American Contemporaries." *American Transcendental Quarterly* 8, no. 2 (September 1994): 211–27.

Bacon, Edwin M. *King's Dictionary of Boston*. 5th ed. Cambridge: Moses King, 1883.

Baillou, Clemens de. "Introduction." In *John Howard Payne to His Countrymen*, edited by Clemens de Baillou. Athens: University of Georgia Press, 1961.

Baker, Samuel. "William Least Heat-Moon: Navigating America." *Publisher's Weekly*, 20 September 1999, 55.

Baker, Thomas N. *Sentiment and Celebrity: Nathaniel Parker Willis and the Trials of Literary Fame*. New York: Oxford University Press, 1999.

Ball, John. *Born to Wander: The Autobiography of John Ball, 1794–1884*. Grand Rapids: Grand Rapids Historical Commission, 1994.

Bancroft, George. *History of the United States, from the Discovery of the American Continent*. (Originally published 1834.) 16th ed. Vol. 1. Boston: Little, Brown, and Company, 1858.

——. *History of the United States, from the Discovery of the American Continent*. 18th ed. Vol. 2. Boston: Little, Brown, and Company, 1860.

Bank, Rosemarie K. "Staging the 'Native': Making History in American Theatre Culture, 1828–1838." *Theatre Journal* 45 (1993): 461–87.

Bartlett, Irving H. "Edward Everett Reconsidered." *New England Quarterly* 69, no. 3 (September 1996): 426–61.

Beach, Lewis. *Cornwall*. Newburgh, N.Y.: E. M. Ruttenber & Son, Printers, 1873.

Beauchamp, William M., ed. *The Iroquois Trail, or Foot-Prints of the Six Nations* [David Cusick's *Sketches of Ancient History of the Six Nations*]. New York: AMS, 1976.

"Beauchamp, William Martin." *Dictionary of American Biography*. Edited by Allen Johnson. New York: Charles Scribner, 1957.

Beck, Theodoric Romeyn, and John B. Beck. *Elements of Medical Jurisprudence*. 10th ed. 2 vols. Albany: Little and Company, Law Booksellers, 1850.

Bellin, Joshua David. *The Demon of the Continent: Indians and the Shaping of American Literature*. Philadelphia: University of Pennsylvania Press, 2000.

——. " 'How Smooth Their Language': Authenticity and Interculturalism in the *Life of Black Hawk.*" *Prospects* 25 (2000): 485–511.

Bergland, Renee. *The National Uncanny: Indian Ghosts and American Subjects*. Hanover, N.H.: Dartmouth College/University Press of New England, 2000.

Berkhofer, Robert. *The White Man's Indian: Images of the American Indian from Columbus to the Present*. New York: Vintage, 1978.

Bieder, Robert E. *Science Encounters the Indian, 1820–1880: The Early Years of American Ethnology*. Norman: University of Oklahoma Press, 1986.

Black Hawk. *Black Hawk: An Autobiography*. Edited by Donald Jackson. 1955; reprint, Urbana-Champaign: University of Illinois Press, 1990.

Boelhower, William. "Saving Saukenuk: How Black Hawk Won the War and Opened the Way to Ethnic Semiotics." *Journal of American Studies* 25, no. 3 (1991): 333–61.

Bolton, Charles Knowles. "Memoir of Francis Calley Gray." *Proceedings of the Massachusetts Historical Society* 47 (1914): 529–34.

Booth, Alison. "The Lessons of the Medusa: Anna Jameson and Collective Biographies of Women." *Victorian Studies* 42, no. 2 (2000): 257–88.

"Boston Academy of Music." *American Magazine of Useful and Entertaining Knowledge* 2, no. 3 (November 1834): 98.

Boudinot, Elias [Buck Watie]. *An Address to the Whites Delivered in the First Presbyterian Church, on the 26th of May, 1826*. In *Cherokee Editor: The Writings of Elias Boudinot*, edited and with an introduction by Theda Perdue, 65–83. 1983; reprint, Athens: University of Georgia Press, 1996.

——. *Cherokee Editor: The Writings of Elias Boudinot*. Edited and with an introduction by Theda Perdue. 1983; reprint, Athens: University of Georgia Press, 1996.

——. Editorial, *Cherokee Phoenix*, 21 January 1830. In *Cherokee Editor: The Writings of Elias Boudinot*, edited and with an introduction by Theda Perdue, 102–3. 1983; reprint, Athens: University of Georgia Press, 1996.

——. Editorial, *Cherokee Phoenix*, 21 April 1830. In *Cherokee Editor: The Writings of Elias Boudinot*, edited and with an introduction by Theda Perdue, 114–17. 1983; reprint, Athens: University of Georgia Press, 1996.

——. "Invention of a New Alphabet," *American Annals of Education*, 1 April 1832. In *Cherokee Editor: The Writings of Elias Boudinot*, edited and with an introduction by Theda Perdue, 48–63. 1983; reprint, Athens: University of Georgia Press, 1996.

——. "Letters and Other Papers Relating to Cherokee Affairs: Being a Reply to Sundry Publications Authorized by John Ross." In *Cherokee Editor: The Writings of Elias Boudinot*, edited and with an introduction by Theda Perdue, 155–233. 1983; reprint, Athens: University of Georgia Press, 1996.

Boudinot, Elias (1740–1821). *A Star in the West: Or, a Humble Attempt to Discover the Long Lost Ten Tribes of Israel, Preparatory to Their Return to Their Beloved City, Jerusalem*. Trenton, N.J.: D. Fenton, S. Hutchinson and J. Dunham, 1816; reprint, Freeport, N.Y.: Books for Libraries Press, 1970.

Bowen, Abel. *Bowen's Picture of Boston, or the Citizen's and Stranger's Guide to the Metropolis of Massachusetts and Its Environs*. 3d ed. Boston: Otis, Broaders and Company, 1838.

Boyce, Douglas Wesley. "Tuscarora Political Organization, Ethnic Identity, and Sociohistorical Demography, 1711–1825." Ph.D. diss., University of North Carolina at Chapel Hill, 1973.

Boyd, Andrew. *Boyd's New York State Directory, 1872–1873*. Syracuse, N.Y.: Truair, Smith & Co., Printers, 1872.

Boyd's Business Directory of Over One Hundred Cities and Villages in New York State. Albany, N.Y., 1870.

Bradford, William. *Of Plymouth Plantation*. In *Norton Anthology of American Literature*, 5th ed., vol. 1, edited by Nina Baym. New York: W. W. Norton, 1998.

Bremer, Richard G. *Indian Agent and Wilderness Scholar: The Life of Henry Rowe Schoolcraft*. Mt. Pleasant: Clark Historical Library, Central Michigan University, 1987.

Bright, Charles C. "The State in the United States in the Nineteenth Century." In *Statemaking and Social Movements: Essays in History and Theory*, edited by Charles Bright and Susan Harding. Ann Arbor: University of Michigan Press, 1984.

Brinton, Ellen Starr. "Benjamin West's Painting of Penn's Treaty with the Indians." *Bulletin of the Friends' Historical Association* 30, no. 2 (Autumn 1941): 99–189.

Brown, Jennifer S. H. *Strangers in Blood: Fur Trade Families in Indian Country*. Vancouver: University of British Columbia Press, 1980.

Bryant, William Clement. "Obsequies at Forest Lawn Cemetery." *Transactions of the Buffalo Historical Society* 3:1–23. Buffalo, N.Y.: The Society, 1885.

Brydon, Sherry. "Ingenuity in Art: The Early Nineteenth Century Works of David and Dennis Cusick." *American Indian Art Magazine* 20, no. 2 (Spring 1995): 60–85.

Buell, Lawrence. *New England Literary Culture: From Revolution through Renaissance*. Cambridge: Cambridge University Press, 1986.

Buffalohead, W. Roger. "Introduction." In *History of the Ojibway People*, by William W. Warren. 1885; reprint, St. Paul: Minnesota Historical Society, 1984.

Burnham, Michelle. " 'How Extravagant the Pretension': Bivocalism and U.S. Nation-Building in *A Narrative of the Life of Mrs. Mary Jemison*." *Nineteenth-Century Contexts* 23, no. 3 (2001): 325–47.

Bushman, Richard L. *The Refinement of America: Persons, Houses, Cities*. New York: Knopf, 1992.

Callcott, George H. *History in the United States, 1800–1860: Its Practice and Purpose*. Baltimore: Johns Hopkins University Press, 1970.

Campisi, Jack. "The Emergence of the Mashantucket Pequot Tribe, 1637–1975." In *The Pequots in Southern New England: The Fall and Rise of an American Indian Nation*, edited by Laurence M. Hauptman and James D. Wherry, 117–40. Norman: University of Oklahoma Press, 1990.

——. *The Mashpee Indians: Tribe on Trial*. Syracuse, N.Y.: Syracuse University Press, 1991.

Canfield, William Walker. *The Legends of the Iroquois*. New York: A. Wessels, 1902.

Carr, Helen. *Inventing the American Primitive: Politics, Gender, and the Representation of Native American Literary Traditions, 1789–1936*. New York: New York University Press, 1996.

Cass, Lewis. Review of *Documents and Proceedings Relating to the Formation and Progress of a Board in the City of New York, for the Emigration, Preservation, and Improvement of the Aborigenes of America*. *North American Review* 30, no. 66 (January 1830): 62–121.

Cayton, Mary Kupiec. *Emerson's Emergence: Self and Society in the Transformation of New England, 1800–1845*. Chapel Hill: University of North Carolina Press, 1989.

——. "Who Were the Evangelicals?: Conservative and Liberal Identity in the Unitarian Controversy in Boston, 1804–1833." *Journal of Social History* 31, no. 1 (Winter 1997): 85–108.

Chen, David W. "Battle over Iroquois Land Claims Escalates." *New York Times*, 26 May 2000, sec. A.

[Cherokee Nation.] *Memorial of the Cherokee Indians*. 21st Cong., 1st sess., 1830. House of Representatives Report no. 311.

——. *Memorial of a Delegation from the Cherokee Indians, Presented to Congress January 18, 1831*. 1831.

——. *Memorials of the Cherokee Indians, Signed by Their Representatives, and by 3,085 Individuals of the Nation*. 21st Cong., 1st sess., 1831. House of Representatives Doc. no. 311.

——. *Memorial of a Delegation of the Cherokee Tribe of Indians*. 22d Cong., 1st sess., 1832. House of Representatives Doc. no. 45.

——. *Memorial of John Ross and Others, on Behalf of the Cherokee Nation of Indians*. 23d Cong., 2d sess., 1833. House of Representatives Doc. no. 71.

The Cherokee Nation v. The State of Georgia. S. Ct. January 1831 Term, 10 U.S. Reports (5 Peters) 1.

Cheyfitz, Eric. "Savage Law: The Plot against American Indians in *Johnson and Graham's Lessee v. M'Intosh* and *The Pioneers*." In *Cultures of United States Imperialism*, edited by Amy Kaplan and Donald E. Pease. Durham, N.C.: Duke University Press, 1993.

Chielens, Edward. *American Literary Magazines: The Eighteenth and Nineteenth Centuries.* Westport, Conn.: Greenwood, 1986.

Choate, Rufus. "The Importance of Illustrating New-England History by a Series of Romances Like the Waverley Novels." In *The Works of Rufus Choate,* edited by Samuel G. Brown. Boston, 1862.

Chow, Rey. *Ethics after Idealism: Theory—Culture—Ethnicity—Reading.* Bloomington: Indiana University Press, 1998.

Clements, William M. "Schoolcraft as Textmaker." *Journal of American Folklore* 103, no. 408 (April–June 1990): 177–92.

Cook-Lynn, Elizabeth. "The American Indian Fiction Writer: Cosmopolitanism, the Third World, and First Nation Sovereignty." *Wicazo Sa Review* 11, no. 1 (Spring 1995): 26–36.

——. *Anti-Indianism in Modern America: A Voice from Tatekeya's Earth.* Urbana: University of Illinois Press, 2001.

——. "Literary and Political Questions of Transformation: American Indian Fiction Writers." *Wicazo Sa Review* 11, no. 1 (Spring 1995): 46–51.

——. "Who Stole Native American Studies?" *Wicazo Sa Review* 12, no. 1 (Spring 1997): 9–20.

Copland, James. *Of the Class, Nature and Treatment of Palsy and Apoplexy: Of the Forms, Seats, Complications, and Morbid Relations of Paralytic and Apoplectic Disease.* Philadelphia: Lea and Blanchard, 1850.

Copway, George. "The American Indians." *American Whig Review* 9, no. 18 (June 1849): 631–37.

——. *Indian Life and Indian History, by an Indian Author.* (Originally published as *Traditional History and Characteristic Sketches of the Ojibway Nation,* 1850.) Boston: Albert Colby and Company, 1860.

——. *The Life, Letters, and Speeches of Kah-ge-ga-gah-bowh.* (Originally published as *The Life, History, and Travels of Kah-ge-ga-gah-bowh,* 1847.) New York: S. W. Benedict, 1850.

——. *The Ojibway Conquest: A Tale of the Northwest.* New York: G. P. Putnam, 1850.

——. *Running Sketches of Men and Places, in England, France, Germany, Belgium and Scotland.* New York: J. C. Riker, 1851.

——. "The Two Cousins: A Mas-s-sanga Legend of Western Canada." *Graham's Monthly Magazine of Literature, Art and Fashion* 35 (1849): 365–66.

Copway, George, and Sherman Hall. *Minuajimouin Gainajimot au St. Luke.* Boston: Crocker and Brewster, for the American Board of Commissioners for Foreign Missions, 1837.

——. *Odizhijigeuinius Igiu Gaanonijig = Acts of the Apostles in the Ojibwe Language.* Boston: Crocker and Brewster, for the American Board of Commissioners for Foreign Missions, 1838.

Corn, Colonel James F. "Sam Houston: The Raven." *Journal of Cherokee Studies* (Spring 1981): 35–49.

Coward, John M. *The Newspaper Indian: Native American Identity in the Press, 1820–1890*. Urbana: University of Illinois Press, 1999.

Cumings, Bradley Newcomb. *Journal, 1828–1847*. Call no. N-223, Massachusetts Historical Society, Boston, Mass.

Cusick, David. *Sketches of Ancient History of the Six Nations*. 3d ed. Lockport, N.Y.: Turner & McCollum, Printers, Democrat Office, 1848.

Dale, Edward Everett, and Gaston Litton, eds. *Cherokee Cavaliers: Forty Years of Cherokee History as Told in the Correspondence of the Ridge-Watie-Boudinot Family*. Norman: University of Oklahoma Press, 1939.

Daniel, G. Reginald. "Beyond Black and White: The New Multiracial Consciousness." In *Racially Mixed People in America*, edited by P. P. Root, 333–41. Newberry Park, Calif.: Sage Publications, 1992.

Dannenberg, Anne Marie. " 'Where, Then, Shall We Place the Hero of the Wilderness?': William Apess's *Eulogy on King Philip* and Doctrines of Racial Destiny." In *Early Native American Writing: New Critical Essays*, edited by Helen Jaskoski. Cambridge: Cambridge University Press, 1996.

Dearborn, Henry A. S. "Journals of Henry A. S. Dearborn." *Publications of the Buffalo Historical Society* 7 (1904): 35–225.

Debo, Angie. *And Still the Waters Run*. New York: Gordian, 1966.

———. *A History of the Indians of the United States*. Norman: University of Oklahoma Press, 1970.

DeForest, John W. *History of the Indians of Connecticut from the Earliest Known Period to 1850*. Hartford, Conn.: Wm. Jas. Hamersley, 1851.

Deloria, Philip J. *Playing Indian*. New Haven: Yale University Press, 1998.

Deloria, Vine, Jr. "Anthros, Indians, and Planetary Reality." In *Indians and Anthropologists: Vine Deloria, Jr. and the Critique of Anthropology*, edited by Thomas Biolsi and Larry J. Zimmerman. Tucson: University of Arizona Press, 1997.

———. *Custer Died for Your Sins: An Indian Manifesto*. Austin: University of Texas Press, 1988.

———. "Intellectual Self-Determination and Sovereignty: Looking at the Windmills in Our Minds." *Wicazo Sa Review* 13, no. 1 (1998): 25–31.

———. "Laws Founded in Justice and Humanity: Reflections on the Content and Character of Federal Indian Law." *Arizona Law Review* 31, no. 2 (1989): 203–23.

———. *Red Earth, White Lies: Native Americans and the Myth of Scientific Fact*. New York: Scribner, 1995.

———. "Relativity, Relatedness, and Reality." In *Spirit and Reason: The Vine Deloria, Jr. Reader*, edited by Barbara Deloria, Kristen Foehner, and Sam Scinta. Golden, Colo.: Fulcrum, 1999.

———. "Revision and Reversion." In *The American Indian and the Problem of History*, edited by Calvin Martin. New York: Oxford University Press, 1987.

———. *Singing for a Spirit: A Portrait of the Dakota Sioux*. Santa Fe, N.Mex.: Clear Light, 2000.

Deloria, Vine, Jr., and David E. Wilkins. *Tribes, Treaties, and Constitutional Tribulations*. Austin: University of Texas Press, 1999.

Densmore, Christopher. *Red Jacket: Iroquois Diplomat and Orator*. Syracuse: Syracuse University Press, 1999.

DePuy, Henry F. *A Bibliography of the English Colonial Treaties with the American Indians, Including a Synopsis of Each Treaty*. New York: Printed for the Lenox Club, 1917.

DiPietro, John. "A Jeep Cherokee History." ⟨http://www.edmunds.com/reviews/generations/articles/46011.article.htm⟩. 19 August 2002.

Dippie, Brian. *The Vanishing American: White Attitudes and U.S. Indian Policy*. Middletown, Conn.: Wesleyan University Press, 1982.

Dirlik, Arif. "Culturalism as Hegemonic Ideology and Liberating Practice." In *The Nature and Context of Minority Discourse*, edited by Abdul R. JanMohamed and David Lloyd. New York: Oxford University Press, 1990.

———. "Culture, Society, and Revolution: A Critical Discussion of American Studies of Chinese Thought." In *Working Papers in Asian/Pacific Studies*. Durham: Asian/Pacific Studies Institute, Duke University, 1985.

———. "History without a Center?: Reflections on Eurocentrism." In *Across Cultural Borders: Historiography in Global Perspective*, edited by Eckhardt Fuchs and Benedict Stuchtey, 247–84. Lanham, Md.: Rowman & Littlefield, 2002.

———. "Is There History after Eurocentrism?: Globalism, Postcolonialism, and the Disavowal of History." *Cultural Critique* 42 (September 1999): 1–34.

———. *Postmodernity's Histories: The Past as Legacy and Project*. Lanham, Md.: Rowman & Littlefield, 1999.

Doty, Lockwood L. *A History of Livingston County, New York*. Geneseo, N.Y.: Edward E. Doty, 1876.

Dowd, Gregory Evans. "Spinning Wheel Revolution." In *The Revolution of 1800: Democracy, Race, and the New Republic*, edited by James Horn, Jan Ellen Lewis, and Peter S. Onuf, 266–87. Charlottesville: University of Virginia Press, 2002.

Drake, Samuel Gardner. *Biography and History of the Indians of North America*. 5th ed. Boston: Antiquarian Institute, 1836.

———. *Biography and History of the Indians of North America*. 5th ed. Boston: Josiah Drake, 1837.

———. *Biography and History of the Indians of North America, From Its First Discovery*. 11th ed. Boston: Benjamin B. Mussey, 1851.

———. *The Book of the Indians of North America*. 2d ed. Boston: Josiah Drake, 1833.

———. *Catalogue of the Private Library of Samuel G. Drake*. Boston, 1845.

———. *Indian Biography, Containing the Lives of More Than Two Hundred Indian Chiefs*. Boston: Josiah Drake, 1832.

———. *Indian Captivities, Being a Collection of the Most Remarkable Narratives of Persons Taken Captive by the North American Indians*. Boston: Antiquarian Bookstore and Institute, 1839.

———. "Indian Miscellany" (scrapbook). Edward E. Ayer Collection, Newberry Library, Chicago, Ill.

———. *Tragedies of the Wilderness; or, True and Authentic Narratives of Captives, Who Have Been Carried Away by the Indians from the Various Frontier Settlements of the United States, from Earliest to the Present Time. Illustrating the Manners and Customs, Barbarous Rites and Ceremonies, of the North American Indians, and their Various Methods of Torture Practised Upon Such as Have from Time to Time, Fallen into their Hands.* Boston: Antiquarian Bookstore and Institute, 1841.

Dubinsky, Karen. *The Second Greatest Disappointment: Honeymooning and Tourism at Niagara Falls.* New Brunswick, N.J.: Rutgers University Press, 1999.

Duncan, John M. *A Sabbath among the Tuscarora Indians.* Glasgow: Printed at the University Press, 1821.

Easton, Hosea. *"To Heal the Scourge of Prejudice": The Life and Writings of Hosea Easton.* Edited by George R. Price and James Brewer Stewart. Amherst: University of Massachusetts Press, 1999.

Enos Ames v. William Apess and Trustee. Barnstable Court of Common Pleas. September 1837 Term. Case no. 1199. Book 2, p. 120. Barnstable Superior Court, Barnstable, Mass.

Ernest, John. "Liberation Historiography: African-American Historians before the Civil War." *American Literary History* 14, no. 3 (Fall 2002): 413–43.

Estes, J. Worth. "Samuel Thomson Rewrites Hippocrates." *Medicine and Healing: The Dublin Seminar for New England Folklife Annual Proceedings, 1990.* Boston: Boston University, 1992.

Evarts, Jeremiah. *Cherokee Removal: The "William Penn" Essays and Other Writings.* Edited by Francis Paul Prucha. Knoxville: University of Tennessee Press, 1981.

———. Review of *Speeches on the Indian Bill . . . in the Months of April and May 1830,* by Theodore Freylinghusen et al., Boston, 1830. *North American Review* 31, no. 69 (October 1830): 396–442.

Everett, Edward. "An Address Delivered at Bloody-Brook, in South Deerfield, September 30, 1835, in Commemoration of the Fall of the 'Flower of Essex,' at That Spot, in King Philip's War, September 18 (o.s.), 1675." In *Orations and Speeches on Various Occasions.* Boston: American Stationers, 1836.

———. "On the State of the Indians." Review of *Report to the Secretary of War of the United States on Indian Affairs, Comprising a Narrative of a Tour Performed, in the Summer of 1820, under a Commission from the President of the United States, for the Purpose of Ascertaining, for the Use of the Government, the Actual State of the Indian Tribes in Our Country,* by Rev. Jedidiah Morse. *North American Review* 16, no. 38 (January 1823): 30–45.

———. *Speech of Mr. Everett of Massachusetts on the Bill for Removing the Indians from the East Side to the West Side of the Mississippi.* Washington, D.C.: Gales and Seaton, 1830.

Ezra Tobey v. William Apess. Barnstable Court of Common Pleas. April 1837 Term. Case no. 1069. Book 2, p. 8. Barnstable Superior Court, Barnstable, Mass.

First Impressions on Reading the Message of the Governor of Georgia, 1830, Relative to the Indians. N.p., n.d.

Fish, Phineas. *Memorial of Phineas Fish, Missionary to the Marshpee Tribe of Indians, in Relation to the Memorial of Sundry of Said Tribe,* 30 January 1834, Senate Doc. no. 17, Massachusetts Archives, Boston, Mass.

Flanagan, Joseph T. "Introduction." In *Tales of the Northwest,* by William Joseph Snelling, edited by Joseph T. Flanagan. Minneapolis: University of Minnesota Press, 1936.

Forbes, Jack. *Africans and Native Americans: The Language of Race and the Evolution of Red-Black Peoples.* 2d ed. Urbana: University of Illinois Press, 1993.

———. "Colonialism and Native American Literature: Analysis." *Wicazo Sa Review* 3, no. 2 (Fall 1987): 17–23.

Ford, Alice. *Edward Hicks: His Life and Art.* New York: Abbeville, 1985.

Foreman, Grant. *The Five Civilized Tribes.* Norman: University of Oklahoma Press, 1934.

———. *Indian Removal: The Emigration of the Five Civilized Tribes of Indians.* 2d ed. Norman: University of Oklahoma Press, 1953.

———. "Introduction." In *Indian Justice: A Cherokee Murder Trial at Tahlequah in 1840,* by John Howard Payne. Oklahoma City: Harlow Publishing Company, 1934.

Formisano, Ronald. *The Transformation of Political Culture: Massachusetts Parties, 1790s–1840s.* New York: Oxford University Press, 1983.

Foucault, Michel. *The Order of Things: An Archaeology of the Human Sciences.* New York: Random House, 1973.

Fraser, Nancy. "Rethinking Recognition." *New Left Review* 3 (May–June 2000): 107–20.

Freeman, Frederick. *The History of Cape Cod: The Annals of Barnstable County, Including the District of Marshpee.* 2 vols. Boston: Printed for the author, 1860.

Freylinghusen, Theodore. "Speech on the Indian Removal Bill," 9–11 April 1830. In *Register of Debates in Congress,* vol. 6. Washington, D.C.: Gales and Seaton, 1830.

Gabriel, Ralph Henry. *Elias Boudinot, Cherokee, and His America.* Norman: University of Oklahoma Press, 1941.

Garrison, William Lloyd. *Thoughts on African Colonization: Or an Impartial Exhibition of the Doctrines, Principles, and Purposes of the American Colonization Society: Together with the Resolutions, Addresses and Remonstrances of the Free People of Color.* Boston: Garrison and Knapp, 1832.

Gaul, Theresa Strouth. "Dialogue and Public Discourse in William Apess's *Indian Nullification.*" *American Transcendental Quarterly* 15, no. 4 (December 2001): 275–94.

Gilman, Chandler Robbins. *Life on the Lakes: Being Tales and Sketches Collected*

During a Trip to the Pictured Rocks of Lake Superior. New York: George Dearborn, 1836.

Goodman, Paul. *Of One Blood: Abolitionism and the Origins of Racial Equality*. Berkeley: University of California Press, 1998.

——. *Towards a Christian Republic: Antimasonry and the Great Transition in New England, 1826–1836*. New York: Oxford University Press, 1988.

Gould, Philip B. *Covenant and Republic: Historical Romance and the Politics of Puritanism*. Cambridge: Cambridge University Press, 1996.

Graymont, Barbara. *The Iroquois in the American Revolution*. Syracuse: Syracuse University Press, 1972.

Gregory, Jack, and Rennard Strickland. *Sam Houston with the Cherokees, 1829–1833*. Norman: University of Oklahoma Press, 1967.

Grover, Kathryn. *The Fugitive's Gibralter: Escaping Slaves and Abolitionism in New Bedford, Massachusetts*. Amherst: University of Massachusetts Press, 2001.

Guillory, John. *Cultural Capital: The Problem of Literary Canon Formation*. Chicago: University of Chicago Press, 1993.

Gustafson, Sandra M. *Eloquence Is Power: Oratory and Performance in Early America*. Chapel Hill: Published for the Omohundro Institute of Early American History and Culture, Williamsburg, Va., by the University of North Carolina Press, 2000.

——. "Nations of Israelites: Prophecy and Cultural Autonomy in the Writings of William Apess." *Religion and Literature* 26, no. 1 (Spring 1994): 31–53.

Halleck, Fitz-Greene. *The Poetical Writings of Fitz-Greene Halleck*. Edited by James Grant Wilson. 1868; reprint, New York: D. Appleton and Company, 1882.

Hallett, Benjamin Franklin. *Oration at Palmer, Hampden County, July 4th 1836*. Boston: Beals & Green, 1836.

——. *Rights of the Marshpee Indians*. Boston: J. Howe, 1834.

Hallowell, A. Irving. "Concordance of Ojibwa Narratives in the Published Works of Henry R. Schoolcraft." *Journal of American Folklore* 59, no. 232 (April–June 1946): 136–53.

Harring, Sidney L. *Crow Dog's Case: American Indian Sovereignty, Tribal Law, and United States Law in the Nineteenth Century*. Cambridge: Cambridge University Press, 1995.

——. *White Man's Law: Native People in Nineteenth-Century Canadian Jurisprudence*. Toronto: Published for the Osgoode Society for Canadian Legal History, by the University of Toronto Press, 1998.

Harris, Sheldon H. *Paul Cuffe: Black America and the African Return*. New York: Simon and Schuster, 1972.

Harvard University. *Historical Register of Harvard University, 1636–1936*. Cambridge: Harvard University, 1937.

Hatch, Nathan O. *The Democratization of American Christianity*. New Haven: Yale University Press, 1989.

Hauptman, Laurence M. *Conspiracy of Interests: Iroquois Dispossession and the Rise of New York State*. Syracuse: Syracuse University Press, 1999.

———. *The Iroquois in the Civil War*. Syracuse: Syracuse University Press, 1993.

———. "The Pequot War and Its Legacies." In *The Pequots in Southern New England: The Fall and Rise of an American Indian Nation*, edited by Laurence M. Hauptman and James D. Wherry. Norman: University of Oklahoma Press, 1990.

Haynes, Carolyn. " 'A Mark for Them All to . . . Hiss At': The Formation of Methodist and Pequot Identity in the Conversion Narrative of William Apess." *Early American Literature* 31 (1996): 25–44.

Heat-Moon, William Least. *Blue Highways: A Journey into America*. Boston: Little Brown, 1982.

———. *PrairyErth (a Deep Map)*. Boston: Houghton Mifflin, 1991.

Herman, Daniel J. "Romance on the Middle Ground." *Journal of the Early Republic* 19 (Summer 1999): 279–91.

Hershberger, Mary. "Mobilizing Women, Anticipating Abolition: The Struggle against Indian Removal in the 1830s." *Journal of American History* 86, no. 1 (June 1999): 15–40.

Hinks, Peter. *To Awaken My Afflicted Brethren: David Walker and the Problem of Antebellum Slave Resistance*. University Park: Pennsylvania State University Press, 1997.

Hoig, Stan. "Diana, Tiana, or Talihina?: The Myth and Mystery of Sam Houston's Cherokee Wife." *Chronicles of Oklahoma* 64, no. 2 (1986): 52–59.

Horan, James D. *The McKenney-Hall Portrait Gallery of American Indians*. New York: Crown, 1972.

Horsman, Reginald. *Race and Manifest Destiny: The Origins of American Racial Anglo-Saxonism*. Cambridge: Harvard University Press, 1981.

Hoxie, Frederick. "Why Treaties?" In *Buried Roots and Indestructible Seeds: The Survival of American Indian Life in Story, History, and Spirit*, edited by Mark A. Lindquist and Martin Zanger. Madison: University of Wisconsin Press, 1994.

Hubbard, William. *A Narrative of the Indian Wars in New England*. Boston: Printed and sold by John Boyle in Marlborough-street, 1775.

Hughes, John. "Tribes Fight Proposal Requiring Local Approval of Townhouse Development." Associated Press state and local wire, 27 August 1999, P.M. cycle.

Huntzicker, William W. *The Popular Press, 1833–1865*. Westport, Conn.: Greenwood, 1999.

Jackson, Andrew. "President Jackson on Indian Removal." In *Documents of United States Indian Policy*, edited by Francis Paul Prucha. Lincoln: University of Nebraska Press, 1990.

Jameson, Anna Brownell. *Winter Studies and Summer Rambles in Canada*. 3 vols. London: Saunders and Otley, 1838.

Jasen, Patricia. *Wild Things: Nature, Culture, and Tourism in Ontario, 1790–1914*. Toronto: University of Toronto Press, 1995.

Jefferson, Thomas. *Notes on the State of Virginia*. In *Writings*. Reprint, New York: Library of America, 1984.

Jemison, G. Peter, and Anna M. Schein, eds. *Treaty of Canandaigua, 1794: 200 Years of Treaty Relations between the Iroquois Confederacy and the United States*. Santa Fe, N.Mex.: Clear Light, 2000.

Jennings, Francis, et al., eds. *The History and Culture of Iroquois Diplomacy: An Interdisciplinary Guide to the Treaties of the Six Nations and Their League*. Syracuse: Syracuse University Press, 1985.

Johnson, Elias. *Legends, Traditions, and Laws of the Iroquois, or Six Nations and History of the Tuscarora Indians*. New York: AMS, 1978.

Johnson and Graham's Lessee v. William M'Intosh. 21 U.S. Reports (8 Wheaton) 573 (1823).

[Johnston, Susan.] "Character of Aboriginal Historical Tradition." In *The Literary Voyager, or, Muzzeniegun*, by Henry Rowe Schoolcraft, edited and with an introduction by Philip P. Mason, 5–7. East Lansing: Michigan State University Press, 1962.

Jones, Dorothy V. *License for Empire: Colonialism by Treaty in Early America*. Chicago: University of Chicago Press, 1982.

Jones, Peter. *History of the Ojebway Indians; with especial reference to their conversion to Christianity*. London: A. W. Bennett, 1860.

———. *Life and Journals of Kah-ke-way-quo-na-by: (Rev. Peter Jones,) Wesleyan Missionary*. Toronto: Anson Green, 1860.

Judkins, Russell A. "David Cusick's *Ancient History of the Six Nations*: A Neglected Classic." In *Iroquois Studies: A Guide to Documentary and Ethnographic Resources from Western New York and the Genesee Valley*, edited by Russell A. Judkins. Geneseo: State University of New York, Department of Anthropology/Geneseo Foundation, 1987.

Justice, Daniel Heath. "'We're Not There Yet, Kemo Sabe': Positing a Future for American Indian Literary Studies." *American Indian Quarterly* 25, no. 2 (Spring 2001): 256–71.

Kah-ge-ga-gah-bowh, a Chief of the Ojibwe Nation of North American Indians, will deliver an address descriptive of the worship or religious belief of the Indian—his poetry, songs and his eloquence. At Lyceum Hall, Old Cambridge, Saturday evening, April 14. . . . [Boston]: Seamens' Press, [1849].

Kalter, Susan. "Finding a Place for David Cusick in Native American Literary History." *MELUS* 27, no. 3 (Fall 2002): 9–43.

Kennard, T. B. *The First White Boy in Otago: The Story of T. B. Kennard*, recorded by J. Herries Beattie. 1939; reprint, Christchurch, New Zealand: Cadsonbury, 1998.

Kent, James. *Commentaries on American Law*. 4 vols. New York: O. Halsted, 1826–30.

Kerber, Linda. "The Abolitionists' Perception of the Indian." *Journal of American History* 62, no. 2 (September 1975): 271–95.

Kidwell, Clara Sue. "Indian Women as Cultural Mediators." *Ethnohistory* 39, no. 2 (Spring 1992): 97–107.

Kilcup, Karen L., ed. *Native American Women's Writing, c. 1800–1924: An Anthology.* Oxford, England: Blackwell Publishers, 2000.

Knapp, Samuel Lorenzo. *Lectures on American Literature, with Remarks on Some Passages of American History.* New York: Elam Bliss, 1829.

Knobel, Dale. "Know-Nothings and Indians: Strange Bedfellows?" *Western Historical Quarterly* 15 (1984): 175–98.

Knox, Henry. "Report of Henry Knox, Secretary of War, to the President of the United States, Relating to the Several Indian Tribes," 7 August 1789. In *American State Papers* I, Class II, Indian Affairs, 12–54. Washington, D.C.: Gales and Seaton, 1832.

Krogseng, Kari. "*Minnesota v. Mille Lacs Band of Chippewa Indians.*" *Ecology Law Quarterly* 27, no. 3 (August 2000): 771–97.

Krupat, Arnold. *Ethnocriticism: Ethnography, History, Literature.* Berkeley: University of California Press, 1992.

———. Headnote to *Experiences of Five Christian Indians of the Pequot Tribe,* by William Apess. In *Native American Autobiography,* edited by Arnold Krupat. Madison: University of Wisconsin Press, 1994.

———. *Red Matters: Native American Studies.* Philadelphia: University of Pennsylvania Press, 2002.

———. "Scholarship and Native American Studies: A Response to Daniel Littlefield, Jr." *American Studies* 34, no. 2 (Fall 1993): 81–100.

———. *The Turn to the Native: Studies in Criticism and Culture.* Lincoln: University of Nebraska Press, 1996.

———. *The Voice in the Margin: Native American Literature and the Canon.* Berkeley: University of California Press, 1989.

Kugel, Rebecca. "Religion Mixed with Politics: The 1836 Conversion of Mang'osid of Fond du Lac." *Ethnohistory* 37, no. 2 (Spring 1999): 126–57.

———. *To Be the Main Leaders of Our People: A History of Minnesota Ojibwe Politics, 1825–1898.* East Lansing: Michigan State University Press, 1998.

Kuper, Adam. *Culture: The Anthropologists' Account.* Cambridge: Harvard University Press, 1999.

Lepore, Jill. *A Is for American: Letters and Other Characters in the Newly United States.* New York: Alfred A. Knopf, 2002.

———. *The Name of War: King Philip's War and the Origins of American Identity.* New York: Alfred H. Knopf, 1998.

Levendosky, Charles. "Once Again, a U.S. Senator Targets Tribal Sovereignty." *Rocky Mountain News* (Denver, Colo.), 20 April 1998, sec. A.

Levin, David. *History as Romantic Art: Bancroft, Prescott, Motley, and Parkman.* New York: Harcourt, Brace & World, 1963.

Lincoln, Kenneth. *Native American Renaissance.* Berkeley: University of California Press, 1985.

———. *Sing with the Heart of a Bear: Fusions of Native and American Poetry, 1890–1999.* Berkeley: University of California Press, 2000.

Linkon, Sherry Lee. "Reading Lind Mania: Print Culture and the Construction of Nineteenth-Century Audiences." *Book History* 1, no. 1 (1998): 94–106.

Littlefield, Daniel F., Jr. "American Indians, American Scholars, and American Literary Criticism." *American Studies* 33, no. 2 (Fall 1992): 95–111.

———. " 'They Ought to Enjoy the Home of Their Fathers': The Treaty of 1838, Seneca Intellectuals, and Literary Genesis." In *Early Native American Writing: New Critical Essays,* edited by Helen Jaskoski. Cambridge: Cambridge University Press, 1996.

Littlefield, Daniel F., Jr., and James W. Parins. *A Biobibliography of Native American Writers, 1772–1924.* Metuchen, N.J.: Scarecrow, 1981.

Longfellow, Henry Wadsworth. *The Poetical Works of Longfellow.* Edited by George Monteiro. Boston: Houghton Mifflin, 1975.

Longfellow, Samuel. *Life of Henry Wadsworth Longfellow.* 2 vols. London: Kegan Paul, Tench and Company, 1886.

Macklem, Patrick. *Indigenous Difference and the Constitution of Canada.* Toronto: University of Toronto Press, 2001.

Maddox, Lucy. *Removals: Nineteenth-Century American Literature and the Politics of Indian Affairs.* New York: Oxford University Press, 1991.

Marshe, Witham. "Journal of a Treaty Held with the Six Nations by the Commissioners of Maryland, and Other Provinces, in Pennsylvania, June 1744." *Massachusetts Historical Society Collections* 7 (1801): 171–201.

Mason, Philip P. "Introduction." In *The Literary Voyager, or, Muzzeniegun,* by Henry Rowe Schoolcraft, edited and with an introduction by Philip P. Mason. East Lansing: Michigan State University Press, 1962.

Massachusetts, Commonwealth of. *Documents Printed by Order of the Senate of the Commonwealth of Massachusetts During the Session of the General Court, A.D. 1834.* Vol. 14. Boston: Dutton and Wentworth, 1834.

———. *Hearing Before the Committee on Indians at Marshpee, Tuesday, February 9, 1869.* House of Representatives Doc. no. 502. Boston: Wright and Potter, 1869.

Mather, Eleanore Price, and Dorothy Canning Miller. *Edward Hicks: His Peaceable Kingdoms and Other Paintings.* Newark: University of Delaware Press, 1983.

Mather, Increase. *Early History of New England.* Edited by Samuel Gardner Drake. Boston: Printed for the editor, 1864.

Mattson, Morris. *The American Vegetable Practice, or a New and Improved Guide to Health, Designed for the Use of Families.* 2 vols. Boston: Daniel L. Hale, 1841.

Maungwudaus. *An Account of the Chippewa Indians, Who Have Been Traveling Among the Whites, in the United States, England, Scotland, France, and Belgium; With Very Interesting Incidents in Relation to the General Characteristics of the English, Irish, Scotch, French, and Americans, with Regard to Their Hospitalities, Peculiarities, Etc.* Boston: Published by the author, 1848.

——. *An Account of the North American Indians, Written for Maun-Gwu-Daus, a Chief of the Ojibway Indians, Who Has Been Traveling in England, France, Belgium, Ireland, and Scotland*. Leicester, England: Printed by T. Cook, 1848.

Mayer, Henry. *All on Fire: William Lloyd Garrison and the Abolition of Slavery*. New York: St. Martin's, 1998.

McFee, Malcolm. "The 150% Man: A Product of Blackfoot Acculturation." *American Anthropologist* 70, no. 1 (December 1968): 1068–1107.

McFeely, William S. *Frederick Douglass*. New York: W. W. Norton, 1991.

McKenney, Thomas L. *Sketches of a Tour to the Lakes, of the Character and Customs of the Chippeway Indians, and of Incidents Connected with the Treaty of Fond du Lac*. Baltimore: Fielding Lucas Jr., 1827.

McKenney, Thomas L., and James Hall. *Indian Tribes of North America*. 3 vols. Philadelphia, 1838–44.

McLoughlin, William G. *Cherokee Renascence in the New Republic*. Princeton: Princeton University Press, 1986.

——. "Cherokees and Methodists, 1824–1834." *Church History* 50, no. 1 (1981): 44–63.

"Meet Chief Panderbear." *U.S. News & World Report*, 30 November 1998, 11.

Merrell, James H. *Into the American Woods: Negotiators on the Pennsylvania Frontier*. New York: Norton, 1999.

Michaelsen, Scott. *The Limits of Multiculturalism: Interrogating the Origins of American Anthropology*. Minneapolis: University of Minnesota Press, 1999.

Mihesuah, Devon A. *Natives and Academics: Researching and Writing about American Indians*. Lincoln: University of Nebraska Press, 1998.

Mills, Charles W. *The Racial Contract*. Ithaca: Cornell University Press, 1997.

Mohr, James C. *Doctors and the Law: Medical Jurisprudence in Nineteenth-Century America*. New York: Oxford University Press, 1993.

Moon, Randall. "William Apess and Writing White." *Studies in American Indian Literature* 5, no. 4 (Winter 1993): 45–54.

Morgan, Lewis Henry. *League of the Iroquois* (1851). Introduction by William N. Fenton. New York: Carol Publishing Group, 1993.

Morton, Nathaniel. *New England's Memorial*. Edited by John Davis. Boston: Crocker and Brewster, 1826.

Morton, Samuel George. *Crania Americana; or, A Comparative View of the Skulls of Various Aboriginal Nations of North and South America: To Which is Prefixed an Essay on the Varieties of the Human Species*. Philadelphia; London: J. Dobson; Simpkin, Marshall & Co., 1839.

Mott, Frank Luther. *American Journalism: A History of Newspapers in the United States through 200 Years, 1690 to 1950*. Rev. ed. New York: Macmillan, 1950.

Moulton, Gary E. *John Ross, Cherokee Chief*. Athens: University of Georgia Press, 1978.

Mumford, Jeremy. "Mixed-Race Identity in a Nineteenth-Century Family: The Schoolcrafts of Sault Ste. Marie, 1824–1827." *Michigan Historical Review* 25, no. 1 (1999): 1–23.

Murray, David. *Forked Tongues: Speech, Writing, and Representation in North American Indian Texts*. Bloomington: Indiana University Press, 1991.

Murray, Laura J. "The Aesthetic of Dispossession: Washington Irving and Ideologies of (De)colonization in the Early Republic." *American Literary History* 8 (Summer 1996): 205–31.

Nell, William C. *The Colored Patriots of the American Revolution, with Sketches of Distinguished Colored Persons: To Which is Added a Brief Survey of the Conditions and Prospects of Colored Americans*. With an introduction by Harriet Beecher Stowe. Boston: Robert F. Wallcutt, 1855.

O'Brien, Sharon. *American Indian Tribal Governments*. Norman: University of Oklahoma Press, 1989.

O'Connell, Barry. "Introduction." In *On Our Own Ground: The Complete Writings of William Apess, a Pequot*, by William Apess, edited by Barry O'Connell. Amherst: University of Massachusetts Press, 1992.

———. " 'Once More Let Us Consider': William Apess in the Writing of New England Native American History." In *After King Philip's War: Presence and Persistence in Indian New England*, edited by Colin G. Calloway. Hanover, N.H.: Dartmouth College Press/University Press of New England, 1997.

———. "Textual Afterword." In *On Our Own Ground: The Complete Writings of William Apess, a Pequot*, by William Apess, edited by Barry O'Connell. Amherst: University of Massachusetts Press, 1992.

Oestreicher, David M. "Unraveling the *Walam Olum*." *Natural History* 105, no. 10 (October 1996): 14–21.

Old Indian Meetinghouse at Mashpee. Library of Cape Cod History and Genealogy no. 20. Yarmouthport, Mass.: C. W. Swift, 1923.

Onuf, Peter S. *Jefferson's Empire: The Language of American Nationhood*. Charlottesville: University of Virginia Press, 2000.

Ortiz, Simon J. "Towards a National Indian Literature: Cultural Authenticity in Nationalism." *MELUS* 8, no. 2 (Summer 1981): 7–12.

———. *Woven Stone*. Tucson: University of Arizona Press, 1992.

Overmyer, Grace. *America's First Hamlet*. New York: New York University Press, 1957.

Parins, James W. *John Rollin Ridge: His Life and Works*. Lincoln: University of Nebraska Press, 1991.

Parker, Arthur C. *The Life of General Ely S. Parker: Last Grand Sachem of the Iroquois and General Grant's Military Secretary*. Buffalo: Buffalo Historical Society, 1919.

Parker, Ely S. "Remarks on Red Jacket." In *Transactions of the Buffalo Historical Society*, 3:41–44. Buffalo: The Society, 1885.

Parker, Nicholson H. "The American Red Man." In *The Life of General Ely S. Parker: Last Grand Sachem of the Iroquois and General Grant's Military Secretary*, by Arthur C. Parker. Buffalo: Buffalo Historical Society, 1919.

———. "Indian Dances and Their Influence." In *The Life of General Ely S. Parker: Last*

Grand Sachem of the Iroquois and General Grant's Military Secretary, by Arthur C. Parker. Buffalo: Buffalo Historical Society, 1919.

Parkman, Francis. *The Conspiracy of Pontiac and the Indian War after the Conquest of Canada*. Introduction by Thomas Seccombe. London: J. M. Dent; New York: E. P. Dutton, 1908.

——. *The Letters of Francis Parkman*. Vol. 1. Edited by Wilbur R. Jacobs. Norman: University of Oklahoma Press, 1960.

Payne, John Howard. "The Cherokee Cause." *Journal of Cherokee Studies* 1, no. 1 (Summer 1976): 17–22.

——. *John Howard Payne to His Countrymen*. With an introduction by Clemens de Baillou. Athens: University of Georgia Press, 1961.

——. "Notable Persons in Cherokee History: Sequoyah or George Gist, by Major George Lowrey, 1835, with Introduction and Transcription by John Howard Payne." *Journal of Cherokee Studies* 2 (Fall 1977): 385–92.

Pearce, Roy Harvey. *Savagism and Civilization: A Study of the Indian and the American Mind*. Berkeley: University of California Press, 1988.

Pease, William H., and Jane H. Pease. *The Web of Progress: Private Values and Public Styles in Boston and Charleston, 1828–1843*. New York: Oxford University Press, 1985.

Pechuman, L. L. "Introduction." In *Ancient History of the Six Nations*, by David Cusick. Occasional Contributions to the Niagara County Historical Society, no. 15. Lockport, N.Y.: Niagara County Historical Society, 1961.

Pekkanen, Sarah. "Measure in Congress Would Remove Tribes' Immunity from Lawsuits." *USA Today*, 8 September 1997, sec. A.

Perdue, Theda. "Clan and Court: Another Look at the Early Cherokee Republic." *American Indian Quarterly* 24, no. 4 (2000): 562–69.

——. "Introduction." In *Cherokee Editor: The Writings of Elias Boudinot*, edited by Theda Perdue. 1983; reprint, Athens: University of Georgia Press, 1996.

Peters, Bernard. "Indian-Grave Robbing at Sault Ste. Marie, 1826." *Michigan Historical Review* 23, no. 2 (Fall 1997): 49–80.

——. "John Johnston's 1822 Description of the Lake Superior Chippewa." *Michigan Historical Review* 20, no. 2 (1994): 24–46.

Peters, Richard. *The Case of the Cherokee Against the State of Georgia*. Philadelphia: J. Griggs, 1831.

Peterson, Carla L. *"Doers of the Word": African-American Women Speakers and Writers in the North, 1830–1880*. New York: Oxford University Press, 1995.

Peyer, Bernd C. *The Tutor'd Mind: Indian Missionary-Writers in Antebellum America*. Amherst: University of Massachusetts Press, 1997.

Phebe Ann Weden (by Pro Ami) v. William Apess. Barnstable Court of Common Pleas. September 1836 Term. Case no. 1168. Book 2, pp. 97–98. Barnstable Superior Court, Barnstable, Mass.

Pierce, Maris Bryant. *Address on the Present Condition and Prospects of the Aboriginal*

Inhabitants of North America, with Particular Reference to the Seneca Nation.
Philadelphia: J. Richards, Printer, 1839.

Powell, Timothy B. *Ruthless Democracy: A Multicultural Interpretation of the American Renaissance*. Princeton: Princeton University Press, 2000.

Prucha, Francis Paul. *American Indian Treaties: The History of a Political Anomaly.* Berkeley: University of California Press, 1994.

——, ed. *Documents of United States Indian Policy.* 2d ed. Lincoln: University of Nebraska Press, 1990.

Putney, Martha S. "Richard Johnson: An Early Effort at Black Enterprise." *Negro History Bulletin* 45 (April–June 1982): 46–47.

Ramsay, David. *The History of the American Revolution*. Vol. 2. New York: Russell & Russell, 1968.

Ratcliffe, Donald J. "Antimasonry and Partisanship in Greater New England, 1826–1836." *Journal of the Early Republic* 15, no. 2 (Summer 1995): 199–239.

Reif, Rita. "A Man Who Traded Everything for an Indian Trove." *New York Times,* 16 May 1999, sec. A.

Remini, Robert. *The Revolutionary Age of Andrew Jackson.* 1976; reprint, New York: Harper, 1987.

Revard, Carter. *Family Matters, Tribal Affairs.* Tucson: University of Arizona Press, 1998.

——. "History, Myth, and Identity among Osages and Other Peoples." In *Family Matters, Tribal Affairs,* 126–41. Tucson: University of Arizona Press, 1998.

Review of "An Address Delivered at Bloody-Brook," by Edward Everett. *New England Magazine* 9, no. 6 (December 1835): 462–68.

Review of *An Address to the Whites,* by Elias Boudinot. *North American Review* 23, no. 53 (October 1826): 470–74.

Review of *Indian Nullification,* by William Apess. *New England Magazine* 9, no. 1 (July 1835): 79.

Review of *A Son of the Forest,* by William Apess. *American Monthly Review* 2, no. 8 (August 1832): 149–50.

Richter, Daniel K. *Facing East from Indian Country: A Native History of Early America.* Cambridge: Harvard University Press, 2001.

Richter, Daniel K., and James H. Merrell, eds. *Beyond the Covenant Chain: The Iroquois and Their Neighbors in Indian North America, 1600–1800.* Syracuse: Syracuse University Press, 1987.

Ridge, John. "John Ridge on Cherokee Civilization in 1826." Edited by William C. Sturtevant. *Journal of Cherokee Studies* 6, no. 2 (Fall 1981): 79–91.

Rinhart, Floyd, and Marion Rinhart. *The American Daguerreotype.* Athens: University of Georgia Press, 1981.

Robertson, William. *History of the Discovery and Settlement of America.* London, 1777; reprint, New York: J. & J. Harper, 1828.

Rorty, Richard. *Achieving Our Country: Leftist Thought in Twentieth-Century America*. Cambridge: Harvard University Press, 1998.

Rose, Wendy. "The Great Pretenders: Further Reflections on White Shamanism." In *The State of Native America: Genocide, Colonization, and Resistance*, edited by M. Annette Jaimes. Boston: South End, 1992.

Ross, John. *Letter from John Ross, Principal Chief of the Cherokee Nation of Indians, in Answer to Inquiries from a Friend Regarding the Cherokee Affairs with the United States*. N.p., 1836.

——. *Letter from John Ross, the Principal Chief of the Cherokee Nation, to a Gentleman of Philadelphia*. N.p., 1837.

——. *The Papers of Chief John Ross*. 2 vols. Edited and with an introduction by Gary E. Moulton. Norman: University of Oklahoma Press, 1985.

Rowe, John Carlos. *Literary Culture and U.S. Imperialism, from the Revolution to World War II*. New York: Oxford University Press, 2000.

Ruoff, A. LaVonne Brown. *American Indian Literatures: An Introduction, Bibliographic Review, and Selected Bibliography*. New York: Modern Language Association, 1990.

——. "Jane Johnston Schoolcraft." In *Dictionary of Native American Literature*, edited by Andrew Wiget, 295–97. New York: Garland, 1994.

——. "The Literary and Methodist Contexts of George Copway's *Life, Letters, and Speeches*." In *Life, Letters, and Speeches*, by George Copway, edited by A. LaVonne Brown Ruoff and Donald B. Smith, 1–21. Lincoln: University of Nebraska Press, 1997.

——. "Three Nineteenth-Century American Indian Autobiographers." In *Redefining American Literary History*, edited by A. LaVonne Brown Ruoff and Jerry W. Ward, 251–69. New York: Modern Language Association of America, 1990.

Said, Edward W. *Culture and Imperialism*. New York: Alfred A. Knopf, 1993.

Saler, Bethel. "An Empire for Liberty, a State for Empire: The U.S. National State before and after the Revolution of 1800." In *The Revolution of 1800: Democracy, Race, and the New Republic*, edited by James Horn, Jan Ellen Lewis, and Peter S. Onuf, 360–82. Charlottesville: University of Virginia Press, 2002.

Salisbury, Neal. *Manitou and Providence: Indians, Europeans, and the Making of New England, 1500–1643*. New York: Oxford University Press, 1982.

Samuel A. Worcester, Plaintiff in Error, v. The State of Georgia. S. Ct. Jan. 1832 Term, 31 U.S. Reports (6 Peters) 515.

Satz, Ronald N. *Chippewa Treaty Rights: The Reserved Rights of Wisconsin's Chippewa Indians in Historical Perspective*. Madison: Wisconsin Academy of Sciences, Arts and Letters, 1991.

Sayre, Gordon M. "Defying Assimilation, Confounding Authenticity: The Case of William Apess." *A/B: Auto/Biography Studies* 11, no. 1 (Spring 1996): 1–18.

——. *Les Sauvages Americains: Representations of Native Americans in French and English Colonial Literature*. Chapel Hill: University of North Carolina Press, 1997.

Sayre, Robert F. *Thoreau and the American Indians*. Princeton: Princeton University Press, 1977.

Scales, Ann. "Few Have Spoken Easily in Nation's Discussion on Race, Clinton Notes." *Boston Globe*, 9 July 1998, sec. A.

Schmalz, Peter S. *The Ojibwa of Southern Ontario*. Toronto: University of Toronto Press, 1991.

Schmitz, Neil. "Captive Utterance: Black Hawk and Indian Irony." *Arizona Quarterly* 48, no. 4 (1992): 1–18.

——. *White Robe's Dilemma: Tribal History in American Literature*. Amherst: University of Massachusetts Press, 2001.

Schoolcraft, Henry Rowe. *Algic Researches: Comprising Inquiries Respecting the Mental Characteristics of the North American Indians*. New York: Harper & Brothers, 1839.

——. *Historical and Statistical Information Respecting the History, Condition, and Prospects of the Indian Tribes of the United States; Collected and Prepared Under the Direction of the Bureau of Indian Affairs Per Act of Congress of March 3rd, 1847*. 6 vols. Philadelphia: Lippincott, Grambo, 1851–57.

——. *The Literary Voyager, or, Muzzeniegun*. Edited and with an introduction by Philip P. Mason. East Lansing: Michigan State University Press, 1962.

——. "Moowis, or the Indian Coquette." *Columbian Lady's and Gentleman's Magazine* 1 (1844): 90–91.

——. *Notes on the Iroquois*. Albany, N.Y.: Erastus H. Pease & Co., 1847.

——. *Personal Memoirs of a Residence of Thirty Years with Indian Tribes on the American Frontier*. Philadelphia: Lippincott & Grambo, 1851.

——. "Reminiscences of Mrs. Jane Schoolcraft." *Michigan Pioneer and Historical Collections* 36 (1908): 95–100.

——. "The Unchangeable Character of the Indian Mind." In *The Literary Voyager, or, Muzzeniegun*, edited and with an introduction by Philip P. Mason, 107–11. East Lansing: Michigan State University Press, 1962.

Schoolcraft, Jane Johnston. "The Forsaken Brother: A Chippewa Tale." In *Native American Women's Writing, c. 1800–1924: An Anthology*, edited and with an introduction by Karen L. Kilcup, 67–69. Oxford, England: Blackwell Publishers, 2000.

——. "Lines Written Under Affliction." In *Native American Women's Writing, c. 1800–1924: An Anthology*, edited and with an introduction by Karen L. Kilcup, 60. Oxford, England: Blackwell Publishers, 2000.

——. "Mishosha, or the Magician and His Daughters: A Chippewa Tale or Legend." In *The Literary Voyager, or, Muzzeniegun*, by Henry Rowe Schoolcraft, edited and with an introduction by Philip P. Mason, 64–71. East Lansing: Michigan State University Press, 1962.

——. "Moowis: The Indian Coquette." In *Native American Women's Writing, c. 1800–1924: An Anthology*, edited and with an introduction by Karen L. Kilcup, 67. Oxford, England: Blackwell Publishers, 2000.

———. "The Origin of the Robin." In *Native American Women's Writing, c. 1800–1924: An Anthology*, edited and with an introduction by Karen L. Kilcup, 66. Oxford, England: Blackwell Publishers, 2000.

———. "Otagamiad." In *Native American Women's Writing, c. 1800–1924: An Anthology*, edited and with an introduction by Karen L. Kilcup, 60–62. Oxford, England: Blackwell Publishers, 2000.

———. "Resignation." In *Native American Women's Writing, c. 1800–1924: An Anthology*, edited and with an introduction by Karen L. Kilcup, 59. Oxford, England: Blackwell Publishers, 2000.

———. "To a Friend Asleep." In *Native American Women's Writing, c. 1800–1924: An Anthology*, edited and with an introduction by Karen L. Kilcup, 59. Oxford, England: Blackwell Publishers, 2000.

———. "To Sisters on a Walk in the Garden, After a Shower." In *Native American Women's Writing, c. 1800–1924: An Anthology*, edited and with an introduction by Karen L. Kilcup, 59. Oxford, England: Blackwell Publishers, 2000.

Scott, Joan W. "Multiculturalism and the Politics of Identity." In *The Identity in Question*, edited by John Rajchman. New York: Routledge, 1994.

———. "Universalism and the History of Feminism." *differences* 7, no. 1 (1995): 1–14.

Seaver, James Everett. *A Narrative of the Life of Mary Jemison*. Garland Library of Narratives of North American Indian Captivities, vol. 41. New York: Garland, 1977.

Simpson, Alan, and Mary Simpson. "Introduction." In *Diary of King Philip's War*, by Benjamin Church. 1716; reprint, Chester, Conn.: Little Compton Historical Society by Pequot Press, 1975.

Sleeper-Smith, Susan. "Women, Kin, and Catholicism: New Perspectives on the Fur Trade." *Ethnohistory* 47, no. 2 (2000): 423–52.

Smith, Donald B. "Kahgegagahbowh: Canada's First Literary Celebrity in the United States." In *Life, Letters, and Speeches*, by George Copway, edited by A. LaVonne Brown Ruoff and Donald B. Smith. Lincoln: University of Nebraska Press, 1997.

———. "The Life of George Copway or Kah-ge-ga-gah-bowh (1818–1869)—and a Review of His Writings." *Journal of Canadian Studies* 23, no. 3 (1988): 5–38.

———. *Sacred Feathers: The Reverend Peter Jones (Kahkewaquonaby) and the Mississauga Indians*. Lincoln: University of Nebraska Press, 1987.

Smyers, Virginia L., and Michael Winship, eds. *Bibliography of American Literature*. Vol. 7. Compiled by Jacob Blanck. New Haven: Yale University Press, 1983.

Snelling, William Joseph. Review of *The Life of Ma-ka-tai-tai-me-she-kia-kiak or Black Hawk, Dictated by Himself*. *North American Review* 40 (January 1835): 68–87.

———. *Tales of the Northwest*. (Originally published 1830.) Edited by Joseph T. Flanagan. Minneapolis: University of Minnesota Press, 1936.

Speck, Frank G. *Territorial Subdivisions and Boundaries of the Wampanoag, Massachusett, and Nauset Indians*. Indian Notes and Monographs, no. 44. Edited by F. W. Hodge. New York: Museum of the American Indian, 1928.

Speeches on the Passage of the Bill for the Removal of the Indians. Boston: Perkins and Marvin, 1830.

Squier, Ephaim G. "Historical and Mythological Traditions of the Algonquins: With a Translation of the 'Walum-Olum,' or Bark Record of the Linni-Lenape." *American Whig Review* 9, no. 14 (February 1849): 173–93.

———. "Manabozho and the Great Serpent: An Algonquin Tradition." *American Whig Review* 8, no. 4 (October 1848): 392–98.

———. "Ne-she-kay-be-nais, or 'The Lone Bird.' " *American Whig Review* 8, no. 3 (September 1848): 255–59.

Stansbury, Philip. *A Pedestrian Tour of Two Thousand Three Hundred Miles, in North America to the Lakes, the Canadas, and the New-England States. Performed in the Autumn of 1822.* New York: J. D. Myers and W. Smith, 1822.

Stern, Madeleine B. *Antiquarian Bookselling in the United States: A History from the Origins to the 1940s.* Westport, Conn.: Greenwood, 1985.

Stevens, Scott Manning. "William Apess's Historical Self." *Northwest Review* 35, no. 3 (1997): 67–84.

Stewart, James Brewer. "The Emergence of Racial Modernity and the Rise of the White North, 1790–1840." *Journal of the Early Republic* 18, no. 2 (Summer 1998): 181–237.

Stewart, Maria. *Maria W. Stewart: America's First Black Woman Political Writer.* Edited by Marilyn Richardson. Bloomington: Indiana University Press, 1987.

Stone, William L. *The Life and Times of Sa-go-ge-wat-ha or Red Jacket.* New York: Wiley & Putnam, 1841.

———. *Life of Joseph Brant.* 2 vols. New York: G. Dearborn & Company, 1838.

Story, Joseph. "History and Influence of the Pilgrims." In *The Miscellaneous Writings of Joseph Story,* edited by William W. Story. Boston: Charles C. Little and James Brown, 1851.

Story, Ronald. *The Forging of an Aristocracy: Harvard and the Boston Upper Class, 1800–1870.* Middletown, Conn.: Wesleyan University Press, 1980.

Strong, Nathaniel T. *Appeal to the Christian Community on the Conditions and Prospects of the New-York Indians.* Philadelphia: J. Richards, 1839.

Sundquist, Eric. "The Frontier and American Indians." In *Cambridge History of American Literature,* vol. 2, *1820–1865,* edited by Sacvan Bercovitch. New York: Cambridge University Press, 1994.

Sweet, Timothy. *American Georgics: Economy and Environment in Early American Literature.* Philadelphia: University of Pennsylvania Press, 2002.

———. "Masculinity and Self-Performance in *The Life of Black Hawk.*" *American Literature* 65, no. 3 (1993): 475–99.

———. "Pastoral Landscape with Indians: George Copway and the Political Unconscious of the American Pastoral." *Prospects* 18 (1993): 1–27.

Tapahonso, Luci. *Blue Horses Rush In: Poems and Stories.* Tucson: University of Arizona Press, 1997.

Tebbel, John. *A History of Book Publishing in the United States.* 4 vols. New York: Bowker, 1972.

Thomson, Samuel. *A New Guide to Health: Or, Botanic Family Physician.* Boston: Printed for the author, 1832.

Tiro, Karim. "Denominated 'SAVAGE': Methodism, Writing, and Identity in the Works of William Apess, a Pequot." *American Quarterly* 48, no. 4 (December 1996): 653–79.

Tomc, Sandra. "An Idle Industry: Nathaniel Parker Willis and the Workings of Literary Leisure." *American Quarterly* 49, no. 4 (1997): 780–805.

Trayser, Donald. *Barnstable: Three Centuries of a Cape Cod Town.* Hyannis, Mass.: F. B. & F. P. Goss, 1939.

Treat, James, ed. *Native and Christian: Indigenous Voices on Religious Identity in the United States and Canada.* New York: Routledge, 1996.

Treaties between the United States of America, and the Several Indian Tribes, from 1778 to 1837. Millwood, N.Y.: Kraus Reprint Co., 1975.

"Treaty with the Indians of the Six Nations." In *The History of the Five Indian Nations of Canada,* by Cadwallader Colden. 1747; reprint, Toronto: Coles Publishing Company, 1972.

Tregle, Joseph G., Jr. "Andrew Jackson and the Continuing Battle of New Orleans." *Journal of the Early Republic* 1, no. 4 (Winter 1981): 373–93.

Tryon, Warren S., and William Charvat, eds. *The Cost Books of Ticknor and Fields and Their Predecessors, 1832–1858.* New York: Bibliographic Society of America, 1949.

U.S. Department of Interior, National Park Service. *Little Bighorn Battlefield Official Map and Guide, Little Bighorn Battlefield National Monument, Montana* (no. 1998-432-903/60345). Washington, D.C.: U.S. Government Printing Office, 1998.

Van Doren, Carl. "Introduction." In *Indian Treaties Printed by Benjamin Franklin,* notes by Julian P. Boyd. Philadelphia: Historical Society of Philadelphia, 1938.

Van Kirk, Sylvia. "From 'Marrying-In' to 'Marrying-Out': Changing Patterns of Aboriginal/Non-Aboriginal Marriage in Colonial Canada." *Frontiers: A Journal of Women Studies* 23, no. 3 (2002): 1–11.

———. *"Many Tender Ties": Women in Fur-Trade Society in Western Canada, 1670–1870.* Winnipeg: Watson & Dwyer, 1980.

Varg, Paul A. *Edward Everett: The Intellectual in the Turmoil of Politics.* Selinsgrove, Pa.: Susquehanna University Press, 1992.

Velikoa, Roumania. "'Philip, King of the Pequots': The History of an Error." *Early American Literature* 37, no. 2 (2002): 311–35.

Vernon, H. A. "Maris Bryant Pierce: The Making of a Seneca Leader." In *Indian Lives: Essays on Nineteenth- and Twentieth-Century Native American Leaders,* edited by L. G. Moses and Raymond Wilson. Albuquerque: University of New Mexico Press, 1985.

A Vindication of the Cherokee Claims Addressed to the Town Meeting in Philadelphia, on the 11th of January, 1830. [Philadelphia], 1830.

Wald, Priscilla. "Terms of Assimilation: Legislative Subjectivity in the Emerging
Nation." *boundary 2* 19, no. 3 (Fall 1992): 77–104.

Waldstreicher, David. *In the Midst of Perpetual Fetes: The Making of American
Nationalism, 1776–1820*. Chapel Hill: University of North Carolina Press, 1997.

Walker, Cheryl. "Guest Expert Transcript," 9 November 2000.
⟨http://www.BeyondBooks.com/chat/2000/walkerarchive.asp⟩ 10 April 2003.

———. *Indian Nation: Native American Literature and Nineteenth-Century Nationalisms*.
Durham, N.C.: Duke University Press, 1997.

Walker, David. *Appeal, in Four Articles: Together with a Preamble to the Coloured
Citizens of the World, But in Particular, and Very Expressly, to Those of the United
States of America*. Edited by Sean Wilentz. New York: Hill and Wang, 1995.

Walker, Willard, and James Sarbaugh. "The Early History of the Cherokee Syllabary."
Ethnohistory 40, no. 1 (Winter 1993): 70–94.

Wallace, Mark. "Black Hawk's Autobiography: Production and Use of an 'Indian'
Voice." *American Indian Quarterly* 18, no. 4 (1994): 481–94.

Walsh, Susan. " 'With Them Was My Home': Native American Autobiography and
A Narrative of the Life of Mrs. Mary Jemison." *American Literature* 64, no. 1 (1992):
49–70.

Walters, Anna Lee. *Talking Indian: Reflections on Survival and Writing*. Ithaca, N.Y.:
Firebrand, 1992.

Warren, William Whipple. *History of the Ojibway People*. With an introduction by
W. Roger Buffalohead. 1885; reprint, St. Paul: Minnesota Historical Society, 1984.

Warrior, Robert Allen. *Tribal Secrets: Recovering American Indian Intellectual
Traditions*. Minneapolis: University of Minnesota Press, 1995.

———. "William Apess: A Pequot and Methodist under the Sign of Modernity." In
Liberation Theologies, Postmodernity, and the Americas, edited by David Batstone,
Eduardo Mendieta, and Lois Ann Lorentzen. London: Routledge, 1997.

Weaver, Jace. *Other Words: American Indian Literature, Law, and Culture*. Norman:
University of Oklahoma Press, 2001.

———. *That the People Might Live: Native American Literatures and Native American
Community*. New York: Oxford University Press, 1997.

Webster, Daniel. *Discourse, Delivered at Plymouth, December 22, 1820. In
Commemoration of the First Settlement of New-England*. Boston: Wells and Lilly,
1821.

Weekley, Carolyn J. *The Kingdoms of Edward Hicks*. Williamsburg, Va.: Abby Aldrich
Rockefeller Folk Art Center, in association with Harry N. Abrams, Inc., 1999.

Weiser, Conrad. "Weiser's Report on the Treaty at Albany." In *Pennsylvania Treaties,
1737–1756*, edited by Donald H. Kent, vol. 2 of *Early American Indian Documents,
Treaties, and Laws, 1607–1789*, edited by Alden T. Vaughan. Lanham, Md.:
University Publications of America, 1984.

Wellburn, Ron. "William Apess." In *Notable Native Americans*, edited by Sharon
Malinowski. Detroit: Gale, 1995.

"The Whale Fishery." *North American Review* 38, no. 82 (January 1834): 84–116.

White, G. Edward. *The Marshall Court and Cultural Change, 1815–1835*. New York: Oxford University Press, 1991.

White, Richard. *The Middle Ground: Indians, Empires, and Republics in the Great Lakes Region, 1650–1815*. Cambridge: Cambridge University Press, 1991.

Wiget, Andrew, ed. *Critical Essays on Native American Literature*. Boston: G. K. Hall, 1985.

Wilder, Alexander. *History of Medicine: A Brief Outline of Medical History and Sects of Physicians, From the Earliest Historic Period*. New Sharon, Maine: New England Eclectic Publishing Company, 1901.

Wilkins, David. *American Indian Politics and the American Political System*. Lanham, Md.: Rowman & Littlefield, 2002.

———. *American Indian Sovereignty and the Supreme Court*. Austin: University of Texas Press, 1997.

Wilkins, Thurman. *Cherokee Tragedy: The Ridge Family and the Decimation of a People*. 2d ed., rev. Norman: University of Oklahoma Press, 1986.

Wilkinson, Charles F. *American Indians, Time, and the Law: Native Societies in a Modern Constitutional Democracy*. New Haven: Yale University Press, 1987.

William Pope v. William Apess. Barnstable Court of Common Pleas. April 1836 Term. Case no. 1035. Book 1, p. 817. Barnstable Superior Court, Barnstable, Mass.

Williams, J. Fletcher. "Memoir of William W. Warren." In *History of the Ojibway People*, by William W. Warren, with an introduction by W. Roger Buffalohead, 9–20. 1885; reprint, St. Paul: Minnesota Historical Society, 1984.

Williams, Raymond. *Keywords: A Vocabulary of Culture and Society*. Rev. ed. New York: Oxford University Press, 1983.

Williams, Robert A., Jr. *The American Indian in Western Legal Thought: The Discourses of Conquest*. New York: Oxford University Press, 1990.

Winthrop, John. *The History of New England from 1630 to 1649*. 2 vols. Edited by James Savage. Boston: Phelps and Farnham, 1826.

Womack, Craig. *Red on Red: Native American Literary Separatism*. Minneapolis: University of Minnesota Press, 1999.

Woods, John. "Long-Running Indian Claims May Hinge on Ashcroft's Stance." *New York Law Journal*, 16 April 2001.

Wyss, Hilary E. "Captivity and Conversion: William Apess, Mary Jemison, and Narratives of Racial Identity." *American Indian Quarterly* 23, nos. 3–4 (Summer 1999): 63–82.

Young, Robert J. C. *Colonial Desire: Hybridity in Theory, Culture, and Race*. London: Routledge, 1995.

Zipes, Jack. "Introduction." In *The Oxford Companion to Fairy Tales*. New York: Oxford University Press, 2000.

ACKNOWLEDGMENTS

Research for this book was completed with the financial help of the Research Board of the University of Missouri system and the Research Council of the University of Missouri–Columbia. I am grateful for the assistance of librarians at the following institutions: the American Antiquarian Society; Boston Public Library; Buffalo and Erie County Historical Society; Chicago Historical Society; Harvard University Archives; Peabody Library of the Johns Hopkins University; Library of Congress; Massachusetts Archives; Massachusetts Historical Society; Bell Collection of the University of Minnesota–Twin Cities Libraries; Ellis Library of the University of Missouri–Columbia; Newberry Library; Archives of the City of New York; New York Historical Society; New York Public Library; State University of New York at Albany Library; State University of New York at Buffalo Library; and Wisconsin Historical Society. Special thanks to Rosemary H. Burns of the Mashpee Historical Commission, who generously copied documents for me, and to Kasia Finkel of the Ellis Library, University of Missouri–Columbia, who found obscure material at the last minute. And then there is my sister, Kathleene Konkle, the archivist, who responded to a desperate plea for information by getting in a car and driving to the Barnstable Superior Court. This was above and beyond the call of duty for even the most dedicated archivist, and I'm lucky to have one in the family.

This book was completed during a fellowship year at the Newberry Library in Chicago, where the collection, the staff, the other scholars in residence, and even the history of the place itself changed the way I think about what I do, for the better I am sure. This book began as a dissertation at the University of Minnesota, under the guidance of Edward M. Griffin, David W. Noble, Paula Rabinowitz, Carol Miller, and Jean O'Brien-Kehoe, who generously supported a project that no one knew much about and asked questions that still matter. Ed Griffin, in particular, is a model of what a scholar and teacher should be, and I am grateful that he was my dissertation adviser. The academic study of Native writing owes much of its existence to the work of two scholars in particular, A. LaVonne Brown Ruoff and Daniel F. Littlefield Jr., both of whom tirelessly supported my research and gave invaluable advice. I'm thankful to them personally, but I'm also thankful for all of the work they've done and continue to do to make Native writing known and accessible to readers and scholars.

In the Department of English at the University of Missouri, my colleagues Catherine Parke and Tom Quirk have been especially supportive in negotiating the sometimes very strange world of the academy. Sharon Black, departmental administrative assistant, patiently answered my too-numerous pleas for files to be sent from Missouri to Chicago posthaste. Thanks to Jessie Lawson, Carol Mason, Charlotte McCloskey, Colin T. Ramsey, Bethel Saler, Jeffrey J. Williams, and Jeffrey R. Williams for putting up with me in various ways while I obsessed about treaties.

Sian Hunter was a generous and understanding editor, and the anonymous readers for the University of North Carolina Press provided encouraging advice.

This book is dedicated to my father, Robert C. Konkle, and my mother, Carol Konkle, who along with her sisters, Jeannette Young and Dorothy Kappauf, were the first readers and critics I knew. They are still the most fun. And thanks to my brothers Michael and Rob for being their excellent selves and often asking, tactfully, when this book would be done.

Finally, I will be forever grateful for chapter 35, title 38, United States Code Veterans' Dependents' benefits and to whoever it was at the Baltimore office of the Veterans Administration who thought it was a good idea to give them to me.

Kathy Malin, the copyeditor of this book, passed away during its production. In her work, Kathy had a passion for the reader and insisted on clarity in the text, from which I hope I have learned. Any mistakes or obfuscations here are despite her efforts.

INDEX

government, 37–38; and Canada, 163; and P. Jones, 163; plan for Indian Territory, 163–64; critiques of, 189; childhood and conversion of, 189, 191; *Life, History, and Travels*, 189–97; accused of embezzlement, 191; excommunication of, 191; and International Peace Conference, 206; as literary entrepreneur, 206; and W. W. Warren, 206; *Copway's American Indian*, 207; and Know-Nothing Party, 207; and Willis, 207; wife's involvement in writing, 207, 209; *Traditional History and Characteristic Sketches of the Ojibway Nation*, 212–22; death of, 223; and Red Jacket, 223, 265–66

Copway's American Indian, 207

Cornplanter, 161, 233, 269

Criticism of Native writing, 27–35

"Crying Indian" public service announcement, 295 (n. 1)

Cuffe, Paul, 157

Culturalism, 26–28; defined, 28; in literary criticism, 28–35 passim

Cusick, David: collects artifacts, 186, 242; family and education of, 240–41; accounts of, 242; artwork of, 242–43; and T. L. McKenney, 242–43; *Sketches of Ancient History of the Six Nations*, 242–51

Cusick, Nicholas, 240

Cusick family, 324–25 (n. 28)

Custer, George, 289

Darley, F. O. C., 206

Dawes Allotment Act (Land in Severalty Act), 8

Dearborn, Henry A. S., 224, 226–27

Deloria, Philip: *Playing Indian*, 39, 259

Deloria, Vine, 8, 26–27, 290, 292

Densmore, Christopher, 233

Dirlik, Arif, 6, 36–37, 46

Douglass, Frederick, 162, 201

Dowd, Gregory Evans, 44

Drake, Samuel Gardner: on Apess, 100; bookstore of, 100–102; reviews *A Son of the Forest*, 102; on pilgrims' violence, 135–36; Apess cites, 136; on authorship of *Indian Nullification*, 148–49, 151–52

Easton, Hosea, 104–5

Eloquence: as Indian trait, 232

Emerson, Ralph Waldo, 154

Erie Canal, 229, 240

Ethnology, 160, 167–68, 177–78, 180–81

Eulogy on King Philip (William Apess): advertising for and venue of, 132; E. Everett and, 132; and missionaries, 132; Jackson and, 132, 146; significance of date of delivery of, 132–34; and misrepresentation, 134, 139–42, 145–46; antecedents of, 135; and pilgrim-republican narrative, 135–38; and "history of New England writers," 139, 142; and Christian hypocrisy, 140–41; and Cherokees, 142, 144; and land sales of King Philip, 142–43; and Mashpees, 143; Mary Rowlandson in, 144; King Philip in, 144–45; sale of King Philip's wife and child in, 145; critiques of, 312–13 (n. 91)

Eurocentrism, 36–37

Evarts, Jeremiah: profession of, 63; on Indian title, 63–64; and William Penn essays, 63–68; on sovereignty, 64–65, 67; and Treaty of Hopewell, 65–66; on Cherokee civilization, 67–68; death of, 71

Everett, Alexander Hill, 132, 154

Everett, Edward: on removal, 97–99; Apess on, 115; elected governor, 132; *Address at Bloody-Brook*, 132–33, 136–37, 140; and Drake, 148, 151

www.ingramcontent.com/pod-product-compliance
Lightning Source LLC
Chambersburg PA
CBHW021807270326
41932CB00007B/90